Dorset

in the shadow of the marble mountain

by
Tyler Resch

Published for the
Dorset Historical Society
by
Phoenix Publishing
West Kennebunk, Maine

Nathaniel "Terry" Tyler reserves all rights to the photographs in this book that are credited to the Terry Tyler Collection.

Library of Congress Cataloging-in-Publication Data

Resch, Tyler.
 Dorset: in the shadow of the marble mountain/by Tyler Resch.
 p. cm.
 Includes bibliographical references.
 ISBN 0-914659-44-8 : $30.00
 1. Dorset (Vt. : Town)—History. I. Dorset Historical Society. II. Title.
 F59.D7R47   1989
 974.3'8—dc20   89-25511
                                                          CIP

Copyright 1989 by the Dorset Historical Society

All rights reserved. No part of this publication may be reproduced, stored in a retrieval system or transmitted in any form or by any means without the prior written permission of the Dorset Historical Society, except for brief quotations in a review.

Printed in the United States of America
by The Knowlton & McLeary Co.
Binding by New Hampshire Bindery
Design by A. L. Morris

Map of Dorset, Vermont (and vicinity)

Labels visible on the map:

- Benson
- W. Hewlett
- Otter Creek
- D. Cook
- H.M. Buffum
- S.M.
- S.H.
- B. Cotrin
- **NORTH DORSET**
- B. Sweet
- DORSET POND
- Joel Wheeler & Co's
- A. Bowen
- Steam Saw Mill
- S.H.
- J. Benson
- J. Benson
- L. Walker
- Williams
- Sexton
- Spring
- French & McDonald's White Marble Quarry
- H. Rowe
- S.M.
- R. Edgerton
- Mrs. Gifford
- G. Whitman
- J. Hewlett
- Mrs. Walman
- W. Belen
- H. Bebee
- J. Sexton
- **DORSET MOUNTAIN**
- S.H.
- B. Ames
- R. Station
- Union Store
- Dwight Brooks
- A. & S. Boyle
- D.G. Williams
- S.M.
- Marble Quarry
- Holley, Fields & Kent's Italian Marble Quarry
- Wilson's
- Union Ch.
- S.M.
- Hotel
- J.M. Daniels
- W. Lamphlerre
- Spout
- S. French
- J. Cochrane
- J. French
- F. Harwood
- Mad Tom
- GREEN PEAK
- Dorset Cave
- Clark's Marble Quarry
- **EAST DORSET**
- H. Morse
- B.W. Wait
- F. Bafsen
- J. Jacobs
- O. Pillsbury
- S.H.
- A. Andrus
- Wilson
- H.A. Sowle
- S.H.
- J. Andrews
- S. Coburn
- **CEMETERY**
- W. Wrightman

Dorset

The principal illustration on the jacket and title page of this volume is an engraving by Lorenzo Hatch, from the collection of the Southern Vermont Art Center, Manchester Vermont. The front endleaf shows the Rice-Harwood map of Dorset published in 1856 which is part of a large hanging wall map of all towns in Bennington County. The back endleaf is the map of Dorset which appears in the Beers Atlas of 1869. The sketches which appear as chapter ends are from The Story of Dorset *by Zephine Humphrey, published in 1924, and drawn by Katherine Field White.*

Contents

Foreword	vii
Preface	xi
Acknowledgments	xv
1. Geology and Geography	1
2. Indians	20
3. The Complexities of Chartering	24
4. Settlement and the First Years	44
5. The Dorset Conventions	70
6. The Mount Tabor Leg	87
7. The Early Nineteenth Century	100
8. The Age of Marble	127
9. The Late Nineteenth Century	153
10. "Summer People"	192
11. The Early Twentieth Century	230
12. Arts and the Artists	263
13. Since 1924	292
14. A Final Word: Cemeteries	344
The Schoolhouses/A Pictorial Portfolio	353
Epilogue	361
Appendices	
State Legislators from Dorset	364
Town Officials	366
Postmasters and Rural Mail Carriers	373
Veterans	378
Population Statistics	383
Bibliography	384
Sponsors	391
Index	392

The Dorset Historical Society, sponsor of this history, has its museum in this former firehouse located between the Dorset post office and home of Mrs. Russell Parks.

Photo by Stetson Fletcher

Foreword

IN 1982 while I was still a member of the Board of Trustees of the Dorset Historical Society Marchen T. Skinner raised the question of having a history of Dorset written. With a demonstrable lack of common sense I volunteered to head a committee of three to explore the feasibility of writing or having a history of Dorset written. After some months, we reported back to the board that a history could and should be written. A History Book Committee was formed and set to work to accomplish the project. Having volunteered before, I was installed as its chairman.

The average person faced with this task would assume that it was pretty straightforward and just press on. Our sentiments exactly, except that we might have thrown in the towel then and there had we known what the next seven years held in store. We began by deciding that we would hire an author to write the book as opposed to writing the history ourselves as a committee. The search for an historian began. As an organization with limited funds we were obliged to be frugal. At first we fondly imagined that we might be able to get a graduate history student to undertake the book as his thesis. No interest was shown in this money-saving scheme by any college or university history department within 200 miles. Professional historians and writers in the local area were canvassed and again no enthusiasm was demonstrated. A local writer finally allowed as how he could be persuaded to undertake the project. He was interviewed by the Book Committee and engaged to write the book at what turned out to be a ludicrously small sum, $1500 up front, $500 halfway through, and $500 at completion. As the Chairman of the Book Committee was patting himself on the back for arranging such an incredible bargain we discovered we got what we paid for which was exactly nothing. We did manage to retrieve our advance so all we really lost was about three years of time and our naivete. We were back to square one and the search began again.

At this point Marchen Skinner suggested that we try to get Tyler

Resch, a Bennington author of several books and a former editor of the *Bennington Banner* and the *Country Journal*. He was ideally situated to do the history because of his writing experience, thorough knowledge of Bennington County if not the town of Dorset, and his enthusiasm and interest. Several more committee meetings produced an acceptable agreement and writing finally got under way in October 1986 with a projected completion date in the Fall of 1987. Here it is in the waning days of July 1989 and the answer to the question of "What happened?" is that nothing ever goes smoothly in the book writing and publishing business.

Two of the problems contributing to the delay were the wealth of photographic material which resulted in doubling the number of pictures in the book and the unexpected amount of interesting information about Dorset which increased the length of the book and the time to write it. The publishers we selected are two most accommodating fellows and in spite of supposedly firm schedules, they extended deadlines, held our hands and told us not to worry. We aren't the worrying kind in any event, but as the costs of writing and publishing the book escalated beyond $50,000, there were some anxious faces around the committee table. The Finance Subcommittee came to the rescue with cash donations, loans, and a $5000 grant from the Town of Dorset which enabled the book to be completed and finally here it is.

I know you will find things about Dorset which you never knew, the story of the Mount Tabor Leg, for instance. I hope you will find bits of the familiar and some pictures of people and places you know or recognize. The writing of the story of Dorset has been an exciting and intriguing time for me and I suspect for the rest of the people involved. There is always that feeling that you want to see how it comes out and how the book looks after you have put some time and effort into it. I hope that the people who read this history will enjoy it but even more do I hope that they gain a better understanding and a deeper feeling about the unique community in which they live. It is not some recently developed, made-to-order seamless village that you will find at the base of Stratton Mt. It has warts, wrinkles, smiles, worry lines, and a beautiful patina of age that only the passage of time can produce and which some communities will never have. Dorset has character.

Putting together this book has been a real labor of love for all concerned. I am not going to enumerate everyone or the particular part he or she played as those acknowledgments appear elsewhere in these pages. I will not say that there was unanimity or even amiable agreement on the Book Committee or its various offshoots. There wasn't. Out of all this came some sort of consensus and also a very valuable insight for me and perhaps all of us. There are a great many people who have deep and strong feelings about Dorset and they are all individuals. They are the ones who give Dorset its character. They are not unwilling to see change as that is inevitable but they are unwilling to see the fabric of the community torn by people who may not have the respect for Dorset that it deserves. This history is for those old or new residents who love Dorset and those passers by who feel the same way and want to know more about this lovely small Vermont town.

Henry A.G. Chapman
Chairman, Book Committee

Dorset Hollow, Vermont
July 26, 1989

Preface

"It is certainly the duty of the present to commemorate the past, to perpetuate the names of the pioneers, to furnish a record of their early settlement, and to relate the story of their progress. The civilization of our day, the enlightenment of the age, and this solemn duty which men of the present time owe to their ancestors, to themselves and to their posterity, demand that a record of their lives and deeds should be made. In local history is found a power to instruct man by precedent, to enliven the mental faculties, and to waft down the river of time a safe vessel in which the names and actions of the people who contributed to raise this region from its primitive state may be preserved."—From the introduction to Portrait and Biographical Album of DeKalb County, Illinois *published by Chapman Brothers, Chicago, 1885, a volume that contains biographies of two of the writer's great-grandfathers.*

DEPENDING on how well it is done, and depending also on the available raw material, tracing the history of a single town can be a fascinating cultural exercise. Or it can be a tedious read. The continuing problem is that the endeavor threatens to drown in provincialism. In the case of the Vermont town of Dorset, the raw material proved fascinating on its own merits and seemed to drive the story with inherent momentum. Certain guarantees against excessive provincialism were provided by interweaving the threads of the Dorset Conventions (which resulted in the creation of the independent Republic of Vermont) along with those of the legendary dispute between New Hampshire and New York at a time when towns like Dorset were being aggressively though illicitly created.

The chapter on the Mt. Tabor Leg indulges in undiluted provincialism, yet the episode churns up rare and revealing slices of life and times and power politics in the very early nineteenth century. But provincialism is again blunted by the "summer people" and "the arts and artists"; both phenomena have insured Dorset a lively cultural diversity. The other special Dorset topic discussed in this book, the marble industry, tends to keep matters interesting of its own weight, so to speak. Two dozen or more large cavities in the ground left by the marble quarriers are now mostly overgrown by foliage that conceals a colorful heritage of an industrial past—useful today mostly as destinations for exploring as well as for their legend-bearing qualities.

Certain mental images spring to mind about "Dorset." In some ways this is a typical Vermont town: small population, numbers that grew quickly, held steady, faltered, and then fell during the great nineteenth-century migration from Vermont, numbers that rose again toward the close of the twentieth century. Typical also is the fact that farming has been disappearing to such a distressing extent that in 1989 there remained only one dairy farm in town that was worked by the owners, the McWaynes. A century ago the *Child's Bennington County Directory* listed 200 farmers or farm laborers in Dorset, along with 181 quarry workers. Now farming, both as a source of income and as a way of life, has almost vanished as completely as marble quarrying.

Undoubtedly the greatest municipal problem in this century's final decade and beyond, a problem shared with many other towns, will be how to deal with the forces of growth and development that seem overpowering. Some communities would welcome this "opportunity," but most Dorseters like things the way they are or, more likely, they have already fled larger and more crowded regions—and they pray that the kinds of growth that happened to nearby Manchester won't happen to them.

For a century now, and with increasing acceleration recently, people have been attracted to Vermont and to places like Dorset for their enduring values and their welcome sense of rural isolation. The rate at which those values are being eroded causes great concern, and many wonder if either the *rural* or the *isolation* elements of this equation can long remain valid.

But to keep matters in perspective, remember that Dorset's ruination has been predicted frequently because of the new people, the new houses, the additional traffic, noise, and commerce. In 1868, pioneering "summer person" Elizabeth Prentiss feared the result if too many people discovered the town's serene charms. Zephine Humphrey, who moved from the busy West Road to the Hollow in the late 1920s to get away from all these distractions, lamented the trends even during the

Depression in her book *The Beloved Community*. In the early 1970s, native William Gilbert drew a despairing picture of a Dorset besieged by flatlanders, second-home transients, and yuppie skiers, whose purchases sent land values dizzily upward. Yet to many others, life seems to go on without noticeable change.

In certain contexts today Dorset implies quiet wealth. (Wealth may be conspicuous but by no means is it universal in Dorset today.) One accepted image conjures up sylvan hideaways, serene settings and attractive architecture—traditional or modern. To some, the Dorset lifestyle means cocktails on an outdoor deck facing a murmuring stream and distant mountains. To many others, thanks to the self-help heritage of AA, established by native son Bill W., Dorset means grateful escape from an alcoholic lifestyle.

In another context, Dorset might have been concocted by an advertising agency to represent "the good life," urbane but not urban, of quiet values, intelligent conversation about literature and the arts, golf and tennis, modest social concerns. In no context is it the southern California fast-lane lifestyle of trendy informality, Jacuzzis, bikinis, freeways, convenient values. Nor is it impersonal American suburbia, daily commuting to the metropolis, social climbing, aggressive money grubbing.

In important ways like this Dorset is different. Visitors marvel at the unspoiled qualities of the place, and they ask why a pseudo-colonial-style Dorset Sheraton Inn or Holiday Inn hasn't been built to cash in on the town's charms and reputation. Indeed, why hasn't there? It might be a great financial success. But Dorseters, who make decisions with their environment as well as their pocketbooks in mind, would never allow it.

Tyler Resch

North Bennington, Vermont
July 4, 1989

ACKNOWLEDGMENTS

Many participants in the research and preparation of this book deserve thanks for their courtesies and for sharing their memories, knowledge, or talents. Special gratitude must go first to Marchen T. Skinner, who long nurtured the concept of this book and who helped to see it through to completion in virtually every detail—editorial, photographic, and fund-raising—and to her husband Calvin for patient encouragement and sunny forbearance.

There were two committees involved, formal and informal. The official book committee was chaired by Henry A.G. "Geoff" Chapman, and included Lucille Fay, Codman Hislop, John A. Kouwenhoven, Donald Johnson, Mildred O'Neal, Marchen T. Skinner, Elisabeth Sturges, and Frederic Taylor. The less formal "picture committee" began meeting on Thursday evenings to mull over and ultimately select two hundred photographs for inclusion, and its members also served as initial readers and sharp-eyed critics of the early drafts of chapters. These included Nathaniel "Terry" Tyler, chairman, Robert "Whitey" Dressler, Nora C. Gilbert, Joe Kucin, Marchen T. Skinner, and Miriam Tifft. In an effort to catch as many errors, gross exaggerations, outlandish claims, and other misstatements as possible, Terry Tyler also served as reader at the galley-proof stage.

Bill Manley, descendant of a Dorset first settler, was extremely helpful on many occasions in locating and appreciating documents and photographs at the Dorset Historical Society museum, where he is the enthusiastic volunteer curator. Special consultations were provided by Charles Gilbert, Arthur W. Gilbert, Robert Cushman, W. Dean Fausett, and Nora C. Gilbert, among others. John A. Kouwenhoven read several chapters and made valuable suggestions. Without Whitey Dressler's curiosity and perseverance there would have been no chapter on the Mt. Tabor Leg. Historian John P. Johnson of Delray Beach, Florida, was generous in sharing his painstaking research on the Manley-Lefevre-Dickenson marble house.

Several committee members appreciated the use of the copying machines so freely offered by Jay Hathaway of Peltier's Store and the Dorset branch of the Factory Point National Bank.

Among offices and institutions that were helpful in addition to the historical society were Dorset Town Clerk Denise Hebert, the Dorset Village Public Library, and Southern Vermont Art Center. Files of the *Bennington Banner* and *Manchester*

Journal were consulted. Resources of the Bennington Museum, Bennington Free Library, Bennington County Courthouse, and Sawyer Library at Williams College were utilized. A special word should be said for the Dr. George Russell Collection of Vermontiana attached to the Martha Canfield Library in Arlington; the region is fortunate to have this collection, and to have David and Mary Lou Thomas as curators.

On a state level, abundant good information was uncovered in the library of the Vermont Historical Society in Montpelier. All the hand-written petitions dealing with the Mt. Tabor Leg controversy, among other documents, were retrievable thanks to Gregory Sanford at the Secretary of State's Archives in Montpelier. Some letters of William Jackson and unpublished manuscripts of Zephine Humphrey were located at the Wilbur Collection of Vermontiana in the Special Collections Division of the Bailey/Howe Library at the University of Vermont in Burlington. The Shelburne Museum kindly provided data and photographs of its "Dorset Castle," and the state Department of Forests and Parks background on Emerald Lake State Park. Details of early relationships with the Yorkers were unearthed at the New York State Library in Albany.

Several residents were interviewed on tape for their recollections of the early twentieth century and in some cases those of their ancestors. These included David Baker, Eugene A. and Jessica Bond, William T. Burns, Sr., Dennis Conroy, Dick Cunningham, Robert Cushman, Ernest G. Edgerton, Arthur W. Gilbert, Connie Harrington, Carleton G. Howe, Beatrice Jackson Humphreys, Donald G. Johnson, Kate Kelleher, Jane Leary, Edwin Lefevre, Jr., William Manley, Ruth Baldwin McWayne, Bea Nichols McWayne, Rene Nolet, Mildred O'Neal, Blanche Parks, Raymond Parks, Walter Read, Ada Williams Rumney, Helen B. Sheldon, and Norma Sheldon Roberts Taft. Of those, four have died at this writing: Jane Leary, Connie Harrington, Kate Kelleher, and Bea McWayne. It was fortuitous that the writer had been acquainted in the 1960s with the late Alfred H. Gilbert and Carl T. Ramsey, among others. Robert R.R. Brooks, the retired dean of Williams College, not only gave advice about writing a town history—based on his experience with the Williamstown history—but also related vivid memories of when he lived in South Dorset in 1920.

Photographic skills were provided by Stetson Fletcher and Chris Alexopoulos. Individual picture credits will acknowledge the many who loaned photos. Preparation of the index, a most painstaking task, became the province of Wyatt Jones, Andy Berkey, Terry Tyler, and Geoff Chapman.

Correspondence was carried on with Rodney A. Barber, Weston L. Cate, Jr., William F. Gilbert, J. Kevin Graffagnino, J. R. Greene, Robert Griffith, Mrs. James Lynch, J. Robert Maguire, Albert L. Ransom, Daniel B. Risdon, Marcia R. Stevens,

Winn L. Taplin, and Robert and Sylvia Warner, among others.

Phoenix Publishing deserves more than a word of acknowledgment, namely the courteous insistence and professionalism of A.A. "Lex" Paradis, editor, the design skills of A.L. Morris, publisher, and the careful work of Anne D. Lunt, copy editor.

A necessary caution is that while many helped, only the writer can take responsibility for the uses, possible abuses, and interpretations of all that help and information. A gestation period of about three years went by between start and finish, and that span of time yielded much enrichment and smoothed out some erroneous judgments. In an effort to nip errors we made use of several kinds of filters, but no doubt some will have escaped our nets. To achieve or even approach perfection would involve so much more delay that a book could never be published.

T.R.

Dorset

Geology and Geography

THE FIRST significant inhabitants of Dorset were the billions of tiny creatures of the Ordovician seas whose bodies, composed of calcium and carbon compounds, eventually were compressed and metamorphosed, during unimaginably long periods of time, by heat and pressure into the solid and useful mineral known as marble that underlies so much of this town's soil, a substance that was to give the town much of its physical and economic character—and, indeed, its dominant personality—for well over a century of the kind of time that is measured in months and years rather than in geological eons.

Dorset's geological underpinnings were described by Zephine Humphrey in a brief and eloquent essay that appeared in her 1924 book *The Story of Dorset*. The state of knowledge about earth sciences has advanced importantly since then, and today's geologists will quibble with some of her terminology and will want to talk in terms of plate tectonics, yet few could improve on the quality of her prose:

> *Geologists think that the foundations of the Green Mountains were laid in Algonkian times and that they emerged from the primeval ocean during the Ordovician period of the Paleozoic age. The first Vermont dry land was probably borrowed from the Adirondacks, debris broken and transported by the storm-driven waves of the Cambrian seas. Sandstone and limestone it was to begin with, later transformed by metamorphism into schists and gneiss. The sandstone was clearly New York's contribution, but the limestone from which our marble was ultimately made must have been our own idea, for it consisted of an accumulation of minute sea shells.*

The Taconic mountains, with which we are especially concerned, were in their youth much higher than they are now, probably boasting an altitude of at least 8,000 feet, and were bolder and sharper. It stirs the imagination to think what a gaunt, haggard place Dorset must have been in those days, bleak and austere, even fierce, very different from the gentle valley we know. Perhaps, indeed, the valley was not yet carven; Green Peak and Mother Myrick may have been one mass. No trees, no grass veiled the ruggedness of the rocky world. Only, by and by, the lichens began to creep and spread.

We have no certain means of knowing how the tremendous changes took place, resulting in folds and elevations, in tiltings and in the metamorphism of the rocks; but there are indications that the process was always slow and gradual. Very well founded is the belief that from the Silurian period the Vermont mountains gave themselves over entirely to the gentle forces of rain and wind, sun and frost, letting themselves be acted upon imperceptibly.

It was a tremendous stretch of time, far and away the longest chapter in Dorset's history. Little by little, the soil accumulated, ferns and flowers, trees and grass were born, animal life developed. During the Tertiary period there were swamps in western Vermont in which grew trees that flourish only in mild climates, so we know that, at least for a time, even the temperature of Dorset was gentle.

But in the Pleistocene age came tumult and trouble enough, extremities of violence and sudden rending change. Down from the north crept a vast glacier, probably more than a mile in depth, covering all the mountains, filling all the valleys, grinding and crushing and distorting them. Again our imaginations are quickened as we try to watch that great wall of ice advancing upon our valley, swallowing hill after hill, relentless, inexorable. If there was animal life here then, how it must have fled in shivering terror! How the whole place must have given itself up for annihilated! That was the sternest chapter in Dorset's history.

But it was a short chapter compared with that which had preceded it. Miraculously, when all seemed over and the valley sealed forever within an icy tomb, the weather conditions changed, the sun reasserted his authority, and summer came back, releasing the dead. Whether the melting of the ice was slow or comparatively rapid we do not know, but we are sure the time must have been one of a wild leaping of waters, huge lakes and rivers, gigantic waterfalls.

How did Green Peak and Mother Myrick look to each other when they once more stood face to face in the good sunlight after their terrific experience? Probably greatly changed. And perhaps the greatest change lay in the soil which the pulverizing glacier had left and which presently proceeded to give birth to new trees and grass, bushes and flowers. Dorset became fertile and beautiful as she could never have been had not the ice sheet passed over her.

For a long time the bowl of the valley was the bed of a lake whose waters gradually receded from terrace to terrace, leaving the long level plateaus on which we now plant

Geology and Geography

The Manley Tavern and Ethan Allen spring on the West Road, circa 1900, with Owl's Head and Mt. Aeolus in background. The building no longer exists.

our orchards and build our hillside homes. The ancient swamp midway between the east and west roads is now all that is left of the Ice Age.

So much for the primeval history of our valley as we can surmise it from the broken, scattered, interfolded records she has kept. A tremendous history, grander than any human records we have yet managed to keep. It is the history of Dorset, the thing we must always bear in mind as we search out or remember our own small doings and sayings and count our few years of habitation. Against this enormous background we all come and go.

The term "pre-Cambrian" is more widely recognized these days than "Algonkian," and it is now known that there were at least three glacial advances and retreats, punctuated by lengthy interglacial periods. An economic resource Zephine Humphrey overlooked was the sand and gravel pits left in valleys by glacial retreats. And there is more poetry than accuracy in remarking that "all that is left of the Ice Age" is Dorset's ancient swamp, for in fact many other land forms and deposits give evidence of the glaciers' achievements.

The point, perhaps, of rereading Zephine Humphrey's geology is that it was not only the heritage of marble that these geological processes bequeathed

A panoramic view of Dorset's mountains, looking northwest from Peru.

to Dorset. The same natural forces also produced those most striking physical features that compose the beautiful panorama of natural landscape and topography—the summits, terraces, moraines, and swamps, as well as hidden caves and crevices. The underlying marbles and dolomites in turn endowed the soil with more than a trace of agriculturally beneficial limestone[1] and gave the town its rugged physical character, qualities that strongly influenced the early settlers and many who followed.

In the 1880s, a century ago, at the peak of Dorset's marble production—which coincided with the town's maximum population, more than two thousand souls—the sources of marble were considered "inexhaustible" by authorities who include Professor Edward Hitchcock, the state geologist; Hamilton B. Child, the compiler of the Bennington County Directory of 1880; and resident Frederick Field Esq., who had written more than a decade earlier about the Dorset quarries for Abby Maria Hemenway's Gazetteer. The assessment of inexhaustibility might have been almost accurate but it did not take into account such economic factors as the widespread use of competing building materials, an unstable stock market in the 1890s, or the preparations for the Spanish-American War or World War I.

It is worth pondering the rugged, varied, and graceful topographical legacy of Dorset, the way the town was divided by geologic forces and glaciation into two fertile and near-parallel valleys, valleys that are accented and shadowed on all sides by magnificent mountain peaks, and with the protected Dorset Hollow just about in the center. The perpetual view of mountains

Mother Myrick is at left, Mt. Aeolus in the center, Dorset Mountain at right.

and uneven terrain—changeless and ever-changing—remains photogenic and also reassuring, and residents who visit other parts of the world always remark about how comforting it is to return to such challenging yet familiar landscape.

All Four Corners

Benning Wentworth could not have anticipated this fact when he first drew the town lines on a map in 1761, but each of the four corners of Dorset is peculiarly defined by topography. At the southwest corner of town, Mother Myrick, named for an early resident, stands at an elevation of 3,361 feet above sea level, and the U.S. Geological Survey map discloses that its summit straddles the Dorset-Manchester town line. Mother Myrick is thus slightly higher than the more conspicuous Mt. Aeolus, which dominates the southern half of the town, reaching an elevation of 3,230. Mt. Aeolus's perpetual companion, the very round and distinctively shaped Owl's Head, stands at 2,481 feet. Mt. Aeolus was first called "Elk Mountain" in 1767 by the Yorker surveyor Will Cockburn, and has been known by several names, most frequently "Green Peak," and also sometimes, confusingly, Dorset Mountain. "Dorset Mountain" itself is subject to various definitions; that term might refer only to the summit itself or, more accurately, to the entire range of elevated lands and peaks that include Netop, Aeolus, and Owls Head.

The highest actual elevation in the town is not a peak so much as it is a ridge on the Dorset-Danby border at the 3,400–3,500-foot level, sloping upward toward an unnamed summit, just over the Danby line, of 3,515 feet. A mile or so to the east rises the highest point of the Dorset Mountain range, located in Danby a few hundred yards beyond the town line. Dorset Mountain's height of 3,804 feet places it in a league with the highest mountains in southern Vermont; competitors are Equinox at 3,816, Stratton at 3,936, and Glastenbury at 3,748.[2]

Dorset Hollow, located in the midst of a majestic array of mountains, constitutes an uncommon scenic and geologic interlude that also figures prominently throughout the town's two centuries of settlement. The Hollow is bracketed by two roads (known logically as the "Upper" and "Lower") and encompasses some of the most aesthetically desirable residential real estate in Vermont. The closest and most conspicuous of its surrounding mountains is the forest-fire-scarred Netop (elevation 2,875) to the east, and a near-twin, Crane Hill (2,782), also known as Dorset Hill, slightly to the south. North and west of the Hollow an undulating complex of high-elevation lands rises abruptly to elevations of between 2,500 and 3,500 feet, leading upward and northward to an even higher series of mountainous masses located in Danby and dominated by Dorset Mountain. The Geological Survey gives few names to the peaks that surround the Hollow, but an informal trail map titled "Dorset, Vt. Her Environs and Her Trails," published in the 1920s, discloses that one of the loftiest, elevation 2,990, is called Jackson Peak, named for that stalwart clergyman, the Reverend William Jackson, who served the

Photo by Otto Pickhardt, from Terry Tyler collection.

The Dorset Hollow forest fire on Netop Mountain, October 26, 1947.

Dorset Village in 1901, looking east from the "lookout" on Reservoir Hill. The village is 1,100 feet above sea level and 210 miles from both New York and Montreal.

Dorset Congregational Church for most of the first half of the nineteenth century.

At the northwest corner a modest mound of only 2,316 feet elevation, called the Scallop, evidently for its distinctive shape, is sandwiched between the Danby Mountain Road and the boundaries of Rupert and Danby.

In the northeast corner an impressive series of steep Green Mountain ridges is climaxed by the summit known as Mt. Tabor, elevation 3,580, located in the northwest corner of Peru. South of Mt. Tabor (the mountain, not the town of the same name) and still in Peru is Styles Peak (3,406), and then south of that is Bromley Mountain (3,260), not so lofty but far better known because of the ski trails that have flourished since 1936 on its southern and eastern slopes. (A separate chapter discusses the unusual geopolitical history of the northeast corner of town, site of the so-called Mt. Tabor Leg.)

The Dorset trails map, again unlike the Geological Survey, identifies several lesser summits by name. Besides Jackson Peak, the northwest quadrant of town also contains Saddleback, Hanks Hill, and Peters Point. Immediately to the northeast and southeast of Dorset village are relatively lowly hills that bear the names of the Pinnacle (about which more is discussed in chapter 10) and Maple Hill, behind the cemetery of the same name.

The lowest official point of elevation in Dorset is 749 feet above sea level, according to a benchmark placed by the U.S. Geological Survey in the south village of East Dorset near the East Dorset Cemetery, and near the town's southeast corner. On the west side of town, Prentiss Pond rests at 929 feet along with most of Dorset village. A benchmark near South Dorset discloses that 879 feet is the lowest elevation on the west side. To traverse the east and west low points one must ascend the foothills of Mt. Aeolus via Morse Hill Road to about 1,100 feet. The difference in elevation between lowest and highest locations in Dorset measures at least 2,750 feet, or more than a vertical half-mile.

The Dominating Mt. Aeolus

Mt. Aeolus, visible from many miles in several directions, is the most dominant mountain in town. It has formed a persistent social and political barrier separating Dorset and East Dorset, and it has forced residents to struggle repeatedly with questions of whether to allow themselves to be divided or united on such fundamental matters as schools, roads, and churches. In the end—that is to say in the late 1950s—this mountain proved to be a unifying force, when voters on both sides of town agreed to tax themselves to build the Dorset Elementary School on a compromise and prominent foothill of Owl's Head just off the Morse Hill Road.

Even the name of this dominating mountain has divided the populace, and perhaps the name Green Peak has been more used by those on the west side and Aeolus on the east. But in recent years Dorset citizens who favor the name

This plaque on the lawn of the East Dorset firehouse proclaims the state of Vermont's official recognition of the name Mt. Aeolus.

Aeolus persuaded the Vermont Department of Libraries, the agency responsible for official names, that on future highway maps it will appear as Mt. Aeolus.

The name Mt. Aeolus has been traced to the visit on a Saturday morning in October of 1860 by the senior geology class of Amherst College, led by Charles H. Hitchcock, son of the noted Dr. Edward Hitchcock, a geologist who had been scrutinizing Vermont's terrestrial underpinnings for many years.[3] Charles Hitchcock's class explored the mountain's geologic structure and its cave. After expounding on these attributes, Hitchcock poured a bottle of pure water on the mountain and christened it Mount Aeolus, for the god of the winds. Frederick Field, who had accompanied the party, accepted this new name on behalf of citizens of Dorset. Someone then read an appropriate poem, and the class sang this song:

We'll tell again that old, old tale,
Of Aeolus of yore,
Who from his cave hard by the vale,
So loudly used to roar.

Chorus:

Blow, blow, blow, blow, blow, blow, blow,
North, South, and East and West,
Blow, blow, blow, blow, blow, blow, blow,
With ne'er a place to rest.

He left that home long years ago,
That home of Auld Lang Syne,
Many a land he's wandered through,
And o'er the ocean's brine.

We've brought him here with us to-day,
We'll leave him here to rest,
While wind and storm shall come alway
And go, at his behest.

Chorus

This mountain grand, henceforth all men,
Mount Aeolus shall call,

*'Till earth shall sink, and loose again
The giant's mighty thrall.*

*Then blow ye winds, ye breezes all,
Obey your king's command,
He sits in this grand marble hall,
Ye are his servant band.*

Chorus

Caves, Pits, and Quarries

Thus far the discussion has pertained to above-ground physical features, but at least two underground caverns deserve special attention: Mt. Aeolus's bat cave, and an eerie place known as Purgatory Pit, explored only by speleologists. In addition, the remains of more than two dozen abandoned marble quarries scattered about the western, southern, and eastern slopes of Mt. Aeolus make for some fascinating explorations on foot. These features of Dorset's landscape bring out the latent geologist or archeologist in almost anyone.

The Aeolus Bat Cave, which opens at an elevation of 2,400 feet, has been the subject of study by another Hitchcock, Harold B. Hitchcock, professor of biology at Middlebury College from 1943 to 1968, whose interest was the natural history of the cave bats of the Northeast.

In a paper published in the *Journal of Mammalogy* in May 1965, Hitchcock, along with Wayne B. Davis, summarized their intensive study of the biology and migration of the bat *myotis lucifugus*. Starting in 1948, they had made fifty-five visits to the Mt. Aeolus bat cave to carry out a project funded by the American Academy of Arts and Sciences. They had banded 73,000 bats, of which 49,000 were found in caves and mines and 24,000 in summer colonies in buildings. An unexpected discovery, they reported, was that a large number of bats visit the Aeolus cave during summer, starting in mid-July: "On August 10, 1961, 663 bats were netted at the entrance of the cave between 9 p.m. and 1 a.m. They appeared to fly out of the woods, beginning nearly an hour before the usual time of emergence from colonies. Bats were most numerous between midnight and 2 a.m., their number gradually decreasing until 4 a.m., when few were flying."

The banded bats from Mt Aeolus were located by the public and scientists—aided by publicity about the project—along a strip that beribboned New England from northwestern Vermont to the southeast, across New

Hampshire, down over Worcester, Massachusetts, and on toward Cape Cod. Hitchcock and Davis described the bat cave as follows:

> *The entrance, about 10 square feet, opens directly into a high-ceilinged room approximately 150 by 65 feet. The floor slopes downward, and at the bottom narrows at one side into a throat, beyond which are crawlways and a few small chambers. In the throat area there has been considerable breakdown. Several passages too small to be crawled through lead from the inner parts. Our collecting normally was limited to the more accessible parts; rarely did we attempt to cover all of the passages known to us, both because of the difficulty of doing so and because relatively few bats were found there.*

Bats travel far and fast, the scientists found. One adult female banded at Aeolus on April 30, 1960, was recaptured near Brookfield, Massachusetts, on May 3, having traveled eighty miles in three evenings.

With few exceptions, the biologists concluded that bats are regular residents in the Aeolus cave in spring and fall, not transients. The female seasonal exodus begins at the end of the first week of April, and most are gone by the second week of May. Males leave in early May and are gone by the first week of June. Hitchcock and Davis estimated that in the winter of 1960–61 the number of bats wintering in the Aeolus cave totaled 330,000 and in 1961–62, 280,000.

In recent years there has been good and bad news at the Aeolus bat cave. The good news is that the Nature Conservancy has acquired the land around it. The bad is that vandals have also discovered it, and to discourage them a most unnatural structure of welded angle irons has been embedded in concrete at the entrance to allow the continued entry of bats but to bar humans, except those with permission to open a locked gate.

An extraordinarily deep cave known as Purgatory Pit, whose opening is high up on Dorset Peak, had often frustrated even the most experienced speleologists until it was explored by Ron Morris of Westminster, Vermont, a member of the northeastern regional organization of the American Speleological Society, and the experience was related in the *Vermont News Guide* of Manchester in June 1974.

Purgatory Pit has not proven popular with hikers or tourists because its opening is characterized by what Morris termed "roll-over edges," over which one cannot even peer without tumbling in. To make his descent Morris was roped and equipped with three sources of light—a miner's carbide, a flashlight, and candles—and he recommended rugged and water-repellent clothing.

He told of descending a series of cavities that could induce Dantesque terror in most rational people. Initially there was a long, straight drop of dozens of feet, followed by a slanting descent of about 45 degrees, a long shaft leading into a dome washed by falling water. Only then could he attempt a record plunge some 200 feet down into another chamber. This, he said, makes Purgatory Pit "the deepest cave explored in the [northeast] region." Morris recommended this kind of exploration only for spelunkers highly skilled in vertical climbing techniques.

Rivers and Watersheds

Dorset's rivers travel unexpected courses. The headwaters of the Battenkill, the Mettawee, and Otter Creek, all well-known trout streams, are located relatively near each other in the northeast region of town, though they flow in three directions and into two watersheds. The Battenkill flows southward through East Dorset, where it picks up waters from Peru's Mad Tom and Little Mad Tom and moves on toward Manchester. A west branch flows through South Dorset and joins East Dorset's Battenkill in Manchester, then cuts through a corner of Sunderland and much of Arlington and flows on toward the Hudson River near Schuylerville, New York. Thus, waters from the Battenkill, much diluted by the Hudson, pass between the Palisades and Manhattan Island before emptying into the Atlantic.

From many small, trickling sources in the mountains the Mettawee accumulates surprising strength and drops sharply down into Dorset Hollow, whence it flows energetically westward. It turns northwest into Rupert, crosses the state line to course through downtown Granville, New York, and about ten miles later pours into the New York State Barge Canal just south of Whitehall, near the southern end of Lake Champlain. The waters of Champlain gradually flow north into the Richelieu River and the St. Lawrence before they, too, join the Atlantic.

The name "Mettawee," also often spelled "Mettowee," has been attributed to a Narragansett word for "black earth" and a Natick term for "poplar trees." It is one of the relatively few Indian names in the region (another being "Netop," which could be Natick for "my friend").[4]

The Mettawee is sometimes called the Pawlet because it traverses much of the town of Pawlet. Ira Allen, who was state surveyor general from 1779 to 1787, referred to it thus in his 1798 *History of the State of Vermont*: "Had the Legislature of Vermont described Powlet (sic) River, instead of Poultney River, in their act of relinquishment of jurisdiction, they would have held a much larger tract, and been equally consistent with the resolve of Congress." In other words, the acreage between Granville and Whitehall would have

The Mettawee River on a spring day in 1963. The children are Tom and Malcolm Cooper and Margaret Skinner.

been part of Vermont instead of New York if only the Mettawee instead of the Poultney had been considered the boundary.

Less conspicuous than the Mettawee, because they pass through no inhabited areas, are the several small headwaters of Otter Creek, also in the mountainous northeast corner of Dorset. These streams feed first into Emerald Lake, formerly known as Dorset Pond and since 1960 a Vermont state park that features swimming, picnicking, and camping each summer. Otter Creek flows out of Dorset almost directly northward to a point near Rutland, where it bears slightly northwest to cut through most of Addison County. It empties into Lake Champlain in Ferrisburg, north of Basin Harbor.

Assuming that the Connecticut River belongs to New Hampshire, which it does in the legal sense, because Vermont's boundary begins not in midstream but on its west bank[5], the 100-mile Otter Creek is the longest river wholly within Vermont. In the days when waterways served as the region's principal highways, Otter Creek was regarded as one of the few navigable rivers.

The Taconics and the Greens

Another important geological phenomenon for which Dorset is known has to do with the distinction between the Taconic mountain range and the Green Mountains. The delineation is clearly evident in Dorset, for the boundary is the so-called Valley of Vermont which, as it transsects Dorset on a north-south axis, follows the Route 7 valley—or, if you prefer, the roadbed of the Rutland Railroad. This was a natural and logical place to locate transportation corridors, and it was unquestionably the route of the Mt. Tabor Turnpike that first linked Manchester and Mt. Tabor in the early days of the nineteenth century. To the west are the Taconics, and to the east the Green Mountains.

Geologically, the whole Green Mountain range represents but a short segment of a rugged and relatively narrow strip of mountain cusps stretching all the way from Mt. Mitchell in North Carolina to the tip of the Gaspe Peninsula. The Taconics are a more regional range, extending into the western Berkshires and part of New York State, where they parallel the Hudson Valley and reach only as far south as northern Connecticut. Differences between the Taconics and Greens are geologically esoteric, but a practical one is that limestone under the Taconics is likely to produce hard water, while water in the Green Mountains tends to be naturally soft.[6]

About the Weather

Although no official records have been kept specifically about Dorset's weather, residents often consider themselves fortunate because of the beneficent climate, the vigorous distinctions among the seasons, and the relative rarity of weather-related hazards. The worst that can be said for the climate is that ambient air often becomes quite cold each winter, on some winter evenings reaching lows of 20 or 25 below zero. But those winters are also considered dry and bracing by those who think that shoveling a little snow is a healthy endeavour and good exercise. Several writers have commented that Dorset receives less snow than neighboring towns. This fact became notably apparent in the early 1930s when Fred Pabst of the Wisconsin beer-brewing family built a ski lift on the James Beebe farm in East Dorset; the site is now the Frost well-drilling business. It took three or four seasons to confirm that snow was going to be insufficient. One reason for that location was the proximity of the railroad, which prompted visions of ski trains from the cities. But snowfall was more important, and Pabst soon moved his ski business over to Bromley Mountain in Peru, Vermont's real snow belt.

Summers in Dorset are refreshingly mild, and the heat almost never be-

Geology and Geography 15

comes intense enough to create a demand for air conditioning. So much has been said about Dorset's idyllic summers that the entire "summer people" industry was spawned by these most pleasurable times (hence chapter 10 in this book).

Autumns are colorful, brisk, and memorable. So attractive are autumns, in fact, that they are responsible for intense levels of tourism—profitable for

Photo by Tyler Resch

A view of Netop from the Upper Hollow Road in 1962, still showing the scar of the 1947 forest fire.

innkeepers and gift shops but sometimes overbearing for year-round residents. After the leaves fall, the sixteen-day deer hunting season is welcomed by many—who tend to be native rather than imported—and Dorset's many square miles of woods, fields, and unpopulated territory offer the kinds of habitat that deer favor. The subject becomes one of classic conflict between natives and flatlanders: the more land that is purchased by outsiders, the more it tends to be "posted" against hunting.

The most variable season is spring. Some years see an awful "mud season" when surface soils thaw but the subsurface remains frozen. More often, spring represents only a brief interlude, first of melting snows and thawing ground and then of the reawakening and blossoming that mark the delineation between winter and summer. One special feature of spring in Dorset is apple-blossom time, when acres of orchards suddenly blaze with color.

Among the many positive attributes of its climate, Dorset regards itself as nearly floodproof because of its high relative elevation and the ample drainage afforded by the Mettawee and the Battenkill. Ernest H. West, best known for his roles as orchardist and marble entrepreneur and as the author of a detailed study of Dorset's marble industry, wrote in 1921 about the climate with true chauvinism:

Dorset has never had a real drought because the mountains catch the clouds; we cannot have a serious flood because we live on the height of land between New York and Montreal; crop failures are almost unknown because the soil is so fertile; hurricanes do not reach us because of our surrounding topography. It is a happy valley in which we live and always has been. The forces which made the marble hundreds of millions of years ago, made Dorset Valley a Garden of Eden.[7]

Over the years there have been so few exceptions to the benign nature of the climate that they become legends. In the winter of 1780-81 snowfall of unprecedented severity served to discourage new settlers. Somewhere in Dorset during 1780—just where is not recorded—"a ponderous rock, about twenty tons in weight" fell some four hundred yards from a precipice and uprooted many trees before it crashed and penetrated about fifteen feet beneath the surface.[8]

A summer of short crops and hard times was experienced in 1789, and in 1805 a major drought resulted when no rain fell between planting and harvest time. In 1826 drought accompanied an infestation of grasshoppers.

The year of 1816 was known throughout Vermont and elsewhere as a time of cold and famine, with frost experienced in every month of the year, caused by massive quantities of atmospheric dust raised by the eruption of a volcano on the other side of the globe. This "great year of famine," also known as "eighteen hundred and froze to death," prompted an exodus of residents seeking more rewarding climes. In neighboring Pawlet this was the experience in 1816: "There was scarcely a bushel of corn raised in town. There was great destitution and distress in the following winter and spring. Many cattle perished and many people were reduced to the last extremity. Benevolent people divided their scanty stores with the more destitute, but the selfish took advantage of the opportunity and put on exorbitant prices."[9]

An exception to the rule of the weather's placidity was an episode in 1856

Fred Pabst's first mechanical ski tow at the James Beebe farm, East Dorset, on the lower slopes of Mt. Aeolus, circa 1935. After discovering that not enough snow fell here, Pabst moved his ski business to Big Bromley in Peru.

when a cyclone downed several maple and elm trees, though it was considered a once-in-two-centuries rarity.

The blizzard of Eighty-eight, which arrived shortly after the March Town Meeting, also affected everyone. Dorset's experience with this notorious storm was reported in the *Manchester Journal*:

The new snow Monday morning was a foot in depth, but it continued snowing with a strong north wind all day Monday and Monday night, and Tuesday morning the drifts were anywhere from 4 to 14 feet high. It is the worst storm for 17 years at least, and the "oldest inhabitant" says he does not remember such another.

Not only all the highways but the railroads were completely blocked. The Monday morning train south managed to pull through, but the 10 A.M. train north, after frequent stops got as far as North Dorset and ran out of coal. The down noon train reached here at 7 o'clock P.M. and proceeded south but got stalled and passed the night and all day Tuesday in Shaftsbury.

The up train was stalled in Schaghticoke where it stayed all night and was all day Tuesday in getting to North Bennington.

Of course all trains were abandoned and all the force that could be obtained was employed in shoveling out the road all along the line. Fortunately the snow was light and easily shoveled, or it would have taken a week, at least, to have cleared the road. Little could be done toward breaking out the highways until Tuesday noon when the wind ceased blowing, and the new commissioners had made no provision for such a storm, at the very commencement of their term of office. [Two road commissioners had just been elected at March Town Meeting.]

... There is no doubt that the old district system was the best for breaking roads, but a little care and foresight on the part of the commissioners might provide for such emergencies. Ordinary storms cause but little trouble, but the avalanche of the present week needs more thorough preparation.

While flood damage has been relatively unremarkable on Dorset's Battenkill, Mettawee, and Otter Creek, such has not always been the case along the Mad Tom in East Dorset. Long-time resident Rene Nolet remembered in 1988 that during the famous Flood of 1927, which did so much damage to the rest of Vermont, the Mad Tom went on a rampage and washed out the lower Morse Hill Road and inflicted heavy disruption on the Rutland Railroad tracks. The flood damaged the mill wheel that Carleton Howe's father had built to generate electricity for Glen Farm at the head of Dorset Hollow; it was later replaced. In the hurricane-induced flood of 1938, however, the town's rivers remained relatively well behaved.

A more recent weather-related incident was a massive landslide in the north end of the Hollow in August 1976. After receiving about 3¾ inches of rain in two days, the steep basin that surrounds the headwaters of the Mettawee simply gave in to gravity. Mud and uprooted trees created an unholy mess, but no one was injured and damage was limited to the uninhabited slopes and valley of the Upper Hollow.

Aside from these exceptional events, few in Dorset have had much reason to worry about the ill effects of drought, heat, floods, earthquakes, hurricanes, typhoons, dust storms, mudslides, or other natural aberrations that plague so many regions of the world.

NOTES

1. "We think we have discovered the reason why Vermont so excels all the other New England States in the agricultural capabilities of its soil," wrote Edward Hitchcock, state geologist, in his 1859 *Preliminary Report on the Geology of Vermont.* "It is the existence, in almost all of her rocks, of lime in such a state that natural processes bring it out in just about the quantity needed by vegetation."

2. Writing about mountains in Vermont involves the pitfall that rarely do two sources agree on official elevations. Dorset Peak, for instance, is 3,804 on the official state highway map and in the Vermont Yearbook, but only about 3,760 on the U.S. Geological Survey map (a figure reached by counting the contour rings, because an official height is not even noted).

3. The tale of the visit of Professor Charles Hitchcock and his geology class to Mt. Aeolus in 1860 was related at length in the history of Dorset by George M. Viall of East Dorset as it appeared in the 1889 history of Bennington county, edited by Lewis Cass Aldrich; a brief

Geology and Geography

version appeared in the Dorset history by Laurel B. Armstrong in the 1868 *Hemenway Gazetteer* vol. 1; and more briefly in Zephine Humphrey's *Story of Dorset*.

4. Esther M. Swift, *Vermont Place Names* (Brattleboro, Vt.: Stephen Greene Press, 1977). Swift attributes the Indian names to the late John C. Huden, an authority on place names that derive from Indian sources.

5. An intelligent discussion of Vermont's waterways is found in Harold A. Meeks, *Vermont's Land and Resources* (Shelburne, Vt.: New England Press, 1987). This book, written by a professor of geography at the University of Vermont, includes among related subjects chapters on the natural landscape, the work of running water and glaciers, floods and flood control.

6. Ibid.

7. Ernest H. West, "A Report on the General History of the Marble Industry in Dorset and Danby . . . " Unpublished monograph, February 1921.

8. John A. Graham, *A Descriptive Sketch of the Present State of Vermont* (London: 1797; rpt. Rutland, Vt.: Vermont Heritage Press, 1987) p. 55.

9. Heil Hollister, *Pawlet for One Hundred Years* (Albany, N. Y.: Joel Munsell, 1867).

2

Indians

HISTORIANS have had a way of dismissing the era of Indian civilization in Vermont—or perhaps it is their way of excusing a shortage of evidence—by saying that Vermont was a "no man's land" that was utilized by the aboriginal inhabitants merely for hunting and traveling through. The more one attempts to learn about Indians in southern Vermont, the more this notion appears to be largely true.

A recent study of Indians in Vermont is *The Original Vermonters*, by William A. Haviland and Marjory W. Power, published in 1981 by the University Press of New England. In their introduction, Haviland and Power attempt to debunk the myth that is expressed in the following quote, from the 1978 *Vermont Atlas and Gazetteer*: "Prior to the coming of the Whiteman, the present state of Vermont was largely an uninhabited no-man's-land. The entire area was a disputed hunting ground claimed by the Algonquin tribes of Indians, who resided in what is now Canada, and the powerful Iroquois federation, whose principal villages were in what is now New York State."

But a few pages after discrediting this assertion, the authors include a map of "major language groups of northeastern North America." The map shows "Eastern Algonquians" throughout the territory between the Delmarva peninsula and the Canadian maritimes and the "Iroquoian" west of the Hudson River—just as the *Vermont Atlas and Gazetteer* claimed.

Further to underscore rather than discredit the myth, Haviland and Power theorize that any Indians who used the southwestern Vermont region as a hunting ground probably retreated along the Walloomsac or Hoosick or

Housatonic rivers back to settlements near the upper Hudson Valley. They acknowledge that "the problem with this theory is that no one has yet found the homes along the upper Hudson to which people from southwestern Vermont would have withdrawn." The authors also declare that Indian sites along the Champlain Valley are known for "sparse materials suggestive of camps or short-term occupations."

A definitional problem that one encounters in the attempt to research possible Indian settlements in the vicinity of Dorset is that scholars tend to use watersheds to define Indian territories, and Dorset is near the point of origin of three watersheds. Not only does the Battenkill drain westerly into the Hudson, and the Mettawee and Otter Creek northward toward Champlain, but nearby in Peru are headwaters of the West and Williams rivers that flow easterly to the Connecticut.

A credible local legend has it that the aboriginals used a trail, known as the Indian Road, that began in Ferrisburg where Otter Creek enters Champlain, and then followed the creek southward, upstream, to its source in Dorset; at that point they crossed the Green Mountains and followed the West River valley to the Connecticut at Brattleboro. The late Tom Daniels of Orwell, who devoted a lifetime to interest in Indian lore and who traced strains of Sioux and Chippewa in his own ancestry, also knew that Indians in Vermont used waterways as travel routes. Along the Indian Road, so called, between Lake Champlain and the Connecticut River, a camping settlement was identified by Daniels on the West River in Jamaica.[1]

Daniels pinpointed about seventy-five locations in Vermont as sites where Indians lived for various lengths of time. The most important of these, he said, was at Mt. Independence in his own town of Orwell, across the lake from Fort Ticonderoga, where excavations have uncovered three different levels of civilization, indicating Indian occupations separated perhaps by centuries. Indian routes that Daniels considered important included the Roaring Brook in Danby, the Otter Creek, and the Lemon Fair, West, Connecticut, Hubbardton, Poultney, Missisquoi, Lamoille, Passumpsic, and White rivers. One caution about Daniels' findings is that scholars today tend to discredit his conclusions as amateurish.

Although there is no evidence that Indians settled specifically in Dorset (the town is not listed in Haviland and Power's index), some conclusions can be drawn from the work of other scholars. Colin G. Calloway, who has done exhaustive recent studies of Vermont Indians, observed that by European standards the Mahican territory, which included much of southern Vermont westward to the Hudson River, may have *appeared* uninhabited. But by Indian standards this land was both inhabited and effectively utilized. Indian villages, which were composed of extended family groupings, responded to weather, food, and the rhythm of the seasons, dispersing in time of scarcity and coming together when supplies were plentiful. The gentle, nomadic nature of the Indians' civilization left little physical evidence to offer proof of permanent settlements.[2]

Arrowheads, or artifacts that resemble them, are not infrequently uncovered, and several found in Dorset are exhibited in its historical society museum. These provide evidence at least of traveling and hunting, not necessarily of settlement.

Before the 1660s, that is, before Europeans arrived in northern New England in significant numbers, the entire Indian population of the region was estimated roughly at ninety thousand, with perhaps only five to ten thousand in all of Vermont. The white man came, introduced epidemic diseases into the vulnerable native population, with disastrous consequences. The Western Abenaki were almost entirely eradicated, with a mortality rate of 98 percent. Among the Mahicans, Calloway estimated that 91 percent succumbed.[3]

The arrival of Europeans was catastrophic for the native Americans for many other reasons. In addition to the devastating new diseases, Indians were occupied with their own intertribal warfare as well as direct confrontation with the new settlers, plus the disruptions caused by the new settlers' own warfare (which might also be considered intertribal). A civilization that certainly had lasted several hundred years—perhaps a thousand or more—came virtually to an end by the time Vermont was settled by Europeans in the mid-1700s. By 1780 the "Indian menace" was considered eradicated from Vermont. One of the last victims was Dorset's first settler, Felix Powell, whose house in Pittsford was burned by Indians in 1777. The only case of Indian depredation occurring in Dorset—this is based on legend—was the burning of the home of Zachariah Curtis, first settler of North Dorset.

Calloway would agree with Zephine Humphrey's contention that Mahican warriors frequented the Battenkill River, spending winters in the valleys of Manchester and Arlington. Humphrey wrote that one of their favorite planting grounds was near Emerald Lake in North Dorset.[4] But in 1987, when the Vermont Department of Forests, Parks and Recreation wanted to locate a picnic shelter and parking lot at Emerald Lake State Park, it conducted archaeological tests on two sites and found no significant artifacts of earlier civilizations.

One author who wrote with confidence about Indian lore and settlements in the region where Vermont, New York, and Massachusetts come together was Grace Greylock Niles, whose book *The Hoosac Valley* was published in 1912. She claimed without documentation that Indian campgrounds had been located around the base of Mt. Aeolus. Despite the heavy toll taken by disease, in addition to the legendary massacre of Abenakis by Rogers Rangers at the village of St. Francis, Quebec, in 1759, enough descendants of Abenaki Indians, mostly residents of Franklin County, emerged in the 1970s to develop a sense of ethnic identity and to litigate to maintain their historic fishing and hunting rights.

A final sympathetic word on the condition of Indians in Vermont might be heeded from Vermont's first historian, the Reverend Samuel Williams, the founder of the *Rutland Herald*, who wrote in 1794: "And wherever the Europeans have settled, misery, calamity, and destruction, have been entailed on that unhappy race of men." Williams concluded, somewhat grandly: "A government of reason and nature ought to attempt to conciliate the affections of a free, brave, independent, and generous people. It would be a greater glory than we have ever yet attained, if we could find out a way to impart the blessings of the civil state, to a people whose greatest miseries and misfortunes have been derived from the superior arts, the policy, and the power of civilized nations."[5]

If only Williams's advice had been taken, and if the white man had dealt more compassionately and understandingly with the red man, there would be much more of substance to report today about Indians in Vermont.

NOTES

1. Arthur W. Gilbert, talk on Indians in early Vermont delivered before the Dorset Historical Society, March 28, 1974.
2. Colin G. Calloway, "Green Mountain Diaspora: Indian Population Movements in Vermont, c. 1600–1800," *Vermont History*, Fall 1986, p. 197.
3. The decade of the 1660s was a turning point not only for the Indians of New England. A legal event took place then that would be cited by the United States Supreme Court almost three hundred years later as the basis for settling a boundary dispute between Vermont and New Hampshire. In 1664 King Charles II of England granted the territory of what is now New York plus Vermont to his brother James, the Duke of York, establishing the west bank, not the center line, of the Connecticut River as the eastern boundary of that grant.
4. Zephine Humphrey, *The Story of Dorset* (Rutland, Vt.: Tuttle Company, 1924), p. 10.
5. Samuel Williams, *The Natural and Civil History of Vermont* (Walpole, N. H.: 1794), pp. 208–209.

3

The Complexities of Chartering

THE ORIGINS of the town of Dorset trace back to two consecutive but independent developments. One was the political creation of the first townships in a neglected region of New York State by the then-governor of New Hampshire, Benning Wentworth. The second is the pattern of settlements of those towns, from south to north, by emigres from the southern New England colonies, as well as a few from New York.

The chartering of a town in the territory that would be called "Ver-mont" because of its Green Mountains was generally separated by several years from its settlement; and several more years might pass before the settlers organized a government. In the case of Dorset, settlement followed chartering by seven years, and organization of town government took place about six years after that. Coincident with those events, the original town proprietors met starting in 1765 to "lay out the lots" to sell to the first settlers.

To begin with a specific episode, let us focus on the occasion in 1749 when Governor Wentworth of the royal province of New Hampshire threw down a gauntlet to Governor Clinton of the royal province of New York by chartering a town. One can ask what business it was of the governor of New Hampshire to charter towns on lands not in his jurisdiction. The answer is that it was none of his business, but he did it anyway.

Governor Wentworth, a plump, wily, enterprising fellow who cherished pleasures as well as profits, took advantage of the fact that New York seemed to be inactive in the unnamed no-man's-land between the Connecticut River and the Hudson, a region that was generally and vaguely regarded as part

The Complexities of Chartering 25

of New York. The ambiguity was partly due to primitive methods of surveying and partly to simple inaction on the part of the provincial government, which was headquartered in New York City.

Wentworth was certainly motivated by aspirations of supplementing his meager annual salary of 500 pounds (about $1,500), and also by visions of territorial expansion. He was most willing, in other words, to fill any apparent vacuum. In December of 1749 he seized the initiative by issuing his first township grant in what is now Vermont, an uninhabited territory difficult to define because it lacked even a name. He followed the king's instructions for chartering towns, though he had no intention of carrying out certain specific provisions. Governor Wentworth drew a six-mile square on a piece of paper, locating its western boundary precisely on the line, twenty miles east of the Hudson River, that formed an extension of the agreed-upon western boundaries of Massachusetts and Connecticut. Boldly he named it for himself: Bennington (Benning was his mother's maiden name). If New York had chosen to retaliate at the time, Wentworth was in such a weak position that he probably would have retreated and the course of history would have been different. He covered his action by sending a letter of inquiry to Governor Clinton, and there followed considerable correspondence back and forth, as New York disapproved but obviously was not prepared to act. After all, both provinces were serving the same monarch, and any dispute between them was a matter for the king to settle. In the confusion and ongoing absence of clear signals from the Crown, Wentworth continued relentlessly to charter towns in the disputed lands.[1]

Courtesy of the artist

A conjectural view of Governor Benning Wentworth of New Hampshire, chartering towns in 1761 in the "New Hampshire Grants," territory that later became Vermont. The sketch is by artist Ellen K. Viereck.

Over the next fifteen years, while New York fussed repeatedly but remained unaggressive, Wentworth chartered the astonishing total of 128 towns in that region of ambiguous jurisdiction north of Massachusetts Bay between the Connecticut River and the twenty-mile line east of the Hudson. He collected fees from the proprietors of the new towns, and the town charters specified that an aggregate of more than sixty-five thousand acres would become the personal property of Benning Wentworth.

On August 20, 1761, Wentworth found himself especially busy chartering towns. It must have been a scene of mass production, carried out with quill pens and parchment, by minions hastily preparing laboriously handwritten documents in overwrought language. On that day the royal governor of New Hampshire chartered Springfield and Weathersfield in what is now Windsor County, east of the Green Mountains, and then as if to balance them west of the mountains, he created the towns of Rupert, Glastenbury, Shaftsbury, and Dorset over in Bennington County. It was the busiest day he had ever experienced in the town-chartering business, though later he would break that record and launch ten towns in a single day.

To elicit favor with King George III, and also to make it as awkward as possible for the Crown to take issue with what he had done, Wentworth selected names for his new townships that would flatter those who held influence in London. Rupert, for example, was named to honor Prince Rupert (1619–82), also known as count Palatine of Rhine, duke of Bavaria, duke of Cumberland, and earl of Holderness, who, although dead for eighty years in 1761, remained a national hero whose memory was beloved by all Englishmen. Shaftsbury was named for Anthony Ashley-Cooper, third earl of Shaftsbury (1671–1713), noted for his philosophical writings. The fourth earl of Shaftsbury, alive in 1761, was a gentleman of substance who held several offices including that of lord lieutenant of Dorset, and who in 1761 became a privy councilor; he was known as a man of letters, music, and the arts.

When Governor Wentworth named the town of Arlington less than a month earlier, he chose one of the several titles of Augustus Henry Fitzroy (1735–1811) of Eustus Hall, near Thetford in Suffolk. That royal gentleman also carried the titles of third duke of Grafton, fourth earl of Arlington, fourth viscount Thetford, and Baron Sudbury. As it happened, Fitzroy favored greater freedom for the American colonies and had urged King George to try to conciliate them; if he had been more persuasive Great Britain might not have driven the colonies to revolt.

Dorset was named, most likely, for an English nobleman, Lionel Cranfield Sackville (1688–1765), the first duke of Dorset, who in the 1760s held great political prominence. He was a son of Charles Sackville (1643–1706), who also held the titles of Lord Buckhurst, sixth earl of Dorset, and fourth earl of Middlesex. The elder Sackville was renowned as a patron of English writers and as poet of the Restoration.[2] Lionel succeeded his father in 1706 and was created duke of Dorset in his own right in 1720. When George I ascended to the throne, Sackville was envoy extraordinary to Hanover, later became a privy councilor, lord lieutenant of Ireland, and president of the Council of St. James, and he was often lord justice of England. Sackville loyally served each of the first three Georges until his own death in 1765.[3]

Dorset's charter was sanctioned by the royal monarch himself, who in turn was authorized "by the Grace of God, of Great-Britain, France and Ireland, King, Defender of the Faith &c." It seems incongruous after invoking such lofty authorities to add a trivial "&c," but that is the way Dorset's charter begins. After addressing a greeting "to all Persons to whom these Presents shall come," the charter's preamble is ornate and fawningly self-serving, especially as it adulates its signer, "B Wentworth." Most of the wording was of course boilerplate, used with few changes in many other town charters, and with blanks for filling in name of town, chief proprietors, and boundary description.

Keep in mind some of these circumstances and motivations as you read the charter of Dorset (spelled *Dorsett* in the original, probably through haste). Reproduced here with its idiosyncratic spelling, punctuation, italicization, and capitalization precisely following the original, it is a wondrous document for reading aloud with feeling:

Know ye, that We of Our special Grace, certain Knowledge, and meer Motion, for the due Encouragement of settling a New Plantation *within our said Province, by and with the Advice of our Trusty and Well-beloved BENNING WENTWORTH, Esq; Our Governor and Commander in Chief of Our said Province of NEW-HAMPSHIRE in New England, and of our COUNCIL of the said Province; HAVE upon the Conditions and Reservations herein after made, given and granted, and by these Presents, for us, our Heirs, and Successors, do give and grant in equal Shares, unto Our loving Subjects, Inhabitants of Our said Province of* New-Hampshire, *and Our other Governments, and to their Heirs and Assigns for ever, whose Names are entered on this Grant, to be divided to and amongst them into Seventy equal Shares, all that Tract or Parcel of Land situate, lying and being within our said Province of* New-Hampshire, *containing by Admeasurement, Twenty Three thousand & forty* Acres, *which Tract is to contain Six Miles square, and no more; out of which an Allowance is to be made for High Ways and unimprovable Lands by Rocks, Ponds, Mountains and Rivers, One Thousand and Forty Acres free, according to a Plan and Survey thereof, made by Our said Governor's Order, and returned into the Secretary's Office, and hereunto annexed, butted and bounded as follows,* Viz.

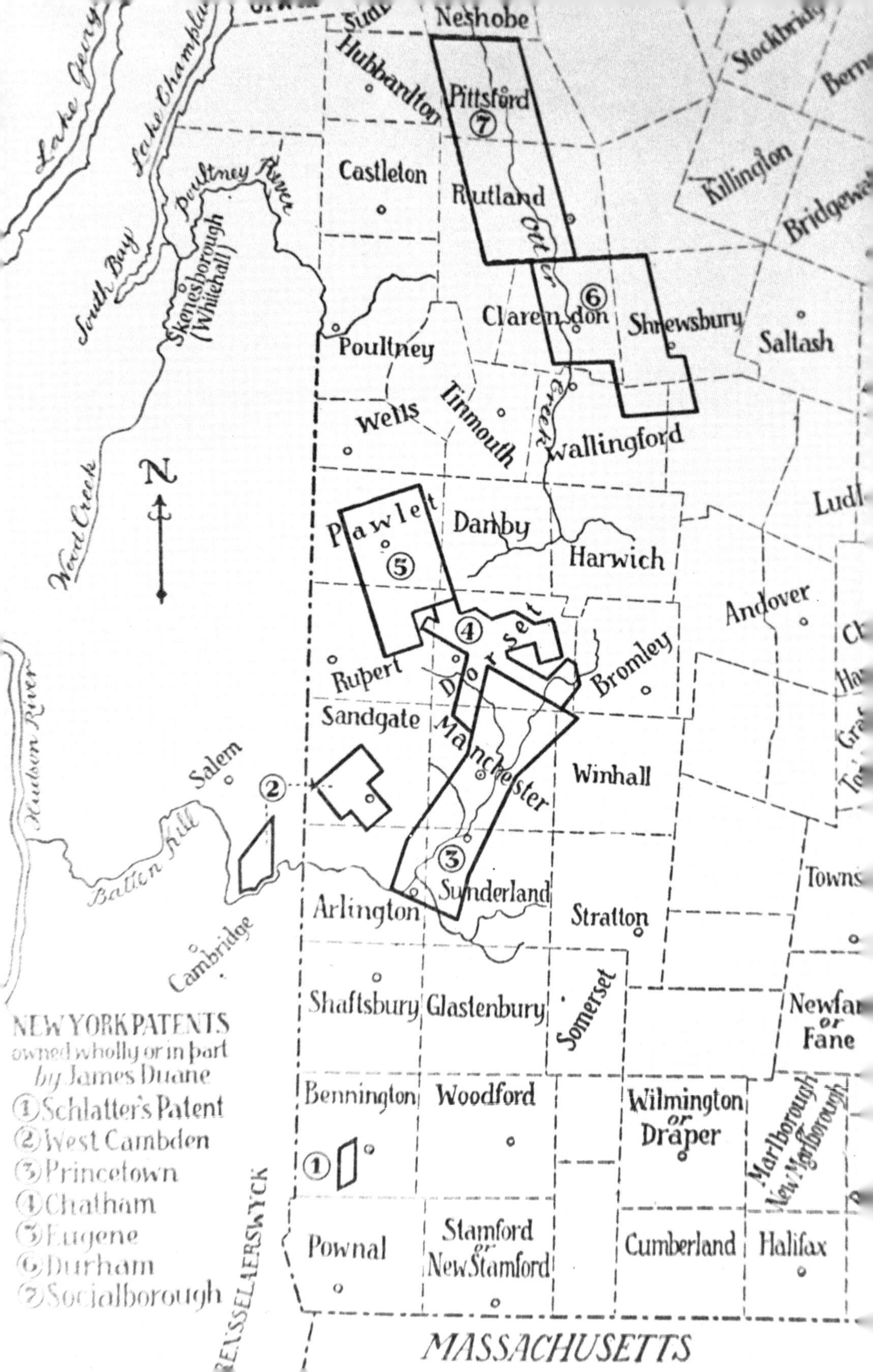

Neshobe
Hubbardton
Pittsford
7
Stockbridge
Castleton
Rutland
Otter Creek
Killington
Bridgewater
Lake George
Lake Champlain
Poultney River
South Bay
Skenesborough (Whitehall)
Clarendon
6
Shrewsbury
Saltash
Poultney
Wells
Tinmouth
Wallingford
Wood Creek
N
Pawlet
5
Danby
Harwich
Andover
4
Dorset
Rupert
Bromley
Sandgate
Manchester
Hudson River
Salem
2
Winhall
3
Batten Kill
Sunderland
Arlington
Stratton
Cambridge
Shaftsbury
Glastenbury
Somerset
Newfane or Fane
Bennington
Woodford
Wilmington or Draper
Marlborough
New Marlborough
1
RENSSELAERSWYCK
Pownal
Stamford or New Stamford
Cumberland
Halifax
MASSACHUSETTS
NEW YORK PATENTS
owned wholly or in part
by James Duane
1 Schlatter's Patent
2 West Cambden
3 Princetown
4 Chatham
5 Eugene
6 Durham
7 Socialborough

The Complexities of Chartering

At the North West Corner of Manchester from thence due North Six Miles from thence due East Six Miles from thence due South Six Miles to the North East Corner of Manchester aforesaid thence Due West by Manchester afore Said to the North West Corner thereof being the Bound first began at—And that the same be, and hereby is Incorporated into a Township by the Name of Dorsett And the Inhabitants that do or shall hereafter inhabit the said Township, are hereby declared to be Enfranchized with and Intitled to all and every the Priviledges and Immunities that other Towns within Our Province by Law Exercise and Enjoy: And further, that the said Town as soon as there shall be Fifty Families resident and settled theron, shall have the Liberty of holding Two Fairs, one of which shall be held on the [blank] And the other on the [blank] annually, which Fairs are not to continue longer than the respective [blank] following the said [blank] and that as soon as the said Town shall consist of Fifty Families, a Market may be opened and kept one or more Days in each Week, as may be thought most advantagious to the Inhabitants.

Also, that the first Meeting for the Choice of Town Officers, agreable to the Laws of our said Province, shall be held on the Fourth Tuesday in November Next which said Meeting shall be notified by Gideon Lyman Esq who is hereby also appointed the Moderator of the said first Meeting, which he is to Notify and Govern agreable to the Laws and Customs of Our said Province; and that the annual Meeting for ever hereafter for the Choice of such Officers for the said Town, shall be on the Second Tuesday of March annually, TO HAVE and to HOLD the said Tract of Land as above expressed, together with all Privileges and Appurtenances, to them and their respective Heirs and Assigns forever, upon the following Conditions, viz.

I. That every Grantee, his Heirs or Assigns shall plant and cultivate five Acres of Land within the Term of five Years for every fifty Acres contained in his or their Share or Proportion of Land in said Township, and continue to improve and settle the same by additional Cultivations, on Penalty of the Forfeiture of his Grant or Share in the said Township, and of its reverting to Us, our Heirs and Successors, to be by Us or Them Re-granted to such of Our Subjects as shall effectually settle and cultivate the same.

II. That all white and other Pine Trees within the said Township, fit for Masting Our Royal Navy, be carefully preserved for that Use, and none to be cut or felled without Our special License for so doing first had and obtained, upon the Penalty of the Forfeiture of the Right of such Grantee, his Heirs and Assigns, to Us, our Heirs and Successors, as well as being subject to the Penalty of any Act or Acts of Parliament that now are, or hereafter shall be Enacted.

This map shows southwestern Vermont towns that Benning Wentworth chartered, along with seven New York "patents." Dorset was of special interest, with the patents of Princetown, Chatham, and Eugene overlapping its borders.

Columbia University Press

III. That before any Division of the Land be made to and among the Grantees, a Tract of Land as near the Centre of the said Township as the Land will admit of, shall be reserved and marked out for Town Lots, one of which shall be allotted to each Grantee of the Contents of one Acre.

IV. Yielding and paying therefor to Us, our Heirs and Successors for the Space of ten Years, to be computed from the Date hereof, the Rent of one Ear of Indian Corn only, on the twenty-fifth Day of December *annually, if lawfully demanded, the first Payment to be made on the twenty-fifth Day of* December, 1762.

V. Every Proprietor, Settler or Inhabitant, shall yield and pay unto Us, our Heirs and Successors yearly, and every Year forever, from and after the Expiration of ten Years from the abovesaid twenty-fifth Day of December, *which will be in the Year of Our Lord 1772* One shilling *Proclamation Money for every Hundred Acres he so owns, settles or possesses, and so in Proportion for a greater or lesser Tract of the said Land; which Money shall be paid by the respective Persons abovesaid, their Heirs or Assigns, in our* Council Chamber *in* Portsmouth, *or to such Officer or Officers as shall be appointed to receive the same; and this to be in Lieu of all other Rents and Services whatsoever.*

In Testimony whereof we have caused the Seal of our said Province to be hereunto affixed. Witness BENNING WENTWORTH, Esq; Our Governor and Commander in Chief of Our said Province, the 20th Day of August In the Year of our Lord CHRIST, One Thousand Seven Hundred and Sixty one And in the First Year of Our Reign.

B Wentworth

On the back of the charter is this important memorandum, almost an afterthought:

His Excellency Benning Wentworth Esq. a Tract of Land to Contain five hundred acres as marked B.W. in the Plan which is to be accounted two of the within shares one whole share for the Incorporated Sosiety for the propagation of the Gospel in foreign parts one share for a Glebe for the Church of England as by Law established—one share for the first settled Minister and one share for the benefit of a school in Town.

The charter was also signed by Theodore Atkinson, secretary of the province of New Hampshire, and dated August 20, 1761. Names of the grantees or proprietors follow (this page of the charter is reproduced as the back cover of this book.) Not only did none of them ever settle in town, but it is probable that few ever set eyes on the place thenceforward known as Dorset.

Of the sixty-four grantees of Dorset listed on the charter, seventeen have the surname of Lyman or Lymon (eighteen if a name spelled "Lem'on" is counted). Of these the name of Gideon Lyman, Esq. appears thrice, and

A view, circa 1901, looking north from Emerald Lake in North Dorset. Note the Rutland Railroad tracks and unpaved Route 7. In his 1765 diary, three years before the town was settled, Yorker James Duane referred to "a large pond" in the northeast section of Dorset.

Gideon Lyman, Jr. once; the name of Captain William Lyman appears twice. Other Lymans include Timothy, Elijah, Gad, Elias, Elijah, Job, Joel, and John. There are several persons with the surname of Olvard, some Pomroys, Hubbards, Parsons, and Ruggleses. None of them settled in Dorset.

It was the role of the grantees to pay the royal governor for the privilege of speculating in land and making money. But it was a legal fiction to suppose that any of them would actually settle on this land drawn six miles square on a piece of parchment, acreage 23,040. The proprietors did meet annually, starting with a meeting in 1765 in Great Barrington, Massachusetts, and after 1769 in Dorset. They divided up the lands they would sell to the settlers, resolved a boundary dispute with Manchester, and laid out the first highways. Using settlers as their agents, the proprietors continued to hold pro forma meetings until early in the nineteenth century.

The charter's description of town boundaries seems truly haphazard. Each town was drawn and described by Wentworth only as it related to a previous town. Dorset's legal description began at the northwest corner of Manchester. Chartered only nine days earlier, on August 11, Manchester began at the northeast corner of Arlington, chartered on July 28. Arlington began "at a Stake Six Miles due North of the North West corner of Bennington." And Bennington, chartered on January 11, 1749, began "At A Crotched Hemlock Tree marked W:W: Six miles Due North of A White Oak Tree

Standing in the Northern Boundary Line of the Province of Massachusetts bay Twenty four miles East of Hudson's River Marked M:C:J:T:."[4]

Like a flower that blooms briefly to offer its pollen to a specific kind of insect and then withers, the language of the Dorset charter blossomed in the hope of fulfilling a precise purpose, then quickly faded. Despite the charter's exacting stipulations, almost none was ever carried out. No one cut tall white pines in Dorset to be used as masts for the Royal Navy; no ear of Indian corn was ever paid on the 25th of December; no annual fairs or weekly markets were held pursuant to the charter's provisions. But the charter did establish Glebelands or leaselands to be used for religious or educational purposes, as did charters in nearly all Vermont towns during Wentworth's time.

Aside from the essential fact that the charter created a municipality that became recognized and legitimized, eventually was settled, and happened to flourish, the charter procedure was an elaborate sham. Benning Wentworth and his aides devised this legalistic verbiage solely to satisfy the Privy Council and Board of Trade attending His Majesty King George III. All circumstances surrounding the charter were designed to flatter and offer obeisance to His Majesty—the very name of the place, the conditions, and most notably the provisions for lands to be allocated to the "Society for the Propagation of the Gospel in foreign Parts," as well as to the official Church of England, and for a school. If the king happened to develop any doubts about the validity or worthiness of the town-chartering adventures of his royal appointee, the governor of New Hampshire, so the strategy went, perhaps those doubts would be laid to rest by knowledge that in each of those towns generous portions of land were designated for religious purposes—to support the propagation of the official faith and for the Church of England—in addition to land set aside for schools. Then as now, it would not be easy for a political figure to appear to oppose religion or education.

Nor is it farfetched to suggest the analogy of an overzealous land developer who makes elaborate promises in order to get his plans past a zoning board and planning commission, then proceeds—because no one is watching—to make all the profit he can in any way that suits him. Governor Wentworth's purpose was to charter towns to earn fees and to reward land speculators—and to beat the royal province of New York to the punch in doing so. He almost failed.

Wentworth's most active year was 1761, when he chartered 63 towns, of which 35 were located west of the Green Mountains and thus more provocative to the New York authorities. In 1762 he slowed down and chartered only 9 towns; but in 1763 he bounced back and created 37 towns, of which 23 were west of the Green Mountains. Only after all this threatening

The Complexities of Chartering

activity was New York prompted to take action, and in the end its actions proved ineffectual.

By December 28, 1763, Acting Governor Cadwallader Colden of New York had had enough of this New Hampshire town-chartering business. He issued a proclamation commanding all his civil officers to exercise New York's jurisdiction over territory that extended to the west bank of the Connecticut River; he wanted a list of names of all settlers on the disputed lands. Less than a month later, Colden issued a formal complaint against Wentworth to the Board of Trade in London and asked for some resolution of the dispute. But Wentworth issued a counterproclamation to assure settlers in what was becoming known as the New Hampshire Grants that their townships and land claims were valid. He sent a copy to the Board of Trade.

The response from London was notably ambiguous. The Board of Trade attempted to resolve this interprovincial dispute by declaring "the Western banks of the River Connecticut, from where it enters the Province of Massachusetts Bay, as far North as the forty fifth Degree of Northern Latitute, *to be* the Boundary Line between the two Provinces." This caused no end of confusion because Wentworth and his followers chose to interpret the phrase "to be" as applying only to the future and thus implicitly confirming what had gone on in the past.

A similarly befuddling order of the king in council was issued on July 25, 1767, based on petitions from Samuel Robinson of Bennington on behalf of more than a thousand alleged grantees in the New Hampshire Grants (a greatly inflated figure) and from the cleverly named "Incorporated Society for the Propagation of the Gospel in Foreign Parts." The order forbade the governor of New York to make any grants on the lands in question "until His Majesty's further pleasure should be known." But this was interpreted by New York as meaning that the prohibition did not extend to lands that had not been granted by the government of New Hampshire.[5]

More was at stake than territorial jurisdiction or political hegemony, for there were basic differences between the social and economic systems represented by the two opposing provinces. Historian Matt Jones describes the situation this way: "This conflict involved two incompatible theories of land ownership and development. New York fostered great manors owned by a few wealthy men and cultivated by tenant farmers, while New Hampshire, like the rest of New England, followed the policy of dividing the land into relatively small farms owned in fee by the men who tilled the soil. In the end the New Hampshire group prevailed."[6]

The dispute raged on and on, and if it had not been for the arrival of Ethan Allen around 1769, in the second year of Dorset's settlement, and the formation of the Green Mountain Boys, Vermont as we know it surely would not have been created. Allen, his brothers and cousins, and assorted rustic allies, provided a vital rallying focus for the settlers of the Grants and established in the minds of authorities of New York an intimidating aura of redneck retaliation. The Green Mountain Boys skillfully manipulated public opinion on both sides of the border by means of the written word, by image-enhancing deeds of retribution and harassment, and by seeming to be in all places at all times. They were skilled propagandists and knew how to use humor, ridicule, and hyperbole as well as legal mumbo-jumbo to achieve their ends. For example, on April 26, 1774, Ethan Allen, Seth Warner, Remember Baker, and Robert Cochran employed the following colorful language to describe Governor William Tryon of New York and his legislature, which had enacted a law to prevent "tumultuous and riotous assembles" in the Grants:

And, inasmuch as the malignity of their disposition towards us, hath flamed to an immeasurable and murderous degree, they have, in their new-fangled laws, calculated for the meridian of the New-Hampshire grants, passed the 9th of March, 1774, so calculated them, as to correspond with the depravedness of their minds and morals:—in them laws, they have exhibited their genuine pictures. The emblems of their insatiable, avaricious, overbearing, inhuman, barbarous, and bloodguiltiness of disposition and intention is therein portrayed in that transparent image of themselves, which cannot fail to be a blot, and an infamous reproach to them, to posterity.[7]

That Ethan and his brothers and cousins were also heavily engaged in land speculation is often forgotten in the telling and retelling of their achievements. Although both the truths and legends about the Green Mountain Boys are of vital significance to the formation of the independent republic of Vermont, the first direct involvement of the town of Dorset would take place because of its geographic location as focal point for the conventions in 1775 and 1776 that led directly to that state of independence.

In the eleven years between early 1764, when Colden proclaimed and Wentworth counterproclaimed, and early 1775, when the Battle of Lexington signaled the outbreak of hostilities between the colonies and Great Britain, a state of open rebellion existed more or less continuously in the New Hampshire Grants against New York. Gradually during this time the idea took root that it might be advisable to break the bonds with *both* tyrannical regimes by advocating the concept of a separate state that was beholden neither to New York nor Great Britain. The germ of this new idea was to quicken and develop at the Dorset Conventions called by settlers on the west side

The Complexities of Chartering 35

of the Grants. But this is getting ahead of the story, for Dorset had not even been settled yet in the early 1760s, nor was it among the first towns to attract pioneers.

Bennington County was opened to exploration and settlement after the end of the French and Indian Wars in 1759. A credible legend about the first settler is that, after serving in those wars, Samuel Robinson of Hardwick, Massachusetts, lost his way returning home and, mistaking the Walloomsac River for the Hoosick, wandered into the vicinity of Bennington; he liked what he saw, and in the spring of 1761 chose to return there with his family. Robinson had other agendas. He was a Congregational separatist who was having trouble with his home church and wished to establish a church based on his own brand of theology. And he was interested, with many others from the southern New England colonies, in speculating in some of that fertile, beautiful, inexpensive, and newly available land in territory that was soon to become the New Hampshire Grants.

Habitations were started in southern Bennington County and proceeded north. Robinson and a few friends settled in what is now Old Bennington in the spring of 1761. Shaftsbury was first settled in 1763, Arlington in 1764, Manchester in 1765.

In 1764, after the Board of Trade's equivocal declaration about where New York's eastern boundary was located, officials of New York decided that they could be doing the same things as Benning Wentworth in lands east of the Hudson. Profits were to be made there, perhaps, if they moved quickly; in case of a showdown, it had been hinted that London would back them and not New Hampshire.

Cadwallader Colden, lieutenant governor of New York, repeatedly served brief terms as acting governor whenever the king decided to appoint a new royal governor—which was fairly often. Colden was especially hard-nosed toward competitive activities in the New Hampshire Grants.

The first town patented by New York inside "Vermont" was Princetown. (New York's terminology was to "patent" a town, while New Hampshire's was to "charter.") The Princetown patent was issued on May 21, 1765, by Acting Governor Colden. At first Princetown was issued to twenty-six patentees for one thousand acres each, or a total of twenty-six thousand acres. But Colden was playing the same kinds of games as Wentworth, and by some legerdemain all of those patentees immediately conveyed their shares to three prominent speculators in what were considered "the wild lands." The three were John Taber Kempe, the attorney general of New York, James Duane, an important lawyer in New York City and Albany, and Major Walter Rutherford, a wealthy merchant speculator.

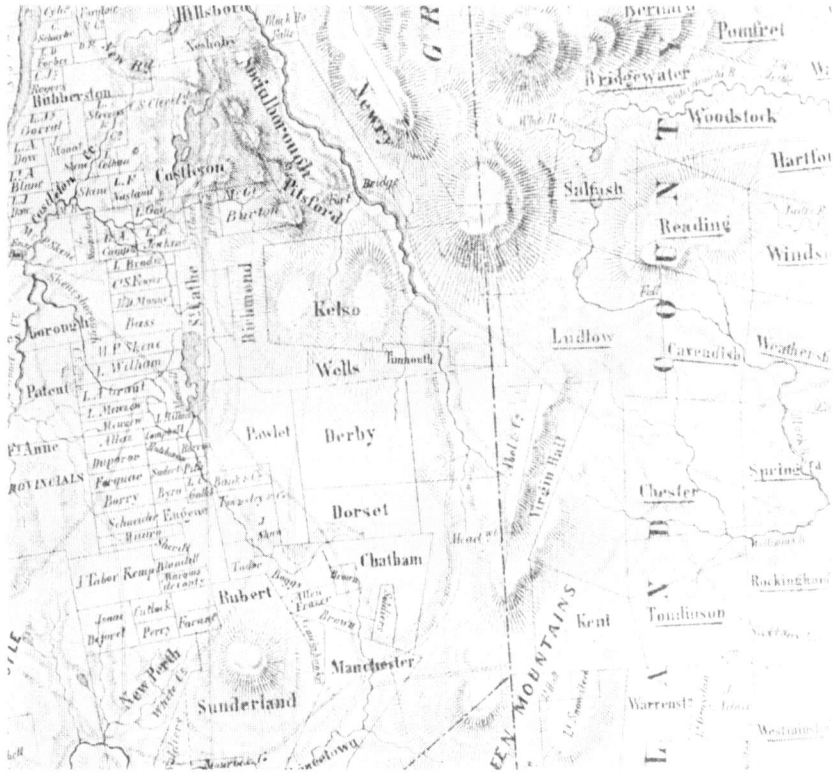

A visual jumble of towns chartered by New Hampshire and patented by New York is evident in this historic 1779 map. By the time mapmaker Claude Joseph Sauthier had done his surveying and the map could be published in London, all of New York's authority over the Vermont territory had disappeared. Dorset is shown as a thin rectangle between New York's "Chatham" and a misspelled "Derby," meaning Danby. Sauthier was hired by William Tryon while governor of North Carolina, who brought him along when Tryon became governor of New York. While surveying for this map, Sauthier also became an active speculator in the New Hampshire Grants.

Colden was equally adroit as Wentworth at playing the game that might be called "flatter the king." Accordingly, Princetown was named for the eldest son of King George III, George Augustus Frederick, who had just been made prince of Wales. The twenty-six thousand-acre patent of Princetown included the best and most fertile land of the Battenkill River valley, and overlapped portions of New Hampshire's towns of Manchester, Arlington, Sunderland, and Dorset. The unusual shape of the patent directly violated instructions from the Crown—as Attorney General Kempe should have known—which declared that the length of each tract must not extend along the banks of any river but that a patent should be of regular shape so it encompassed both profitable and unprofitable acres. Princetown was hardly square; it was almost hourglass-shaped, and it tilted, as does the Battenkill, in a northeast-southwest direction.

Several other towns or territories in the vicinity were patented in Duane's name. One that was planned but never officially granted by New York was the bizarrely shaped town of Chatham, as the accompanying map shows, centered precisely on New Hampshire's Dorset. Slightly to the northwest of that was Eugene, covering most of what Wentworth chartered as Pawlet but also overlapping into Rupert and touching the northwest corner of Dorset. Several miles north, in what Wentworth created as Rutland and Pittsford, was New York's town of Socialborough, formed for Duane with the intention that it would become a social club catering to wealthy New York businessmen. Overlapping Clarendon, Shrewsbury, and Wallingford was another Duane-inspired speculative town known as Durham. On a portion of Sandgate, and also on a noncontiguous parcel between Cambridge and Salem, New York, Duane patented still another town called West Cambden.

In all, between May 21, 1765, when Princetown was patented, and January 12, 1776, New York issued 101 patents covering more than two million acres inside what is now Vermont.

A Tour of Princetown

Duane and Rutherford knew that a place called Dorset existed, but they knew it only as a name given to a putative township chartered by the governor of New Hampshire. Almost immediately after Princetown was patented, during the good weather of June and July 1765 Duane and Rutherford visited their new possession. They rode over from Albany on horseback and hired as their reluctant guide none other than the most prominent settler on the Grants, Samuel Robinson, first inhabitant of Bennington. Surely Robinson wanted as much as anything to size them up and figured that there was no harm in showing the Yorkers how many settlers already had started to clear land and build habitations.

(Robinson would travel to London in the winter of 1766–67 to make a personal appeal to the King asking him to legitimize the new settlements in the New Hampshire Grants, and to plead that settlers be allowed to retain their lands as well as the townships Wentworth had granted. After meeting with modest success in this quest, Robinson took ill with smallpox and died while in London, and thus the effectiveness of his journey was negated.)

Duane and Rutherford both kept diaries of their tour of Princetown. Duane recorded in the summer of 1765 that forty persons had built houses or started settlements within the boundaries of what they considered to be Princetown.[8] Duane's diary describes their arrival in Bennington on Monday, July 1, when they dined at the home of Captain John Fassett and traveled over land in Bennington and Pownal, some of it good and some of it "in general rough & uneven & its produce mean." They found Pownal not very appealing: "In the Evening we got to the Tavern—a Miserable Hut! filled with the Miscreant Inhabitants of this Town who are a Mixture of Dutch & English. We lodged at Wrights where our accommodations were tolerable."

On Tuesday, Duane and Rutherford turned northward, visited the house, barn, and cleared land of Mr. Walbridge (located in what is now Papermill Village near North Bennington), and observed the sawmill and gristmill of Mr. Robinson. Then they continued north into Shaftsbury, and on Wednesday went to Arlington, where they "found the land very hilly & uneven, the quality not extraordinary." It was there they first viewed the centerpiece of their territory, about which Duane wrote: "There we had a view of the Batten Creek, which is a very fine rivulet two or three chains wide, the stream at this Time Rapid & Water pretty deep."

On July 4 (eleven years before the date had reason to become a national holiday) they continued northward into Sunderland and Manchester where Duane found the land "extraordinary fine" except for a mountain "which is steep and I believe barren." He must have been referring to Mt. Equinox.

They met Captain Jehiel Hawley, one of the first settlers in Arlington, "but he was shy of treating with us tho we made advances. Old Robinson shewed the same behavior." Hawley, known as "the father of Arlington," and Robinson, who could be called the same for Bennington, were willing to guide the aristocratic New York speculators; but their anxiety showed.

Finally the visitors reached Dorset, and to quote Duane's journal (retaining his spelling):

Several People are beginning their Improvements in our part of Arlington, Sunderland & Manchester—tho theres no Building of value & very little yet cleared.

One—a young man behaved with much Civility & respect, he has begun to clear a Farm & we promised to encourage him.

From Pownal to Crown Point theres a Road cut. But when it comes to about the Middle of Dorset there's a mountain, which is extremely difficult to pass over with a Horse.

From Information of a Proprietor in Dorset [not a settler, but a proprietor, and he is not named] I suppose a Road may be made by passing thro' on the West side of the last mentioned Mountain where theres an Intervail.

The Complexities of Chartering 39

On each side of this mountain theres good Land. In or near the North East bounds of Dorset is a large Pond where theres good fishing; but it is difficult of access. Near this place we suppose is the common source of Batten Kill & Otter Creek, the first emptying itself into Hudson's River at Sarghtoga (sic) the other into Lake Champlain.

Otter Creek runs from the said North East Corner of Dorset towards the center of Hardwyck and there takes a turn to the westward, cutting by the North East corner of Danby. In Hardwyck, Danby & Pawlet are very good Lands. [Duane's references to Hardwyck means Harwich, later changed to Mt. Tabor because it was constantly confused with Hardwick, in Caledonia County.]

By the best Information we could collect there were about 45 families in Prince Town, fifty in Bennington, seven or eight in Shaftsbury, the like number in Arlington, two in Sunderland and not more in Manchester, in Dorset none. This night lodged again at Waters' in Shaftsbury.

Rutherford's only recorded comments about Dorset were that while no houses had been built yet, there were "several Improvements begun by Kinderhook [New York] men and a Road is open clear thro the Interval quite as far as Crown Point, being laid up 60 Miles from Bennington." Rutherford continued: "Several Waggons went up this Spring in 18 days from said Town [Bennington], a fine Pond of 100 Acres in this Town [Dorset] full of Perch and Trout. Said to be Head of Otter Creek. Battons Kill enters said Town, and comes from a Gully in the Green Ridge. Indians say that the North Branch of B. Kill and Otter Creek come both out of an Ash Swamp to the West of Green Mountain."

Duane and Rutherford returned to Manhattan by way of Walloomsac, New York, and the Hoosick River, where Duane observed that farmland belonging to Colonel Van Courtland and his brothers "will probably be worn out by too constant tillage." They journeyed through Stillwater and Saratoga to stay overnight in Albany, then in another day went to inspect Duane's new personal patent, known as Duanesburg, a few miles west of Schenectady. From July 9 to 16 they continued "for a passage"—down Hudson's River—and back to New York City.

These diary comments form a remarkable description of Dorset and surrounding towns three years before Dorset was settled. The early visitors knew all about the Battenkill, Otter Creek, and Dorset Pond (later to be called Emerald Lake) and how their sources originated in a common region up in the mountains. A grand perspective is obtained by trying to envision traveling northward into Dorset before there was any civilization at all, and to imagine riding a horse, in the absence of roads, over that big mountain.

The municipal entity known as Princetown eventually faded away, as did Chatham, Durham, Eugene, Socialborough, and all the other towns New

York patented in the Grants, after the Green Mountain Boys made it their business to threaten and harass away all attempts by the Yorker surveyors or sheriffs to measure boundaries or assert jurisdiction.

A few other events are known about the years between the visit of Duane and Rutherford in 1765 and Dorset's settlement in 1768.

In the same month that New York created Princetown, Dorset's proprietors held their first known meeting, though not in Dorset. They met on April 17, 1765, in "Grate Barrington" (Massachusetts) at the home of John Bogart and proceeded to elect Lieutenant Hendrick Bogart as moderator and Israel Dewey as clerk. To a committee "to lay out the lots" they named Asa Alger, Jacob Vosburgh, and Casparus Conyne Jr. As assessors they elected Peter Vosburgh, Larrance Goose, and Harmon Pruim.[9]

On June 10, 1766, many of the same Dorset proprietors' names appeared on a petition to Sir Henry Moore, then governor of New York, to confirm with him their patent of the town. Dorset was by no means alone in that condition for during this time speculative proprietors from ninety-two of the New Hampshire-chartered towns, by seeking confirmation of patents, took the calculated risk that New York might end up on the winning side of the dispute. But only eighteen towns "passed the seals," to use New York's term for confirmation.[10]

Though the spelling of the names of these proprietors was crude, some appeared to be the same as those mentioned in the first meeting of proprietors in April of 1765. Based on their handwriting, these names included Hendrick Bogard, Matthew Goes, Peter Vosburgh, Johannis Van Alen, Wyndert Vosburgh, John Leggett, Casparus Conyn, Jeremiah [also spelled Jeremye] Miller, Cornelius van Hoesen, John Bongheart [probably Bogart], and [indistinct] Pruyn. In their petition to Governor Moore, they acknowledged that Benning Wentworth on August 20, 1761, had granted to Gideon Lyman, Esq. and others a parcel of land that was incorporated into a town by the name of Dorset, and they reiterated those basic facts and the boundaries.

They asserted that they had purchased the rights of the patentees "for a valuable consideration," and claimed to have made "very considerable improvements." (It is likely that some of them were the "men from Kinderhook" whom Rutherford mentioned in his journal as having "begun improvements.") The petitioners to Governor Moore phrased their plea this way: "But now as it is—may it please your Excellency that your petitioners have lately received information that the said lands lye—within this province and not within the province of New Hampshire of which your petitioners are not competent judges but willing and desirous to secure their possession and improvements uninterruptedly and to avoid all future trouble and controversy are inclineable to obtain his majesty's grant of confirmation under the proud seal of this province of New York for the same."

Nothing ever came of this petition. The Dorset proprietors probably exaggerated the amounts of their payments and the extent of their "improvements," and the whole episode can be regarded as a gamble that did not pay off. Dorset was in good company. Other Wentworth-chartered towns for which New York confirmation of patents was sought but not obtained included Brandon, Burlington, Danby, Pawlet, Peru, Pittsford, Rupert, Rutland, Sandgate, Shaftsbury, Sunderland, Wallingford, Winhall, and Woodford.

In the winter of 1767, the year before settlement, New York surveyor William Cockburn had completed explorations of lands north of Princetown for the royal province of New York. He was lucky during this particular venture, for in the course of his surveys a couple of years later in Durham and Socialborough, he was subjected to considerable harassment by settlers and by the Green Mountain Boys, who broke his surveying instruments and sent him packing toward Albany. In any case, in sworn documents dated February 13 and 15, 1767, Cockburn certified that there were still no settlers and no improvements to his knowledge in Dorset.[11]

Cockburn was a deputy to New York surveyor general Alexander Colden, son of the Vermont antagonist Cadwallader Colden, who himself had been surveyor general for many years prior to his elevation as alternate lieutenant governor and acting governor. Cockburn's knowledge of Dorset was centered around its most conspicuous physical feature, which he called "the Elk Mountain." Cockburn's February 13 statement was as follows:

THESE are to certifie, That in my Survey of a Tract of Land on the Northward of Princetown, and East side of the Elk Mountain, I found no Settlers, & was likewise informed by the Neighbouring Inhabitants There was none—and as I understood they proposed to make some Improvements in Dorset I put up an Advertisement at Capt. Hawley's [in Arlington], Intimating that agreeable to an order of the Lieut. Governor and Council—if any persons had made Improvements there and would apply to me, I would survey there respective Lots, and make a Return of them to the Surveyor General in order to there obtaining a Confirmation Thereof in the Province of New York. But none apply'd.

Two days later Cockburn made the following statement, and on February 16 had it notarized by Dan Horsmanden, chief justice of the New York colony:

THESE ARE TO CERTIFIE, That by virtue of warrants from his Excellency the Governor I did, in the months of October and November last, Survey and lay out several Tracts of Land, to wit, two thousand acres for Lieut. John Cruickshanks. The same quantity for Lieut. John Bowen: The same Quantity for Ensign Alexander Fraser: The same Quantity for Surgeon James Boggs: All lying to the northward of Princetown, in the County of Albany, and, except a small Part thereof, within what I understood to be the Limits of a Township formerly erected by the Government of New-Hampshire by the name of Dorset.

THAT at the same time I did run out another tract of 2500 Acres of Land, petitioned for by Henry Biram, and other non-Commission Officers and soldiers, also lying with the Limits aforesaid, and to the Eastward of a Mountain there called the Elk Mountain; And 250 acres more petitioned for by Charles Hughes & Robert McCullogh, within those limits to the Northward of James Boggs.

THAT, I found no Letters on any Part of the said Lands so surveyed and set out; and was likewise informed by the Neighbouring Inhabitants, that there were none.

THAT, before I went upon the said Survey, I put up an Advertisement at the House of Captain Hawley, the most Public Place among the Settlements in that part of the Country: Intimating, that if any Person had made Improvements, within the intended Surveys, and would apply to me, I would, agreeable to an Order of the Lieutenant Governor and Council, survey their respective Lots, and make a Return of them to the Surveyor General; in Order to their obtaining a Confirmation thereof under this Government; but none applied to me.

Up to this point in time the deer, bear, beaver, and partridge that for centuries had had Dorset all to themselves remained blissfully undisturbed while jurisdictional disputes raged to their east and west among political leaders of the species known by a name which, translated from the Latin, means "wise man." In 1768 the wild creatures were about to be rudely intruded upon.

NOTES

1. An amusing and interpretive exploration of Benning Wentworth's town-chartering experiences is provided by Frederick F. Van de Water, *The Reluctant Republic* (New York: John Day Company, 1941), notably a chapter titled "His Excellency the Realtor." A relevant volume that makes fascinating reading is *State Papers of Vermont, Vol. VII, New York Land Patents 1688–1786, Covering Land Now Included in the State of Vermont* (Montpelier, Vt.: Rawson C. Myrick, Secretary of State, 1947, ed. Mary Greene Nye), for its recitation of the dispute between New Hampshire and New York as bumblingly adjudicated by London.

2. Brice Harris, *Charles Sackville, Sixth Earl of Dorset: Patron and Poet of the Restoration* (Urbana, University of Illinois Press, 1940). This is a biography of the father of the nobleman for whom Dorset was probably named, and it helps explain the aura of arts patronage that became synonymous with the name "Dorset" in fifteenth-century England.

3. Most of this discussion of the English noblemen for whom Benning Wentworth named

The Complexities of Chartering 43

towns in Vermont is based on the research of Esther M. Swift in *Vermont Place-Names: Footprints of History* (Brattleboro, Vt.: Stephen Greene Press, 1977).

4. Secretary of State's Archives, Montpelier.

5. Matt Bushnell Jones, *Vermont in the Making* (Cambridge, Mass.: Harvard University Press, 1939), contains the best modern account of the sequence of the dispute between settlers of the New Hampshire Grants and the royal province of New York. A longer, drier, more traditional study of this era, written with a strong anti–New York bias, is found in Hiland Hall *Early History of Vermont* (Albany, N.Y.: Joel Munsell, 1868). Chapter VII.

6. Jones, p. vii.

7. *State Papers of Vermont*, 1779–86, (Montpelier, Vt.: William Slade, Jr., Secretary of State, 1823), p. 50.

8. The journals of Walter Rutherford and James Duane on their trip to Princetown, from the James Duane Papers in the New-York Historical Society, appear as appendices D and E in Jones *Vermont in the Making*.

9. The names of proprietors as listed represent the writer's best attempt at deciphering the handwriting of Dorset Town Clerk John Underhill, who in 1817 transcribed all known accounts of proprietors' meetings into a document called the Proprietors' Book of Records. Some of these names appear on the list of original proprietors and some do not.

10. New York Land Papers 21:11, a list of New Hampshire Grants west of Green Mountains that sought confirmation from New York. Albany, N.Y.: New York State Library, 1766).

11. Sworn certificate of William Cockburn, a copy of which is in the possession of Arthur W. Gilbert, Dorset.

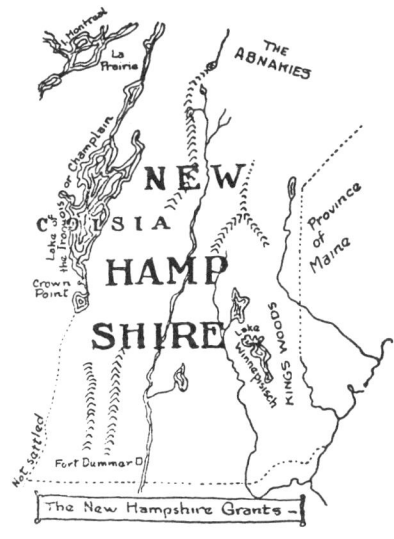

Settlement and the First Years

AS DORSET'S first settler, Felix Powell won fifty free acres, granted at a meeting of the proprietors on May 23, 1769, at the Dorset home of Isaac Lacey. Powell's lands were to be selected from any of the untrammeled wilderness that had not been already divided, wherever he saw fit.[1]

A member of a Welsh family that migrated early to Gloucester in the Massachusetts Bay Colony, Powell was a peripatetic pioneer in the New Hampshire Grants perhaps because of the promise of free land for each "first settler" of a new township.

Powell was not only Dorset's first settler in 1768, but he was also the first settler of Burlington in 1773 and a founding settler of Pittsford. Powell is mentioned in Crockett's history of Vermont and also in Caverly's history of Pittsford, though they do not agree on when he came to Pittsford. After his death, Powell's remains were returned for burial to Dorset. "He seems to have left no mark upon the community life, but to have come—and to our mortification gone—like an illusive shadow," wrote Zephine Humphrey.

In Dorset in that first year of habitation, Powell was joined by Isaac Lacey, from Connecticut, and Benjamin Baldwin, Abraham Underhill, John Manley, and George Page from New York.

Ira Allen first surveyed Burlington in 1772 (where nearly twenty years later he would found the University of Vermont). In 1773 for thirty pounds Felix Powell purchased a tract of Burlington land near Appletree Point extending nearly to the Winooski River. He bought it from Samuel Avery of Litchfield County, Connecticut, an original Burlington proprietor and large-scale land speculator. Powell cleared some of this land, built a cabin, stayed four years, then sold his property in 1778 to James Murdock of Saybrook, Connecticut, at a profit of 160 pounds—recording the first of many real-estate profits that would follow in Vermont's Queen City.[2]

Wilderness life was rugged, and Powell experienced severe personal losses before succumbing to disease. While living in Pittsford in 1777 Powell lost his house to Indian depredations, and his wife suffered a terrifying trauma. In September of 1777—after the patriots' victory at the Battle of Bennington but before Burgoyne's surrender at Saratoga—Pittsford was having trouble with Indians. One night two brothers, John and Joseph Rowley, aged eleven and fifteen, were seized by Indians and taken to Canada. A few nights later, while Felix Powell was away, his house was attacked by Indians. The pregnant Mrs. Powell managed to flee, and from the cover of darkness and foliage she watched the plundering and burning of their home. Then before morning dawned she gave birth to a daughter—the first white child born in Pittsford, though she lived only a few weeks. Powell forfeited his fifty acres in Pittsford by failing to meet a stipulation that he build a sawmill and keep it in repair for five years.[3]

Powell must have sold his Dorset property before moving on. His other movements have been lost to time except for the final act: after his death, during the American Revolution, his feelings for Dorset were strong enough to cause his kin to bury him there. His grave, along with those of ten others who died of "plague," was in a tiny cemetery near the West Road and Route 30, though there is no evidence today of a burial ground there.

This was a time when epidemics were frequent, diagnoses primitive, and treatments mostly ineffective. It is likely that the "plague" was smallpox, which is known to have struck the Bennington region in 1773, 1777, 1783, and again in 1794. Starting in 1800, Dorset would authorize town-funded inoculations against smallpox. The affliction known as fever or "ague" was common, and dysentery was "universally epidemic" in 1776 and 1777, affecting Burgoyne's army and mercenaries as they marched southward from Canada.[4]

The Pioneering Families

After Dorset's first six settlers had led the way, others of European stock recognized the attractions of this fertile and stimulating environment. Benjamin Baldwin attracted his brothers Asa, Eleazer, and Elisha, along with relatives Silas and Thomas Baldwin. Benjamin was "a man of almost herculean strength," who settled about a mile east of the village in the Kirby Hollow section and raised the first apples in town.

Dorset artist Wallace W. Fahnestock painted this mural of early settlers; it was on a wall of the old Arlington High School that burned in 1941.

Some of Benjamin's many children—Guy, Edward, Benjamin Jr., Asa, Benjamin II, William, Deborah, Rachel, Sarah, Ruth, Thomas K., Lorena, and Mary—migrated westward, though Benjamin, Jr., an infant, was the first person to be buried in the Maple Hill Cemetery when he died, in 1772, twelve years before a church was established there. Benjamin the elder lived until 1830, to the age of eighty-six. The house of "Uncle Ben and Aunt Ruth" was one of warmth and kindness, with Baldwin known for his spicy stories and good cheer, and his benevolent wife taking in many poor children.[5]

Asa Baldwin established himself as a man of culture and education, and became Dorset's first town clerk and one of its first selectmen. He also remained loyal to Great Britain, and thus saw his property seized by the Court of Confiscation in the early days of the Vermont Republic. Unlike many other Tories, Baldwin was allowed to return; he came back to Dorset in 1783 with his reputation intact, and was considered a useful and respected citizen. He died 1827, at the age of sixty-three.

Pioneer Abraham Underhill was thirty-eight when he settled in South Dorset in 1768. His home, an inn on the east side of the present Route 30 near the Morse Hill Road, soon became the unofficial town hall, where early town meetings were held. Captain Underhill was active in the revolutionary cause and raised a company of militiamen which he commanded. He is said to have been "a man of very humane feelings" who could reconcile persons of differing viewpoints. He served on the Vermont Council of Safety that preceded the first state government.

Underhill thrice represented Dorset in the legislature, starting in the fall of 1778 when he succeeded Cephas Kent who had attended Vermont's first legislative session that spring. Underhill went to the session of 1780–81, and he shared those duties with Benjamin Baldwin in the 1784 session. After Underhill died in 1796, at the age of sixty-six, his home, then identified as that of "the widow Marcy Underhill," continued to be used for town meetings.

John Manley, Jr., a cabinetmaker, was followed to town by his father, Deacon John Manley, who settled in what is now Dorset Village with his wife, a half-sister of Benedict Arnold. (Many members of this family spelled the name *Manly*, and some still do.) A legend about John Manley, Jr., is that when he first arrived in town he camped for the night along the West Road and awoke in the morning to find his oxen missing. Searching, he found them browsing beside a spring (later called the Ethan Allen spring because Allen was reputed to have camped there on his way to capture Fort Ticonderoga in 1775). Manley liked the spot and built a log house there. Commented Zephine Humphrey of his decision, "We suppose it was hard to tell one place from another in those early days, for the woods were everywhere and the general 'lay of the land' must have been invisible." The Manley house became a tavern that was known by soldiers on both sides of the American Revolution. Therein lies another tale handed down for two hundred years and related in Humphrey's *Story of Dorset*: "Apparently Mrs. Manley cooked and washed dishes until she was exhausted and there was no food left in the house. For she gave up finally and went to bed, calling down to the next batch of soldiers, 'Open the pantry window and take some bread off the shelf. That's all there is.' In the morning she was thanked by the lingering soldiers. 'We dipped the bread in the soup and it was very good.' Soup! Let us hope she did not tell them that they had dipped their bread in the pan of dish-water which she had been too tired to empty out."

Deacon John Manley built a small marble house (now part of the Elam Miller home) along the East Road (now Route 30), and various dates are given for it: 1773, 1779, and 1780. Whichever year may be correct, if any, Manley thus made use of that noble native material, marble, several years before Reuben Bloomer and Isaac Underhill wedged the white stone out of the ground in 1785, the beginning of the first commercial marble quarry in the nation.

An important early settler was Thomas Farwell, whose family was to build four houses in Dorset village. Farwell came to town with a land agent who could have been one of the many Lymans who were Benning Wentworth's proprietors. Farwell selected some land and built a crude cabin, then went back to Connecticut for the winter. He returned in the spring of 1770 with his brothers Isaac, Asa, and John, and their families. They drove their yoke of oxen through Massachusetts, up the Connecticut River valley, and were astonished when they crossed the Green Mountains near Peru to encounter massive snowdrifts. There was also plenty of snow inside their bark-roofed cabin, located on the south corner of the West Road and Church Street. But they shoveled out the place and heated it, and then they began to thrive.[6]

Soon four Farwell farms were located around that intersection, and by 1792 Asa Farwell was granted a license to operate a tavern in the house he built in 1777 on the northeast corner [now owned by Bea Jackson Humphreys]. The West Road was then a post road connecting Bennington and Vergennes; some of its original milestone markers are still in place.

Reuben Bloomer married Susannah Paddock on April 22, 1761. Susannah, according to family records, came from "South East, Mass.," which her descendants interpret to mean Cape Cod. The couple lived in northern Westchester County, New York, and is reputed to have settled in Dorset in 1774, the probable year of the first town meeting. But Bloomer was around before that because his name appears in state records as having purchased land in Dorset from Asa Alger on July 12, 1769. Bloomer's purchase was confirmed by the General Assembly in 1782 because the original deed had been witnessed by one Samuel Wright, who had "deserted the county and joined the enemy."

Bloomer's name would remain prominent in Dorset not only for his role in opening the first marble quarry but also for the fact that he and Susannah raised a large and "robust" family. The legend has been passed along that they had nine sons and eight daughters, but the Bloomer family Bible carefully, and probably more truthfully, lists three sons, Coles, Reuben II, and Robert, and ten daughters, Mary, Mercy, Deborah, Elizabeth, Susannah, Nancy, Chloe, Keziah, Jerusha, and Roxey.

Bloomer served as an army teamster in the Battle of Hubbardton in 1777. Later that summer he remained on his farm after many had fled because of the threatened invasion by Burgoyne's army marching from Canada toward Albany. In early October, Bloomer had the lonely task of finding a burial site for his eldest son, Coles, age seven. In this effort he was assisted by a stranger who came along the road. Only a week later Bloomer's daughter Susannah, age nine, died. The cause has not been recorded, but there was a smallpox epidemic in Bennington County in 1777. Bloomer himself lived to be eighty-six, and died May 2, 1824, and his wife lived to be ninety-one. The name Bloomer would remain in Dorset until the 1890's though other descendants reside elsewhere in Vermont.

The name Paddock would be significant too. Prince Paddock was among the first settlers in Dorset Hollow in 1769, followed in 1780 by brothers John, Isaac, and Asa from Mansfield, Connecticut. Isaac had served in the French and Indian Wars and later fought for the Revolution as a commissioned officer in the Battle for Bunker Hill. The extent to which these early families intermarried is dramatized by the fact that three Paddock sisters, Mercy (or Marcy), Susannah, and Mary, were married to Abraham Underhill, Reuben Bloomer, and John Manley. Prince Paddock died in 1833 at seventy-six, and his wife Lucy died a decade later at eighty-six.

While 1769 was only the town's second year of habitation, a vital political turning point took place nearby. Down in Bennington on the farm of James Breakenridge, which adjoined the "twenty-mile line" east of the Hudson, the first of a series of disturbances took place between New Hampshire claimants and New York officials. On October 19, 1769, Breakenridge and several settlers engaged in an armed standoff against some New York commissioners and surveyors, accompanied by their "chainmen," who intended to take land measurements. The patriots' intransigence provoked New York to indict several Bennington settlers as "rioters." Though no one was arrested, the episode was the first phase of a lengthy dispute with New York authorities that was resolved only by statehood in 1791.

What happened at the Breakenridge farm was later sanctified as the first evidence of a spirit of pioneer independence. In 1927 the Daughters of the American Revolution placed a commemorative stone marker on the Murphy Road not far from the Henry covered bridge near North Bennington, declaring the site "the birthplace of Vermont."

The first settler of East Dorset was Zachariah Curtis, who arrived in 1769. Born in England, he migrated to Connecticut at the age of eighteen before deciding to head northward. Curtis bought a large quantity of land—most of what is known as the Route 7 valley, for a distance of five miles north of East Dorset—where he raised a family, supposedly, of twenty-five children. Legend has it that the original Curtis house, located at the outlet of Dorset Pond or Emerald Lake, was once burned by Indians.

There was no census of the Grants in 1770—there would be no official census until statehood in 1791—but the territory's population was estimated by historian Lewis Stilwell at seven thousand. In wilderness conditions nearly every stream was capable of being tapped for power, Stillwell observed. Only after tree roots and other vegetation were removed from channeled banks did streams become subject to erosion and flooding, minimizing their usefulness for power.

The first gristmill and sawmill in town were believed to have been built by Deacon Israel Bostwick, using the power of the Mettawee River near the lowest point of elevation in Dorset Hollow, where Kirby Hollow Road joins the Hollow Road.[7] Another early Mettawee sawmill site, that of Ira Sykes, was to become one of Dorset's most enduring industries, later known as the Edgerton sawmill, then Bearpaw Lumber.

An important early industry in Dorset, as in all of New England, was the production of potash salts—achieved by boiling down the lye leached from ashes of trees that were cut to clear the land—the end product of which was soft soap. As late as 1820 an ashery was operated in Dorset village (near the site of the Field Club) to collect ashes from fireplaces and wood-burning stoves. In the 1820s the American potash business dwindled because of the discovery in Europe of chemical substitutes for the cleaning of wool.

In October of 1772, settlers of the Grants took an important preliminary step toward independence. Representatives of towns on the west side of the Green Mountains (Bennington, Manchester, Sunderland, Dorset, Rupert, Pawlet, Wells, Poultney, Castleton, Pittsford, and Rutland) held a convention in Manchester. They selected James Breakenridge of Bennington and Jehiel Hawley of Arlington as agents to appeal to the king in London to settle the dispute with New York and to confirm their claims under the Wentworth charters. This effort, which probably was endorsed by the provincial government in Portsmouth, had the effect for a while of causing New York to ease up on its land patents.[8]

About 1772 Titus Sykes, Jr., aged nineteen, arrived in Dorset from Suffield, Connecticut, and thus became the pioneer settler of a family that would expand greatly in numbers, influence, and acreage. Titus settled at the northern end of the West Road. He was followed by his father, Titus, Sr., and brothers Sylvanus, Ashbel, Jacob, Israel, and Victory.[9]

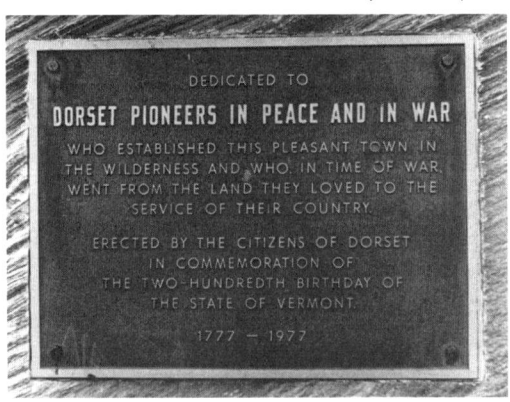

Photo by Chris Alexopoulos

The 1977 Bicentennial Memorial Rock at the Dorset Elementary School on Morse Hill Road. The plaque's inscription was written by Kathleen Ludlam of East Dorset

Titus Sykes, Sr., aged forty-six, first came to town in 1772 but decided to go back to Connecticut, then returned to Dorset, where he settled on a large farm on the East Road (Route 30) and died in 1811. Family tradition holds that his eldest son, Sylvanus, slept his first night in Dorset at Cephas Kent's inn with Ethan Allen as his bedfellow. Another family anecdote relates that during the flight from Burgoyne's army in 1777, one Sykes wife in her haste abandoned a wooden washtub full of water in her kitchen, later to discover that her wedding ring was missing. When she returned weeks later the tub was dry and its staves had fallen in but the ring was safe on the bottom of the tub.

Unlike the large Farwell family, who tended to cluster in the same neighborhood, the Sykeses spread out, as if to conquer the northwest quadrant of town. After two or three generations, in 1856, there were more Sykeses on the Grand List than any other name. In 1861 there were ten Sykes farms in Dorset; the 1869 Beers Atlas lists 13 Sykes households; and the 1880 Child's directory enumerates nine. Among Sykeses who served as town representative were Sylvanus, in 1832–3, Gilbert, in 1867–68, and Dwight, in 1882. In 1880 Gilbert M. Sykes was elected a Bennington County state senator.[10]

Back in Suffield, several members of the Sykes family had intermarried with Kents. According to family research, Sykeses also married Baldwins, Barrows, Bloomers, Childs, Crandalls, Crantons, Duntons, Edgertons, Gilberts, Grays, Harwoods, Hogebooms, Holleys, Jenks, Manleys, Pratts, Sheldons, Smiths, Towsleys, Underhills, and Williamses.

In 1773 a serious gentleman arrived in Dorset from Suffield who would play a strong role in the development of Dorset as well as Vermont's coming struggle for independence from New York and Great Britain. He was Cephas Kent, Sr., who migrated at age forty-eight with a wife, six sons, and three daughters, to claim the property of an uncle, Samuel, who had died in Dorset in 1772.

Cephas Kent, Sr., was known as deeply religious. A legend has been handed down that he came to town on a Friday, and by Saturday had made arrangements with Deacon John Manley for a service of religious worship that Sunday—the first such service to be held in Dorset. Then Deacon Kent and the settlers waited more than a decade to attract the first minister to town.

Deacon Kent was known for expressing himself sternly and frequently by stating, "Verily, I will have it so." He and his wife, Hannah Spencer, who married in 1747, had the following children: Mary (who died at an early age), John, Hannah, Cephas, Jr., Moses, Daniel, Mary 2nd, Alexander, Deborah, and Martin, all of whom were born before he settled in Dorset, and most of whom remained in town. At least three of the sons fought in the Battle of Bennington.

Son Daniel Kent, who served in Seth Warner's regiment at Bennington, chose a career as a clergyman and in 1791 became the first "settled minister" of the Old First Church in Old Bennington. Much is known about the life and especially the military career of the Reverend Dan Kent, because in 1832 at the age of seventy-four in applying for a pension he prepared a document to recount his Revolutionary War service. The application was filed with the probate court in Fair Haven, near the Rutland County town of Benson, where he served as a minster for thirty-six years. He got his pension.[11]

Another immigrant from Connecticut, in 1774, was Deacon Ebenezer Morse, who became an active Whig during the Revolution and was on the Committee of Safety and a deacon of the Congregational church. His son, Dr. Alpheus Morse, served Dorset as a physician for some thirty years, in addition to being proprietor of the Dorset Inn, before he moved on to northern New York state, where he practiced medicine for another twenty-four years.

In 1780, at the age of sixteen, Justus Holley came to town from Richmond, Massachusetts, about seventy miles down the road. Holley served as a fifer in Captain Robinson's Bennington militia, where his request for a gun instead of a musical instrument was refused because of the regiment's need for a musician. He married Elizabeth Field, who was a babe in arms when her family migrated from Mansfield, Connecticut. The Holleys raised eleven children. They lived on the West Road where Holley combined farming with tailoring; he would travel the valley each fall to cut garments and prepare them for women to sew during the winter. Holley died at the age of eighty-six in 1849, his wife nine years later at eighty-five. The Holley family intermarried with several other prominent Dorset families.

Jonathan Armstrong settled in Dorset Hollow in the fall of 1779 from Norwich, Connecticut. Two years earlier he had served in the Battle of Bennington along with five brothers of his wife, Abigail Haynes, a Bennington resident. At Bennington he made a name for himself for having taken as prisoner the injured mercenary Colonel Francis Pfister, who later in the day died of wounds. Armstrong was thus depicted in a painting by Roy Williams of Weston, commissioned by the Bennington Museum, carrying the injured Hessian into a house. Armstrong was also a veteran of an early military expedition to Cuba, where he fought at the age of sixteen. He lived to be eighty-three and was buried in Maple Hill cemetery in 1826.

Other post-Revolution settlers included Titus Kellogg, a veteran who became the town's principal carpenter; Eliakim Deming, who with his half-brother, Tory William Marsh, owned most of the valley south of East Dorset, including Deming Pond; and William Ames, progenitor of a large family, who came from Wethersfield, Connecticut. Noah Morse arrived in 1778 from Massachusetts and in 1783 acquired a farm that was confiscated from accused Tory Price Bardslee.

From Mansfield, Connecticut, came Amos Field, who settled a farm near the north end of West Road that remained in this family for many years. (Field was a descendant of Zacharias Field, a founder of Hartford, Connecticut; he was related to the Chicago family that developed the Marshall Field department store, to the poet and critic Eugene Field, and to financier George Field.)

Colonel Stephen Martindale settled in Dorset in 1783 from Stockbridge, Massachusetts. He had volunteered to serve in the Battle of Bennington at the age of sixteen, weighing only sixty-six pounds. He was in Seth Warner's regiment, and when Warner saw the stripling he ordered him to take care of some horses—to the mortification of Martindale, who was thus prevented from engaging initially in the action. He did serve in the victorious action led by Warner. He later fought in the War of 1812. Laurel B. Armstrong recalled in 1868, "He was very tall and spare, courteous and gentlemanly in address, very energetic and active in all his movements, and one of the most graceful riders we ever saw mounted on horseback." Martindale was Dorset's legislator in 1794, 1801–02, and 1828. He died in 1845, at eighty-six.

In 1784 Captain John Shumway arrived in town from Mansfield, Connecticut, a veteran of army service since 1775. He served in the Battle of Monmouth, of which he reported that participants had orders to strip to their shirtsleeves and charge bayonet, and after the charge "the blood was shoe-deep" and "the dead lay on the ground like a flock of sheep." Later, Shumway was Dorset town clerk, a probate judge, and between 1783 and 1807 served nine times as town representative. He was the Dorset delegate to the 1791 state convention held in Bennington that approved Vermont's entry into the Union. Born in 1735, he died in 1829 at ninety-three.

The First Town Meeting?

The question of when Dorset's first town meeting was held seemed buried in history's haze when Zephine Humphrey investigated it in 1924, as it had earlier when writers for the William J. Fuller Woman's Relief Corps No. 23 researched the historical booklet they published in 1896.

On the basis of the number of settlers who arrived starting in 1768, followed by many more arrivals in the next five or six years, one could assume that municipal meetings must have been held before 1774; but if so the records are lost. In fact, current town records do not show a town meeting until March 14, 1797. Evidence that the first meeting *was* that of 1774 is found in *Demings's Vermont Officers* and in state confiscation papers that refer to Asa Baldwin's election as town clerk "at the organization of the town in 1774."[12] Wherever the truth lies, the 1774 town meeting was uneventful. It was called as follows:

Warning; these are to notify and warn the freeholders and inhabitants of the township of Dorset to meet at the house of Abraham Underhill, Innholder at Dorset, on Tuesday, the 8th day of March, at two of the clock in the afternoon for the following purpose: First, to choose a Moderator to govern the meeting; second, to choose town officers agreeable to the charter of said Dorset. Given under our hands this 26th day of February, A.D. 1774.
Asa Baldwin
Town Clerk

Asa Baldwin
Abraham Underhill
(selectmen)

Other first officers, besides Asa Baldwin as clerk and selectman, were selectmen Cephas Kent and John Manley and first constable George Gage. The first townwide Committee of Safety was chosen in 1778: Cephas Kent, John Manley, Asahel Herman, Ebenezer Morse, and Ephriam Reynolds.[13]

The Court of Confiscation

When the Republic of Vermont was formed in the summer of 1777 with the signing of the constitution at Windsor, substantial revenues were needed. A statewide Council of Safety was formed "to manage the affairs of the State until the government should go into operation under the newly adopted Constitution" and its powers encompassed executive, legislative, and judicial branches. The first meeting of the Council was held in Manchester on July 11, 1777, when Thomas Chittenden was elected president and Ira Allen treasurer.

The creative Allen proposed that state revenues could be raised without resorting to taxation by seizing the property of those who remained loyal to the British at the outbreak of the American Revolution. His scheme had the advantage of eliminating adversaries while it consolidated political support for those who held power. Furthermore, in the summer of 1777 the new state desperately needed funds to equip its militia, because Burgoyne's army was advancing south from Canada.[14]

The treatment of suspected Tories—those considered to have committed "notorious and treasonable acts"—was rough, but Ira Allen's plan adhered at least to a token degree of due process. Alleged Tories were brought into

Settlement and the First Years 55

a court where their views were examined. The term "Tory" was liberally interpreted, and justice was swift and ruthless.[15] The loyalty test was whether a person subscribed to this association adopted by the Dorset Convention of July 1776:

We the subscribers inhabitants of that District of Land, commonly called and known by the name of the New Hampshire Grants, do voluntarily and Solemnly Engage under all the ties held sacred amongst Mankind at the Risque of our Lives and fortunes to Defend, by arms, the United American States against the Hostile attempts of the British Fleets and Armies, until the present unhappy Controversy between the two Countries shall be settled.

By 1777 all males in the Grants over the age of sixteen either accepted that covenant or risked being regarded as an enemy. If judged the latter, judicial action would declare their property sequestered to prevent its removal, or confiscated and sold at auction. Joseph Bowker of Rutland, who chaired the third and fourth Dorset Conventions, was named commissioner of sequestration.[16]

On April 23, 1778, the Court of Confiscation of Bennington County, with John Fassett, Jr., as commissioner and Matthew Lyon as clerk, ordered evi-

Courtesy of Robert Dressler

This stone chimney was the last remnant of an early Masonic Temple on Morse Hill Road. The photo was taken in 1920, and little can be seen here now except a beautiful southerly view.

dence examined against several dozen alleged Tories, most of whom were from Pownal and Arlington. Suspects from Dorset were Enoch and Ephraim Mallary, Israel and Price Bardslee, and William Marsh. (The name Bardslee was spelled several ways but appears here as it does on family gravestones.) Though Dorset's most prominent Tory was town clerk-selectman Asa Baldwin, he was not summoned by the court at this time.

According to a law enacted on February 26, 1779, "certain persons" who were declared to have joined "the enemies" would also be ejected from Vermont. In case a declared Tory attempted to return, he would be arrested and brought before a justice of the peace. Whereupon "if they are found to be the person sought" the justice would "order him to be whipped on the naked Back, not more than forty nor less than twenty Stripes; which Punishment shall be inflicted, and the Delinquent shall be ordered to quit this State immediately." If any such person had the temerity to return again, after conviction by the Superior Court, "he shall be put to death." The penalty for harboring an enemy was five hundred pounds, to be divided so that two-thirds went to the state and one third to "whoever prosecutes the case."

In 1777 William Marsh moved to Dorset from Manchester, where he had settled before 1770. Even though Marsh was a prominent member of the Dorset Conventions, he later chose to remain loyal to the Crown and fled to Canada, leaving his family in Dorset. His wife Sarah was a daughter of Jeremiah French, a pioneer settler and large landowner in Manchester. French was also a Tory and was included with Marsh on the list of persons proscribed by legislation of February 26, 1779, and the property of both was confiscated and sold.

After Marsh fled, Sarah filled a brass kettle with her pewterware and silver spoons, and sunk them in a pond for safekeeping. But the pond, located in the south village of East Dorset, later proved "bottomless" and the treasures were never recovered. Marsh had not returned by January of 1781, and Sarah Marsh petitioned to the legislature in February, claiming that she never had the benefit of Colonel Marsh's estate and was now left with nine children. But in 1797 Marsh was identified as one of two "leading characters" of Dorset by Rutland lawyer John A. Graham.[17]

Asa Baldwin had made no secret of his allegiance. While Burgoyne was embattled at Saratoga in the fall of 1777, Baldwin rode his finest horse to the British camp to declare his loyalty. After being entertained by the genial, pleasure-loving Johnny Burgoyne, Baldwin called for his horse the next morning. "Surely," the general reportedly suggested, "a loyal subject will be glad to give a good horse to the king." Baldwin demonstrated his fealty in a generous and tangible way, and returned to Dorset on a sorry old nag, no doubt nurturing his rationalization for having been such a good fellow.

But the patriots caught up with Baldwin, arrested him at his farm, and he was jailed in Bennington. His wife, Chloe, fled their home and followed him on horseback, taking one child in her arms, with another on a second horse. Though the couple were united briefly in Bennington, she was torn from his embrace and journeyed on to the home of her parents in Dutchess County, New York. The nineteenth-century Dorset historian Laurel B. Armstrong, a grand-nephew of Baldwin who resided in Baldwin's house at Kirby Hollow, wrote of the incident: "The strong man, who had unflinchingly met the contumely and reproach which was heaped upon him in consequence of his attachment to the royal cause, melted and wept like a child, to see his lone defenseless wife and babes thus depart."[18]

Baldwin was later allowed to join his wife, and on February 19, 1779, he petitioned from exile in Dutchess County to Governor Chittenden and the Council asking to be permitted to "resume his station and assist the state of which he considers himself a member." His reentry was not easy. On October 22, 1781, another petition from Baldwin, which asked "Liberty to return to the State from Banishment," was rejected by the General Assembly.

On February 23, 1782, by resolution of the Assembly, Baldwin's case went before the governor and council, which ordered that all papers belonging to him be returned. Finally, on February 20, 1783, a resolution of the General Assembly gave him "liberty to return into this state and enjoy the priviledges of the same."

The lands and house on the west side of Dorset that were confiscated from Tory Ephriam Mallary "and forfeited by his treasonable conduct" were purchased by one Lieutenant Peter Roberts for 120 pounds. This transaction was certified on December 1, 1778, by Reuben Harmon, a justice of the peace from East Rupert about whom we shall learn more.

The confiscated East Dorset lands of William Marsh were bought by his half-brother, Eliakim Deming, on September 20, 1780. Some lands of Price Bardslee were sold to Joseph McIntire on March 20, 1781, and others to Noah Morse on June 5, 1783.

At a session of the General Assembly held at Bennington in October 1780, Hannah, the widow of Israel Bardslee, petitioned to use thirty acres of the farm that was confiscated so she could support herself and her children. But the papers of the Court of Confiscation offered no reference to the disputed thirty acres as they recorded the sale of Israel Bardslee's property to Abel Geer on June 4, 1783.

If Asa Baldwin lost a horse for his loyalties, Deacon Cephas Kent gained one for his. On January 29, 1778, Kent bought at public auction a horse that had been seized from one of the Arlington Tories, Phineas Hurd.

The First Churches

Ever since it was founded on September 22, 1784, the Dorset Congregational Church has been the most important continuously operating institution in the town. A cohesive social influence on the west side, it was given consistent leadership for almost the entire nineteenth century by two prominent clergymen. The reverends William Jackson and Parsons S. Pratt served in the pulpit for a combined total of eighty-six years. Pratt was one of the few residents who kept written accounts about the town and its people, and he compiled genealogies of all members of his congregation. Few others in Dorset's first century bothered to do much writing; what Heil Hollister declared in his 1867 history of Pawlet could be said with equal validity of Dorset: "Whatever the inhabitants of this town for the last hundred years may have been, and whatever they may have done, they are not chargeable with much waste of printer's ink."[19]

In 1784 the Reverend Elijah Sill was called from New Fairfield, Connecticut, where he had served from 1751 to 1779, to become pastor of the Dorset Congregational Church. (It is not known where he preached during the five unaccounted-for years.) As Dorset's first "settled minister" he was given land set aside in the town charter for those religious purposes. Sill was a graduate of Yale, was probably in his sixties, and stayed in Dorset for five years before he was dismissed for reasons that have not survived the stresses of time. Little is known about his theology or his life, except that his daughter Dorcas was Dorset's first teacher and married Thomas Manley, second son of John, in 1790.

About the only contemporary recollection of Sill comes from a source known for his haughtiness. The Reverend Nathan Perkins, for more than sixty-five years pastor of the Third Church of West Hartford, Connecticut, kept a diary of his 1789 horseback journey from Hartford to Burlington, Vermont, and back. Everywhere he tarried—mostly with fellow clergymen and their families—Perkins privately recorded not only his disdain for the raw wilderness conditions he encountered but also his dismay at the fact that the inhabitants seemed to be enjoying life so exuberantly in the midst of their crudeness and sacrilegious squalor.[20]

Perkins visited Manchester, which he termed "a loose town." His description of Dorset, Rupert, and Pawlet is brief, and sour:

Went on to Dorset, called on Rev. Mr. Sill, a good friendly man, extremely poor—poor looking family,—poor land,—got some directions of him, as to my route,—passed to Pollet, through Rupert, called on Revd. Mr. Bebee, a serious man, who left honor & ye prospects of wealth for ye Gospel, sensible, of little reading,—of narrow sentiments,—a weakly

An 1890 view of the Waldo Sykes mill on the Mettawee River north of Dorset, torn down about 1910. Sykes is wearing a suit; Charles Wade is on wagon at left. The mill, powered by a water wheel, made cheese boxes.

wife, a poor hut,—a friendly heart,—mean victuals,—destitute of neatness. Wednesday 5th May, set out from Pollet for Middletown, preached at one Reed's in a dark room—to a small collection of people, chiefly Connecticut Separates, very serious & attentive, put up at Mr. Minor's, a kind man,—a kind wife,—wretched fare,—wretched bed,—eat up with fleas,—no hay,—my horse starving.

Other founders of the Dorset church were John Manley, Cephas Kent, Mary Manley, Hannah Kent, John Gray, Nathan Wheeler, Betsey Wheeler, Israel Bostwick, Seth Smith, and Noah Holcumb. John Manley was elected first deacon and Cephas Kent second deacon in 1785. The church then had about forty members, a number that doubled by 1796, the year Jackson was installed as minister.

The original meetinghouse itself was located in what is now Maple Hill Cemetery, though no trace of its foundation can be seen. Near the century's end the building was moved to what is now Church Street, across from the present church. It was repaired in 1816. A controversy in 1832 over whether to repair it again or build a new one was settled by a fire. The building's loss was blamed on hot coals emptied from the women's "footstoves," then fanned by strong winds.

In 1783 the legislature had granted citizens the right to establish religious societies that could tax residents to build a church and appropriate land for a minister. Perhaps the first legislative matter pertaining to Dorset was a bill adopted by the General Assembly on October 20, 1785, "for dividing the town of Dorset into two distinct parishes." The act followed a petition from Cephas Kent, Jr., and fifty-five others on both sides of Dorset "praying that said town might be divided into two societies . . . " the dividing line of which was "the heighth of land" on the road over what is now known as Mt. Aeolus. It would not be the last time that the mountain's "heighth of land" would be used as a demarcation point. The petition's wording is of interest: "The Petition of the Town of Dorset humbly sheweth that the Township being disadvantaged by a high and almost impassible Mountain Situate near the Middle of said Township by reason whereof the People inhabiting said Township, cannot without great inconveniency meet and Enjoy the benefits, or transact such matters as are Necessary in Town or Society."

Kent's petition was referred to a legislative committee composed of representatives Gideon Ormsby or Manchester, Jonathan Robinson of Bennington, and Joseph Bradley of Sunderland, who reported it favorably. With concurrence of the governor and council, the bill was enacted. Clearly, any right of the state to specify churches' jurisdictions blurred the lines between church and state; this authority was repealed in 1807 upon recommendation of the Vermont Council of Censors.

Curiously, in spite of the large mountain in its center, there was never an attempt to divide Dorset into two municipalities as was the case where mountains caused Weston to be split off from Andover or Baltimore from Cavendish, to use two Windsor County examples.

The geographical outlook of Dorset's Congregational church was again the subject of legislation a few months after Vermont became a state. On November 3, 1791, an act was adopted to create "the United Societies of Dorset and Rupert, uniting the First Society of Dorset and the east society of Rupert." And that has been the official name of the church ever since: the United Congregational Church of Dorset and East Rupert.

Congregationalists did not have the only active church in the eighteenth century, though there were no non-Protestant denominations. An Episcopal parish was organized in Manchester in 1782 by settlers from western Connecticut and Dutchess County, New York. Then followed the building of a church in Arlington in 1784, which sent missions to Sandgate, Dorset, Pawlet, Tinmouth, and as far as Shelburne, Jericho, and Alburg. In Dorset an Episcopal parish was formed in 1791 and was served by the Reverend Daniel Barber from Manchester, though no church was ever built. Members included Asa and Benjamin Baldwin; John, Isaac, and Asa Farwell; Jonathan Armstrong, Grove Moore, Isaac Squires, and the Dunton family. Epis-

Settlement and the First Years 61

copal church services were suspended and never revived after moderator Eleazer Baldwin died in 1797.

Another Protestant church would be built in East Dorset, first on a union basis in 1839 and later organized as a Congregational church in 1867. But the cohesion that existed in Dorset village was absent in East Dorset. The reason was partly because of the spread-out north-south geographic nature of the east village, and partly also because of the development of a strong Roman Catholic population following the arrival of the Irish in the late 1830s and the 1840s.

Little information seems available about the ways in which theology shaped the behavior of residents toward the end of the eighteenth century, but some clues are found in the records of Justice John Strong, who kept a "Book of Records for Crimenals [sic] and Delinquents" between 1779 and 1781. Justice Strong's family had been driven by Indians from their home in the town of Addison, and settled in Dorset in 1777 on the farm of Asa Baldwin during his exile as a Tory. Strong, who lived from 1738 to 1816, was Dorset's legislator from 1779 to 1782.[21]

Justice Strong's first entry, on August 11, 1779, recorded the conviction of one Peleg Sunderland for "profain Swearing." The fine was 12 shillings. After that case, Strong decided that the correct spelling for the word *fine* should be *foin*, which must have been the way he pronounced it, for he then used that spelling consistently. His cases convey a sense of what was acceptable and what was not (the spelling is Strong's):

—*on the 26th of June 1780 Worter Gage of Danby Confest himself guilty of traveling on the Sabath or Lord's Day. Foined 3 pounds.*

—*On the 17th day of Sept. 1781 Comes Charles Bullis of Manchester in Bennington County and Confesses himself Guilty of Speaking wordes at the house of James Stewart in Dorset on the 12th day of May Last which has a Direct Tendency to Discourage the good People of this State from Nervisly Exerting themselves in the Cause of America (viz). that he the said Bullis was Now and allways was one of Georges men being asked whether he ment George Washington, answered Damn your washington for which wordes and many others he is ordered to Pay a foin the Sum of Six Pound. Confest.*

—*August 18th 1780. William Manly Confessed Guilty of making Disturbance on the Lordes Day by Laughing. foin 2 pounds.*

The First Schools

If Dorset's first school was organized in 1785, as Zephine Humphrey contended, it happened at a time strong emphasis was being given to education throughout Vermont. That first school was taught by Dorcas Sill, daughter of the minister, and was located on the West Road, either opposite Cephas Kent's or further north near Gilbert Brook. It was built of logs, with oiled paper for window lights. Humphrey may have obtained her information from an article in the April 1908 issue of *The Vermonter* magazine by Elizabeth Sykes Lee, who reported that teacher Sill was paid 50 cents a week, probably in the form of farm produce, because cash was in short supply in the era of Vermont's Republic and most commerce was carried on by barter.

The state constitution of 1777 provided for schools to be established in each town by the legislature, "for the convenient instruction of youth, with such salaries to the masters paid by each town . . . thereby to enable them to instruct youth at low prices." Thus, the organization of schools was placed in the hands of the legislature but financial support was strictly up to the towns.[22] Vermont's new 1786 constitution removed the provision that "schools shall be established" and replaced it with: "A competent number of schools ought to be maintained in each town."

In keeping with New England tradition that towns were self-governing autonomous democracies, the first state school law in 1782 contravened the clause, "A school or schools shall be established in each town by the legislature" by empowering towns "in any legal town meeting by such ways and means as they shall devise, to divide into so many districts as they shall find convenient and the same to alter from time to time."

The school law of 1782 was amended in 1787 to favor the district system. This provided for school districts controlled by resident committeemen, sometimes acting with selectmen in finding a means for raising and dividing money among districts. The law mandated nothing but did acknowledge the right of the state to supervise if not control schools.

What Dorset did about school districting at first is unclear, but at the next town meeting for which records exist, on March 14, 1797, when there were three schools, voters divided the town into six school districts. It is difficult to envision where these districts were located but the method of delineation can be perceived from this description of District No. 1: "Beginning on Rupert East line at Amos Fields N.W. corner thence easterly on said Fields North line Untill it intersects the Creek that Leads from the Swamp thence southardly through the Center of Sd swamp or with the creek that leads through Sd. swamp to the North line of John Manleys Junior Land Thence Westerly on Sd. Manly's North line to his N.W. corner thence a Southwesterly course to Rupert east line Northerly on Sd. line to the bounds Began at."

Other districts followed in like fashion, descriptions becoming more concise as they referred to previously defined districts. Town meetings often adjusted district lines to favor the convenience of residents. Ultimately there would be as many as twelve school districts in the town after the Civil War. Nearly a century would pass for the district system to settle down before agreement was reached on a townwide school district and a single central school.

Reuben Harmon's Mint

The year 1785 was particularly active in Dorset. The first marble was quarried, the first public school opened, and the legislature authorized a division of Dorset's church into two "societies." It was a time of rampant inflation—unskilled labor was receiving 79 cents a day in 1780, an alarming increase over the 22 cents paid in 1772. Currency was in short supply, not only in the Republic of Vermont but throughout the American Confederacy of nonunited states. Money consisted of "rag tag copper and silver coins, British, Spanish, a host of private tokens, counterfeits, and a paper money not worth putting in your pocket."[23]

These conditions prompted Vermont to mint its first and only official coins, and to issue paper currency. The new system did not solve any problems; the paper money was redeemed shortly after it was issued in 1781, and the copper coins were never sufficient to remedy the shortage of money. In any case, in June 1785 the legislature granted the exclusive right to mint copper coins to Reuben Harmon, Jr., of East Rupert, for two years. The law was quite specific:

That all copper by him coined, shall be in pieces weighing not less than four penny weight, fifteen grains each; and the device for all copper, by him hereafter coined, shall be, on the one side, a head with the motto auctoritate Vermontensium, *abridged—on the reverse a woman, with the letters* INDE: ET LIB: *for independence and liberty.*

Said Reuben . . . shall pay, for the use of this State, two and one half per cent of all the copper coin for and during the remainder of the aforesaid term of eight years.

The law also required security, and on June 16, a day after the law was enacted, Harmon executed a bond for 5,000 pounds to State Treasurer Ira Allen. His sureties were Judge David Sheldon of Rupert and two of the Dorset pioneers, Abraham Underhill and Benjamin Baldwin.

Harmon had come to Vermont with his father from Suffield, Connecticut, in 1768, and was a delegate at the Dorset Conventions. He established his mint in a rough, unpainted 16-by-18-foot frame structure on the east bank of Hagar Brook, a tributary of the Mettawee River, not far from the Dorset line. In one end of the building a furnace melted copper and a device rolled it into bars, and at the other end the cut coppers were stamped into coins by means of an iron screw attached to heavy timbers moved by hand-pulled ropes. At top speed it was possible to produce sixty coins a minute, though the more usual rate was thirty, according to a recollection in 1855 by Harmon's grandson, Julian Harmon.

The first pennies, struck during 1785 and early 1786, clearly proclaimed "Vermont." The obverse side showed the sun rising from behind wooded mountains, a plow in a field underneath, and the legend "Vermons Res. Publica. 1785." The reverse side depicted an eye within a circle from which issued 26 rays—thirteen long, their points intersecting a circle of thirteen stars, and thirteen short—representing the original states of the American Confederation. The Latin motto "Stella Quarta Decima"—the fourteenth star—expressed Vermont's aspiration to join them.

Harmon petitioned the legislature in October of 1786 to extend his contract for ten years and suggested: "the present scarcity of a circulating medium the coining of coppers within the State may be very advantageous to the Public." Instead of ten years, he was granted a generous eight. Bondsmen Underhill and Baldwin were succeeded by Nathaniel Chipman and Lemuel Chipman.[24] One witness to the new bond, executed on February 23, 1788, was a young Rutland attorney, John A. Graham.

In all, Harmon coined about a ton of copper. Harmon's coins were not of especially good quality. Their many defects have made them extremely valuable to coin collectors, who study their flaws and categorize minute variations. The largest collection of Reuben Harmon's Vermont coppers is at the Bennington Museum.

It must have been heady business to mint money under authority of the state, and Harmon entertained visions of expanding operations beyond the Republic of Vermont. He entered into a grand gamble with Captain Thomas Machin of Newburgh, New York, a former British army officer and former American army engineer who is remembered for having forged a chain that once spanned the Hudson River at West Point to bar the British fleet.

With several partners, Machin and Harmon proposed in April 1787 to become coinmakers to the new nation. Fragmented systems of coinage, after all, were among reasons for failure of the Articles of Confederation. But miscalculations and new circumstances foiled their plans. The Revolution ended, a new Constitution was devised, and plans matured for a United States Mint at Philadelphia that did not involve Harmon.

Harmon's mint at East Rupert ceased operation in 1788, and he abandoned his hard-won contract. Harmon left Vermont in 1790 and went to Ohio,

where making salt seemed more profitable than minting money. It is not certain what happened to the crude building in which Harmon's pennies were minted. Some say it burned. Others claim it was moved and used for many purposes. Part of it may be one of several red outbuildings on the Robert Graf farm, near the Rupert-Pawlet line.
Terry Tyler collection

A 1900 view of the Amos Field house, built in the late 1700s on what later became the Foote Road. The house was later owned by Homer Williams, an ancestor of Mrs. Ada Williams Rumney, then by Mrs. Susan Lord who named it "Elmsleigh" for the two stately trees. The last of the trees died in 1980.

Some Early Houses

There is no agreed-upon answer to the question of which is Dorset's oldest house. Houses were often moved, disconnected, joined, added onto, rescued from fires, and otherwise altered. [Brackets indicate who owned the house at the time this book was prepared.] The oldest house acknowledged by a 1976 bicentennial map is that of John Farwell, built in 1769 just north and west of the corner of West Road and Church Street [Tom Warren farmhouse].

Other eighteenth-century houses include the John Kent house, built in 1773 diagonally across from the Cephas Kent Inn, which was built the same year. The John Kent house [Mabel Gilbert, now Paul Schwint] was moved

Dorset

Courtesy of Peter Palmer

An early view of the Deming-Viall-Benedict house, one of the oldest in East Dorset, at the foot of Morse Hill. A marble block in the chimney bears the initials E D (for Eliakim Deming) and the date 1786. In the late 1800s the west side of the house was a cheese factory. The Benedict family used to move into the south part of the house each winter. In 1988 Peter Palmer of Manchester bought the handsome house and has been painstakingly restoring it.

Photo by Stetson Fletcher

The Deming-Viall-Benedict house as it looked in 1988 after restoration by Peter Palmer.

to the corner of West Road and Lane Road, and later added to by John's son, Juba Kent. Part of the original Kent inn was probably incorporated into Martin Kent's house, now at the corner of West Road and Nichols Hill Road [Raymond Kopituk]. As noted earlier, the marble John Manley house was built between 1773 and 1780. The Amos Field house [Roseanne Foote Smith] off the West Road, almost on the Rupert line, has been attributed to 1776; and the Hodge house [Warren Murray] in Dorset village, next to today's library, is said to date to the Vermont statehood year of 1791. The Asa Baldwin house, which later became the Hart house in Kirby Hollow, dates to 1774, though it too has seen several changes. The Harvey Holley house, in the village, dates to about 1790. In South Dorset, a portion of the Abraham Underhill house, built about 1773, still exists [Helen B. Sheldon].

Other candidates for the title of oldest house might be the Burt Harrington house in the Hollow [David Sirak]; the Edson Holley house [Dorothy Weston] near the golf course; a house [Fred O. Whittemore] once owned by Major Dunton, north of the former Burr Philips store; and the building that housed the old telephone office west of Peltier's store [Peter Zecher]. The earliest East Dorset house is no doubt that built by Eliakim Deming, whose date, 1786, is carved in stone [Peter Palmer].

Not to be overlooked as an eighteenth-century institution is the grand Dorset Inn, built in 1796 and believed to be the oldest hostelry in Vermont still in continuous operation.

The Statehood Convention

In March of 1791 Vermont became the fourteenth state of the Union, fulfilling the aspiration expressed on Harmon's copper coins. The dispute with New York was settled on terms negotiated by commissioners from both states and by payment of $30,000 from Vermont to New York to settle all residual land claims.

Formal achievement of statehood was preceded by a state convention held January 6, 1791, in Bennington. John Shumway was Dorset's delegate, and the chief issue was ratification of the U.S. Constitution. But debates also took place over the more fundamental question of whether to join the Union at all. Ratification was finally approved by a vote of 105 of the 109 delegates, with only those from the Windsor County towns of Chester, Andover, Bridgewater, and Rochester dissenting.

Nathaniel Chipman and Lewis R. Morris were designated commissioners to secure acts of Congress so that Vermont formally could become a state. The law they drafted would have given the new state three congressional districts, though only two districts prevailed. (Between 1812 and 1822, Vermont would have six congressional districts, before it lost population in relation to the other growing states. Its representation in the U.S. House gradually narrowed by 1932 to one at-large district.)

John Graham's Travelogue

The most enduring description of life in Dorset at the end of the eighteenth century appears in the travelogue written by Rutland lawyer John A. Graham. Graham harbored several motives for offering thumbnail sketches of each town and tried to make Vermont as appealing as possible. His phrases "excessive crops of hay" and "prodigious quantities of honey" are typical exaggerations, but in general his glimpse of Dorset was probably accurate.[25] Graham wrote:

The principal grain raised in this town is rye and Indian corn—the land also produces excellent flax, and the meadows excessive crops of hay and good pasture. The face of the country is beautifully diversified with hills and vallies; it has a mountain exceedingly high, the top of which, for at least three parts of the year, is enveloped in clouds: it is not unfrequent to see its top rising a great height above them, and the rain descending in cataracts down their sides with almost the velocity of the falls of Niagara, while the sun beams shoot their brightest rays on the adjacent fields and neighborhood . . . .

The inhabitants of Dorset are very industrious: they enclose their land with strong fences of stone walls and timber; yet they are terribly annoyed by the wolves, which pour down from the mountains and often destroy whole flocks in a single night. This makes the breeding of sheep extremely hazardous; however, they are amply compensated in another respect, by the prodigious quantities of honey they take every year, one farmer often procuring five hundred weight in a season. They also raise immense numbers of geese, turkies, ducks, and fowls, and have salmon trout in as great abundance as the people of Manchester.

They have a Dissenting Meeting-house, but are much divided in their religious tenets. They have three Schools. The number of inhabitants is about eleven hundred, and the value of land from three shillings to twenty pounds per acre.

NOTES

1. Dorset's second "proprietors' meeting," May 23, 1769, attended by settlers as agents of the proprietors, was recounted in a history by George M. Viall of East Dorset that appeared in Lewis Cass Aldrich's *History of Bennington County* (Syracuse, N.Y.: D. Mason & Co., 1889.) The minutes appear in the original Book of Records of the Proprietors of Dorset as transcribed in 1817 by John Underhill, town clerk.

2. Walter Hill Crockett, *History of Vermont* (New York: Century History Co., 1921), vol. 1, pp. 232–33, and vol. 2, p. 256. Powell's was not the only connection between Dorset and Burlington, for editor Abby Maria Hemenway in the 1861 *Vermont Historical Magazine* noted: "In an early day, several families from Dorset, removing north, settled in the eastern part of the town of Burlington, giving to their district the name of their native town: Dorset Street,

Settlement and the First Years 69

so-called, is one of the most interesting sections of Burlington."

3. A. M. Caverly, M.D., *History of the Town of Pittsford, Vt.* (Rutland, Vt.: Tuttle Company, 1872).

4. Lewis D. Stilwell, *Migration from Vermont 1776-1860* (Montpelier, Vt.: Vermont Historical Society, and Brattleboro, Vt.: E.L. Hildreth & Co., 1937).

5. Viall, in Aldrich, *History of Bennington County.*

6. From Edith V. Harwood, paper on the Farwell family and its houses, presented June 8, 1964, to the Dorset Historical Society.

7. "Dorset Industries and Mills," papers presented to the Dorset Historical Society by Anna E. Gilbert on February 26, 1968, and Arthur W. Gilbert on November 18, 1974. The latter was a development of the former.

8. Hiland Hall, *Early History of Vermont* (Albany, N.Y.: Joel Munsell, 1868), p. 147.

9. The Sykes material is based on a paper dealing with this family written mostly by Anna E. Gilbert and delivered before the Dorset Historical Society by Mrs. George Albert Lewis, nee Margaret Sykes Child, on September 8, 1964.

10. Vermont's thirty-member state senate was formed in 1836, and Bennington County has always had two members elected at large. Tradition has been that one resides in the North Shire (Arlington and towns north), the other in the South Shire.

11. "Action in Vermont During the Revolutionary War: Dan Kent's Narrative," *Vermont History*, Spring 1971, p. 107.

12. Mary Greene Nye, ed., *State Papers of Vermont, Vol. 6, Sequestration, Confiscation and Sale of Estates* (Montpelier, Vt.: Vermont Secretary of State's Office, 1941).

13. *Gazetteer and Business Directory of Bennington County, Vt. for 1880-81* (Syracuse, N.Y.: Hamilton Child, 1880).

14. Nye, ed. *State Papers of Vermont*, Vol. 6.

15. Aleine Austin, *Matthew Lyon: 'New Man' of the Democratic Revolution—1749-1822*, (Harrisburg, Pa.: Pennsylvania State University Press, 1981).

16. Sarah V. Kalinowski, "Sequestration, Confiscation and the 'Tory' in the Vermont Revolution," *Vermont History*, Fall 1977, p. 236.

17. John A. Graham, *A Descriptive Sketch of the Present State of Vermont* (London: 1797; and rpt. Rutland, Vt.: Vermont Heritage Press, 1987) An amusing account of Graham's motives is related by Noel Perrin in an introduction to the reprint.

18. Laurel B. Armstrong wrote a history of Dorset that was included in vol. 1 of Abby Maria Hemenway's *Gazetteer*, published in 1861.

19. Hollister, *Pawlet for One Hundred Years.*

20. Nathan Perkins, *A Narrative of a Tour Through Vermont, 1789* (Woodstock, Vt.: Elm Tree Press, 1930; rpt. Woodstock, Vt.: Yankee Bookshop, 1937).

21. Edward Sprague Marsh, "Justice Strong's Book of Records" *The Vermonter*, vol. 28, October, 1928. Zephine Humphrey related the experience of John Strong's reunion with his wife: "John Strong had been absent when Addison had been raided, and he returned to find his house in ashes and his wife and children gone. For weeks he hunted for them, going down into Connecticut and wherever he thought they could possibly have fled. Finally, by the merest chance, he arrived in Dorset toward dusk one afternoon and applied at a log house for shelter. 'Moses, take the gentleman's boots,' said a voice which smote him by its familiarity and, turning, he found himself face to face with his wife."

22. John C. Huden, *Development of State School Administration in Vermont* (Montpelier, Vt.: Vermont Historical Society, 1944). Huden was a state education commissioner. Data on Vermont schools are scarce because many files were destroyed in the statehouse fire of 1857 or the flood of 1927.

23. Much of this discussion of Harmon's mint is gratefully appropriated from "The Coinage of Vermont 1785-1788" by Codman Hislop in *Rare Coin Review*, April-May 1984, Vol. 51, published by Bowers and Merina Galleries, Inc., Wolfeboro, New Hampshire.

24. George S. Hibbard, *Rupert, Vt.: Historical and Descriptive* (Rutland, Vt.: Tuttle Company, 1899).

25. Graham, *Descriptive Sketch.*

5

The Dorset Conventions

BY THROWING off the oppressions of both the New Yorkers and the British, and also by ignoring their New Hampshire origins, the four Dorset Conventions of 1775 and 1776 boldly set the stage for the creation of the independent republic and later the state of Vermont.

These conventions can be seen as links in a chain of at least nineteen impromptu meetings called by settlers of the New Hampshire Grants between 1766 and 1777 to oppose the unwanted authority of New York State. The first, a huddle at Bennington, designated pioneer settler Samuel Robinson to travel to London to meet with King George in an effort to resolve the incipient dispute between the New Hampshire Grants and province of New York; results of the meeting were encouraging but ultimately ineffectual because of Robinson's death by smallpox. The last of the nineteen sessions were held near the symbolically important Connecticut River at Westminster and Windsor, where independence was declared by the state of "New Connecticut, alias Vermont," and a constitution was signed.[1]

Of those nineteen meetings of assorted delegates of pioneers, who were also attempting to glean a living from primitive subsistence farms in near-wilderness conditions on the New Hampshire Grants, the most important were the four at Dorset. It was here that the first regiment of "Green Mountain Boys" was formed, and it was here that delegates from towns on the Grants voted to become "a separate district," an initially ambiguous term that was later emboldened by use of the sovereign word "state."

The fact that the first of the four Dorset Conventions was initiated by the

The Dorset Conventions

Continental Congress in Philadelphia lends them a certain national significance. The second, third, and fourth conventions were all logical outgrowths—and adjourned sessions—of the previous meetings.

There was no compelling reason these conventions were held in Dorset except that the town was a geographic center of gravity west of the Green Mountains, a kind of fulcrum for the territory's three drainage basins—the Champlain, the Connecticut River, and the Hudson River. It is possible, too, that the location was related to the legend that the Green Mountain Boys may have camped at what is now Kent Meadows on their way to seize Ticonderoga in May of 1775. The four Dorset Conventions were all held at "the dwelling house of Cephas Kent, innholder," often referred to as "Cephas Kent's tavern."[2]

Frictions between the New Hampshire Grants and the New York authorities had been heating up for several years. An immediate provocation for the conventions at Dorset occurred on March 9, 1774, when the New York legislature passed "An Act for preventing tumultuous and riotous Assemblies . . . and for more speedy and effectual punishing [of] the rioters." This law was aimed at a recent "spirit of licentiousness" in parts of the counties of Charlotte and Albany. (From New York's point of view, Albany County then extended to the north border of Manchester, Vermont, and Charlotte County was north of that and west of the Green Mountains.)

Photo by Tyler Resch

This Cephas Kent marker, made of marble, at the foot of Nichols Hill was designed to indicate the site of the Dorset Conventions. Its wording has since been corrected, and the marker moved across the road.

The "principal ring-leaders" were identified as Ethan Allen and Seth Warner of Bennington, Remember Baker of Arlington, Robert Cochran of Rupert, Peleg Sunderland, John Smith, and Silvanus Brown of "Socialborough" (New York's name for a town it patented near Rutland and Pittsford), and James "Brackenridge" (correctly spelled Breakenridge) of "Wallumshack" (Walloomsac), a New York patent that included parts of Bennington, plus Hoosick, New York, and traced back to 1739. The New York Provincial Assembly offered rewards for the apprehension of these Green Mountain Boys, who had employed some mischievous techniques for chasing Yorker surveyors off the Grants and for harassing Yorker justices who attempted to perform their duties of office.

"With this act," wrote the Reverend Samuel Williams of Rutland in 1794, in the first history of the state of Vermont, "all prospect of peace, or submission to the government of New York, ended."[3]

The Riotous Assemblies Act provoked the calling, only six weeks after its passage, of a convention of towns of the New Hampshire Grants held at the house of Eliakim Weller in Manchester, later adjourned to that of Jehiel Hawley in Arlington. This April 24 convention, one of the series of nineteen, elected Nathan Clark of Bennington chairman; the secretary was Dr. Jonas Fay, a physician and the son of owner Stephen Fay of the Catamount Tavern in Bennington. "At the expense of our lives and fortunes," members of the convention resolved to stand by their indicted friends and neighbors, and urged the New York Assembly to await a decision of the king and thus "desist from taking us as rioters, to prevent the unhappy consequences that may result from such an attempt."

Pledging to act defensively only, the Grants convention at Manchester affirmed its allegiance to King George, asserted that the settlers had purchased their lands in good faith from one of His Majesty's governors, and declared that New York was acting contrary to the spirit of the laws of Great Britain. The settlers' determination was steadfast, though their professed loyalty to the king was also, in fact, near the breaking point. The Manchester convention resolved: "That for the future, every necessary preparation be made, and that our inhabitants hold themselves in readiness, at a minute's warning, to aid and defend such friends of ours, who, for their merit to the great and general cause, are falsely denominated rioters."

The alleged rioters, Green Mountain Boys Allen, Warner, Baker, Cochran, Smith, Sunderland, and Brown, also made clear their intentions, in a lengthy open letter issued to all people of the New Hampshire Grants: "We will *kill* and *destroy* any person or persons whomsoever, that shall *presume* to be accessary, aiding or assisting in taking any of us."[4]

Another provocation took place in the same time span that has come to be known as the Westminster Massacre. It was not a massacre in the usual sense, for only two persons were killed; but the power of the royal province of New York was forcibly broken, and blood was shed in the process. Westminster was the seat of so-called Cumberland County, and on March 13, 1775, the populace by force of arms prevented sheriffs and other officers of New York from holding court. This event "served still further to exasperate all parties," Samuel Williams wrote.[5]

A convention of committees on the east side of Vermont met on April 11 and voted to resist the administration of the government of New York until they could appeal "to the royal wisdom and clemency, and till such time as his Majesty shall settle this controversy."[6] This was the last declaration of loyalty to the king by a convention in Vermont, for reasons outlined below:

1. On March 11 Patrick Henry delivered his "Liberty or Death" speech in the Virginia House of Burgesses, predicting that hostilities would soon break out in New England. He was correct, for between the time of the April 24 convention at Manchester and the first Dorset Convention on July 26 and 27, 1775, alarming events were taking place on the national scene.

2. On April 19, with the outbreak of hostilities, at the Battle of Lexington the patriots declared their determination to overthrow the motherland. The American Revolution was launched.

3. On May 10 Ethan Allen, accompanied by Seth Warner, Robert Cochran, Matthew Lyon, and others—joined by Benedict Arnold—took it upon themselves to capture Fort Ticonderoga, the strategic key to the southern end of Lake Champlain. Uncommissioned and obedient to no authority but their own, Allen and Warner later traveled to Philadelphia and met with the Continental Congress. The Congress resolved that not only should the men and officers who took Ticonderoga be rewarded by payment but that, indeed, a regiment should be raised of these legendary "Green Mountain Boys"—the Congress's own name for them. Going through proper channels, the Continental Congress sent a resolution to the New York Provincial Congress, which it recognized as having authority over the Green Mountains. Though the jurisdiction rankled, Allen exulted in the prospect of a brilliant military career.[7]

Accordingly, on July 27 at Cephas Kent's Dorset dwelling delegates assembled who were appointed by the committees of safety of towns west of the Green Mountains. Their mission was to choose officers of the regiment that was authorized both by the Continental Congress and the Provincial Congress of New York. Chairman of the convention was Nathan Clark, and the clerk was John Fassett, Sr., the father-in-law of Dr. Jonas Fay, who would be clerk of the three remaining conventions.

This was the first Dorset Convention. It also proved to be the low moment in Ethan Allen's lifetime of exuberance, imprudence, and vanity, because the delegates passed him over by casting forty-one votes for Seth Warner as regimental commander, with the rank of lieutenant colonel. Warner's unnamed competitor (presumed to be Allen though the record does not specify), received only five votes. Other officers elected were Samuel Safford, major; Weight (or Wait) Hopkins, Oliver Potter, John Grant, William Fitch, Gideon Brownson, Micah Vail, and Heman Allen, captains; John Fassett, Jr., Ebenezer Allen, Barnabas Barnum, Jellis Blakely, Ira Allen, Gideon Warren, and David Galusha, first lieutenants; John Nobles, James Claghorn, John Chipman, Nathan Smith, Jesse Sawyer, Joshua Stanton, and Philo Hard, second lieutenants.[8]

Ethan Allen chalked up his defeat to "old Farmers on the New Hampshire Grants who do not incline to war." He wrote this explanation to Governor Trumbull of Connecticut in a letter dated at Ticonderoga on August 3, to which he penned this postscript: "How the old men came to reject me, I can not conceive inasmuch as I saved them from the encroachments of New York."[9]

It was also possible that bad feelings between Benedict Arnold and Allen over their authority at Ticonderoga figured in the vote at the first Dorset Convention, for one of Dorset's two delegates, John Manley, was the husband of Arnold's half-sister.

Winds of national and regional change continued to swirl about the coming Dorset Conventions. The year 1775 had ended in despair for the Americans after the Green Mountain Boys' militia was defeated in the Canadian campaign. After taking most of Montreal, General Richard Montgomery died of wounds in the arms of his aide-de-camp, Cephas Kent, Jr., of Dorset. Montgomery was succeeded by General David Wooster, who on January 6 wrote to Lieutenant Colonel Seth Warner asking for help. Ethan Allen, ever impetuous as he rushed to assist in the taking of Canada, was captured by the British and would spend the next couple of years in uncomfortable and unaccustomed humility either aboard prison vessels or in a London jail. Though the leadership of Ethan Allen was absent throughout the Dorset Conventions and the Battle of Bennington that followed shortly afterward, his brothers did their utmost to make up for it.

As the Yorkers became embroiled in the far more serious dispute with the Crown, lower priority was given to criminal prosecutions against "riotous" settlers of the Grants. The latter hoped that a new government in New York might right the wrongs of the old regime, but such was not to be the case; the old politics still prevailed. James Duane, for instance, was a member both of a New York constitutional convention and of the Continental Congress,

The Dorset Conventions

and he had many political allies. In fact, settlers on the Grants had reason to conclude that their plight would be worse under New York than under the Crown.

Nationally, the first clear call for American independence was issued by Thomas Paine in his pamphlet called *Common Sense* which appeared in Philadelphia in January 1776. It attacked that "Royal Brute" George III as chiefly responsible for obnoxious measures against the colonies, and skewered his monarchical form of government.

A planned second Dorset Convention was postponed until Warner could return to participate. On December 20, 1775, a warning was issued for a convention to take place on January 16, 1776, again at the dwelling of Cephas Kent. The warning, dated at Arlington and signed by Moses Robinson, Samuel Robinson, Jr., Seth Warner, Jeremiah Clark, Martin Powell, Daniel Smith, and Jonathan Willard, announced four agenda items of potential revolutionary import:

I. To see if the Law of New York shall have free Circulation where it does not infringe on our properties or Title of Lands, or Riots (so-called) in defense of the Same.

II. To see if the said convention will come into some proper Regulations, or take some method to Suppress all Schismatic mobbs [sic] *that have, or may Arrise* [sic] *on Said Grants.*

III. To see if they will Choose an Agent, or Agents to send to the Continental Congress.

IV. To see whether the Convention will Consent to Associate with N. York, or by themselves in the Cause of America.

Some historians, notably Thompson, surround the Dorset Conventions with a certain illegitimacy: the delegates were not duly elected by their constituents; they did not represent all towns in the Grants. But the initial convention at least was authorized by *two* proper authorities, provincial and federal; and delegates were appointed by local committees of safety. Indeed, it might be asked what "legitimacy" the other three conventions enjoyed. The territory of the Grants itself was unrecognized. Its inhabitants were secessionists who sought to form their own government, to split away from another government that itself had joined forces to separate from its "legitimate" motherland. As for the matter of representing all towns in the Grants, members of the second Dorset Convention, it is true, came from only eighteen towns. Representation was recognized as a serious issue, and by the fourth convention efforts would be made to enlist support from towns in the so-called counties of Cumberland and Gloucester along the Connecticut River.

Proceded viz.

This Convention being fully sensible that the importance of the business which Occasions their Meeting at this time requires the most serious deliberation, are therefore disposed to make the following Votes viz.

1st. That not more than One person be Allowed to Speak at the same time, and only by leave of the Chairman.

2d. That the business of the Meeting be closely attended to, and that the several Articles contained in the Warrant for this Meeting, be severally followed in Course (Except otherwise over-ruled.)

3d. Voted to pass over the fourth, fifth and sixth Articles of the Warrant till tomorrow at 10 OClock at this place

Voted Col. William Marsh, Col. Thomas Chittenden, John Burnam junr., Capt. Micah Vial and Lieut. Joseph Bradley, be a Committee to examine the Account of Capt. Heman Allen for his Service for the Publick, and report their Opinion thereon to this Convention 9 OClock tomorow Morning.

Adjourn'd to 7 OClock tomorow Morning at this place.

Meeting Opened at time and place.
Proceeded to the Consideration of the fourth Article of the Warrant and after due Consideration it was dismissed.
Proceeded to the Consideration of the fifth Article of the Warrant and Resolved that Application be made to the Inhabitants of said Grants to form the the same into a Seperate District, discentients only One.
Proceeded to the Consideration of the sixth Article of the Warrant, and Voted to recommend it accordingly.

The Dorset Conventions

Some delegates, it is also true, did not even reside in the towns they purported to represent. This was most egregiously the case with Heman Allen, who played a dominant role throughout the conventions. Heman, younger brother of Ethan and older brother of Ira, was a resident of Salisbury, Connecticut. But as a partner in the Onion River Land Company (the Onion is now known as the Winooski River) he held title to vast acreage in the disputed lands. Heman was a convention delegate from Middlebury. Dorset's two delegates were Deacon John Manley of the Congregational Church, and Captain Abraham Underhill, who would later lead a company of Dorset Green Mountain Boys.

Chairman of the second convention was Joseph Woodard and the secretary was Dr. Jonas Fay. The delegates took no action on the proposal to control "Schismatic mobbs" or to concede to the "circulation" of New York laws in the Grants, two moves that might have hinted at conciliation. Instead the convention, at all times under the control of the Allens and their relatives and allies (known as the Allen Junto, or the Bennington Party) focused on the matter of sending a delegation to the Continental Congress in Philadelphia. Those selected were James Breakenridge, Dr. Jonas Fay, and Heman Allen; but only Allen actually traveled to Philadelphia.

The convention's memorial to Congress began with this preamble: "The humble petition, address and remonstrance of that part of America being situated south of Canada line, west of Connecticut river, north of Massachusetts Bay and east of a twenty mile line from Hudson's river; and commonly known by the name of the New Hampshire Grants . . . "

The petition restated the history of the dispute with New York and described how the governor of New Hampshire after the end of the French and Indian wars had granted many townships, towns that were now inhabited by a great number of the petitioners, who were "men of considerable substance." The document described the settlers' hardships in the desolate wilderness, and how some monopolizing land traders from New York had threatened the validity of their hard-earned homesteads. The petitioners made it clear that they were: "entirely willing to do all in their power in the general

A page of the proceedings of the Dorset Conventions in the handwriting of its secretary, Dr. Jonas Fay. It is difficult to read, but near the bottom this page records that the conventions voted that the New Hampshire Grants be made into "a separate District." That "district" became first the independent Republic, then the state, of Vermont. This is page 43 of the book, Early Vermont Conventions, 1776-1777, *published in 1904 by Redfield Proctor.*

Photo by Tyler Resch

cause of the colonies, under the Continental congress, and had been, ever since the taking of Ticonderoga, in which the petitioners were principally active under Col. Ethan Allen, but were not willing to put themselves under the honorable, the Provincial congress of New York, in such manner as might, in future, be detrimental to their private property."

As to evidence of their willingness to come to the military aid of the national cause, the Grantsmen added:

We are called on this moment by the committee of safety of the county of Albany, to suppress a dangerous insurrection in Tryon county. Upwards of ninety soldiers were on their march, within twelve hours after receiving the news, all inhabitants of one town, inhabited by your petitioners, and all furnished with arms, ammunition, accoutrements and provisions. Again we are alarmed by an express from Gen. Wooster, commanding at Montreal, with the disagreeable news of the unfortunate attack on Quebec, requiring our immediate assistance by troops; in consequence of which, a considerable number immediately marched for Quebec, and more are daily following their example.[10]

On May 8 Heman Allen presented the petition to Congress and it was referred to a committee of congressmen from the presumably neutral South. The petitioners were advised "for the present, to submit to the government of New York . . . but that such submission ought not to prejudice the rights of them or others to the lands in controversy" until after the dispute with Great Britain was resolved, when the matter might be adjudicated.

After consulting privately with several sympathetic congressmen, including John Adams of Massachusetts and Roger Sherman of Connecticut (New Englanders would always support the cause of an independent Vermont), Allen decided that the resolution offered no protection against the New Yorkers, and he shrewdly chose on June 4 to withdraw the Dorset petition. He claimed, as the congressional journal reported, "that he had left at home some papers and vouchers necessary to support the allegations therein contained."

The third Dorset Convention was warned on June 24 to be held a month later. On July 24 forty-nine delegates from thirty-one towns convened and elected as chairman Joseph Bowker of Rutland, who at the previous convention had survived a credentials challenge. Dr. Jonas Fay was reelected clerk. Between the time of the warning and the actual convention the dramatic news arrived that on July 4 the United Colonies had declared their independence to become the United States of America!

Heman Allen's report from Philadelphia, disingenuous but politically effective, did not mention that the Continental Congress had recommended that the Grants should join New York for purposes of defending the nation.[11]

Instead he told the delegates at Dorset that he had withdrawn the petition on the advice of important persons who warned that the New York delegates might decide to have the Congress act upon it at a time when no agent of the Grants was present. These advisers, Allen told the convention, suggested that the Grants not "connect or associate with the honorable Provincial Congress of New York or any authority derived from, by or under them, directly or indirectly, but that the said inhabitants do forthwith consult suitable Measures to Associate and unite the whole of the inhabitants of said Grants together."

Thus, by Allen's interpretation, the delegates were encouraged to take steps to transform the New Hampshire Grants into "a separate district," a clever phrase that perhaps had the effect of meaning one thing to the timid and another to the bold. With only one dissenting vote, the convention agreed to form the separate district. That great excitement prevailed on the convention floor throughout this discussion is evidenced by a vote that "not more than one person be allowed to speak at the same time and only by leave of the chairman."

Too, the separate-district advocates had been encouraged by a resolution of the Congress on May 10 that advised the "assemblies and conventions" of the continent "to adopt such government as shall in the opinion of the representatives of the people best conduce to the happiness and safety of their constituents in particular, and America in general." No doubt the intention of this resolution was to promote self-determination rather than separatism, but the delegates of the Grants at Dorset were entitled to read it the way they wished.

The convention, aligning itself again with the national cause, also resolved to recommend that the field officers already nominated in the district "see that their men be forthwith furnished with suitable arms, ammunition and accoutrements, etc., agreeably to a resolve of the Continental congress." But because the delegates were also properly concerned that they lacked representation from towns on the east side of the Green Mountains, a committee was named to persuade influential persons in the Connecticut River valley to join the cause of the separate district. On this committee besides Heman Allen were Jonas Fay, Colonel William Marsh of Manchester, and Colonel Samuel Fletcher of Townshend, the only east side spokesman to attend the July convention. Marsh may have been a Tory, but he was also steadfast in his opposition to the Yorkers.

One other significant action taken at this third Dorset Convention was the adoption of an oath of loyalty in an effort to unite residents of the New Hampshire Grants and to assure the world that this district was an unyielding friend of the new American republic. This oath, or "association," was agreed to by all but one delegate, Thomas Brayton of Clarendon, who later became an active Tory. All males above the age of sixteen were required to subscribe to the oath or face the prospect of being branded a Tory and have their property confiscated to raise funds for the new Republic of Vermont.

The third Dorset Convention was adjourned until September, and the committee that was delegated to negotiate with east side towns began to do some effective work. There were several factions on the east side that also had their own reasons for opposing New York, and the third Dorset Convention's committee had only to draw them into a common fold. On August 26 the town of Rockingham approved the formation of a separate district. On September 2, "at the fullest meeting ever known in Chester," another important town approved it also. Halifax rejected the scheme.[12]

At the fourth and final Dorset Convention, held on September 25, there were fifty-one delegates from thirty-five towns, twenty-five west of the mountains and ten east. Joseph Bowker was again chairman and Jonas Fay clerk. Loyalty was expressed anew for the American cause, and this time members also declared that "no law or laws, direction or directions" from New York would be acceptable to them. The convention adopted the following resolution:

We the subscribers, inhabitants of that district of land commonly called and known by the name of New-Hampshire Grants, being legally delegated and authorised to transact the public political affairs of the aforesaid district for ourselves and constituents, do solemnly convenant and engage that, for the time being, we will strictly and religiously adhere to the several resolves of this or a future convention, constituted on said district by the free voice of the Friends to American liberties, which shall not be repugnant to the resolves of the honourable the Continental congress, relative to the cause of America.

It was also resolved "to take suitable measures, as soon as may be, to declare the New Hampshire Grants a separate district." Yet, on the important matter of petitioning directly to the Congress for support for statehood, the convention decided to wait until even more representatives from east side towns were in evidence. So the convention was adjourned to a location on the vital east side: the delegates would meet on October 30 in Westminster, a place of symbolic importance because of the "massacre" there in March 1775. But by October 1776 Sir Guy Carleton was advancing on Lake Champlain and it seemed inappropriate for a sparsely attended convention on the Grants to be petitioning to "the Great Council of the United States of America."

At a second Westminster meeting, on January 15, 1777, Carleton had retreated to Canada and the immediate military threat was past, yet attendance was still thin. Bowker was chairman and Ira Allen convention clerk. A committee was appointed to determine how many persons in Cumberland and Gloucester counties favored setting up a new government. Ira Allen best knew the answer because he had been proselytizing there for two months. The committee's report was really misleading because its conclusion (to which italics have been added for emphasis) was: "We find by examination that more than three fourths of the people of Cumberland and Gloucester counties (both east of the range) *that have acted*, are for a new state; the rest we regard as *neuters*."

The report was meaningless unless one knew how many had *acted* and why the remainder were considered *neuters*. Yet the delegates blandly accepted the report and went on to formulate a historic declaration of independence. A committee chosen to draft the declaration made specific reference to the resolution of Congress that called for the adoption of regimes that would "best conduce to the happiness and safety of their constituents in particular and America in general."

The convention proclaimed that the New Hampshire Grants was from now on to be considered "a Separate Free and Independent jurisdiction or State by the name to be forever hereafter called and known and distinguished by the name of New Connecticut, alias Vermont." The precise form of government was promised "to be established at the next session adjourned of this convention."[13]

The January 15 convention also sent two letters. One, signed by Joseph Bowker, went to delegates to the New York constitutional convention and announced smugly that Vermont's declaration of independence was derived from the "full authority to make such laws as they shall from time to time

Photo by Stetson Fletcher

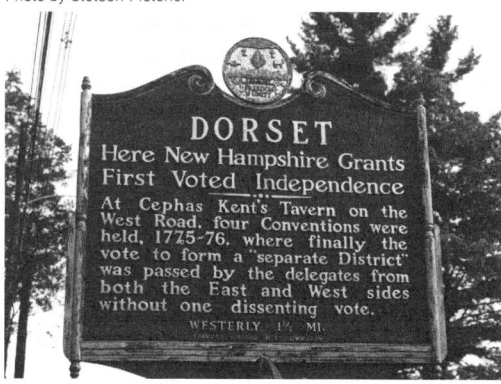

This state marker on Route 30 in Dorset Village describes the origins of the state of Vermont.

think fit." The other letter, signed by Jonas Fay, Thomas Chittenden, Heman Allen, and Reuben Jones, notified the Congress of their action and asked that the new state be privileged to send delegates to it. The response to these declarations was predictable in the sense that friends were satisfied and foes were not.

The designation "New Connecticut" proved short-lived, partly because of the discovery that a territory on the Susquehanna River in Pennsylvania was calling itself by that name, but more importantly because of the influence of Dr. Thomas Young, a Philadelphia physician, mentor of Ethan Allen, and distinguished citizen. Dr. Young not only suggested the name "Vermont," from the French for "Green Mountain," but he also fanned the flames of independence at a crucial moment by writing, on April 11, an open letter "to the inhabitants of Vermont a free and independent state." The letter heartened Vermonters by assuring them that their cause was honorable and would eventually have to be accepted by the Congress: "Your friends here tell me, that some are in doubt, whether delegates from your district would be admitted into congress. I tell you to organize fairly, and make the experiment, and I will insure you success at the risk of my reputation, as a man of honor and common sense. Indeed, they can by no means refuse you. You have as good a right to choose how you will be governed, and by whom, as they had."

It was also Dr. Young who suggested adapting the Pennsylvania state constitution, which at a three-day convention in June 1777 at Windsor was accepted with relatively few changes as the original Vermont constitution. Attending that convention were seventy-two delegates from twenty-three towns on the west side of the mountains and twenty-seven on the east side. Captain Joseph Bowker of Rutland was again chairman and Dr. Jonas Fay secretary. In an effort to underscore the seriousness of this convention's task, it adopted a declaration that June 18 would be "observed as a day of public fasting and prayer throughout the state."

Meanwhile, news arrived that on May 8 the New York Constitutional Convention had adopted provisions that were so odious that friends of the new Republic of Vermont were actually given encouragement. Based on a concept of landed aristocracy that was anathema to New Englanders, the new New York constitution annulled all township grants made by New Hampshire, and it accepted and even increased the hated feudal quitrent as a permanent source of state revenue. Vermont was not recognized, of course, and another fourteen years would pass before a resolution of disputes between the two territories.

During this summer of 1777, as part of a grand scheme of the British to cut off New England militarily from the rest of the continent, the forces of General John Burgoyne were marching and sailing southward from Quebec with such aggressive and alarming intent that many residents along the western borders of Vermont, including most in Dorset, fled for safer ground.

The Battle of Bennington, which took place during a hot August afternoon on a hillside in Walloomsac, New York, provides a logical culmination to the tale of the complex series of events that took place during the several conventions at Manchester, Dorset, Westminster, and Windsor.[14] Timely pleas from Vermont to militia units in New Hampshire and Berkshire County, Massachusetts, enabled the patriots to gather strength and strategy under the leadership of General John Stark.

On August 16 the Americans routed the forces of Burgoyne and his Hessian mercenaries who were poorly advised by Philip Skene that supplies and horses could be obtained easily from pro-Tory citizens of Bennington. The supplies were located in the village later known as Bennington Centre, where in another 110 years a massive three-hundred-foot obelisque would be erected to commemorate the patriots' grand victory of 1777. That victory in a three-hour battle, climaxed by the arrival of the fresh forces of Seth Warner, who reached the scene from Manchester, badly stung the confident Burgoyne, who would suffer an even greater defeat two months later after a series of bloody battles near Stillwater on the Hudson. Burgoyne's surrender at Saratoga in October 1777 proved to be the truly fateful turning point of the American Revolution.

The national impact of the Dorset Conventions was the subject of a doctoral thesis written in 1955 at the University of Michigan by Winn L. Taplin, Jr., a native of Bennington. Titled "The Vermont Problem in the Continental Congress and in Interstate Relations, 1776–1787," the thesis was made available to the writer by Dr. Taplin, a fellow trustee of the Vermont Historical Society and a resident of Stowe. The following discussion summarizes the Taplin thesis and quotes liberally from it.

The existence of a state that claimed independence from one of the new American states—in the same way that Congress claimed independence from the Crown—would continue to raise nettlesome questions at the federal level about sovereignty and the limits of jurisdiction. In the Continental Congress there was little overt interest in Vermont, largely because most delegates did not wish to stir up the wrath of powerful New York.

Seth Warner's regiment of 1,833 "effectives" also nettled New York, which felt deprived of proper recognition from Congress. Warner's force, instigated and recognized by Congress, ended up in poised opposition to New

York on territory claimed by New York. The mere existence of this regiment would remain a continuing irritant between New York and the Congress during the later years of the American Revolution.

When hostilities broke out between the colonies and Great Britain in 1775, just as the Dorset Conventions were about to take place, both problems and opportunities were created for Heman Allen and "the Bennington Party," the best-organized political grouping in Vermont. With the disappearance of the Crown from the American scene, Vermont evolved toward independence and looked for support to the Continental Congress. The significance of Vermont's action was felt on the American military struggle against the British just as it was on Congress's effort to organize a unified government.

Vermont's profession of fidelity to America's common cause, so long as it could be done without subordination to New York, continued to underscore the conflicts within the Congress itself about sovereignty and jurisdiction. Congress preferred to avoid the Vermont issue, because Vermont was insisting that it had the same right to claim independence from one of the new American states as Congress had to claim independence from the Crown.

The Vermont policies launched at Dorset, so troublesome to New York, were also disruptive of relations between New York and the New England states, which would always support the Vermont cause. Bitter feelings between New York and New England traced back to the seventeenth century and Dutch control of the Hudson River valley. "New Netherland" had been a geographic stumbling block to New England's westward expansion. First the English of New Haven and Connecticut had pressed for war against the Dutchmen, and later Massachusetts also had tried to push its boundaries westward. In the mid-1700s New Hampshire took up the same challenge. Now its place was taken by a brash new self-proclaimed state, Vermont, settled mostly by New Englanders whose behavior "was colored throughout by the old New England animosity toward New York, the province that was in the way."[15]

"The Vermont problem" proved divisive throughout the Revolution, for the Continental Congress never grappled successfully with the extent of its legislative, judicial, and procedural powers, matters that were more carefully analyzed and resolved by the Constitution that was drawn up in Philadelphia in 1787. The Vermont issue remained one of the principal questions over which such jurisdictional issues were debated. Thus the foundation was laid at Dorset for controversy in Congress and at the interstate level until Vermont's formal entry into the Union in 1791.

NOTES

1. "Conventions of the people of the New Hampshire Grants," a list of nineteen meetings compiled by Hiland Hall February 18, 1869; Montpelier, Vermont Historical Society Library.

2. With his wife and nine children, Kent settled in Dorset in 1773 to claim the property of an uncle, Samuel Kent, also from Suffield, Connecticut, who had died the year before. Controversy long has surrounded the question of whether the building still exists in which the Dorset Conventions were held, that is, the Cephas Kent dwelling house. The matter was considered "one of confusion and contradiction" in 1924 by Zephine Humphrey. In more recent years this topic has focused on W. Dean Fausett, who insists that the central portion of the house in which he has lived since 1945 on Nichols Hill Road is the same structure which, when located down the hill near West Road, was the Cephas Kent dwelling.

Fausett has conducted a fifteen-year campaign to prove his case because he contends that the "birthplace" of Vermont, as he calls it—the building in which the Dorset Conventions were held—should be recognized for its historic associations. Fausett has many critics, some of whom say that these arguments only add to the value of his house; yet none of the critics has contested his documentation. He has offered diaries, wills, probate records, family genealogies, letters of Kent descendants, obituaries, town proprietors' meeting minutes, records of land transfers, title searches, early surveys, maps, nineteenth-century photographs, recollections of previous owners and other old timers, statements from preservation experts, physical samples of material from his attic and cellar, and copies of accounts of the Dorset Conventions.

Figuring heavily in his rationale for pursuing this case was Fausett's discovery that his ancestors were involved in events of the revolutionary era. Two were John Fassett, Jr. and Sr. (the spelling was changed over the years). The elder Fassett was clerk of the first Dorset Convention and the father-in-law of Jonas Fay; the younger Fassett was a captain in Seth Warner's regiment, created at the First Dorset Convention. Another ancestor Fausett claims was William Dean of Windsor, whom the Yorkers prosecuted for cutting pine trees that should have been reserved, it was charged, for the Royal Navy. The diary of John Fassett, Jr., can be found in the Bennington Museum, and accounts of the Dean brothers' legal problems are found in Henry Steele Wardner, *The Birthplace of Vermont, A History of Windsor to 1781* (New York: Charles Scribner's Sons, 1927) and in B.H. Hall, *History of Eastern Vermont* (New York: D. Appleton & Co., 1858).

Fausett exhausted his case at the state level, and at this writing was appealing to the Keeper of the National Register in the office of the Secretary of the Interior.

The final word at the state level, that of the Vermont Division of Historic Preservation, came in a letter to Fausett on June 29, 1987, following a meeting of the Advisory Council on Historic Preservation in Dorset on June 18, when council members inspected Fausett's house. Nancy E. Boone, architectural historian, outlined reasons for the state's rejection of Fausett's pleas about (a) the name of the Kent historic district, (b) whether the district is considered to have state or national significance, and (c) the provenance of the house as the 1773 Cephas Kent dwelling.

All these matters hinge on a concept of the building's "integrity," wrote Ms. Boone. "Although the Dean Fausett House may be the dwelling of Cephas Kent, Sr., it does not retain sufficient physical integrity to convey that association."

While the state council acknowledged that the Dorset Conventions were indeed of national significance, it would not agree to modify the designation of the district, because to have national significance a property "must have a direct association with events, people and trends of national significance *and* it must retain integrity of the material culture (buildings, structures and objects) that relates to that national significance . . . If the Fausett House does not have sufficient integrity to be significant for association with Cephas Kent, Sr., and the Dorset Conventions, it necessarily follows that the District itself cannot be deemed nationally significant for association with the Conventions. The National Register program relates to material culture that reflects history, and not the facts of history alone, in the abstract."

The state council voted to support the erection of a historic site marker at Nichols Hill Road and West Road acknowledging the site as the location of the Dorset Conventions. (The original location of the Cephas Kent dwelling, according to an 1814 survey by Stephen Martindale, Jr., was where the Nichols Hill Road is now; the road was located just to the south.) But the advisory council voted to retain the name "Kent Neighborhood Historic District" instead of changing it to the "Dorset Conventions Historic District."

The council agreed to add to the nomination an acknowledgment associating the house with "Dean Fausett, the internationally known muralist."

Ms. Boone's letter concedes that "a few 18th century features were observed" in Fausett's house but concludes that "most of its historic detail and material dated to the 19th century." But Manchester restorer Peter Palmer, who accompanied the state council's inspection, said there was no doubt of the house's eighteenth-century origins, with its square nails, mortised joints, and hand-adzed beams.

The controversy over the Cephas Kent dwelling must remain unresolved at this writing while Fausett pursues his appeal.

    3. Samuel Williams, *The Natural and Civil History of Vermont*. (Walpole, N. H.: Isaiah Thomas and David Carlisle, Jr., 1794), p. 223.

    4. Vermont State Papers, (Middlebury, Vt.: comp. and pub. by William Slade, Jr., Secretary of State, 1823, p. 53.

    5. Williams, *Natural and Civil History*, p. 224.

    6. E. P. Walton, ed. and pub., *Governor and Council* (Montpelier, Vt.: 1873), vol. 1, p. 4.

    7. Charles Miner Thompson, *Independent Vermont* (Boston: Houghton Mifflin, 1942), pp. 214 et seq.

    8. Walton, *Governor and Council*, contains biographies of the members of Seth Warner's regiment who were chosen at the first Dorset Convention, pp. 6 et seq.

    9. Hiland Hall, *Early History of Vermont*. (Albany, N.Y.: Joel Munsell Co., 1868), p. 212.

    10. The ninety men mentioned, Hall explains, (ibid., pp. 228-29) were all from Bennington, and they joined General Philip Schuyler at Albany, then marched to Johnstown, New York, to deal with the hostile intentions of five hundred Tories and a body of Indians who had assembled on the Mohawk. Schuyler resolved the conflict with a treaty he later violated when he fled to Montreal.

    11. Thompson, *Independent Vermont*, p. 254.

    12. Benjamin H. Hall, *History of Eastern Vermont* (New York: Appleton & Company, 1858).

    13. Redfield Proctor, arr. and pub., *Record of Conventions in the New Hampshire Grants for the Independence of Vermont 1776-1777* (Washington, D.C.: 1904), p. 65.

    14. Heman Allen, who played such a key role in the Dorset Conventions, died at the age of thirty-eight on May 18, 1778, of a disease he picked up at the Battle of Bennington.

Ethan Allen was freed during an exchange of prisoners in May 1778 and returned to Vermont, but not as the vigorous and strident leader he had been before his captivity. He devoted much of the final decade of his life to writing, and died of "apoplexy" in Burlington in February 1789, aged fifty-two.

Ira Allen went on to be state treasurer and surveyor general of the new Republic of Vermont. He was involved in the so-called Haldimand negotiations with Canada in an effort, it was widely believed, to leverage Vermont into statehood by hinting that it might even reconcile with Britain. Ira donated some of his Onion River land holdings to found the University of Vermont, then went to France and England in pursuit of a series of unsuccessful business deals. He later wrote a lengthy history of Vermont, largely to justify his own conduct. Eventually he moved to Philadelphia, where he died in poverty in 1814.

    15. Dixon Ryan Fox, *Yankees and Yorkers* (New York: New York University Press, 1940.) This book generally presents the New York side of the Grants controversy.

6

The Mt. Tabor Leg

EXPLORING the tale of the Mt. Tabor Leg draws open a curtain on a distant era that has never been documented in history books. The Leg, or what remains of it, is that enigmatic notch of Dorset's northeast boundary in which a parcel of about 325 acres of Mt. Tabor jurisdiction thrusts down into Dorset. Originally, the full strip of land known as the Mt. Tabor Leg was six miles long and 200 rods (about three fifths of a mile) wide.

The Leg's remnant is visible on nearly every map of Vermont, though its configuration is often depicted differently. It is most noticeable on maps that show county lines, because the boundary oddity also affects the Rutland-Bennington county line.[1]

Topographically, the land in question is remote, steeply mountainous, and sparsely populated. It is accessible by automobile by following the Mad Tom Road east into East Dorset, staying on the road as it bends around to the north, and continuing for four or five miles, rejoining Route 7 near an old Mt. Tabor cemetery.

With a variety of elevations, views, and landscapes, the territory of the Mt. Tabor Leg is ruggedly beautiful. The meeting ground between the Taconic mountain range to the west and the Green Mountains to the east, it shows evidence of geological upheavals of millions of years. At one point a panorama looks southwest, with a spectacular view of Mt. Aeolus, toward the rest of Dorset, while to the north and east a different mountainside pitches steeply heavenward. At the site of the farm of Caleb Buffum, an early-nineteenth-century citizen of Mt. Tabor, a mountain rises steeply from a field

This extreme enlargement of a 1796 map by Vermont Surveyor General James Whitelaw shows Dorset and its neighbor "Bromley," which was renamed "Peru" in 1804. The road indicated at their boundary became part of Mt. Tabor (town to the north) in 1805, then was annexed to Dorset in 1825. Details on the map include a cavern on Mt. Aeolus, Emerald Lake, and a depiction of the Congregational church.

as if thrust there by a gargantuan; and a dramatic view to the north reveals an array of mountain peaks far away in Rutland County.

Surely this is the road described in Ira K. Batchelder's *History of Peru* as the first one laid out in that town. Batchelder wrote that it was built in 1787 "on the west side of the mountain, (now in Dorset)."

These boundary manipulations assume importance as they reflect the political and social life of Dorset and its neighboring towns when the nineteenth century was young. The episode that created the Leg entails much instructive and even amusing history, for it involved the shifting and reshifting of town lines between 1805 and 1825. For a while west side residents of Dorset were pitted against those on the east side in a raging dispute. Dorset's 1826 representative, Reuben H. Blackmer, over whose opposition the Mt. Tabor Leg was annexed to his own town in 1825, angrily attributed the move to "lust for power."

The Mt. Tabor Leg provoked more local citizen involvement with the state legislature than any other issue ever pertaining to Dorset, Peru, or Mt. Tabor. This was a time when legislators were elected annually, and citizen petitions were common.

The root cause of this whole problem was an unforeseen consequence of Governor Benning Wentworth's drawing of lines on a map in the early 1760s to delineate townships he never saw in territory that was mostly unexplored. In some places the drawing of an arbitrary boundary will coincide with appropriate geographic features, and in others it will make no sense at all; that's the luck of the draw.

Because of the extraordinarily mountainous topography of Dorset and its neighbor to the east—first known as Bromley but often spelled "Brumbley" to echo the pronunciation of the day, but in any case changed in 1804 to "Peru"—the boundary that Wentworth drew with his quill pen was especially impractical for the pioneer settlers. The arbitrariness of the line caused difficulty in traveling to town meetings or to interact in other ways with their own towns, so the boundary problem gave them all something in common. Those in East Dorset had a mountain to cross to reach Dorset village; those on the Peru side of the border had about sixteen miles to travel, over steep trails, to reach Peru village.[2]

Of equal interest to the geophysical facts are the reasons and emotions behind those facts. The saga of the Mt. Tabor Leg was one of the most unusual of the estimated five hundred attempted changes in place names or boundaries among Vermont's towns, counties, and gores between the early 1700s and 1890.[3] A master's degree thesis completed for the University of Vermont in 1985 by Steven S. Farrow concluded, in harmony with Blackmer, that the most important common factor behind these changes was "politics." Politics, or the quest for political power, was the basis of these boundary entanglements of Peru (nee Bromley), Mt. Tabor (nee Harwich), and Dorset.[4]

The reasons for the boundary changes are disclosed in a remarkable series of more than a dozen citizens' petitions now found in the secretary of state's archives in Montpelier. These two- or three-page petitions are all hand written and addressed to the Vermont General Assembly as it sat each fall in various locations before the seat of state government was finally anchored in Montpelier in 1808. On each petition, notes indicate when it was filed and how the legislature handled it.

One solution to the early Dorset-Peru boundary problem might have been to create a new town out of the valley that constitutes the eastern portion of Dorset and western part of Peru. This is precisely what was proposed by a petition dated September 23, 1802, to the General Assembly that was to convene at Burlington on the second Thursday of November. The signers, who identified themselves as "inhabitence of the East Society of Dorset and the West part of the Town of Brumbley," declared that their petition "humbly sheweth that their situation is very peculiar in configurance of the Green Mountains or height of land from East to West running through said Brumbley." They complained that the terrain was "incapable of affording a rode [road] fit for any carriage whatever from East to West." Residents of western "Brumbley," they pointed out, must travel thirteen to eighteen miles to attend a town meeting (though at that point there had been only one, on March 1, 1802). Residents of the east side of Dorset were cut off from communication with their townsmen "by a mountain extending almost the whole length of this town."

They suggested that the answer would be to "form us into a New Town by the Name of Lebenon." The petition was signed by 21 "Brumbley subscribers" and 22 from Dorset. An addendum signed by another 22 from Bromley suggested that the new line be drawn between the sixteenth and seventeenth tier of lots from north to south, "which will be the height of land as near as they can judge." (For some reason Peru divided its territory into north-south "tiers" and Dorset did not.)

The proposal to create the town of "Lebenon" did not get far. Filed on October 18, 1802, the petition was first tabled, then received an adverse committee report, and its sponsors were allowed to withdraw it.

Only a few days after the "Lebenon" proposal, a petition dated September 27, 1802, sought to resolve a larger geopolitical problem by suggesting that *four* new towns be carved out of parts of Rupert, Dorset, Bromley, and Landgrove by conforming to the realities of topography. Signed by 108 persons, this plea asked to have the land known as the West Society of Rupert be incorporated into one new town; territory identified as the United Society of Dorset and Rupert would become a second town; the East Society of Dorset plus "so much of the town of Bromley as lies west of the height of land" would be a third town; and the portion of Bromley east of the height of land would be combined with Landgrove for a fourth. No names were suggested for the proposed towns. The petition explained the purposes succinctly: "Which would remove all the inconvenience under which the inhabitants now suffer by reason of the aforesaid mountains and would also leave the inhabitants of Each Town much more compact."

The legislature tabled the proposal and referred it to the next year's session, and it was never acted upon. Yet the idea was an ingenious and logical solution to problems imposed by arbitrary town lines drawn where mountain ranges interlock. This four-town rearrangement might have worked had it been adopted well before 1802. But forty years after the original charters were granted, and some thirty years after settlement, too many municipal procedures and legal mechanisms had had time to harden—grand lists, assessment and taxation, records of land transactions, checklists of voters, actions taken by town meetings, creation of school districts, and so forth.

Municipal boundaries in Vermont are not changed for whimsical reasons. That is why the experience of the Mt. Tabor Leg is so unusual, for it involved shifting town lines not once but three times, among three towns and two counties, and it left a jigsaw-puzzle shaped boundary.

Early in the year 1802, before the four-town solution was proposed, settlers of Bromley had appealed to Justice Joseph Curtis of Dorset to help them organize their first town meeting. This he did, and town officers were elected. At the second Bromley town meeting, in the fall of 1803, held at Butterfield's Inn near the height of land on the road between Peru and Manchester, west side residents expressed reluctance to attend because of the distance and hardship of travel. They did attend, but they "then petitioned to be set off to Dorset."

A year and a half later their plea was rejected at a Dorset town meeting. On March 12, 1805, this question was warned in Dorset: "Whether the West Part of Peru, formerly Brumley, shall be annexed to the town of Dorset." (The only other municipal concern at that Dorset meeting was whether to restrain sheep rams from running at large between September 10 and November 10, the penalty being that any ram thus found would be forfeited to the finder.)

At a Dorset town meeting on September 3, 1805, it was "Voted that the Town will not have the West Part of Peru annexed to the town." That meeting was held at the request of the General Assembly, which on November 5, 1804, had been divided on a bill to annex part of Peru to Dorset. The House passed the bill, but the Council (predecessor of the state Senate) balked because "It would be highly injurious and a violation of corporate privileges to annex a part of any town to another without the free assent of the majority of the inhabitants of each . . . at a legal meeting of the inhabitants convened for the purpose. This does not appear to have been the case in the present instance."

Two days later, November 7, the House passed the bill on second reading, but in view of the Council's reluctance, and at the request of Representative Reuben Bigelow of Peru, it was agreed to postpone matters until the 1805 session so that both Peru and Dorset could hold town meetings on the question.

After Dorset's 1805 rejection the settlers of western Peru, still eager to make a change, immediately asked to become part of Mt. Tabor to the north. Mt. Tabor favored that idea and the General Assembly quickly adopted, on

Dorset

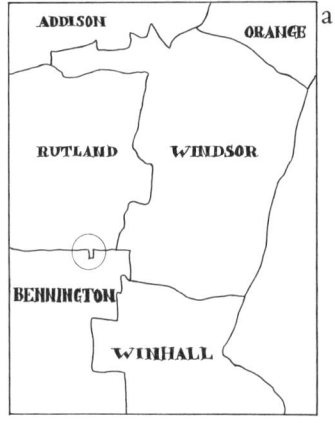

Mt. Tabor Leg

a. This notch on the boundary of Rutland and Bennington counties is the so-called Mt. Tabor Leg. It is seen on nearly all maps that show town or county lines.

b. Governor Wentworth of New Hampshire originally drew identical town lines in the 1760s in southwest Vermont, then known as the New Hampshire Grants. All towns were identical squares of six by six miles. Mt. Tabor was originally known as Harwich, and Peru was called Bromley.

c. Residents living in the shaded portion, those in the western strip of Peru, petitioned in 1802 to become part of Dorset because their East Dorset neighbors were so near, and Peru village was so far, over mountainous trails.

d. But voters in Dorset rejected the proposal in 1805, so residents of western Peru asked to be annexed to Mt. Tabor, to the north. The change was enacted by the legislature in 1805. The resulting outline of Mt. Tabor's boundaries then appeared to be a town that sprouted a leg six miles long and three-fifths of a mile wide. The leg stayed with Mt. Tabor for twenty years.

e. In 1825, after petitions from residents of the leg, plus those on the east side of Dorset, the legislature amputated the leg from Mt. Tabor and joined it to Dorset—except for about 100 acres at the north end owned by Caleb Buffum, who insisted on remaining in Mt. Tabor. Residents of western Dorset were angered at not being consulted. In 1832 Buffum claimed that a mistake had been made, that another 225 acres he owned should be in Mt. Tabor also, and the legislature confirmed his wish. Thus was created the jigsaw puzzle piece that has been known ever since as the Mt. Tabor Leg.

Sketches by Joe Kucin

The Mt. Tabor Leg 93

October 25, 1805, a law titled "An act annexing part of the town of Peru to the town of Mt. Tabor."

A petition to annex the western slice of Peru to Mt. Tabor, signed by Representative Bigelow as agent for Peru residents, had been filed only a week earlier and was favorably received by the General Assembly. Wrote Bigelow about his townsmen: "That for purposes of attending town meeting, doing military duty and other public occasions they have no communication by roads across said mountain and no mode of access to the main body of the inhabitants except by travelling through parts of the towns of Dorset, Manchester, & Winhall, a circuitous rout [sic] of about sixteen miles . . . It would be convenient for them and would obviate most of their present local difficulties if they could be annexed to & made part of the Town of Mount Tabor, who they suggest are ready to receive them."

The speed with which matters moved in 1805 was remarkable. The Dorset town meeting that rejected annexation took place September 3; the Mt. Tabor town meeting that accepted the annexation of part of Peru was also in September, though the date is not known; Bigelow's petition was signed October 5, filed with the legislature on October 21, and the law was adopted on October 25. In an era of primitive communication, there had been little time for consultation. Bigelow, as a citizen who held a variety of town offices as well as that of legislator, clearly had clout.[5]

The resulting shape of the town of Mt. Tabor was now a geographical oddity consisting of the original square, six miles in each direction, plus the six-mile-by-two-hundred-rod appendage dangling from its southwest corner. The town's new configuration looked on a map precisely like a table leg, and that is what it was called from the start—the Mt. Tabor Leg. The Rutland-Bennington county boundary also presented a bizarre appearance—a straight line with a huge niche cut into it.

This solution did not please everyone. Drawbacks began to dawn, in particular, on those who resided on the Leg itself. In the fall of 1812, eighteen residents of the Leg complained to the General Assembly "that we labour under many great and grevious disadvantages by being annexed to said Mount Tabor."[6] They claimed that they must travel twenty-seven miles to the courthouse in Rutland rather than to Bennington County's court at Manchester, which they said (with some exaggeration) was only five miles away—neglecting to mention that half the time Bennington County's court sat in Bennington, at least as great a distance from the Leg as Rutland.[7]

More plausibly, residents also contended that the very shape of the Leg imposed educational difficulties. "We are wholly deprived from the benefit of schools by reason of the said strip being so narrow East & West and so long North & South that we cannot form ourselves into a District." Schooling, they said, was "verry essential to the well being of every well regulated society," and they explained that even if a schoolhouse should be "erected in the center of the strip some of us would then have three miles to send our children to said center, which is utterly impossible especially in the snowy season of the year under the foot of our Green Mountain." They reverted to the idea of asking to be annexed to Dorset, "which directly joins west and we can be accommodated with the priviledge of schooling."

The legislative committee that received this plea noted that residents of Dorset had not been notified, and asked that the matter be postponed. It would be another dozen years before action was taken.

In September 1825 two petitions were prepared for the October session of the legislature. One was from the Albees—William, Addison, James, and Eleazer—and other residents of the Leg, formally asking to become a part of Dorset; the other was from residents of the original territory of Mt. Tabor, including several persons named Tabor, asking for the same thing— that is, seeking to have the Leg amputated from Mt. Tabor and joined onto Dorset. Both petitions were viewed favorably by legislative committees, and suddenly on November 17, Legislative Act. No. 18 was adopted. It was simply titled "An Act, annexing a part of the town of Mt. Tabor, in the county of Rutland, to the town of Dorset, in the county of Bennington." Evidently there were no public hearings, and no town meeting vote either by Dorset or Mt. Tabor.[8]

The new law specifically provided for the exception of "about one hundred acres, on the north end of said piece, owned and occupied by one Caleb Buffum." This land was to remain in Mt. Tabor even though it was considerably south of the straight line that should have been the Dorset-Mt. Tabor boundary.

Buffum was "a man of sound morals, and was a highly respected citizen," according to J. C. Williams's 1869 history of Danby. He was also "a man of strict integrity and uprightness of character." Buffum had come north in 1797 from Providence, Rhode Island, settled first in Danby, then moved in 1818 to his Mt. Tabor farm where he remained for many years. He was a justice of the peace for twenty-nine years, and served as town clerk and selectman. His ties with Mt. Tabor were so strong that one can understand why he would oppose a law that would change the town in which he resided.

To many in Dorset, the annexation of the Leg came as a surprise and shock. Evidence that voters were never consulted is found in the fiery petitions that followed the 1825 annexation. These petitions, written for the next legislative session, drew the lines between Dorset factions; it was strictly a matter of east versus west, one side of the mountain against the other.

From the east side came three petitions—all in identical handwriting and all dated October 2, 1826. One was signed by citizens of Mt. Tabor, another by residents of the Leg, and the third by those in "the original charter limits of Dorset," noticeably residents of East Dorset. All asked that the status quo be retained—that is, that the Leg remain a part of Dorset. They referred to another petition that was making the rounds seeking reannexation of the Leg to Mt. Tabor.

From the west siders came a bombast, three and a half lengthy pages written in a fine hand that spelled out a series of festering injustices claimed by a majority of Dorset citizens. Signed by 184 persons and dated October 13, 1826, this protest contended that "a large majority" of the inhabitants of the original town of Dorset, as laid out and chartered by Benning Wentworth, never had been consulted to see whether they would agree to adding this new territory and extra population.

"Your petitioners have ever been, and are still of the opinion, that the Legislature have no more right to alter the Jurisdictional limits of a chartered & incorporated town without the consent of the former than they have to alter the charter of an incorporated company without the consent of said company," the petition charged. The signers cited violations of the United States Constitution, the Bill of Rights, and the Vermont Constitution.

Residents of the east side of Dorset comprised less than one-third of the population and paid less than one-fourth of the town's taxes, they claimed, and this minority should not be allowed to overpower the voice of the majority of west siders.

The 184 Dorseters argued that "in presenting the subject before the Legislature, their attention was directed to the local situation of Tabor Leg, so called, and the accommodation of its inhabitants; and the local situation of Dorset, and the feelings and interests of its inhabitants [were] more studiously kept from view." Further, they alleged, nearly half the residents of the Leg itself had opposed annexation, were not consulted, and did not sign a petition to be joined to Dorset.

The west side petition concluded darkly "that the accommodation of the inhabitants of Mount Tabor Leg was not the moving spring of action; it was only a cloak under which a grasp was made at power."

The nature of the power play was indicated by petitioners' references to east siders who were envisioning great growth in their section of town: "It is supposed that the furnaces built and building on the east side will tend to increase the number by the addition of wood-cutters, colliers, oar-diggers [sic], teamsters, furnaces, etc., etc., so much, that with the addition of Mount Tabor Leg the east side will have the majority." They observed wryly about

Caleb Buffum that the north line of the Leg had been "so calculated as to leave the most wealthy man resident on the leg still in Mt. Tabor."

The list of signatures of the west siders was headed by Alonzo Selden and Reuben H. Blackmer, and constitutes virtually a checklist of the most prominent early Dorset families, including Manleys (Edmund, John, Alonzo, William, Isaac, George, Hiram, and Martin); Grays (Alvin, Elijah, Paddock, Oliver, Raleigh, John, Anson, and William); Sykeses (Lyman, Silvanus, Horatio, Israel, Titus, Orville, and Simeon); Kents (Juba, John, Jacob, and three others whose first names are indecipherable); Underhills (William, John, and Nathan); and Duntons (William, Henry L., and Richard), among many other names. On the final page is the practised signature of the Reverend William Jackson, minister of the Dorset Congregational Church. The names of a few illiterates appear in the official-looking handwriting along with an X and the notation "his mark." Many signatures are distinct, while others are the scrawls of persons unaccustomed to writing.

The bombastic petition met with no success at all in Montpelier. The Judiciary Committee reported it out unfavorably. It was recommitted with the same result, then withdrawn. Clearly the legislature was unwilling to reverse a law it had passed in the previous session.

From the east side of Dorset, relevant to this dispute, there was an attempt by one Johnson Marsh, a surveyor, to overturn the 1826 election of Representative Blackmer. Blackmer had been the town's legislator for the sessions of 1823 and 1824, but was defeated by Marsh in the annual election of 1825; then in 1826 Blackmer defeated Marsh by three votes. On October 17, 1826, Marsh petitioned to have Blackmer unseated on the basis that he, Marsh, had been a candidate for that office and that about fifteen Dorset freemen "who reside in that part of the town which was formerly a part of Mt. Tabor" offered to vote for him, but that those votes had been challenged by the town constable. Marsh said that in view of Blackmer's election by only three votes, Marsh would have been elected if the fifteen votes had been counted.

Marsh was not successful in unseating the incumbent. But he did initiate still another east side petition, dated October 2, 1826 and signed by about 75 residents, asking the General Assembly not to make any changes in the 1825 law that annexed the Mt. Tabor Leg to Dorset.

Blackmer came back with a petition on November 3, 1826. Blackmer wrote that the 1825 law, for which his adversary Marsh had voted, "was an unwarrantable interference of the Legislature to further the political views of the minority of Dorset, was a most flagrant innovation upon the rights of its citizens and is totally repugnant to every principle of just and equitable legislation." Blackmer claimed that the law was "sanctioning deceit and falsehood and rewarding the offender with the spoils of his offence." He concluded: "With a full knowledge of all the facts and a thorough conviction of the injustice of said vote, I utterly disapprove of the same, and enter my solemn protest against it on the journals of the House."

A year later, on October 1, 1827, in the same handwriting as the lengthy petition from the 184 west side residents, came a protest from Dorset selectmen Silvanus Sykes and Paddock Gray. (There was no word from the third selectman, John Chapman.) Still feeling the heat from citizens who were outraged by the 1825 annexation, the two complained that "there had been no expression of the feelings of the town on the subject since 1805, when the town voted that they would not have said tract of land annexed." The selectmen said the subject had not been even talked about in town, that the Leg annexation was "secretly managed," and that few in Dorset had the slightest intimation about annexation "until nearly a fortnight after the session of the [1825] legislature commenced." By that time, they argued, there was no chance to obtain an expression of opinion at a town meeting. "Under these circumstances the majority of Dorset believed that the Legislature of 1825 had been deceived, not only as to the feelings of Dorset on the subject, but as to the actual situation of the inhabitants on the Leg."

The two selectmen sputtered on about the law being unconstitutional and not binding. They threatened to bring suit and warned the legislature that "to avert litigation, to allay the present excitement, and to prevent further trouble," the whole subject should be reexamined by the General Assembly so that, they suggested, the law could be repealed.

The selectmen concluded wryly, "But if upon a full examination, your honorable body shall be of the opinion that the whole transaction has been fair, just, and legal, comporting with the principles of just and equitable Legislation and consistent with the spirit and meaning of our valuable constitution, then your memorialists, with their fellow citizens of Dorset, be content to be left to the anarchy which said act has created."[9]

Even this plea was given no consideration in legislative circles. It remained the last official word on the subject until the powerful Caleb Buffum weighed in, on September 25, 1828, with a request to have the General Assembly annex still more of his farm to Mt. Tabor. Buffum claimed that a mistake was made in the 1825 law in that only one hundred acres of his land was retained in Mt. Tabor, whereas the entire farm, contiguous to his home, included 262 more acres. Because his land always had been assessed and taxed in Mt. Tabor, that fact should be ratified by legislation, he said.

As before, what Buffum wanted Buffum got. And so the final act in the saga of the Mt. Tabor Leg controversy consists of a law passed on November 3, 1832 titled, "An act, in addition to, and in explanation of an act entitled 'An act annexing a part of the town of Mount Tabor, in the county of Rutland, to the town of Dorset, in the county of Bennington,' passed Nov. 17, 1825." In necessarily convoluted language, the new legislation read: "It is hereby enacted by the General Assembly of the State of Vermont, that the words *excepting about one hundred acres, on the north end of said piece of land, owned and occupied by Caleb Buffum* in the act aforesaid [the 1825 law], shall be so taken and construed, as to include all the lands owned by the said Caleb Buffum, at the time of the passage of said act, included within the limits of that part of Mount Tabor annexed to the said town of Dorset, by the act aforesaid."

Thus endeth the tale of the Mt. Tabor Leg. The original residents of the west side of Peru, in concert with the east siders of Dorset and with help from the prominent Reuben Bigelow of Peru, had achieved their goal—at the expense of the majority of west side residents of Dorset, two of their three selectmen, and their town representative, Reuben Blackmer. The other victor was the honorable Caleb Buffum, owner of the enigmatic jigsaw-puzzle piece of Mt. Tabor land, once part of Peru, which ever since 1825 (and enlarged in 1832) has thrust itself down into Dorset.

NOTES

1. Town boundaries are intended to be straight—north, south, east, west, with right angles. Sometimes reality intervenes, and this is the case with the Mt. Tabor Leg. A few maps depict the Leg with right angles, but most show it slanted on a slight northeast-southwest tilt. The tilt seems to be a case of reality overpowering the wishes of map makers, for the natural direction of the mountain ridges that define the Leg provides their own northeast-southwest slant.

2. All municipalities—whether towns, cities, villages, or fire and light districts—are creatures of the state and may be created, joined, divided, abolished, or changed in any manner only by the legislature.

3. The typical Vermont town six by six miles contains about 23,500 acres. Ever since the 1832 law fixed the Mt. Tabor Leg, Dorset has had more acreage (28,756) and Peru has had less (20,977) than towns like Danby (22,746) or Rupert (23,312) that retain their original borders. Figures are from the National Survey Company's *Vermont Yearbook 1969*.

4. Bromley's name was changed because of a feeling that the name itself was holding back the town's development. Bromley was chartered in 1761 and settled in 1773, but not organized as a town until 1802, when only fourteen families resided there. Settlers thought that growth might be hastened by a reputation-enhancing name, and "Peru" seemed to ring of gold and romantic riches in far-off South America. Something worked, for the population, a mere 72 in 1791, grew to 239 in 1810. After recovering from a time of sickness between 1809 and 1814, Peru's population then soared, reaching an all-time maximum of nearly 600 in the 1840s before it declined. By 1980 Peru's numbers had declined to half of the 1840 peak.

Mt. Tabor was chartered in 1761 as Harwich (often spelled Harwick). Because of confusion with Hardwick in northern Vermont, the name was changed in 1803 to Mt. Tabor. The namesake was Gideon Tabor, a pioneer settler, first town moderator and legislator and town clerk for twenty-eight years.

5. Reuben Bigelow was Peru's most influential citizen. Besides being legislator and constable, he was the town's first postmaster, town clerk and treasurer from 1812–34, and a lifelong justice of the peace, and starting in 1803 taught in Peru's first school. Before the organization of town government, he was proprietor's clerk. He came from Westminster, Massachusetts, in 1797 and brought his family to Peru in 1800.

6. Names of residents of the Mt. Tabor Leg who signed this petition included Simeon Hurlburt, John Wellman, Eleazer Albee, John Collson, Jonathan Hulet, Thomas Hulet, James Lincoln, John Brocke, James Hathaway, Henry Baker, David White, Jonathan White, and Seth Allen. It goes without saying that in those days only men signed petitions.

7. Bennington County is Vermont's only county with two "shire" towns, a town in which a courthouse is located. A compromise in 1781 spurned the centrally located town of Shaftsbury and settled on the two-shire approach—sometimes called "half shire"—so that both Bennington and Manchester would have courthouses. The courthouse at Manchester was built in 1822.

8. Town meeting records of 1825, among other years, are missing for both Mt. Tabor and Dorset.

9. Both of these selectmen later served in the Vermont House of Representatives. Sylvanus Sikes (spelled Sykes in the legislative records and nearly everywhere else), who lived from 1775 to 1840, was Dorset's legislator in 1832 and 1833. Paddock Gray was elected for the 1834 and 1835 legislative sessions. Gray was born in 1793 and died in 1858.

7

The Early Nineteenth Century

VERMONT entered the nineteenth century at a time of peace, prosperity, and unparalleled growth. Compared to the first census only a decade earlier, the state's population in 1800 had nearly doubled, from 85,539 to 154,465. (When Vermont joined the Union, in 1791, its population was larger than that of Rhode Island, Georgia, Delaware, or Kentucky.) The rancorous controversy with New York was resolved, the hardships of pioneer life gradually lessened; land values were rising, and settlers continued to migrate to a new land of opportunity. The future appeared promising.[1]

Dorset grew rapidly during the first decade of statehood and became known as one of the more prosperous towns, along with Bennington, Shaftsbury, Westminster, and Guilford. The 1800 census counted 1,286 souls (the same population Dorset would have in 1970). During the 1790s the town grew at a rate of 25 percent, the greatest in its history.

The population was incredibly young, with half the residents under the age of sixteen. Growth came from immigration and a surplus of births over deaths. Teenage marriages were the rule, birth control was unknown and for a time epidemics were mild, so families simply exploded with offspring. Zachariah Curtis in North Dorset sired twenty-five children; Reuben Bloomer had thirteen "husky" sons and daughters; Cephas Kent, Sr., came to town with nine children between the ages of four and twenty-four, and most of them stayed and multiplied.

In 1800 a young man with the unusual name of Experience Barrows settled in town from Hartford, Connecticut. In 1804 he married Lucretia Wales, also from Connecticut, and they raised a family of eight sons and three daughters. Their farm was located at the far end of the Hollow where the rushing Mettawee River could be harnessed by a millwheel to generate energy. Barrows lived to the age of eighty-four, his wife ninety-three.

After 1800, however, Dorset's population suddenly stabilized as if brakes had been applied: the census of 1810 reported an increase of only eight residents. (In nearby Rupert the population followed a most unusual pattern. Rupert in 1791 was slightly larger than Dorset and had 1,034 residents, then for some twenty years Rupert grew to 1,600 before declining sharply. By the time of Dorset's peak of 2,000 in the 1870s and 1880s Rupert had dwindled to less than 1,000.)

In 1800 Vermont's independence had been subordinated in the federal Union, and new political leadership replaced the rustic Allen gang and Thomas Chittenden, who died in 1797 after being governor for nineteen years. Although most Congregationalists leaned politically toward the aristocratic Federalists, all of Vermont's western counties in 1800 voted for the party of Jefferson, which favored the common laborer, farmer, and mechanic.

The new state's economy gained in self-sufficiency, with industries mostly home based: sawmills, gristmills, tanneries, asheries. Small-farm products were wheat, rye, corn, pork, beef, mutton, lard, butter, and cheese. Imports included crockery and textiles as well as coffee, tea, salt, sugar, molasses, rum, and spices. Goods of English or German steel or iron were hauled overland or by boat. Within its own borders Dorset would soon produce two important commodities—crockery and iron.

Town records show that Dorset began the nineteenth century with concerns about smallpox, the status of glebelands, and the ejection from town of undesirables. On March 4, 1800, a town meeting was held at the dwelling house of the widow Marcy Underhill (Abraham Underhill having died in 1796) with a distressing issue: "to see if they will grant libberty for a pest house to be opened in Sd. Town under the direction of the Select Men and authority of said Town for the Enoculation of such inhabitence and others as shall chose to be Enoculated [original spelling retained]."

Dorset was keeping up with the times—immunization against disease had first been demonstrated to the western world only four years earlier by Briton Edward Jenner. Ira Allen reported in 1798 that inoculation was introduced to Vermont with great success, "and by this means thousands of lives are preserved to the community." Measles were no longer so dangerous, Allen wrote, because "the treatment of this disorder has deprived it in a great degree of its malignity."[2]

A town meeting vote in 1803 confirmed that the sickness was smallpox.

Two local physicians, Dr. Jonathan Blackmer and Dr. Alpheus Morse, were authorized by selectmen to inoculate persons at town expense.

Dorset acted on a different issue on September 21, 1802, when selectmen Jonathan Armstrong, Benjamin Baldwin, and Price Bardslee ordered nine persons "to depart said town with their families and effects." No reasons were given for the ejection of Frances Bagley, John Kelly, John Robinson, Joy Babit, Theodora Not, Simeon Lackey, Noah Dunn, Jonathan Engel, and Eunice Ingraham. The next day Constable Stephen Martindale recorded that he had served notice on all nine (though he misspelled most of their names). For his labors he charged $2.16. Many other "undesirables" ejected from town during this era, though reasons were never specified.

A footnote to the era of Dorset's original proprietors, relating to the Dorset-Kinderhook connection noted in chapter 3, is found in federal records showing that in 1817 one Alexander M. Martine of Kinderhook, New York, for failure to pay taxes, was ordered by the U.S. District Court to sell some 650 acres in town. The buyer was Daniel Boardman, who in like manner acquired parcels in Sandgate, Arlington, Bennington, and Pownal.

Not all conditions were rosy. In 1811, two-thirds of Vermont's water-powered mills, weakened by erosion of the soil that surrounded them, were washed away in a series of cloudbursts.[3] Vermont's nineteenth-century out-migration is often traced to the calamitous year of 1816, often called "Eighteen hundred and froze to death." Snow or frost was experienced every month, wiping out crops and making seed scarce. The phenomenon was caused when volcanic ash from the massive 1815 eruption of Mount Tamboro in the East Indies blanketed the earth's atmosphere.

There were other natural calamities—floods, forest fires, and diseases. In 1813 an epidemic of "spotted fever" (some say it was spinal meningitis) took a toll of six thousand statewide; among its local victims were brothers Alexander and Cephas Kent, Jr. Hollister's history of Pawlet told how a major grasshopper infestation ruined crops in 1826.

The Dana Hart farm in Kirby Hollow, site of Asa Baldwin's eighteenth-century cabin, has remained in the Hart family since the late 1700s, and is now owned by Mrs. Edna Mylott (daughter of Mr. and Mrs. Dana Hart) and her husband Robert. It is known as Spring Brook Farm.

Photo by Tyler Resch

The George B. Holley house as depicted on the 1856 Rice-Harwood map. It was later owned by Gilbert Sykes, and is now owned by Peter Zecher.

Education

Benning Wentworth's charter set aside land for the Church of England, for the propagation of the gospel, for the first settled minister, and for schools. After the victory over Great Britain the Vermont legislature specified that lands designated by Wentworth as church oriented would be used in fact for education.

A town meeting in 1798 agreed that a deed to ministerial lands originally granted to the Reverend Elijah Sill, as the first settled minister, be transferred to the town of Dorset "for the benefit of schooling forever." Next year the warning asked voters "to see if the town will direct the Select men to collect the rent now due for the use of the glebe and appropriate the same for the use of schooling." At a special meeting on May 5, 1800, trouble between town and church over glebe lands was hinted when it was voted "that the town will not give up the glebe to the Church Wardens." Then it was also voted "to chose [sic] a committee of 3 to defend the suit if it is brought." But town records shed no more light on litigation.

At the 1801 town meeting selectmen were directed "to prepare a work house in Dorset, if necessary, and not to expend more than Sixty Dollars without further orders from the town."

Numerous town officials were elected at each meeting. These typically included a sealer of weights and measure, a leather sealer, fence viewers, a deer reeve (often spelled *Dear Reef*), grand jurors, petty jurors, four listers, three tithingmen, pound keepers, and several surveyors of highways. The first recorded election of school directors took place in 1802, when seven "trustees of the several school districts" were named. At the 1801 meeting it was clear that boundary lines of the six school districts approved in 1797 were not satisfactory to all, for it was agreed "that Joseph Grover, Samuel Allen and Charles Purday be transferred from their former school district and be anexed to the schol [sic] district south of where they now live."

In 1804 a "publick grammer school" was created, which in 1807 became the Dorset Academy. The following petition for a school, signed by John Shumway, Humphrey Richardson, and James Underhill, was filed with the General Assembly at Windsor:

Dorset, January 7, 1804

That a number of inhabitants of the town of Dorset and Manchester have mutually agreed to raise a sum of money for the purpose of building an academy or publick grammer school on that tract of land formerly known on the proprietor records by the name of Underhill's Grant and lies north of Humphrey Richardson's land west of the highway leading from the meeting House in Dorset to the court house in Manchester south of the highway between Abraham Underhill's and Cooks Mills so-called, and east of the streem on which the said Cooks Mills and Humphrey Richardson's Fulling Mill now stands, and having subscribed a sum which they deem sufficient for the erection of said building they pray that they may be incorporated into a body politic for the purpose of carrying the said institution into effect under such rules and regulations the Honorable General Assembly in their wisdom shall think proper.

Another petition to incorporate the Dorset Academy was enacted into law in October 1807, the final year that John Shumway, the town clerk, who had signed the 1804 petition, was Dorset's representative. Academy trustees were Reverend William Jackson, Stephen Martindale, John Vail, Asa Baldwin, John Shumway, Titus Sikes, and Samuel Collins, all of Dorset, Reverend John Griswold and John Sargent of Pawlet, Richard Skinner of Manchester (who would become governor of Vermont in 1820), and Josiah Rising and Grove Moore of Rupert. Shumway was Dorset's legislator off and on for eleven sessions between 1783 and 1807, followed in 1808–11 by Samuel Collins.

This twelve-man board found it difficult to secure a quorum of eight, as the 1807 law provided, and the law was amended in 1808 to provide that "a majority of the members present, at any legal meeting . . . shall be considered a quorum to do and transact any business."

On the state level, a Board of Commissioners of Common Schools was created in 1827 to oversee the operation of local schools. But the board's zealousness in attempting to dictate textbooks soon prompted the legislature to abolish it.

The account book of jack-of-all-trades Allen C. Roberts mentions that in 1834 Elizabeth Bromley began teaching school in Dorset for 50 cents a week, with board provided by the town.

By mid-century the state superintendent of common schools reported that Dorset had eleven school districts attended by 511 scholars. The 1849 annual report to the legislature compared the number of male and female teachers in terms of total weeks taught during the year. In Dorset, male teachers taught for a total of 90 weeks, compared with 263 weeks for female teachers. There was vast disparity in pay: men received $13.66 a month, women $6.02, both including board at private homes. At least the town was paying more than the Bennington County average, which was $13.36 for men and $5.90 for women. The average length of the school year was twenty-eight weeks. In 1849 Dorset spent $704.64 on teacher salaries and a grand total of $1,275.39 on schools.

In higher education in the region, Middlebury College graduated its first class in 1802, the University of Vermont in 1804. Dartmouth, chartered in 1769, opened in 1770. Williams College was chartered in 1793. The first Dorset resident to attend any of them was the Reverend William Jackson, who graduated from Dartmouth in 1790.

Transportation

Better roads than mere tracks through the wilderness were repeatedly demanded. In 1797 Dorset roads were supervised on a local level by the fourteen elected "surveyors of highways." The first coordinated townwide roads were planned by selectmen and surveyors in 1804, 1805, and 1806. Precise locations are obscure to anyone who scrutinizes these records 180 years later, for roads were designated by various residents' fields, by certain beech or maple trees, and stakes and stones, and were described in surveyors' language with sightings measured in rods.

Since 1783 lotteries had been a popular Vermont method for raising funds for roads and bridges, as well as for churches. In 1800 Vermont also authorized turnpike companies and granted them the powerful right of eminent domain: the state could seize land for highway purposes and compensate the owners. The legislature retained control of toll rates.

In October 1802 about seventy-five citizens asked the legislature for a road "from Danby through Harwich, Brumly [sic] and Dorset into Manchester." They complained that the existing road was in poor condition, "and requires a large sum of money expended to make it tolerably good." But the growing state faced similar pleas from many other regions and the matter was postponed. In October 1804 several Dorseters sought improvements in the stage road through Manchester, Dorset, Peru, Mt. Tabor, Danby, Wallingford, Clarendon, Rutland, Mt. Holly, and Shrewsbury. Their petition pleaded that the road: "is in many places almost impassable with carriages and that for many miles on said road the inhabitants are so thinly settled as to render it wholly out of their power to keep it in repair by means of the ordinary mode provided by law."

In the fall of 1805 another petition demanded a turnpike from Danby to Manchester. One signatory to all three mentioned petitions was Eliakim Deming of East Dorset, the erstwhile Tory. By 1806 the Dorset Turnpike Company was having trouble completing the job it had undertaken. Company officials met in September and named attorney Nathaniel Chipman as agent to seek legislative authorization for: "an alteration and extension of the grant of said company from the south end of the said road heretofore granted through Dorset, Manchester, Sunderland and Arlington by the Battenkill to the west line of this state and from the north end of said road on or near the public or county road from Rutland."

In fact, the Dorset Turnpike Company in 1806 reported "great discouragements" and so the General Assembly granted a one-year extension, "provided the company shall agree with the persons through whose land such alterations are proposed to be made."

Long-distance transportation was best accomplished by boat along Lake Champlain, the Hudson, or the Connecticut. In 1809 the first steamboat, *The Vermont*, was launched on Champlain, creating new business for the port of Burlington. By 1823 the twenty-eight-mile Champlain Canal linked Whitehall on Lake Champlain with Fort Edward on the Hudson River, and in 1825 the Erie Canal opened waterways to Buffalo and the Great Lakes. Both canals were vital to the flourishing of Dorset's marble industry (see chapter 8).

Commerce and Industry

The extent to which trade and barter formed an accepted medium of exchange is disclosed in the account book of Allen C. Roberts, which details his transactions between 1828 and 1844.[4] Roberts did practically anything for a living: he built houses, repaired schools, drove wagons to the Champlain Canal, made shingles, farmed, slaughtered hogs, boarded indigents, and ran a tavern. Born in 1804, Roberts married Hannah Farrar of Rupert in 1826. The pair moved often, living in Rupert, Danby, and Dorset.

Earliest accounts in Roberts' book are dated at Danby soon after he and his wife moved there in May 1828, when they apparently ran a tavern. The account with Isaac Hillyard, a Danby shoemaker, was listed as follows (using Roberts's spelling):

May 24, 1828	to one glass of lemmon punch	$0.13
	to two drinks of lemon biters	0.12
May 31	to one drink of lemon biters	0.06
June 3	to four crakers	0.04
	to four dinners and rum bill	1.55
	to half dozn crakers	0.06
	to sour punch	0.12
	to ginger bread for your boys	0.10
June 3	to lemons and sugar fifty cents	0.50
July 7	to two drinks of lemmon biters	0.10
July 21	to one gallon cider brandy	0.50
	to one drink of biters	0.04
Aug. 15	to half gallon cider brandy	0.25
Aug. 30	to two quarts of brandy	0.25

These charges totaled $4.32 and were offset with the following credits:

by one iron kitle	1.50
by making one pair of shoes for my wife	0.87
by making one pair of shoes for myself	0.87

(and later, in 1832:)

by making one pair of thick boots for Caleb	1.25

This totaled $4.49, or seventeen cents more than Hillyard owed Roberts, but evidently the seventeen cents was considered earned interest on the four-year-old indebtedness, for the account was then closed.

Roberts recorded trips he made in 1838 to the canal. For carrying a load of marble weighing 2,060 pounds from "Dorset to canal," Roberts was paid twenty cents per hundred, or $4.12, by Seneca Smith & Co. At other times he earned $5.38 for hauling 2,670 pounds, and $5 for 2,500 pounds. On return trips Roberts charged Smith & Co. for "fetching in one load of goods from canal"—1,496 pounds the first time, 2,310 and 1,244 pounds the next two trips.

The nature of the arrangement was made clear in a letter preserved with the account book, from Seneca Smith & Co. to "Friend Allen C. Roberts" on June 9, 1838, after the first trip to the canal: "We should like to have you take another load of stone and go to the canal and get a load of the goods—Get the small articles, and then fill up with Fish to make up the load."

Usually Roberts would be paid in cash, but his final payment was "by one barrel of pickled fish seven dollars and half."

One of the early retail stores was that known today as Peltier's, across from the Dorset Inn. Research by its current owner, Jay Hathaway, places its establishment at about 1816, in a building believed moved from East Rupert, by owners thought to be Norman Blackmer and Harvey Holley. Early records are sketchy, but for several years it was known as the Dorset Union Store, operating like a co-op, with members owning shares; it was associated with the New England Protective Union, which offered uniform bookkeeping and inventorying. In 1839 the store was bought by Moore Holley & Co., a six-man partnership. Then it took on several identities, including S.F. Holley & Co. and Holley & Gray Co. In 1851 its name again became the Dorset Union Store.

According to documents found in the store attic, in 1845 the store was known as Underhill & Gray, for on September 27 a firm in Troy wrote to Underhill & Gray of Dorset that they had "shipped this day to the care of C.W. Kellogg, Fort Ann [New York], per 'Northern Transportation Line'" six sheets of zinc—88 pounds at 9 cents per pound, or $7.92. And on October 17, 1845, at Comstock Landing Charles W. Kellogg wrote to Underhill & Gray saying, "We ship your wool to Greenbush." In 1847 the store was known as Clark Gray, for in October of that year Olcott, McKenon & Co. of New York City billed Clark Gray for blue vitriol, cloves, nutmegs, corks, cologne, and other items that they had shipped "care of C.W. Kellogg, Fort Ann, per Comstocks M.T. Line."[5]

By 1819 Barzilie Hudson was operating a blacksmith shop on a stream at Nichols Hill. Among the boyhood recollections of Laurel Armstrong, dating to 1810–15, was a description of an old man, Amos Thompson, who built a sawmill north of the village on the Mettawee. John Shumway owned it until about 1840, selling to Ira Sykes, who with his son Waldo later passed it to a cousin, Ernest Edgerton, Sr.[6] The mill in 1840 boasted the first circular saw in Bennington County when it was operated by Ira Sykes and Return Underhill. Underhill also had an interest in a sawmill in the Hollow, where still another mill was run by Timothy Rideout.

A descendant, Norma Taft, believed the first shoemaker in town was Bruneau Roberts. His shop was located on the Dorset Hollow Road and in the early 1900s became the blacksmith shop of E. E. Kent, and later that of Fred Seymour.

Williams' Brothers harness shop as it looked in 1899. It is now the H.N. Williams Department Store on Route 30 south of Dorset village. The business began in 1840 and remains in the same family after five generations, owned and operated by Ada Williams Rumney and her husband, Austin, and Ruth and Dennis Brownlee.

Between 1825 and 1830 William Williams acquired a shop on the West Road and converted it to a tannery, thus launching one of the town's most durable institutions. Williams used a horse-powered mill to grind chips of bark to create tannic acid. By the 1840s the shop was making shoes and boots that sold for $1.25 a pair, and leather harnesses. Williams was a son of Oliver Williams, who came to town in the 1790s from Connecticut and married Abigail Kent, a granddaughter of Cephas, Sr.[7] Later in the century the store would expand not only its leather products but also to carry a wide variety of merchandise (about which more in chapter 9).

(The story of East Dorset's iron works is also related in chapter 9.)

In North Dorset some time between 1832 and 1840 a substantial Greek Revival-style house was built by Welcome Allen which, more than a century later and eighty-five miles away, would bring a certain renown to the town. The Welcome Allen house consisted of a central section measuring thirty-four feet, with a large ell at each end, giving it a total width of sixty-three feet. The roof was of long-lasting slate, and an unusual veneer of marble slabs concealed the foundations.

The house was usually a two-family residence, and during the twentieth century it was allowed to fall into disrepair. In 1953 the architecturally distinguished but shabby house caught the eye of Mrs. J. Watson Webb, founder and president of the Shelburne Museum, while she was driving to visit a sister in Manchester. Making inquiry of a local friend, Sidney Whalen, she learned that the owner was Aubrey N. Shaw of Dorset. He sold it to her for $50.

The "Dorset Castle," as the Shelburne Museum calls it, was dismantled, moved to Shelburne, and painstakingly restored in 1954. Some residents of Dorset have been disappointed that the house was not used for relevant local furnishings and memorabilia. Instead it holds the museum's extensive and rare collection of wildfowl decoys. Perhaps it is well that the house is not used for totally authentic purposes, for a legend that the museum passes along has it that one occupant of the Welcome Allen house "used to take a couple of bottles of liquor and hole up in the bedroom and not come out for a week."

The Fenton Potteries

The name of Christopher W. Fenton has been long associated with the well-known Bennington pottery, but not until the 1970s did research by the late Alfred H. Gilbert and others document Fenton's Dorset origins.[8]

Jonathan Fenton, father of Christopher, founded a pottery to produce redware in 1800 or 1801 near the first bridge leading to Dorset Hollow. By 1810 he had moved to East Dorset, probably because of better access to clay deposits in the foothills of the Green Mountains. The East Dorset pottery site was on land occupied more recently by the homes of Jane Leary and Walter B. Read, where for a quarter of a century Jonathan and sons Richard Lucas and Christopher Webber Fenton carried on the potter's art. In 1828 Richard and Christopher moved to Bennington to join Luman Norton, son of Captain John Norton, who had established the first pottery in Bennington in 1793. But the Fenton brothers returned to Dorset in 1830 and formed the partnership of R. L. Fenton and Co., as attested by several stoneware jars and jugs that bear the inscription: "R. L. Fenton and Co., East Dorset."

Jonathan Fenton continued his East Dorset pottery for a while, and deeds in 1833 and 1835 indicate that he conveyed at least half of his property to his son-in-law, Job Cleveland of nearby Hebron, New York.

The existence of two two-gallon jugs inscribed "R. & C. [Richard and Christopher] Fenton, Dorset" led Alfred Gilbert to conclude that the brothers must have reactivated their Dorset Hollow pottery at an early date. Gilbert quoted a reminiscence by Laurel Armstrong in 1858 about a potter's wheel and kiln of the Fentons from the days of Armstrong's childhood in the Hollow, placing that time at about 1800 to 1810.

The Fenton brothers sold their share of the East Dorset pottery and made a final move to Bennington in 1833; Richard died the next year, and Christopher married the daughter of Luman Norton to become a partner in

Photo by Nancy H. Otis

the Bennington enterprise. The Norton-Fenton connection lasted until 1847, when Christopher dissolved the partnership, then with his brother-in-law, Julius Norton, and went into business for himself. Fenton became widely known for his mass production of fine pottery that included Staffordshire, Parian, Rockingham, and flint enamel wares.

After Fenton's Bennington pottery works were destroyed by fire he rebuilt them, in 1845. He described the new facilities as "the most extensive pottery works in the country . . . We produce a much better, handsomer and stronger stoneware, than is made in this country." There was little exaggeration in Fenton's boast, for his creative output in the years 1847–58 was described by a Bennington Museum curator as "the most dynamic" in New England nineteenth-century pottery: "There was an explosion of design, color, and variety. While the Norton company continued to turn out its traditional stoneware line, the Fenton pottery leaped ahead with its Parian, Rockingham and flint enamel pieces. Daniel Greatbach, an English designer, came to Fenton's pottery via the Jersey, City, N.J., Pottery, and created many of the high-quality animal designs (lions, poodles, cows, deer) and Toby bottles that were to receive wide popular acclaim."[9]

Sales flourished after Fenton acquired a partner-manager named Oliver Gager, who exhibited Fenton wares at the important 1853 Crystal Palace Exhibition in New York, using the clever name United States Pottery Company. Fenton's fame was further enhanced by an elaborate statue of himself

The Early Nineteenth Century

Far left: Ed Slanetz and Dr. Alfred H. Gilbert examine pottery shards they uncovered in the late 1960s at the site of the 1800 Fenton Pottery near the "cheese factory bridge" on Dorset Hollow Road.

Left: This Fenton jug dates from the moving of the Fenton Pottery works from the Hollow Road over to East Dorset in 1810. It is on exhibit at the historical society museum.

that was created for the great exhibition. The Parian bust of Fenton, on a base of scroddleware, surrounded by flint enamel columns, surmounted by a figure of Charity, stood for many years in an exterior niche of a home on Pleasant Street in Bennington built in 1838 by Luman Norton. This ceramic confection is now on permanent exhibition in the Bennington Museum's pottery gallery.

Despite these successes, only five years later the Fenton works were in decline, afflicted by high prices of cordwood that heated the kilns and by frequent breakage involved in shipping fragile wares by horse-drawn wagons over primitive roads. Though the Norton Company continued production until 1894, the United States Pottery Company closed in 1858. Fenton moved to Peoria, Illinois, where a new pottery venture proved unsuccessful. He died in Joliet, Illinois, in 1865.

Sheep

Sheep did not become a major source of income until the 1830s—but as early as 1801 loose rams were a nuisance. Controls over "sheep rams" running on the Dorset commons, as noted in chapter 6, were voted at a town meeting on March 10, 1801, the ban in force between September 1 and November 1 "with a fine of 50 cents for the first offense and one dollar for the second."

By 1823 there were thousands of sheep, and town records evoke the ways in which animals grazed freely. Each sheep owner had a registered ear mark, but unlike many other towns, which recorded a small picture of the actual marking, Dorset's livestock marks were described only in words. The first registered were those of Anson Shumway: "His mark a crop of the end of the right ear. His mark [signature]. Recorded 4th January 1823." The mark of Stephen Taylor was "a swallow tails on the right ear & a happenny on the upper side of the same & a slit in the end of the left ear." Artemus Sheldon's was "a hole in the right ear and a happeny [sic] on the upper side of the same. Recorded the above 2 marks June 5, 1824."

Sheep in Vermont flourished in extraordinary numbers throughout the 1830s, until protective tariffs were removed in the 1840s. The origin of these flocks—at least of the prolific merinos—was traced to William Jarvis, a Boston merchant who while U.S. consul in Lisbon from 1802 to 1811 violated an export ban and shipped four hundred woolly Merinos to his newly purchased farm in Weathersfield, Vermont.

Though sheep pastures changed the landscape dramatically, little visual evidence remains, because by the time sheep were gone photography had been barely invented. But many late-nineteenth-century landscape photographs demonstrate that much of the land remained clear, even high up on the mountainsides. Sheep were so numerous that about 70 percent of the land was opened for grazing, the rest forested. By the 1970s that ratio was reversed so that it again resembles the mix of open versus forested land of the eighteenth century.

Photo by Nancy H. Otis

Ada Rumney displays patterns of harnesses that were manufactured in the early nineteenth century by her grandfather, William Williams.

In 1836 Vermont counted more than one million sheep—about four for every person. This compared to 4.2 million in New York State, including 412 in New York City. Bennington County alone had a sheep census of 69,828 (again, four for every person); the county's greatest sheep town was Shaftsbury, with 12,084, the smallest Glastenbury, with 13. Dorset had 4,022.[10] By 1840 Vermont was a nationally important sheep-raising state, with 1.6 million of the productive animals. But times changed abruptly and the sheep craze ended in the 1840s, when competition was felt from the American West and from Australia.

Churches

On March 7, 1838, the East Dorset Union Society was organized to encompass various religious groups, none of which was large enough to afford its own church. What each group could not achieve alone was done by the entire society, which voted to build a meetinghouse that measured 44 by 34 feet.[11] The society owned the building and apportioned times for various members to use it. The moderator was former legislator John Cochran, with Benjamin Ames as clerk. Subscribers numbered forty-seven, and in 1839 $1,654.50 was raised, front pews selling for more than rear.

Early records are sketchy, but by 1865 the "slips" (pews) were taxed, and $63.50 was spent for shingles, $31.50 for laying same, and $20.41 for a new chimney. More was spent the next year for a platform and steps (probably a choir loft), paint, whitewash, and pulleys for ringing the bell. In 1877 a cellar was dug, and marble steps and an organ were installed.

There were Baptists and Methodists in the society, but it was the Congregational Church Society that became the largest, and eventually the only, group using the building for religious services. In 1867 a group gathered at the East Dorset home of Frederick Field [now George Ludlam] to organize a Congregational Church. Articles of faith were adopted on October 1 that year. The East Dorset Union Society retained title to the meetinghouse for more than a century longer until it was formally passed to the Congregational Church Society in December 1975.

At the Dorset Congregational Church, official records are mostly missing for the years between 1809 and 1830 but, as noted earlier, the first church burned in January 1832. Originally located in the Maple Hill Cemetery, and made of logs, the building was often known as "the Lord's Barn" for its draftiness. Moved to a location across from the present building, it succumbed to fire caused by hot coals from footwarmers.

Not everyone regretted the loss. "I'm glad on't, I'm glad on't!" shouted

The East Dorset Union Society built the predecessor of this church about 1838 at Village Street (old Route 7) and the Mad Tom Road. The present East Dorset Congregational Church was organized in 1867.

Haratio Sykes as he plowed through snowdrifts to reach the disaster. "I only wish the old school house had been in the middle of it."

Plans for a new church were drawn by a committee of three headed by Experience Barrows, who had earned a reputation for efficient construction when he built his own house in the Hollow in 1829. But he was also influenced by the Temperance Association that was founded in 1826, and both his house and the new church were built without the assistance of spiritous beverages.

The new edifice was raised during a community-wide effort. The church cost $3,250 and was dedicated February 6, 1833, at a meeting of the Pawlet Congregational Association, held in Dorset.

Dorset and Pawlet had other connections. A twenty-four-page hand-sewn pamphlet survives of the text of a sermon delivered by Amos Pettengill of Manchester to the Moral Societies of Dorset and Pawlet at their annual meeting in Dorset on June 6, 1815. A notation by Dr. Alpheus Morse, who was clerk of the society, records that the group voted to thank the speaker for his sermon, and asked him "to grant them a copy for the press."

The Reverend William Jackson and Henrietta

Some understanding of early eighteenth-century Dorset can be gained by reviewing the life of a towering figure of that age, the Reverend William Jackson, who arrived by horse-drawn sleigh in February 1797 with his bride Susannah Cram. He remained pastor of the Congregational church until his death in 1842.

William Jackson was born in Cornwall, Connecticut, on December 14, 1768, to a family that migrated while he was a child to Wallingford, Vermont. He prepared for college by attending an academy in Norwich, Vermont, then entered Dartmouth, graduating in 1790. After teaching in Wethersfield, Connecticut, "his mind became settled upon the Christian ministry as the employment in which he could most usefully serve God and his generation," according to an 1842 posthumous biography by Joseph D. Wickham, principal of Burr Seminary in Manchester, a school Jackson helped to found.[12]

Jackson studied with theologians in Massachusetts and earned a license to preach the gospel at age twenty-five. He returned to visit friends in Vermont and by chance stopped in Dorset, where members of the church, then without a minister, invited him to preach. Worried about his health, always fragile, he declined to "accept a call to the pastoral office." Instead he preached for a season in New Jersey. But he returned to Dorset, where the congregation again asked him to stay. He agreed, and was ordained in the Congregational Church of Dorset and East Rupert on September 27, 1796.

Jackson had been courting Susannah Cram of Brentwood, New Hampshire, whom he addressed in love letters as "My Dear Sukey." They were married the next winter and left Brentwood for Dorset by sleigh. Jackson wrote to his in-laws, Mr. and Mrs. Samuel Cram:

Weathersfield, Vermont, February 10, 1797

Dear Parents

We are now on the west side of Connecticut River, in the New State, about 50 miles from home. We shall proceed about a dozen miles further today and with a smile of providence we hope to reach Dorset tomorrow. Sukey appears to endure the journey dominably well. She enjoys very good spirits . . . I had no idea that she could support such a journey with so much strength and fortitude.

William Jackson[13]

Jackson's pastorate in Dorset was marked by scholarly attention to the classics, and his pulpit manner was one of "marked solemnity." Principal Wick-

The Welcome Allen House on Route 7 in North Dorset, built about 1840, was allowed to deteriorate to this condition until it was purchased in 1953 by Mrs. J. Watson Webb, founder of the Shelburne Museum, for $50. (Welcome supposedly got his name because of his tardy arrival at his parents' home.)

The Welcome Allen House after its removal and reconstruction at the Shelburne Museum in 1954. The museum calls it "the Dorset Castle" and uses it to hold a large collection of wildfowl decoys.

ham penned this description of Jackson's first sermon:

An aged member of the church, now in his ninety-third year, remarked to the writer that when the preacher rose in the pulpit and uttered these words his aspect was so serious, and his tone and manner so solemn and impressive, that the bare announcement of the text produced an instantaneous and perceptible effect upon the whole assembly. "I shall never forget it, I never can," he added with a trembling voice. "We thought it a solemn business then to have a gospel minister."

Jackson worried about a shortage of clergymen, and in 1804 founded a Western Vermont Evangelical Society "for the purpose of forming a benevolent society, to aid pious and needy young men, in acquiring education, for the work of the gospel ministry." The society, described as the first in the nation, loaned money to "pious and Calvinistic" students who wished to pursue the ministry, using funds donated by the "charitably disposed."

Jackson's tenure was marked by a series of religious revivals. One took place in 1795, while he was preaching but before his ordination, and it enlisted 22 new members. Wickham described a "general revival" in 1803–1804 that lasted for eighteen months and recruited 101 new members. Revivals were slowed by the War of 1812 and the distraction of the Embargo Acts. But protracted church revivals occurred in 1818–19 with 80 more members, others in 1821 and 1826, and three "distinct revivals" in 1830, 1832, and 1833, with 77 more members. At the time of Jackson's death there were 152 resident church members and 16 nonresidents. Thirteen young men went from Jackson's church to become preachers, and Wickham wrote in 1842 that, "several others are in a course of preparation."

The 1830s was a decade notable in Vermont for its social ferment, often couched in causes that involved self-improvement or zealous altruism. In addition to religious revivals there was a wave of temperance organizations (one was formed in Dorset in 1826) and antislavery societies, some utopian communes were formed, and the anti-Masonic movement, fearful of mysterious foreign influences, grew so strong that it actually elected a governor, William A. Palmer, from 1831 to 1835.[14]

Jackson's feeble health prompted him by 1837 to ask either to be dismissed or to have a colleague in the pulpit. The congregation called in a series of interim pastors, though none stayed long. One, the Reverend Ezra Jones, suggested that Jackson was not easy to get along with. In a letter years later to Parsons Pratt he wrote: "When Dr. Jackson requested the church to seek out a proper successor in his work, the neighboring pastors who were best acquainted with the whole situation, expected that *whoever* should be the man, his pastorate there would be brief."

The Jacksons had seven children, including a son and a daughter who died in childhood. The surviving son became a minister, the Reverend Samuel C. Jackson, and three daughters married ministers: Margaret, wife of the Reverend John Maltby of Bangor, Maine; Elizabeth, wife of the Reverend Nathaniel Beach of Milbury, Massachusetts, and Henrietta, wife of the Reverend Cyrus Hamlin. Daughter Susan lived with her mother in the Dorset family homestead next to the original location of the church, a home known in the twentieth century as the Barrows House.

Henrietta Anna Lorain Jackson, born in 1811, was named for her older sister, who died at the age of five. Henrietta was a mystical child, living in her own spiritual world, bewitched by the beauties of nature. From her window in the parish house she became especially attached to a lone elm tree. The Spirit would often visit her there as she sat beneath its high branches to read, dream, and pray. When neighbors began calling it Henrietta's Elm a Dorset legend was born that would endure far longer than the tree itself. Henrietta's biographer, Margaretta Woods Lawrence, wrote of it this way:

[The tree was] a towering elm, whose immense trunk, rising to a great height without branch or bough, finally terminated in a splendid crown of gracefully drooping branches, clothed with the densest and most verdant foliage. It was a noble relic of the primeval forest. As Henrietta sat at her window in the dreamy twilight, this magnificent tree seemed to stand as one of the pillars of the firmament; and, as it proudly rose toward heaven, it bore her thoughts upward to Him that sitteth above the firmament. At this beloved tree she gazed and gazed, until her rapt spirit became almost engrafted upon it . . . Being thus associated in the hearts of her family with her sweetest communings, it received the name of Henrietta's elm.

In 1835, during a visit to her sister in Bangor, Maine, Henrietta, then twenty-four, met Cyrus Hamlin, a theological seminary student. The next year Hamlin, assigned to take charge of a seminary in Constantinople for the education of Armenian youth, felt "authorized to look for a companion" and asked for Henrietta's hand in marriage. She agonized over the decision (her letters disclose more concern about distance and logistics than any considerations of love for Hamlin). But after consulting her parents she was guided by the religious calling of the enterprise and decided to marry him—and then waited another year.

The marriage was conducted by the Reverend Mr. Jackson in the new church on September 3, 1838. Old Deacon John Kent, almost deaf and blind, said it was the happiest day of his long life (he lived to the age of ninety-nine, in 1849). But for everyone else it was a day of sorrow and tears, because all sensed that Henrietta would never return to her beloved village. Jackson rode part of the way with the couple as they departed, and Henrietta "nearly died of a broken heart" when she left her father and saw Green Peak (not yet named Mt. Aeolus) for the last time.

Many letters were exchanged between Constantinople and Dorset. That December Henrietta Jackson Hamlin gave birth to her first child, a daughter; three more soon followed. But in July 1850, just before delivering her fifth daughter, Henrietta was seized with "a violent influenza." She never recovered, and died in November, aged thirty-nine. Burial took place on the Isle of Rhodes.

Hamlin, a first cousin of Hannibal Hamlin, vice-president in Lincoln's first term, went on to an illustrious career. In 1860 he founded Robert College in Constantinople, and in 1877 became a professor at Bangor Theological Seminary. In 1881 he was named president of Middlebury College, which would have made his father-in-law proud, for Jackson had been the first elected member of the Middlebury College corporation. At his Middlebury installation Hamlin was introduced by Principal Wickham. Hamlin was also a close friend of Dorset clergymen Parsons S. Pratt and George L. Prentiss, a Bowdoin College classmate. Hamlin belonged to the Portland (Maine) Second Parish Church when the Reverend Edward Payson, father of Dorset's first "summer resident," Elizabeth Payson Prentiss, was its minister. Hamlin retained close associations with Dorset and returned in 1884 to celebrate the church centennial and to reminisce about Henrietta and the Jacksons.

Meanwhile the stately elm flourished in the meadow just south of Dorset village. Even after it died it remained standing for many years. On July 7, 1966, the following haunting article appeared in the *Bennington Banner*, written by its Dorset correspondent, Marchen T. Skinner:

Lightning Storm Fulfills
Strange Request at Dorset
The towering 70-foot dead tree "Henrietta's Elm," one of Dorset's most beloved landmarks, burned Wednesday night in its meadow on Vermont 30.

Struck by lightning during an early evening storm, it became a fiery pyre. Almost eerily the bolt of lightning at last fulfilled the wishes of the tree's namesake, Henrietta Anna Louise Jackson, who asked in her will in 1850 "that my tree never be cut by the hand of man."

. . . On Wednesday night, word of the burning tree spread without aid of sirens or fire engines. All evening villagers gathered sadly at the south end of the village or wandered to the wet pasture to watch and wait for the stark old landmark to go. Some estimated its age at 200 years.

This magnificent photograph of Henrietta's Elm in its prime was taken by Harriet Gilbert on August 21, 1910. The view looks west from West View Farm, now Village Auberge, on Route 30.

Spectators watched the fire creep from remaining jagged stumps of branches that had refused to yield through the years to winter winds but had served as roosts for migrating birds. As they burned they fell like flaming pinwheels to the ground.

Slowly the fire slipped down the trunk to the old bee hole the height of which had precluded all desires for honey. Then helped by a slight breeze, the fire continued until the whole length of the mighty tree was ablaze—a torch in the night.

Burning slowly but brightly until around midnight, the tree finally fell helpless to the ground—and then suddenly changed, and not by the hand of man, from reality to memory.

But the tree will always flourish when the sun lights up a stained glass window on the west side of the Dorset church where its crown and stout trunk have been immortalized.

The Militia, and Resistance

In 1807, legislation created the "Columbian Band of Music of Rupert and Dorset." It became an official military band, though not all was peaceful in its first decade because some members signed a petition, dated at Rupert October 4, 1817, asking for voting equality among the membership. They asked that at least one vote be granted for field officers of the 2nd regiment, 1st brigade, 2nd division, Vermont Militia. The petition contained the noble thought that "in free governments all ought to be entitled to equal privileges and that those who govern ought to derive their power from the governed." But the legislature's military committee rejected the plea.

In 1813 William S. Martindale of Dorset was captain of the same regiment. He and six others that year petitioned the legislature for authority to increase the company, by enlistment, to sixty-four privates and one second lieutenant. The petition received a favorable committee report but legislation did not follow.

Strong antimilitary sentiment came to light in the century's third decade. On September 25, 1826, Austin Johnson and nine others declared themselves to feel "in common with our fellow citizens the Friends or Quakers" and asked the legislature for exemption from military duty as well as taxation that supported the military. The petition was signed by 24 other Dorset and Rupert residents of like mind. They pleaded:

We the undersigned inhabitants of the towns of Dorset and Rupert and the adjoining towns beg leave respectfully to represent that while in common with our fellow citizens the Friends or Quakers we believe that the principals [sic] of Christianity forbid our bearing arms, yet unlike them we are exposed to penalties on account of our religious sentiment.

But your Honorable body will be sensible that to men believing as we do this affords no real relief—the money we thus pay goes to support the system of war . . .

We cannot doubt but that your candor will lead you to feel that every principal of justice and equity require that we and others in like circumstances as ourselves should be placed on the same footing as the Friends whose conscientious scruples are founded on the same divine authority—and probably no stronger than ours.

But the petition was rejected by the legislature. Signers besides Austin Johnson were John Underhill, Asa Baldwin, Buckley F. Bartlett, William S. Southworth, Noah Fuller, Jr., Orson Fuller, G. B. Southworth, Joel Bartlett, and Robert Wilson.

A similar petition on September 14, 1827, met the same fate. Joshua Judson and about ten others from Dorset sought exemption from military service. They wrote: "We the undersigned citizens of this state, being thoroughly convinced of the incompatibility of war with the precepts of the Gospel, feel, that we are bound by the sacred ties of Philanthropy and Religion, to dissent from the popular opinion in relation to, and to withhold our support from, the present mode of adjusting national disputes."

Other signers whose names are legible were Alphons Morse, Noah Fuller, Joel Bartlett, Buckley Bartlett, Phineas F. Smith, and Moses Kent.

The Boorn-Colvin Case

Much has been written about the Boorn "murder mystery" of 1819. Jesse Boorn of Manchester and his brother Stephen, of Dorset, were accused, arrested, indicted, tried, convicted, and sentenced to die by hanging for the murder of their brother-in-law, Russell Colvin. There was no body, but there were parts of a body, and circumstantial evidence seemed ironclad. Stephen Boorn had signed a confession, the case had gone to the Vermont Supreme Court, and the brothers were languishing in a "loathsome dungeon" ready to die when to everyone's surprise the victim, Russell Colvin, showed up in town alive and well.

In October 1820 a plaintive petition by Stephen Boorn for remuneration was cold-heartedly rejected by the legislature—*after* the reappearance of Colvin clearly proved that the Boorns, despite the state's best judicial proceedings, were innocent. Several popular versions of this tale have been published,[15] but the following petition has not previously seen print:

The petition of Stephen Boorn of Dorset in the County of Bennington humbly sheweth unto your Honorable Body that on or about the 7th day of May 1819 your petitioner was arrested at Denmark in the County of Lewis in the State of New York, and brought in Irons from thence to Manchester in this State, a distance of about two hundred miles, leaving his family consisting of a wife and three children in destitute circumstances, that immediately on your petitioner's arrival in Manchester he was delivered into the hands of the civil authority upon a charge of having been guilty of the horrid crime of murder *and such proceedings were held that your petitioner was committed to a loathsome dungeon until some time early in the month of November 1819 when together with Jesse Boorn were jointly tried, convicted and sentenced to execution for the supposed murder of one Russell Colvin before the Hon. Supreme Court of this State and that your petitioner pursuant to his sentence was recommitted and Ironed as aforesaid where he remained untill the January term of the Supreme Court holden at Bennington for said County when your petitioner was liberated in manner that has been already made known to the world; and your petitioner further saith that by reason of his longstanding confinement his health hath become impaired and his own vigorous constitution has become broken to the degree that since his liberation he has been unable to perform any hand or fatiguing labor on which himself and family wholly depended for their daily bread; and altho your petitioner is not disposed to cast any censure upon those persons by whose means the said prosecution against him was brought about but*

Fred Whittemore and Arthur Gilbert consult in October 1977 as the Dorset Historical Society opened its museum in the former firehouse.

would in charity hope that no one was activated by any other than motives to public good yet the sufferings of your petitioner have been sore and grievous.

Stephen Boorn's plea for relief from "pecuniary embarrassment" was endorsed by citizens Eli Pettibone, Joseph Bishop, David Briggs, Oramell Chamberlin, Elisha Petty, Daniel Curtis, Orra Gifford, Ham Gifford, and Joseph Curtis, but to no avail. Evidently the state's judicial embarrassment was the stronger force. Boorn's petition was dismissed. Another plea by brother John Boorn was given the same disposition.

That the legislature in this era was tight with the state's dollar was also indicated by a petition by Almond Curtis of Dorset in 1827. Curtis sought remuneration for expenses incurred in apprehending a felon, Nathan Shipley, who had absconded with some articles he stole from Curtis. The petition claimed that Curtis pursued Shipley, apprehended him in Saratoga, New York, brought him back to Manchester where he was tried, convicted, and sentenced to prison. Curtis itemized expenses of $17.75 including 75 cents for "vitualing said felon untill commitment."

Not only were the expenses certified by Jabez Hawley but the petition was endorsed by a note from former Dorset legislator Johnson Marsh to incumbent Representative John Cochran saying, "I wish you to do the best you can with the above petition." But Curtis's plea was rejected.

NOTES

1. Lewis D. Stilwell, *Migration from Vermont, 1776-1860* (Brattleboro, Vt.: E. L. Hildreth & Co.), p. 95.
2. Ira Allen, *History of the State of Vermont* (Rutland, Vt.: Tuttle Company, 1969 [reprint of original 1798 edition], p. 166.
3. Stilwell, *Migration from Vermont*; p. 124.
4. The faded and difficult-to-read account book of Allen C. Roberts, in the possession of Raymond G. Fisher of Rupert, was studied and "translated" in 1987 by John A. Kouwenhoven of Dorset, and a copy provided to the writer.
5. Also quoted by Kouwenhoven in his paper on the Roberts account book.
6. From Arthur W. Gilbert, paper on early industries presented to the Dorset Historical Society November 18, 1974.
7. From Mary Williams Rowland, "The Story of the H.N. Williams Store" presented to the Dorset Historical Society August 11, 1983.
8. Alfred H. Gilbert, "The Fenton Potteries," *Vermont History* (October, 1966), p. 268. This research was also presented by Gilbert in a paper to the Dorset Historical Society on May 21, 1965. Gilbert's research, in turn, referred to two earlier studies: John Spargo, *Early American Pottery and China* (New York, 1948) and Lura Watkins, *Early New England Potters and their Wares* (New York: Archon Books, 1950).
9. Peter W. Cook, "The Potteries," in *The Shires of Bennington*, Tyler Resch, ed. (Bennington, Vt.: *Bennington Banner* for the Bennington Museum, 1975), p 94.
10. C. Benton and S.F. Barry, *A Statistical View of the Number of Sheep* . . . (Boston, Folsom, Wells, and Thurston, 1837). This tiny book was dedicated to Henry Clay, "the early and steadfast friend of the manufacturing and agricultural interests of this country," and contains detailed statistics for numbers of sheep in 1836 throughout eastern states and counties, with a discussion of the introduction of merino and saxony sheep.
11. Donald G. Johnson, paper on the East Dorset Congregational Church presented to the Dorset Historical Society April 7, 1976.
12. Joseph D. Wickham, "Discourse Delivered at Dorset, Vt., at the Funeral of the Rev. William Jackson, D.D., on Tuesday, Oct. 18, 1842" (Andover, Mass.: Allen, Morrill and Wardwell, 1843). Bassett 4057.
13. The original Jackson letters are preserved at the Wilbur Collection of Vermontiana, University of Vermont.
14. Movements such as anti-slavery, religious revivals, temperance, anti-Masonry, and utopianism that marked much of the early nineteenth century are described in David Ludlum *Social Ferment in Vermont: 1791-1850* (Montpelier, Vt.: Vermont Historical Society, 1939 [rpt. 1966]).
15. The two best-known accounts of the Boorn-Colvin case are John Spargo *The Return of Russell Colvin* (Bennington, Vt.: the Bennington Museum, 1945) and Richard Sanders Allen, "The Boorn Mystery" in *Mischief in the Mountains*, Walter Hard, Jr., and Janet C. Greene, eds., (Montpelier, Vt.: *Vermont Life Magazine*, 1970), p. 103.

8

The Age of Marble

The business of quarrying, hauling, and finishing marble flourished, faltered, rebounded, and struggled for 130 years, dominating the life, livelihood, and reputation of the town of Dorset. At the industry's transitory peak in the 1880s nearly two hundred residents—in addition to almost two hundred other laborers from nearby towns—worked in the Dorset quarries and mills, or about the same number who made a living from farming. Though far from a steady industry, marble contributed vitally to the town's economy until the exigencies of World War I and other economic factors elevated this regal building material to luxury status. From the beginnings of Dorset's marble business in 1785 until its demise before 1920 a grand total of 15,805,000 cubic feet of nature's beautiful pressure-treated calcium carbonate was extracted from the town's approximately twenty-five quarries.

By attracting dozens of Irish families to town, starting as early as the 1830s, marble was responsible for contributing to the only real ethnic diversity Dorset has known. It also prompted the construction of one of Vermont's colorful short-line railroads, the Manchester, Dorset & Granville (known familiarly as the Mud, Dirt & Gravel).

For a few years in the twentieth century, a historic marker on Route 7 near the foot of Morse Hill Road proclaimed, "Westerly near Mt. Aeolus, Isaac Underhill opened the first marble quarry in 1785." A traveler looking westward would see the rising mass of Mt. Aeolus that conveyed the general direction; it was probably the first commercial marble quarry on the North American continent. The slopes and vegetation of Mt. Aeolus now mostly conceal

A state historical marker on Route 7, no longer standing, recognized that the oldest marble quarry in the nation was located on Mt. Aeolus.

the remains of two dozen abandoned marble quarries, plus an uncountable number of "working holes" where attempts were made to determine whether profitable quantities and qualities of marble could be extracted.

No marker now designates the actual location of the nation's oldest marble quarry, yet it remains within clear view of the traveling public along Route 30. This site blossoms with life each summer as a popular swimming hole. There is irony in the fact that Dorset's first primitive quarry is also the location of its last commercially successful one, known when it was abandoned in 1917 as the Norcross-West, source of the building material of the New York Public Library at Fifth Avenue and 42nd Street.

For swimmers, the water that filled the Norcross-West quarry remains clean, green, and refreshing, and the now-weathered white blocks of abandoned marble on its banks offer inviting crevices and platforms for sunbathers. Near the north end of this quarry a short trail leads to the Plateau quarry, used by swimmers seeking more seclusion. From the Plateau came cornices and columns for the Harvard Medical School building, and monoliths for the Daughters of the American Revolution building in Washington and the Montreal Art Association building.

Marble from the Norcross-West also went into the John Hay Memorial

Library at Brown University in Providence, Rhode Island; and the Temple Israel in Boston.[1] More prominently, Dorset Mountain marble from the Danby quarry was used to build the U. S. Supreme Court building in Washington and the Arlington National Cemetery Memorial. In the Beineke Rare Book Library at Yale University, architectural advantage was taken of light-transmitting qualities of thinly sliced Danby Imperial.
Courtesy of Ernest G. Edgerton

A turn of-the-century view of the Elam Miller house in South Dorset, when it was a boarding house for quarry workers. Note the tracks of a rail spur that led to the Plateau quarry. The house was built by Deacon John Manley about 1773 as the first made of the native material.

In the 1920s a network of mountainous trails was thoughtfully cleared by members of the Dorset Science Club to connect many of the quarries. The abandoned marble pits offer fascinating destinations for curious hikers, but few seem to take advantage of this asset and today the trails are mostly overgrown.[2]

Dorset's marble forms one layer of a massive, undulating Taconic cake. The mammoth slab of limestone and marble underlies most of Dorset Mountain including its southern adjuncts known as Aeolus, Owl's Head, Crane Hill, and Netop. This layer has been quarried both on the floor of the valley near the 800-foot level and, in the case of the Freedley quarry, at elevations as high as 2,040 feet above sea level.

Although marble is no longer shipped from Dorset, commercial quarrying continues inside the same stratum through an aperture on the northeast side of Dorset Mountain in Danby. Millions of cubic feet of stone have been extracted by the Vermont Marble Company—headquartered in Proctor but now owned by a Swiss firm—from the interior of this mountain, much of which is supported by stout pillars left by the quarriers.

In 1785 Isaac Underhill of South Dorset, a member of one of the pioneer

Terry Tyler collection

Loading a multi-ton block of marble, by crane and chain, onto a flatcar at the Plateau quarry in South Dorset in 1905. Note size of the chain links.

families, began to split out hearthstones, fire jambs, hearths, lintels, and chimney backs from a marble ledge on lands of Reuben Bloomer, part of the quarry on Route 30 later known as the Norcross-West. Underhill was joined by Bloomer, and John Manley echoed their work on the other side of the road. Bloomer had help from his family of thirteen children. A thriving trade developed, and people came to buy these fireplace stones from as far away as Troy, New York.

Part of the John Manley (Elam Miller) house, as noted in chapter 4, was made of marble around the first decade of settlement, and any of the various years ascribed to it, 1773, 1779, or 1780, predate the commercial beginnings of the Underhill-Bloomer marble business. Another alleged pre-1785 use of Dorset marble was a slab set in a Bennington cemetery in 1768, the very year of Dorset's settlement, to mark the grave of one John Pratt.

Others besides Bloomer and Underhill saw opportunity and dug at primitive quarries elsewhere on Mt. Aeolus, seeking beds where marble could be

Horses hauled blocks of marble on wooden tracks in this view, circa 1873, of the Vermont Italian Marble quarry 1,200 feet above East Dorset. This quarry was also known as that of the Hollister, Tyrel & Co., and the Holley, Field & Kent.

split away easily. For many years the slabs were worked laboriously with mallets, wedges, and chisels. In 1790 Jonas Stewart, a manufacturer of slate and granite headstones in Claremont, New Hampshire, applied his craft in Dorset and taught others to carve designs on marble. One of the most artistic gravestone carvers was Zerubabel Collins, whose elaborate designs, including faces, flowers, verses, and scrollwork, are still widely admired on eighteenth-century headstones in cemeteries in Dorset, Shaftsbury, Bennington, and elsewhere.

A business developed for traveling salesmen whose horse-drawn wagonloads of Dorset-extracted headstones would go from door to door over long distances to peddle these memorials. One can imagine with amusement the nature of the sales pitch the salesman-carver might use to entice a buyer. After a sale was clinched, down to the selection of designs and inscriptions, the carver would proceed to prepare everything but the date of death. Ed McDevitt pursued this trade well into the twentieth century.

Marble entrepreneur Ernest H. West wrote with confidence in 1921: "A trip to nearby cemeteries shows how surprisingly well this surface marble has withstood the wear of the elements during a century and a quarter of exposure." Alas, his observation is no longer valid because the ravages of acid rain have caused irreparable deterioration to inscriptions on many marble headstones. Unlike granite, which is igneous and siliceous, marble, a meta-

The Norcross-West Company's marble mill at the southern terminus of the Manchester, Dorset & Granville Railroad in 1905. Note the 30-ton traveling crane. The site is now that of the CVPS Richville Road station in Manchester Depot.

morphic and calciferous rock, is subject to gradual decay by acids. With measurable increases in rainfall acidity due to fossil fuel exhaust in the atmosphere, marble monuments are slowly melting, almost like ice in the sunshine.

In 1818 the first attempt was made to saw blocks of marble instead of drilling into the strata and breaking off slabs. That year Josiah Booth and Spafford Field started a marble finishing mill near what later became the T. D. Manley quarry. In 1827 Dan Kent and Barnum Thompson built other mills, and later Edmund Manley opened one, but they all awaited the development of more efficient methods for quarrying and finishing the stone.

The first derrick was erected in a Dorset quarry in 1848 by S.D. Manley, according to an 1861 account by Frederick Field, who counted ten other derricks then in use. Field summarized the state of the industry, noting that a total of sixty-two gangs of saws were in operation, annually cutting about 750,000 feet of two-inch-thick marble. Total annual sales of Dorset marble in 1861 were estimated at $200,000.

Explosives were rarely employed in Dorset quarries because they tended to do more damage than good. An exception to that rule was the "Deaf Joe" quarry, named for Joseph French, who opened a pit in 1817 and worked it alone for many years. [This quarry, on the south side of Mt. Aeolus, is now owned by Orla Reed.] He was so deaf he could not trust his ears to tell him when a blast had gone off, so he watched carefully. Once a piece of flying marble took off a tiny bit of one ear, and according to legend, in telling the boys about it that evening he said, "I look out behin' tree to see her pop and by Gosh, she miss me jus' on time."[3]

It is a source of wonder that in a town best known for its marble Dorset has so very few marble residences, though there are several marble foundations, cellar floors, and sidewalks. The late architectural historian and photographer Herbert Wheaton Congdon of Arlington expressed this sense of curiosity succinctly when he commented that Vermont is the center of the marble and granite industries of the United States, yet it has very few stone houses. "Shoemakers' children go barefoot," he said.[4]

One modest early marble house was originally a one-story toll gate in North Dorset on the old Dorset Turnpike, later Route 7, made of marble from the Danby quarry, and probably built in the first decade of the nineteenth century. (This house was restored in 1948 when a second story was added; it is now owned by Mr. and Mrs. Sylvester Ford.)

The most conspicuous marble residence is the grand estate on the West Road known for years as "the old stone house," and since 1908 as the Lefevre estate. The builder of the original portion of this house is not known, though it was probably a Manley. The blocks of rough-cut marble that compose the original 30-by-40-foot Federal-style house were probably taken from an outcropping of marble about 200 feet behind the house. (That outcropping later became a quarry, opened by Martin and George Manley in 1840 and purchased by Nelson J. Sanford in 1852; it was usually known as the Sanford quarry.) The blocks were placed with precision by a master stonemason to create a house that resembles no other in material, craftsmanship, or design—in Dorset or elsewhere in Vermont.

Despite exhaustive research on this house, the date of its construction is not known for certain, as is the case with the Manley-Miller marble house. Edwin Lefevre, Jr., who owned the house for many years, said that to the best of his knowledge it was built in 1812. The late Anna Gilbert, no stranger to Dorset history, said it was built in 1824. Zephine Humphrey said it was built by George Manley but proffered no date. An 1813 deed from father to son, George (1752–1835) to Martin (1783–1856) Manley, mentions two houses, one of which might have been the one in question. A will dated 1822 from George to Martin also mentions a dwelling. Research in 1986 by a descendant, Judson Manly of Dalton, Georgia, concluded that the house was already on the West Road in 1816.

The name of William Corey is listed in the 1880 *Child's Bennington County Directory* as a marble polisher and farmer. He came to Dorset from Ireland in 1868, but could not have been too impoverished an immigrant, for he bought the Manleys' West Road marble house from the partnership of Hawley, Kent & Root, the owner of the Sanford quarry, in 1879. Corey died of an illness he contracted while slating the roof in 1904, and was buried in St. Jerome's Cemetery in East Dorset. His widow, unable to maintain the house, sold it in 1907 to Ernest H. West, who sold it to Edwin Lefevre, Sr., the following year. Chapter 11 provides more details about Lefevre's transformation of this once-modest marble house into a palatial country estate.

Until 1837 the quarrying of Dorset marble was limited mostly to hearthstones and headstones. In that year a contract was signed with the firm of Underhill & Strong to provide marble for a new U. S. Customs House in Erie, Pennsylvania. The stone came from Underhill's main quarry and from "the gulch" between it and the Plateau. With the discovery that it could be used successfully as a building material, the Erie Customs House became a major commercial turning point for Dorset marble.

This item in the *Erie Observer* on August 5, 1837, related the news:

Local improvements:- The United States Bank is about commencing a banking house; which we are informed will be of white marble and built at a cost of not less than $20,000 and will be one of the richest specimens of architecture in the western country. It will be located in State, one of the most delightful streets in our Borough, and will be a splendid ornament to our place. The contract for furnishing the marble is taken by Messrs. Underhill & Strong, who are already beautifying our country with the rarest and richest specimens of marble from the Vermont Quarry.

Courtesy of the Bennington Museum

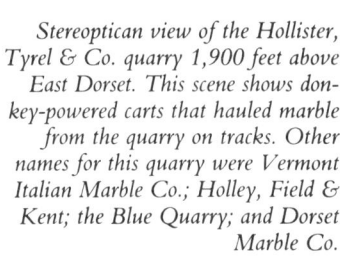

Stereoptican view of the Hollister, Tyrel & Co. quarry 1,900 feet above East Dorset. This scene shows donkey-powered carts that hauled marble from the quarry on tracks. Other names for this quarry were Vermont Italian Marble Co.; Holley, Field & Kent; the Blue Quarry; and Dorset Marble Co.

Both quarrying and transportation remained laborious. Hand channeling was not yet practised, and hauling was still by teams of horses or oxen from Dorset to the Champlain and Hudson Canal landings. The three trips Allen C. Roberts made in 1838 for Seneca Smith & Co. carrying loads of marble "from Dorset corner to canal" were undoubtedly for the Erie customs house job.

Ernest West became acquainted with one of the drovers who had accompanied the four-horse teams on the trips to Comstock Landing. West wrote: "In 1910 I learned that Brazil Ladd was the only surviving teamster of those early days. So I lost no time in getting an interview with him." Ladd, born in 1837, was then seventy-three, and lived to be eighty-five. West's interview with him forms a rare personal glimpse of early Americana that dates probably to the late 1840s:

When I was a small boy I used to hang around the quarry and watch the men shape up stones with the hammer and chisel, and once in a while I'd get a chance to ride to Comstock Landing on one of the rigs drawing marble to ship on the canal. A fellow named Waite used to take me along. He drove a four-horse team and could handle the reins as well as anyone I ever see. The first day we'd get as far as Wing's Hotel in Granville, but had to leave Dorset at daylight to make the trip.

At night the boys would have a big time. New England rum was only 35 cents a gallon and it was a sight to see Waite pour out a tumbler full and drink it down in four swallows. First some molasses was put in the tumbler and then the rum was run in from the keg. Waite was always up at five in the morning as chipper as could be and never any worse for getting pickled the night before. The rum in those days wouldn't hurt no one and I never knew Waite to have a cold or any other ailment.

The next morning we would curry off the horses and rub their coats until they would shine like a bottle, and by seven o'clock we would be under way again.

Waite would holler at the horses so people heard him for half a mile, but he did it just to show off. I never knew him to hit a horse with a whip. By night time we would get to Comstock and see that the marble was unloaded onto a canal boat.

Waite would put up for the night at the hotel. He had a lot of friends there and they would play cards and drink "blackstrap" half the night.

One morning I couldn't wake Waite up so I went out to the barn and fed the horses. That was the time I got the idea in my head that I'd hitch the teams up all alone. I stood up on a box and managed to lift the harnesses onto the horses. It was about all I could manage, but I was sure a proud boy when Waite came out at seven o'clock and found his teams all ready. He was mighty tickled and he let me try driving a part of the way home.

That was the time I had the ambition to have a team of my own some day, and it

Bill Tobin's six-horse team hauls a twelve-ton block of marble.

wasn't many years before I did own one. I never did care for oxen. I'll admit they worked out pretty well on the Comstock haul, but give me a horse every time . . .

I want to tell you one thing and that is them old days were the best Dorset ever saw or ever will see. Everybody was working and you should have seen the village green every fine summer evening. There would be about thirty or forty of the boys out and the big sport would be the standing broad jump with weights. They used to rastle a lot, "catch as catch can." I was quicker than a cat when I got my growth and I often flopped the best of 'em.

There were six blacksmith shops in the township and three grist mills. Dorset made right around 200,000 pounds of cheese every year and three saw mills turned out a million feet of lumber. They made our boots and harnesses right here in town and a lot better than any you can buy now. That was the golden day for Dorset, I tell you.

Comstock was not Dorset's only shipment point, for the Allen C. Roberts account books never mention Comstock, or Comstock Landing. Roberts specified Fort Ann and also Fort Miller several times in the early 1830s. Roberts's description of his itinerary in 1832 from Dorset to the canal via Tinmouth and Poultney is interesting compared with Ladd's late 1840s route through Granville. These records, plus papers of Spafford Holley found in Peltier's store, suggest that the landing at Comstock might have been estab-

The Age of Marble 137

This marble-finishing mill of the Tyrel & Kent Company in East Dorset produced thousands of headstones throughout the 1890s.

lished in the late 1830s to handle large shipments that were not so easily accommodated at Fort Ann.

In 1852 the Bennington-Rutland Railroad was completed through East Dorset to Manchester, greatly simplifying the task of transporting marble to major markets and making obsolete the tedious haul by horse- or ox-drawn wagon to the Hudson River or to the canal landings.

Between 1840 and 1855, seven marble-finishing mills were built in Dorset, seven in Danby, and four in Manchester, all working on Dorset-extracted marble. The number of gangs totaled ninety, sawing a million feet a year of two-inch slabs, and employing more than 385 sawyers, stone cutters, and quarrymen. One of the major mills was that of Dan Kent in East Dorset village, which employed forty men. By 1855, eight quarries were being worked vigorously, finding ready sale for their output. A list of Dorset quarries that year was as follows:

	Number Employed
Wilson, McDonald & Freedley	12
McDonald & Freedley	20
Holley, Field & Kent's Vermont Italian	35

A wood engraving depicts hand channeling of marble before the steam channeler was invented in 1863. The illustration is from Ernest H. West's study of the Dorset quarries. Note the sun shields at right, which protected the men's eyes from brilliant sunlight on white marble.

Gray, Wilson & Sanford	15
M. & G. B. Holley	20
Fulsom & Barnard	6
Bloomer	20
Holley, Field & Kent's Extra White	15

The Freedley quarry, located high up on the east side of Mt. Aeolus between East Dorset and North Dorset, was first opened in 1808 by Elijah Sykes, and another section of it was started by Abraham Underhill and John Chapman in 1810—the two openings then merged both physically and corporately. But when the Freedley quarry was expanded in 1841 hand channeling was employed, and this method of cutting was soon adopted by other quarries. Ernest West said of this practice: "The workmen of this day must have been sturdy and industrious, for we find from old quarry records that they channeled between five and ten feet square per day at an average cost of 28 cents per channel foot. It must have been a stirring sight to see all these quarrymen striking their long drills into the channel cut."

West said it was the custom to throw cotton sheets over wooden racks in summer to shade the cuts, enabling the drillers to see what they were doing and to protect their eyes from the glare of sunlight on white marble.

For many reasons the Freedley quarry was Dorset's most fascinating. Not only was it the highest in elevation, it was also the only quarry that tunneled into the mountainside instead of remaining an open pit. The Freedley produced the greatest quantity of any Dorset marble, a total of 4,250,000 cubic feet, most of which was lowered to what is now Route 7 by means of a mile-long funicular railroad.

Courtesy of Howard Bowen

The Freedleyville mill in East Dorset, at the foot of the funicular railway, was where marble was cut to size and finished. This photo was taken several years before the mill burned in October 1923.

The Freedley operations were also closely associated with Irish immigrants, whose very lives came to revolve around the quarry, with workers' houses, school, church, and cemetery. The first Catholic mass was celebrated in 1838, on East Dorset Hill, though no Catholic church would be built until St. Jerome's opened in 1874. More Irish settlers came to work on the construction of the Rutland Railroad and when that was completed many remained and took up quarrying and farming.

Curiously, the quality of the Freedley output was not outstanding. Some Freedley marble was used in the Soldiers' and Sailors' Monument, the old Drexel Building at Wall and Broad streets, and the Plaza Hotel, all in New York City, and the multi-columned State Education Building in Albany, but no entire buildings or monuments were made from it.

In 1859 the tunnel began to be cut into the steep face of the Freedley, high up on Mt. Aeolus, where horizontal strata that dip somewhat into the moun-

tain presented opportunities to support overhanging material. Eventually the tunnel, supported by pillars, would extend for several hundred feet, north-south, and 160 feet wide. At its north end the tunnel leads into an open quarry 110 feet deep, though the full depth of the marble stratum was estimated by Ernest West to be 165 feet.

Still visible from Route 7 near North Dorset are the rock outcroppings that mark the Freedley quarry and the raised right-of-way of its abandoned rail line. Marble foundation stones and side walls of the Freedley finishing mill are seen near the U.S. 7 highway bridge over the Vermont Railroad tracks. The Freedley closed all operations by about 1920.

Completion of the railroads released cheap labor to work the quarries. The first marble quarry in West Rutland had been organized by W.F. Barnes in 1849. Ten years later a strike of quarriers at West Rutland was the first large-scale work stoppage in Vermont. The workers were paid 65 cents a day in winter and 90 cents in summer, and struck for rates of 10 cents more.

The patenting of the Wardwell Steam Channeler in 1863 revolutionized marble quarrying. These clumsy mechanical channelers could cut more square feet of marble in a day than a dozen men; and thereby many were put out of work. The devices aroused such antagonism, in fact, that they could not be operated at night because cursing workers, under cover of darkness, would bombard them with stones.

"Bad luck to ye, ye old steam engine, cheating an honest man out of a day's work. But be-jabbers ye can't vote," swore one of the hand drillers after heaving a rock at the monster.

The steam channeler was followed by the Black diamond channeler, even more efficient for cutting blocks of marble.

One Dorset quarry that is, strangely, unmentioned in Ernest West's accounts, except for a reference in a picture caption, is the Gettysburg, high above Dorset village. The Gettysburg takes its name from the fact that as many as twenty-thousand headstones were extracted from it for the graves of soldiers at Gettysburg and other Civil War cemeteries. Wrote George Holley Gilbert of the Gettysburg quarry region, "As late as the sixties of last century there was a little settlement near this quarry, with substantial houses, well kept gardens and numerous children."[5] In April 1989 an Associated Press news item quoted the maintenance director of the Gettysburg National Mili-

Like a Vermont Stonehenge, part of one of the Freedleyville mills, made of marble, still stands just off Route 7. This photo was taken in the 1960s.
Photo by Tyler Resch

A reflective view from inside the Freedley quarry in the 1960s. In winter, this sheltered quarry becomes an occasional destination for skaters because the water freezes into smooth black ice that needs no shoveling.

tary Park as saying that its marble headstones were being seriously eroded by acid rain.

Paralleling the national economy in the latter half of the nineteenth century, the Dorset marble business slumped in the early 1870s, and by 1875 several quarries and mills were forced to close, including the T. D. Manley, Bloomer, Sanford, and Edmund Manley quarries; in Danby the Imperial and Symington quarries were also closed. But the industry quickly rebounded and during the 1880s more than three hundred men were employed and the number of gangs "swinging" at Dorset marble totaled forty-eight.

Using the diamond channelers, other quarries became large producers, and the volume of business during the 1880s was greater than ever. D. L. Kent & Co. employed fifty men and had annual sales of $75,000; the East Dorset Italian Marble works of Hollister, Tyrel & Co. employed 125 men, with annual sales of $150,000. J. K. Freedley Sons shipped between three and five thousand tons a year, and Kent & Root Marble Co. employed about 100 men, while S.F. Prince & Co. employed 45.

Marble quarrying had a severe impact on the environment, and in 1882 First Selectman William D. Ames of East Dorset did something about it. He

The Age of Marble 143

Terry Tyler collection

Quarriers in 1905 stand on a 43-ton block of white marble from the Plateau quarry, on the west side of Mt. Aeolus. The block became one of thirteen columns of the D.A.R. Constitution Hall in Washington, D.C. At left are Ira Glover, Jack (Wee Willie) McDevitt, and Tom Burns. On the block, from left: Bill Morrow, Joe Hanlon, Art Bolster, Mike Kelly, Will Johnson, George McBride, Plynn Stannard, Bernie Connell (black hat), Charles McWayne, Ed Towsley, Punk McCormick, Seymour Wilkins (wide hat), Fred Reed, Joe Wade, John Stewart, Larry Malloy, Ed Bowen, Charles McBride, John Nichols, Fred Stannard, Ed Conlon, Jo Italian. At right are A.W. Phelon, Dighton Lee, and Billy Rubadeau.

filed suit in Chancery Court against Dorset Marble and D. L. Kent companies for blocking and diverting the headwaters of the Battenkill River with large quantities of sand and leftover marble slabs. The blockage interfered with Ames's seventy-six acres of "rich, fertile productive farmland," he complained. In 1890 the court ordered the companies to remove their walls, stones, sand, pipes, and other debris, and restrained them from obstructing the river in the future.

In 1891 D.L. Kent & Co. published an elaborate catalogue. The company specialized in "East Dorset Italian, Florentine, New East Dorset Variegated, South Dorset White, and Foreign Italian" marbles. The catalogue cited an office and mills located in East Dorset and a branch yard at 2214 Chestnut Street, Philadelphia. Prices were listed for a great variety of cemetery posts, turned crosses, coping, urns, tiles, headstones, and monuments of scores of different designs. The list contained no illustrations but noted that photographs could be obtained at $2 per dozen. The preface to D. L. Kent's catalogue conveys a kind of Victorian sense of what made this company tick:

We hand you our Price List for 1891, and congratulate our many patrons on the successful opening and encouraging prospects of trade this season.

We have added to our List many new and attractive designs and left out some of the old styles, which seem to have become unsuitable to the present requirements of the trade . . .

We take pleasure in calling your attention to our new variety of Marble—the New East Dorset Variegated—possessing both the dark and medium cloud—very handsome and susceptible of high polish.

Our Extra Dark Florentine fully sustains its high popularity, while its demand seems to be constantly increasing. The East Dorset Italian is too well known to need more than this passing notice.

Soliciting a continuance of your patronage and wishing you a prosperous year, we remain,

Respectfully yours,
D. L. Kent & Co.

January 1st, 1891

But this company's prosperity was short-lived. After the Panic of 1893 the marble business entered a severe decline and by 1897 almost all of Dorset's quarries and mills were closed again. Part of the reason was that better qualities of marble were being exhausted in Dorset, and business gravitated toward Rutland and Proctor, where superior stone of more varied colors was being extracted. Another geographic-geologic difference was that until about

Terry Tyler collection

Spafford H. West (1846-1906), a founder of the Norcross-West Company. He is holding a marble test core.

The Age of Marble 145

1870 quarrymen had to work vertically from the surface, a handicap at first in Rutland County, where the beds incline steeply. But with the perfection of the Ball Diamond channeler and gadder it became possible to follow sloping beds, vastly increasing production in the Rutland region. Too, superior quality of interior and monumental marbles enabled Rutland, West Rutland, and Proctor to dominate the market at the same time Dorset was declining.

At the start of the twentieth century, when the Dorset marble industry was still depressed, Orlando W. Norcross of Worcester, Massachusetts, an ingenious building contractor and notorious eccentric, located a source of marble for the proposed New York Public Library and thus came into partnership with Dorset entrepreneur Spafford H. West. Forming the Norcross-West Marble Company, they reopened the old Underhill-Manley quarry, which had closed in 1876 and had languished long before. The decision to build the new library of marble put Dorset back on the map, because an impressive half million cubic feet would be required.

Spafford West was someone "who knew marble as well as any man who ever lifted it out of a mountain," his son Ernest recalled. He sported a keen Vermont sense of humor and was a superb story teller, popular among his associates and employees. He was heavily involved in the Dorset marble business, owning part of the Kent and Root Marble Company in addition to Norcross-West. But in 1907, at the age of sixty, Spafford West died unexpectedly while engaged in supplying the New York Public Library, and Ernest took over.

Courtesy of the Bennington Museum

Ernest H. West (1875-1950), quarrier and orchardist, succeeded his father at the Norcross-West Company. His grandchildren are still Dorset residents.

Norcross was a different kind of character—profane, absentminded, energetic. He was president of twenty different corporations involved in machinery, slate, granite, steel, bricks, and railroads as well as marble in Dorset. Though he had made some handsome profits during his long construction career as far back as the Civil War, he also invested too speculatively. When he died, at the age of eighty, he left an estate worth only a few thousand dollars.

Ground was broken for the New York library on May 1, 1900, and after a few large blocks of marble were hauled from South Dorset quarry to Man-

Terry Tyler collection

Orlando W. Norcross in 1905.

chester Depot finishing mill, it was decided to build a railroad to connect them. This was the origin of the Manchester, Dorset & Granville, stimulating grandiose dreams that the rail line might also be used for profitable common-carrier traffic carting agricultural and commercial freight, and even for passengers making connections with the Delaware & Hudson in Granville and the Rutland Railroad at Manchester Depot.

The opening of the Norcross-West quarry and building of the railroad, plus new discoveries from the Imperial and Symington quarries in Danby, conspired to generate a short-lived economic boom, Ernest West reported: "A regular gold craze struck Dorset about 1902. A number of us started prospecting and coring ledges in Dorset, Danby and Wallingford. I shall never forget the excitement that came with the pulling of a core. Some fortunes

Blocks from which the marble columns were cored for the New York Public Library are contemplated by William Gilbert and sculptor Ben Karp. A pair of these may be seen at the entrance to the J.K. Adams company parking lot.

were made and some were lost, but . . . in 1910 building operations rapidly declined and once again the lack of monumental marbles brought the Dorset industry to a low ebb."

The MD&G Railroad was incorporated June 21, 1902, with capital stock of $350,000, of which $72,500 was issued, with a $260,000 5 percent bond issue (paid off in 1930). The first step was to build a rail line for the 5.09 miles between quarry and mill. The first train ran in July 1904.

The railroad, of course, never went to Granville, sixteen miles away and across the state line. It never even reached Dorset village, a mile and a half away. Completion of the New York library in May 1911 halted the primary traffic for which the railroad line was built. But other jobs, plus twice-a-day passenger service, kept the little MD&G going for a few more preautomobile years in spite of heavy snows, flooded streams, and roaming livestock. One dramatic brush with death became fixed in many memories. To quote G. Murray Campbell's account:

During the morning of July 6, 1906, two empty Rutland Railroad flat cars, preceded by one MD&G flat car, were placed on the 4,000-foot Plateau or Upper Quarry

148   Dorset

This was MD&G locomotive No. 1 at the quarry railroad station in South Dorset, 1904. Today the site is near Tim Baker's home.

siding, of which the grade was so steep that the locomotive was taxed to handle them. The two Rutland cars were placed under the quarry derrick. The MD&G car was ahead, and it was planned to use the hand brake and let this car down the grade a short ways to the woodpile, to load after the two cars of marble had been loaded. It was customary to hold the cars on the siding with a ¾ inch cable attached to the uppermost car and looped over a 3-inch holding pin on the ground.

Two large blocks of marble, each weighing over 25 tons, had been loaded on the forward Rutland car, and one block of 30 tons had been loaded on the uppermost car. Another 20-ton block was being hoisted to load, and while it was about 45 feet in the air, the hoisting engineer noticed the cars moving. The car holding the cable [surely the cable, not the car] had broken.

In the confusion that followed, no one attempted to set the hand brakes; so the hoisting engineer tried to drop the suspended block on the car to disable it, but was prevented from giving a full blow because he had to stop the drop to permit laborers on the car to scamper. He did allow the lowering block to hit the rear end of the last car hard enough to damage it, but the cars continued to move slowly forward. The hoisting cable was allowed to run out about 250 feet, but there was little more. The brake on the hoisting drum had to be applied, and the taut cable then pulled the marble block off the car, to the ground. The runaway cars were on their way to Manchester.

The regular 11 A.M. trip of the passenger coach southbound had left about 20 minutes earlier, and there were about 40 school children with accompanying teachers, along

The Age of Marble

Nobody was hurt on July 6, 1906, when this passenger coach was struck by a runaway flatcar, loaded with marble, which escaped from a South Dorset quarry and careened into Manchester on the MD&G tracks. This coach had just unloaded forty schoolchildren and assorted passengers.

with other passengers. When the loaded freight cars broke away, a telephone call was quickly made to Manchester Depot, where it was learned the passengers had arrived and had unloaded about four minutes before. The engine had gone to the enginehouse, and the passenger coach was left standing on the main line.

Possible death and disaster had been averted. The runaway cars, with the empty MD&G flatcar ahead, hit the coach and tore it from its wheels, landing it atop the flatcar. Only a window in the coach door was broken. It did, however, end the career of the passenger coach, which became a tool storage car. For a while benches were put on a flatcar to give an open air ride to passengers, until a second-hand car was purchased from the Rutland Railroad, to fill out the passenger-carrying life of the MD&G.

One survivor of the runaway, Seymour Wilkins, a native of Dorset Hollow, was interviewed in 1964 by the *Bennington Banner* because of a sign he had painted in front of his house near the Battenkill Locker in Manchester. His sign read: "A few flowers, a little paint, will make this old place look like what it ain't. For Sale." Wilkins, then seventy-seven, attributed his longevity "to the fact that he has never smoked nor had a drink." (His mother was ninety-two at the time.) The interview went on: "Wilkins remembers working at the Norcross-West marble quarry, where everyone now swims, and he recalls being paid $1.35 for eight hours of work. It was Wilkins, along

Photo from Grace Wilcox, in Terry Tyler collection

with a man named Glover, who jumped to safety on that scary day, July 6, 1906, when a flatcar bearing that fateful 40-ton block of marble, got away and ran undirected down the track from Dorset to Manchester on the old Manchester, Dorset & Granville Railroad. It injured no one, but frightened everyone who saw it pass."

The Norcross-West quarry was sold in 1913 to the Vermont Marble Company, which also took title to the MD&G. But this combination of businesses never made sense again. The quarries at South Dorset closed in 1917, the railroad ceased on June 1, 1918, and Vermont Marble shifted attention to its Rutland County quarries, which yielded stone of higher quality that could be extracted more efficiently. For a while in 1924–25 Pat and Tom McCormick ran a flange-wheeled truck on the rusty rails to haul marble from the Kent & Root quarry to Manchester Depot. After a decade of silence the rails were sold for scrap in 1934, and a certificate of dissolution was granted in 1936.

A quantitative grand-total summary of the cubic feet of marble ever taken from Dorset quarries, and compared with the quantity extracted from the Imperial quarry in Danby, was calculated by West in 1936 as follows:

The Age of Marble

Photo by Catharine Resch

Far left: The Norcross-West main quarry on Route 30 is now best known as "Dorset's swimming hole." This was the way it looked in 1902 when marble was being excavated for the New York Public Library. The view looks toward the highway.

Left: Enjoying the Norcross-West quarry on a hot summer day, Liz Resch is caught in mid-air, her reflection seen on the block of marble from which the 1902 photograph was probably taken.

Freedley	*4,250,000 cubic feet*
Norcross-West	*3,300,000*
Sanford	*2,500,000*
Blue Ledge	*2,000,000*
S. F. Prince Co.	*1,500,000*
Kent & Root	*1,000,000*
Fulsom	*775,000*
T. D. Manley	*480,000*
Total Dorset	*15,805,000*
Danby Imperial	*29,000,000*

Ernest West repeatedly expressed the judgment that Dorset marble of good quality still awaited attempts at quarrying. But the only serious revival effort took place in 1963, when the Georgia Marble Company of Tate, Georgia, organized itself as the Green Mountain Marble Quarry and hired a crew of six to drill some "blue cloud" from the old Pat McCormick quarry near South Dorset. A year later, after having dug horizontally into the vein, marble described as "dark cloud, golden vein, and pure white" had been extracted. But the venture did not prove profitable and was soon abandoned.

NOTES

This chapter derives gratefully and quotes liberally from three documents. One is a monograph that virtually exhausts the subject of Dorset marble, written by Ernest H. West in 1921 and revised in 1936, copies of which are available at the Dorset Historical Society. The second is "Dorset's Marble Mountain," a pamphlet published in 1972 by the historical society, also adapted from records kept by Ernest West with material supplied by Arthur Gilbert, Jr., a geologist. The third is a 1951 paper on the MD&G Railroad by G. Murray Campbell, a resident of Manchester who was a vice-president of the Baltimore & Ohio Railroad.

Ernest West, in turn, recycled much information contained in the earliest account of the Dorset marble business, that of Frederick Field, which first appeared in the *Vermont Historical Magazine* in 1861, later to be incorporated into Abby Maria Hemenway's *Gazetteer* for Bennington County.

Gratitude is expressed here to Nathaniel "Terry" Tyler for providing a copy of the D.L. Kent & Co. price list of 1891.

Details about the Manley-Lefevre marble house on the West Road derive from the research of historian John P. Johnson of Delray Beach, Florida, who was engaged by David and Katharine Dickenson, owners of the house since 1983. Johnson graciously shared his research with the writer.

— —

1. A directory of the Dorset quarries, including the many different names by which they were known at different times, the years in which they operated, their various owners, the buildings to which they contributed, and a map of their locations, can be found in the monographs written in 1921 and 1936 by Ernest H. West, available at the Dorset Historical Society.

2. George Holley Gilbert, "The Dorset Trail," with photographs by Carl T. Ramsey, (Dorset, Vt.: Dorset Science Club, 1928).

3. Edwin B. Child, "The Marble Mountains" in *Scribner's Magazine* vol. 37, no. 5, May 1905, and rpt. in *Tales of Old New England* pub. by Castle Books, 1986. Known primarily as a painter and illustrator, Child wrote this important account of the use of explosives and the realities of rugged work in Dorset's quarries. He illustrated his own article.

4. Herbert Wheaton Congdon, *Old Vermont Houses: 1763–1850* (Peterborough, N. H.: Noone House, 1968), p. 89.

5. Gilbert, "The Dorset Trail," p. 9.

9

The Late Nineteenth Century

PROFOUND CHANGES came to Vermont and to Bennington County at mid-nineteenth century. Among these were the railroads, a statewide Roman Catholic diocese, and the brief flourishing of an iron industry in East Dorset. The 1860s were dominated by the turmoil of Civil War, and there followed a maturing of outlook generated by the stern realities of war and by a new age of information and awareness. With the shock of war's severity, the divisiveness of public issues—notably slavery—and newly efficient transportation, many opened their eyes to the world around them.

The first regular passenger train in Vermont traveled twenty-seven miles between White River Junction and Bethel on June 26, 1848. The next year the Vermont Central and the Rutland & Burlington tracks opened and connections could be made between Burlington, Montpelier, Rutland, and Middlebury with Boston and Montreal. The Western Vermont Railroad Company was incorporated November 5, 1848, and the section of track between Rutland and Manchester, with stops at East Dorset and North Dorset, was completed in December 1851 and the first regular run started a month later.[1]

East Dorset grew in importance as a stop for mails, freight, and passengers. The arduous business of hauling marble was transformed. The age of railroads had a predictable impact on agriculture, and the rails also facilitated disturbingly strong outmigration from Vermont, to the Midwest in particular and to greener fields in general. A major step had been taken to alleviate Vermont's sometimes oppressive rural isolation. Suddenly the entire continent

Mr. and Mrs. Rollin Sykes in 1898 demonstrate a new-fangled butter churn at their home on West Road (now that of Mr. and Mrs. Eugene Bond). The wall calendar advertises the DeLaval cream separator. The Sykeses were known for the sugaring-off parties held in their saphouse.

Photo by Bertha M. Pratt from Charles Gilbert collection

seemed to beckon those who toiled on hardscrabble Vermont hill farms.

The urge to go elsewhere was widely evident. Reuben Bloomer II, son of the pioneer marble quarrier, left town early. Born in 1771, Bloomer left town in 1817 to take his wife, Lois Able, and their seven children to Huron County, Ohio. There he bought 137 acres and built a substantial brick house (reputed to be the oldest in Sherman township).

Milutus Barrows, born in Dorset in 1806, moved his family to western New York in 1849, then to Trumbull County, Ohio, in 1873. He died in 1884 in Connersville, Indiana, having outlived two wives and six daughters, though four sons survived.

Homer Gray, born in Dorset in 1816, moved to Rhinebeck, New York, where for thirty years he made marble monuments, then in 1868 settled on East 48th Street in Manhattan, where he worked for New England Granite Company. He died in 1884.

A variation was the case of Marley Griffith, born in Dorset in 1834. After graduating from Burr Seminary, where he learned some surveying, he migrated in the 1850s to Minnesota, then went on to California. As elected surveyor of Amador County he made its first map in 1866. He kept a diary that recorded how he and a partner staked a gold mining claim. He returned to East Dorset in 1870 intending only to visit, but became enamored of one Mary A. Kelley, married her, bought the general store, and remained until his death in 1912.

While some were emigrating elsewhere, one of the more durable families arrived in town to stay. Zephine Humphrey wrote of them, "And then there were the Gilberts. They are now so integrally a part of our life that we find it hard to believe that they came here only in 1855." The Gilberts moved south from Cavendish; Sophronia and Diana were already in town as wives of Alfred Field and Colonel Newton Sykes. Brother Oliver, with wife and children, first moved to the Field homestead, and in 1861 built their own home on the West Road. Oliver's son Charles married Carrie, a daughter of Parsons Pratt. Many of their offspring thrived, and the name Gilbert has remained strongly identified with Dorset and its history.

The Irish Catholics

The arrival of railroads coincided with the consecration in 1853 of Louis de Goesbriand as first Roman Catholic Bishop of Burlington This energetic thirty-seven-year-old priest from Cleveland recruited other priests from his native Brittany, Ireland and Canada and established parishes, convents, and parochial schools throughout Vermont.[2] In East Dorset Catholic mass had been celebrated for the first time in 1838 by Father John

St. Jerome's Roman Catholic church in East Dorset, built in 1874, replaced an earlier church that was located on Village Street where the firehouse is now.

D. Daly for about thirty Irish families who settled in town amid much hardship. There was no church, and mass was first held in the home of Michael McGuigan, then in other homes until a former cheese factory was converted to a church.[3]

Father Daly was based in Middlebury but traveled wherever there were Catholics for whom mass could be celebrated, baptisms administered, and confessions heard. He stayed with families of the faithful. Father Daly retired in 1854 and was succeeded by Father Druon from Rutland, who arranged for construction of the first church building.

Property for the present, larger church, was acquired in 1868 on a small hill overlooking East Dorset, from Plyn D. Ames, a dealer in dry goods, groceries, and medicines. Six years later men of the parish built the church, to minimize expenses. One of them was Michael McGuigan of Dorset Hill, then age twelve, according to a church history by Rose Burns Koch; perhaps he was a son of the parishioner in whose home mass was first held. St. Jerome's Church was consecrated by Bishop de Goesbriand on August 25, 1874, and came to be a central church for Catholics throughout Bennington and Rutland counties.

Among those who attended the cornerstone laying was Mrs. William Kelly of the Hollow, showing that parishioners were not limited to East Dorset. Indeed, Catholics were widely dispersed throughout town. According to one of the eldest residents in 1988, William T. Burns, Sr., names of the earliest Irish families in Dorset included (with occasional variations in spelling): in Dorset Hollow, Kelly, Collins, and Dalton; in Dorset village, McBride, McPhillomy, Daly, and Connell; on Nichols Hill, Houlahan and Kenny; on West Road, Sennett, Corey, Burns, Kelleher, and McDevitt; on McNamara Road, McDevitt and McNamara; in South Dorset, Malone, Carney, Burns, McDevitt, McBride, Cody, Bowen, Sullivan, McCormack, Hill, Wallace, Molloy, Gallagher, Tully, and Joyce; on Morse Hill Road, O'Connor, Hagen, Stuart, Sheridan, McDevitt, and Tuohy; on Dorset Hill, Tully, McDonald, Cox, McLaughlin, Casey, Cooper, Leary, McGuigan, Regan, Callahan, and Cunningham; in North Dorset, Condon, Flynn, Cooney, and Dunn; and in East Dorset, Sherlock, Leary, O'Leary, Gormley, Whalon, Hoctor, and O'Neal.

Construction of the railroad through East Dorset provided employment for Irish immigrants, and many stayed on to work in the marble quarries, toiling for $1.10 to $1.25 per ten-hour day. Others joined descendants of pioneer settlers by farming.

The Catholic parish was furnished with priests from Bennington until 1868, when Father Thomas J. Gaffney was assigned as first resident pastor. He remained until 1887. The original Catholic cemetery was on Dorset Hill until land was acquired in 1860 next to the new church site. At its height in the 1870s parishioners numbered nine hundred, nearly all of whom were of Irish origin. The number was reduced to about 250 when the quarries suffered reversals and members of the parish sought work elsewhere.

In 1887 Father Gaffney became pastor of St. Peter's Church in Rutland and Father Anthony J. Glynn, D.D., came to East Dorset and missions in Arlington, Manchester, Danby, Wallingford, and Mt. Holly. He was followed in 1900 by Father J. J. Boyle, and in 1902 by Father J. H. Maillet, who helped undertake extensive church repairs.

The Iron Business

In East and North Dorset in the mid-nineteenth century the mining and smelting of iron ore enabled craftsmen to produce some useful objects that previously had to be imported. In the long run, the making of iron stoves and hardware proved marginal, because raw materials did not exist in necessary qualities or quantities. But iron was an interesting and briefly viable business before and after the Civil War. Now-rare examples of East Dorset stoves and plows attest to the skill, practicality, and design sense of these iron makers.

Matthew Lyon began Vermont's first production of iron in blast furnaces

The East Dorset Hoyt mine, which produced iron ore, in an 1887 photo. The mine was located at the base of the mountain between Big and Little Mad Tom rivers.

at Fair Haven in 1785. Furnaces operated at Orwell, Pittsford, Bennington, and Sheldon, followed in the early 1800s by operations at Tinmouth, Vergennes, Highgate, Woodford, Brandon, Troy, and St. Johnsbury. Iron was being worked in Dorset as early as the 1820s.[4]

In the late 1840s Francis Draper built a blast furnace in East Dorset. He made iron there for about eight years, then the furnace was permanently idled. Several attempts were made at restarting it, but research has failed to uncover any evidence of production there after 1854.[5]

The 1856 map shows a "furnace" and a Draper residing just north of it, but the 1869 map shows the same furnace next to the "Dorset Iron Co." and no Draper. The 1880 Child Directory lists Francis Draper of East Dorset as owner of "cupola furnace in Windsor" and of one thousand acres of timber in Dorset and two thousand in Peru. In any case, the pile of stones known as the East Dorset furnace has survived the test of time, and it stands as one of the best preserved in the state, a curiosity. The site, bypassed by U.S. Route 7, has become Mr. and Mrs. Dennis Conroy's "Kiln Guest House."

In 1864 the Draper furnace was purchased by the Dorset Iron Co., which evidently hoped to make iron for the Civil War. But by 1866 the furnace was not "in blast," though its facilities included a hundred-foot marble casting house and cupola furnace designed for casting stoves and water power. The company owned a hundred acres of hardwood. In 1875 Draper bought the

The Late Nineteenth Century 159

furnace back and no doubt intended to repair it and resume smelting, perhaps to support the furnace he owned in Windsor, a center of machine-tool manufacture, but he did not resume East Dorset operations.

In North Dorset on Otter Creek, a jumble of stones today marks the site of a furnace that once had an annual iron-making capacity of a thousand tons, operated by Welcome Allen as early as 1849. Nearby the remains can be seen of Allen's foundry that made Dorset stoves. An example of a "W. Allen" stove is shown in an accompanying photograph. A later North Dorset stove of al-

Dorset Historical Society

An 1890s photograph of the East Dorset iron furnace, built in the 1840s. The marble shop at right and the tall chimney no longer stand, but the furnace itself is one of the best preserved in Vermont.

most identical design, made by Welcome's son Florenz R. Allen, has been acquired by the historical society.

Between the blast furnace and foundry lie ruins of the sawmill of Silas L. Griffith of Danby, a legendary lumber operator who among other pursuits converted immense amounts of waste wood from his sawmills into charcoal for ironmaking. (The Griffith sawmill site and Allen foundry and machine shop are located on the North Dorset map in the 1869 Beers Atlas.)

Researcher Victor Rolando tried to find remains of an earlier blast furnace in North Dorset operated by Daniel Curtis, one of many sons of Zachariah Curtis. In his 1980 thesis Rolando had been unable to locate it, though he concluded: "I still believe there to be an unrediscovered blast furnace in North Dorset. Too many good references point to it." Among these was the first *Annual Report on Geology of the State of Vermont* in 1845 by Charles Baker Adams, which stated: "Mr. Curtis has a furnace in North Dorset, the ore coming from a few rods east of his furnace and Otter Creek. This furnace is supplied with ore partly from Wallingford, but mostly from the bed in East Dorset, three miles south."

Another foundry buff, Richard Sanders Allen, in 1982 confirmed Rolando's findings about the missing North Dorset furnace and located what appeared to be its remains near Otter Creek and an east-west trail off Route 7 north of Emerald Lake.[6] Allen raised the further question of which Curtis operated the furnace. A "D. Curtis" was proprietor of a North Dorset hotel in 1869, and a John Curtis was North Dorset's "postmaster, mechanical engineer and farmer" in 1880.

In a 1969 paper on Dorset iron, Alfred Holley Gilbert quoted a 1943 *Rutland Herald* interview with Mabel T. Herrick:

My grandfather, Paris Buffum, and two other men owned and operated an iron foundry in the south village of East Dorset. Their trademark was "Manufacturers of stoves and Hollow Ware." The hollow ware was, I suppose, iron kettles large and small . . .

This firm got its iron ore by digging into the foothills of the Green Mountain on the Walker lot, Cochran's pasture, and the Torrey farm. I have seen these tunnels many

Dorset Historical Society

This "W. Allen" stove was made in North Dorset in 1874 by Welcome Allen (1811-1885). A similar stove made by his son Florenz R. Allen (1844-1893) was acquired in 1988 by the Dorset Historical Society.

times and they are probably visible at the present time. To smelt this ore they used charcoal which they burned in kilns.

When competition could not be met from the Pennsylvania foundries, where hard coal and iron were found in quantities near together, this firm was dissolved, and two of the partners moved to Pennsylvania, leaving grandfather behind. He had bought or built a house, had a patch of land, and babies. At that time some of the patterns were sold to an Allen family [Welcome Allen] of North Dorset where the chunk stoves were manufactured for some time afterward, but I think not the hollow ware. These stoves were used in the Little Red Schoolhouses that dotted the country districts, also in depots, bar rooms and barber shops until quite recently. The Allens also manufactured plow points.[7]

Related to iron was the business of providing charcoal needed to smelt iron ore, and several charcoal kilns were located in Peru, Mt. Tabor, and elsewhere in mountainous regions. One owner of the East Dorset blast furnace, Alfred Gilbert wrote, was Timothy Ridehout (also spelled Ridout), who later operated sawmills in Dorset with his son Samuel. These mills were purchased by Welcome Allen, who also owned much mountain land, source of his charcoal.

Cheese Factories

Another important business was cheese, a salable and relatively long-lasting product made from perishable milk. There were at least two factories in town after the Civil War. One was started about 1869 by Augustin B. Armstrong near the first bridge to the Hollow. The other was that of the Dorset Dairy Association, owned by a stock company whose officers included Joseph H. C. Hodge, Freeman Paddock, Harmon N. Paddock, Rollin Sykes, E. Farwell, and Philetus Barrows. In its prime it handled twelve thousand pounds of milk a day.

In 1871 Augustin B. Armstrong, a half-brother of Laurel B. Armstrong, patented a method for heating cheese vats by means of fire arches under the vats. His pamphlet described and promoted his invention, including testimonial letters from users. "My improvement," he explained, "consists in the use of plates of cast and wrought iron under the forward portion of the bottom of the water vat; said plates running back past the middle of the bottom of the water vat." An even temperature in the vat reduced the need to stir the curd, and made available a source of hot water for cleaning. The fuel was "ordinary fire wood."

Testimonials came from Mrs. A. D. Caprin of Danby Four Corners and from Nelson Jones, who said he used Armstrong's invention to make forty

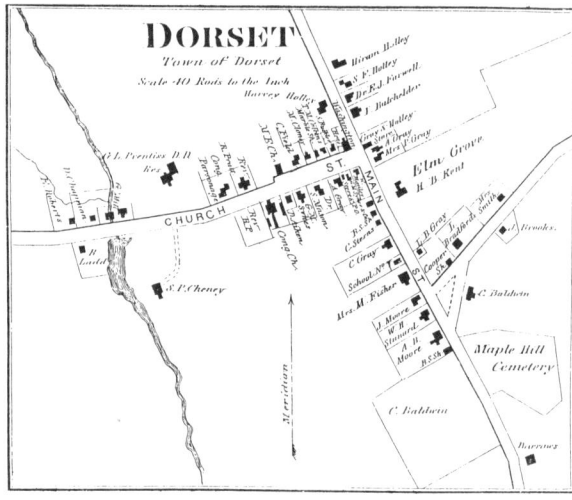

thousand pounds of cheese during a 160-day season in 1870 for the Dorset Dairy Association. Jones's letter was notarized by I. N. Sykes, justice of the peace, as was one from Merrill T. Baker. There were letters from Dorset listers, William D. Ames of East Dorset, and Nelson J. Sanford and George W. Farwell, verifying the uniform temperatures achieved. Dwight Taylor wrote from East Rupert to praise Armstrong's devices used by both the Dairy Association plant and Armstrong's factory.

The cheese factory at the Hollow bridge was later owned and managed by Moses Sheldon, an all-around citizen. A graduate of Burr & Burton, Sheldon was a farmer who held offices of selectman, lister, constable, tax collector, and deputy sheriff. Born in Rupert in 1850, he was Dorset's 1884 Republican representative in the House, and in 1902 went to the Senate.

A Flowering of Information

A kind of information explosion took place during the late nineteenth century as Vermonters grew more aware of their surroundings. Maps showing where everyone lived, with schools, rivers, sawmills, and other comprehensive data, were published before and after the Civil War.

The 1856 Rice & Harwood wall map attempted to depict each residence and object of interest in every Bennington County town and village. A good copy can be seen in the Bennington Museum's genealogy library. Rice & Harwood included detailed maps of Dorset and South Dorset and two of East Dorset including its south village. Engravings of the town's finest homes in-

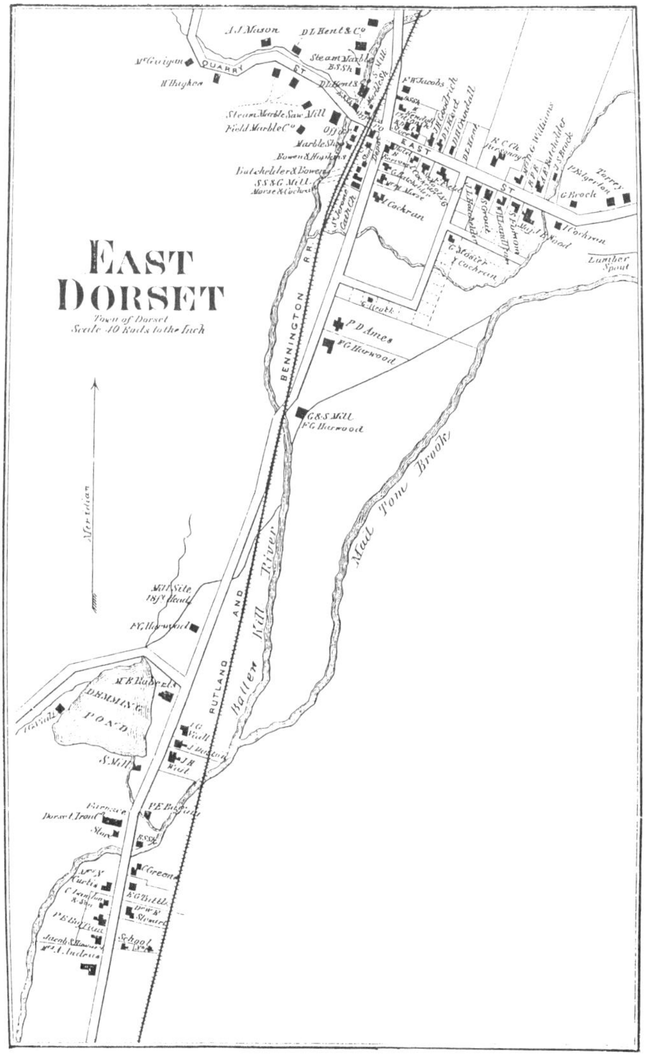

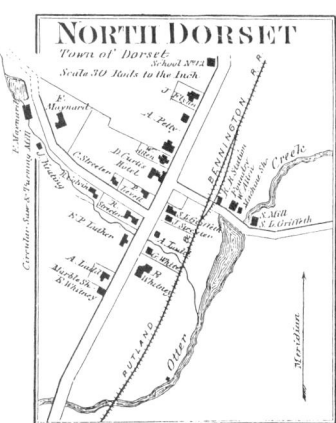
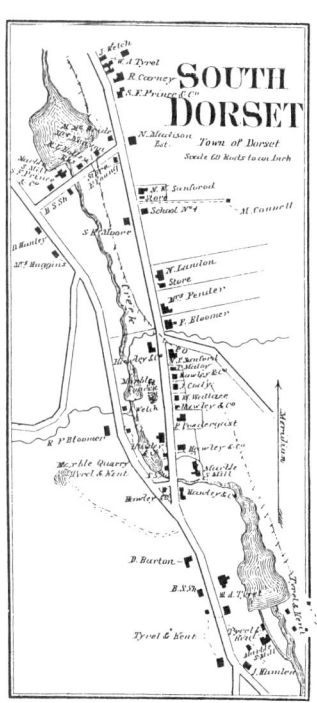

Detailed maps of Dorset's villages from the 1869 Beers Atlas.

cluded those of Charles Field, Dr. Sylvester Mason, George B. Holley, and Charles Baldwin, also identified as the former home of the Reverend William Jackson (Barrows House). One engraving shows "The Vermont Italian Marble Quarry" of "Holley, Fields & Kent, proprietors."

"Dorset Mountain" is shown as a north-south ridge that divides the town, ending in a hillock misspelled "Geene Peak" and accompanied by "Owls Head." The odd shape of the Mt. Tabor Leg is not shown.

The 1869 *Atlas of Bennington County, Vermont*, by F. W. Beers, was more sophisticated. Its Dorset map includes residences, sawmills, churches, roads, rail lines, mountains and hills, caves and quarries, streams, cemeteries, a "Subscriber's Business Directory," as well as the Mt. Tabor Leg. The most striking aspect of the Beers map is the colorful way the approximately fourteen school districts are shown—in pink, tan, and green. We say approximately, for no numbers 11 or 13 are shown though there is a 14. Within each district the school location is indicated. (The Rice-Harwood map appears as a front endpaper to this book, the Beers map at the rear.)

Public education in Vermont between 1827 and 1870 was considered "the period of slow development" by state school historian John C. Huden.[8] An 1864 law provided for free, tax-supported common schools in Vermont, and in 1867 "normal schools" were launched to produce "a better class of teachers." In 1869, the year of the Beers Atlas, Governor Peter T. Washburn asked the legislature to abolish the multitude of subdistricts in favor of townwide districts, a move that began in 1870. So the Beers Atlas became quickly outmoded.

The Beers "business directory" of Dorset contributors included marble firms, merchants, physicians and surgeons, and a long "miscellaneous" list. Physicians were E. J. Farwell in Dorset and W. E. Stewart in East Dorset. "Miscellaneous" included thirty-three sponsors.

Town histories

Dorset's first history was written in 1861 by Laurel B. Armstrong (1806–96), who was a state senator in 1858 and 1859. Armstrong, a resident of the Kirby Hollow homestead of Asa Baldwin, his great-uncle, was also a founder and early officer of the Vermont Historical Society. Armstrong's history found its way into Hemenway's *Bennington County Gazetteer*, one of a series of countywide histories to which Abby Maria Hemenway of Ludlow devoted her life. Miss Hemenway began alphabetically with Addison County. She published the *Bennington County Gazetteer* in 1868, and died in 1890 before she could complete Windsor County.

Municipal information multiplied with publication of the 1880 *Child's Ben-*

The Late Nineteenth Century 165

nington County Directory and the Lewis Cass Aldrich *History of Bennington County* in 1889. The Aldrich volume carried a history written by George M. Viall (1849–1912) of East Dorset, who was in the state senate in 1882. Some of Viall's account was lifted from Armstrong's, but Viall included lists of ministers, legislators, town clerks, town treasurers, selectmen, and delegates to state constitutional conventions.

The Vermont Senate was created in 1836 to succeed the Governor's Council. Then as now, Bennington County elected two members at large in the thirty-member Senate, and with one exception those two senators were divided between North Shire (Arlington and towns to the north) and South Shire. In 1870 Vermont abolished the old Council of Censors and also switched from a one-year term for state officers to a two-year term.

The first volume of town history was published in 1896, a fifty-six-page booklet titled "1768-1896. Dorset, Vermont." It was prepared by the William Jackson Fuller Woman's Relief Corps No. 23, the women's auxiliary of the unit of the Grand Army of the Republic, named for the soldier who died at Andersonville. The 1896 history explained itself this way: "'Dorset Night' Entertainment. Sketches of Dorset, Vermont, from the date of its charter August 20th, 1761, and settlement in the year 1768. A series of historical, biographical and literary papers, pertaining to the development and progress of the town where the corner stone of the independence of Vermont was laid."

Corps president Elizabeth C. Dunton wrote an introduction, and contributors were Mrs. Olive S. Roberts, Mrs. Jennie A. Williams, Mrs. Helen E.

Courtesy of Bea McWayne

Sherman Nichols, who marked his 100th birthday on March 3, 1920, then died the next month, was a Bennington County side judge. He was born in Sandgate. Many of his descendants have remained in Dorset, including the lender of the picture, his great-granddaughter.

Williams, Mrs. Lillian A. Sheldon, Miss Belle Roberts, Mrs. Susan F. Armstrong, Mrs. Pluma G. Harrington, Mrs. Mary A. Fisher, Bessie A. Dunton, and Mrs. Emma J. Towsley. Mrs. Mamie E. Norton wrote about the Woman's Relief Corps, whose motto she expressed as "Fraternity, Charity and Loyalty; but the greatest of these is Charity."

In a section called "The Future of Dorset," Olive Roberts looked ahead 125 years—because the book looked back 125 years—to the year 2021 and

Gift of Allan Sheldon to Dorset Historical Society

A "Gay Nineties" group in front of Mrs. Arvin W. Harrington's house (later that of Dr. and Mrs. Jerry McGinnis) on Church Street. Next door is Tom Collins' undertaking parlor and marble shop, no longer standing.

a grand city of 50,000 souls that nobody in 1896 would recognize. She foresaw an "aerial car" to take passengers to places like the Pinnacle. If only she could have known that her late-nineteenth-century town would be fully recognizable to those almost a century hence.

Olive Roberts's inventive and imaginative eyes foresaw this twenty-first-century view from the Pinnacle:

Please turn your eyes now in each direction and notice the beauties of this natural amphitheatre, nestled among the everlasting hills, that rise on either side terrace-like; no more beautiful spot greets the eye of man than this scattered city, for as you see, it is a city. We learn from looking back over the history of the place that it became noted as a place of resort some 150 years ago, and attracted the seekers of health, pleasure and beauty from the large cities near the seaboard, and from a straggling settlement of farms mostly, in the valley, it became the thickly settled seat of happy homes which you now see.

Castle-like in some places, surmounting hills, and overlooking the valley are the more pretentious ones, while surrounded by trees and amid glistening miniature lakes are the other and not less beautiful ones. You ask in wonder where all the water comes from. Look to the Southeast and see the large lake lying under the shadow of "Owls-head" and see the surrounding hills. The ancient Mettawee or Pawlet river was dammed at a narrow opening in its course, and turned into a lake or reservoir that supplies much of the water; away to the Westward, and across the main valley, is another reservoir hidden among the hills, that is supplied by the old "Sheldon" brook or Gilbert brook later called. This last supplies the potable water fountains, etc., and is second to none in the world in purity, while the supply is ample for the probable increase of a century in population.

You will notice in this glance several prominent buildings, monuments, etc. Among the most striking in location and appearance is one near the Cemetery; a building of native stone, plain in exterior, but strong like our early people, it rises in simple grandeur to commemorate the service of Dorset men in the Wars of our beloved Country. It is called "Dorset Memorial Hall." It was erected by the Woman's Relief Corps, a patriotic organization of women that had its origin soon after the civil war of 1861 to 1865; this organization, though the actual need that prompted its inception has passed, still exists, and is widely recognized as a powerful influence in the education of our youth in patriotism, and preserving the memories of that great war in our history; a war that emancipated a people. The organization has its hall in the building, you must learn, and is a veritable historic museum and library! the latter containing more than 20,000 volumes.

Mrs. Dunton told of the Grand Army of the Republic, "whose members live only in enduring marble and bronze, and in the memory of a grateful people, whose country they saved." She foresaw a gleaming white monument marking the site of—as she called it—"The ancient 'Cephas Kent Tavern Stand' " and said 150 years were allowed to pass before the monument was erected.

A mile south of the Kent monument, Mrs. Dunton envisioned a "glittering mausoleum" to mark the burial place of the first eleven white people to settle in the valley—also a project of the ambitious Woman's Relief Corps and the G.A.R.

She foresaw three railroad trains charging through the Dorset valleys—"operated by electricity instead of outmoded steam." There would be thirty schools in the Dorset of 2021, the finest of which would rank with "the universities of 100 years ago." Chauvinism ran strong in her prediction that these schools would offer a course in patriotism, "taught by the symbol of our Country's Flag, as expressing national unity, power and glory, for we are to-day a Nation without a peer on earth in either political, moral, social or intellectual greatness."

The Arrival of Telephones

Ample fuel for the explosion of information was provided in 1883 when the first telephone was installed in Dorset, at the Kent & Root Marble Company, connecting the firm with Burr & Manley's Store in Manchester Depot. By November 1887 several private homes in Dorset had telephones, with "central" located again in Manchester Depot. A 1906 diary noted the installation of telephone poles along the eastern route, between the Barnumville section of Manchester and East Dorset. But these were for local calls only, because the only "long distance" connection in 1900 was located at Young's shoe store in Manchester. By 1901 there was a total of thirty-eight telephone subscribers, including Manchester and Dorset.

The telephone line on the west side of Dorset was split in 1907 between Route 30 and the West Road for the convenience of Edwin Lefevre, Sr., among others. Dorset's telephones remained anchored in Manchester until 1932, when Dorset got its own exchange. But not until 1953 was the toll charge removed between the two towns. Within a month of that changeover the number of toll calls rose by 70 percent.[9]

The Irrepressible Si Clone

In the 1890s a tradition arose that seemed peculiarly adapted to Dorset when Andrus L. Bowen under the pseudonym of "Si Clone" wrote Dorset news for the *Londonderry Sifter* and the *Manchester Journal*. Competition came from H. C. Sheldon, who penned Dorset items for the *Granville Sentinel*, and from *The Southern Vermont Mirror & Advance* in Danby.

Si Clone reported a pot pourri of news tidbits: court cases, fires, obituaries and funerals, marriages, accidents, who was painting a house, school events, and organizations and churches. On occasion Si would go on a verbal rampage, mixing political and social concerns with personal tirade, as in the following eccentric report. From the *Manchester Journal* of December 31, 1897:

I would like to ask your Peru scribe what newspapers he would have our teachers read and what political platforms he would have them study; and if they are expected to know

The Late Nineteenth Century

A family portrait from about 1906 includes cyclist Ed Bowen, Mrs. Carl (Hulda) Henning, Mr. and Mrs. A.L. Bowen, and their daughter Helen. Bowen, at right, wrote under the pseudonym "Si Clone." The Bowen home is now that of Mrs. Helen Sheldon, "Si Clone's" granddaughter.

who has been or is to be appointed to office, where they can get a copy of the list of those who contributed the most and who got the biggist [sic] *boodle-trust backing in electing the appointing power, in fact get the time table on which this boss-ridden country is run. But is it not enough that our appointive offices are filled as payment for boodle furnished to run political machines but that even our lady teachers, who are not competent to vote, who are a degraded part of the human race and never should vote, according to the present views of the powers that be, must become clairvoyants and tell the secret workings of this administration, which promised before election to free Cuba, to establish bimetalism, to break up trusts, to support civil service, to produce revenue to run the government, and, in fact, do just what they have not done, and let alone just what they have done. No, This tomfoolery of such questions is all rot and is got up simply to catch good scholars and good teachers and leave them out while some forward ones who have accidentally got hold of the key can flippantly answer enough conundrums to squeeze through. Give us less red tape and more common sense—less sham reform—and our schools and country will be better off.*

The same column contained this gossipy item: "The Josie Gibson variety show busted up here in Dorset and sold their effects at auction on Saturday.

Two important nineteenth-century North Dorset buildings, the railroad depot, right, and schoolhouse, across Route 7, were both being used for new purposes when this photo was taken in 1975.

Their advance agent went on a drunk and failed to bill them farther."

Aside from Si's outbursts, the phenomenon that seems most peculiar to Dorset is the personal news note, the who-just-returned-from-where or who's-visiting-whom item: "Miss Lauderdale of Geneseo, N.Y., is the guest of her aunt, Miss Vance, at the 'Hemlocks.' "

There is nothing unique to Dorset or to the *Manchester Journal* about such items. But the personal news note was particularly adapted to Dorset. It formed the basis of news reportage from Dorset for nearly a century, and the close-knit neighborliness that Dorset fostered made these items especially compatible and appropriate. Dorset thrived, after all, on "boarders," "summer people," and people "from away" for many years, and for those involved in such businesses it was necessary to know who was in town or had just returned from where, or had visited whom. The format rarely varied—almost always a single sentence. One rule seemed to be that an item would report that someone had just returned; it never said someone was about to go away, because advance notice could invite burglary.

Some of H. C. Sheldon's reports also had character. Take this tidbit from the *Granville Sentinel* of March 3, 1899: "The Shakespeare reading club met on Monday evening of this week at the home of Miss Louise Sykes. Hamlet was finished. Their next attack will be on Julius Caesar, at the home of Miss Pratt."

Sheldon could force his sense of humor too far, as in this report of May 12, 1899: "George Harrison of Troy is an occasional visitor here and for a number of years has been a summer boarder here. His last visit was of a piscatorial nature. There are fewer trout here after his invasion of our brooks than before. He returned to Troy Tuesday."

One could devote endless time and space to the stuffed books of clippings of published Dorsetiana in the historical society. These items are informative, witty, evocative of the times in which they were written, varied yet unchanging.

The Book Club

"At a gathering of ladies and gentlemen at the residence of Rev. P. S. Pratt Jan. 17, 1871, Mr. Pratt being chosen moderator, it was resolved to organize the Dorset Book Club. . . . Miss Carrie G. Pratt was appointed librarian."

Thus began the records of the Dorset Book Club, which evolved into the Dorset Public Library and was a vital element of information flowering in the late 1800s. In Carrie G. Pratt's hand it is recorded that $25 was realized "from a public exhibition at the close of Mr. William J. Gilbert's school, Feb. 18, 1870" and that amount was appropriated "to buy books and periodicals for a circulating library."

Gilbert taught in a private school and in the village school's upper class for the previous winter term. A son of Oliver Bowen and Harriet Holley Gilbert of Dorset, he graduated from Middlebury in 1870 and was among emigrants who perceived greener grasses elsewhere; he became a lawyer in Niles, Michigan.

The first club president was Theophile Comba, a native of Italy who found his way to town with a brother employed in the East Dorset quarries. Comba had wandered over to Dorset village, boarded with the Gilberts, attended

Burr & Burton, and then taught school. He later married Mattie Gray, an original book club member.

At that first meeting a list of rules was devised; "any person in this parish" could belong with payment of a 50-cent annual fee. Nonmembers could take books not already in use for 2 cents a day, later amended to 5 cents a week.

Parsons Pratt wrote in his diary that others present at the launching of the book club, besides members of his own family, were Mrs. Charles Field, the Misses Vance, Angie Gilbert, Ellen Hilliard, Mary Sheldon, Nettie Wing, Mattie Gray, Aurelius Sykes, Ira Hilliard, and Fred Gilbert.

The creation of a public library in Dorset coincided with a trend throughout Vermont. The St. Johnsbury Athenaeum in 1871 was said to be the first free village library in the state, followed by the Bennington Free Library in 1872.

Dorset's book collection was first kept in Pratt's home, then moved in 1875 to that of Marcia Gray, the librarian until 1877. From 1877 to 1894 the books, numbering about one hundred, were kept in various homes. The club met monthly and there was great interest in "reading circles" and Shakespeare readings, especially during winter. In 1894 Gilbert M. Sykes made space for a library above his store, now Peltier's, and Henry Baldwin, who lived in adjacent quarters, became librarian. "Mr. Baldwin was a genial soul who loved books, his violin and garden," and he added books from his own library to the collection until poor health forced him to quit in 1903.[10]

Charles Gilbert collection

"Deacon Sykes'" store, now Peltier's Market, in a photo taken by Harriet Gilbert in 1910. The public library was upstairs here between 1894 and 1913.

From 1915 to 1928 the library was located in the home of Merritt Chapman, an uncle of Perry Peltier, next door to the store. The building became a branch of the Factory Point National Bank in 1974.

Sykes kept the library above his store until 1913 and his daughter, Louise, became acting librarian until 1905, when Miss Hattie Gray took the job. Louise Sykes then became the wife of the widowed Dr. F. C. Liddle and remained a guiding spirit of the library. From 1915 to 1928 the library was housed in Chapman House, next to the Sykes store. When Bernard Sykes purchased the former John Gray Tavern building in 1928 and presented it to the Dorset Library Association, Louise Sykes Liddle prepared a paper tracing events from the founding.

The Civil War

"Volumes could be written of the services of Dorset men in the Civil War, which would compare favorably with that of any other town in the state," wrote Mary A. Fisher in the 1896 Woman's Relief Corps history. "But much of the experience of these brave men who suffered death, or braved the hardships of soldier life will never be written or told."

Dorset indeed contributed heavily, because in the war Vermont lost more of her sons to the cause of the Union, relative to population, than any other northern state, according to G. G. Benedict's *Vermont in the Civil War*.

Locally, the most shocking news of the war came in July 1862 when it

A painting by an unknown artist shows North Dorset, looking north, about 1860. Note the train, the schoolhouse, and the woman posed in foreground with a parasol. This painting has been on permanent exhibit for many years at the Vermont Historical Society in Montpelier.

was learned that of the fifty-nine members from Dorset and Manchester of Company E, Fifth Regiment, First Brigade, forty-four were killed or mortally wounded during a battle at Savage's Station, Virginia.

Solomon Bulkeley of Dorset was Company E's official letter writer. He kept the home front informed of its activities through the *Manchester Journal*, and pleaded for warm blankets, food, and linens. Company E took part in twenty-five battles of fifteen major engagements, including Gettysburg, Fredericksburg, Antietam, and Rappahannock Station. Then, according to Benedict, the entire regiment, which rendered "important and memorable service . . . in half an hour suffered the greatest loss of men killed and wounded ever endured by a Vermont regiment in a single action."

The William J. Fuller Woman's Relief Corps account stated that 144 Dorset men volunteered. Of this number 28 died, either of wounds or disease. One of them was William Jackson Fuller, whose name was immortalized by the Woman's Relief Corps. Fuller died August 25, 1864, in the notorious prison at Andersonville, Georgia. Two years later his remains were returned to Dorset and buried in the Maple Hill Cemetery family plot of his namesake, the Reverend William Jackson.

The inscription on Fuller's marble obelisk gravestone conveys the story of his brief life. It reads:

Wm. Jackson Fuller Co. G. 1st Reg
Vt. Cav. born Alden, NY 1842
Volun. Dorset Oct. 8, 1861, captured
near Petersburg Va. June 29 '64
died Andersonville Ga. Aug. 25 1864 ae.22

Faithful Firm,
Kind in spirit, calm in danger,
Brave in Battle, Honored & loved,
Dying in prison with 13 thousand
loyal men—a victim to treason
and barbarity—a martyr for Freedom.

A youthful soldier who, in Christian
patriotism, promptly gave himself,
For liberty & the Union, in the grate [sic]
War against slavery & its rebellion.

Parsons Pratt, his admirer and mentor, in writing the family genealogy, reported that Fuller was born in Alden, New York (near Buffalo) in 1842, the year William Jackson died, and was named for the esteemed clergyman. Little was known of the family except that Fuller's father Orson, was born in Hampshire, Illinois, in 1779 and died nearly a century later, on April 6, 1875. As an infant Fuller lost his mother, was adopted by a relative in Illinois, then was sent at the age of ten to Dorset, traveling part of the way alone. He was taken in by Susanna (Jackson) Baldwin, a daughter of Reverend Jackson, who with her husband Charles lived in her father's former parsonage. Young Fuller remained there until he joined the army at age nineteen.

Pratt wrote of Fuller's enlistment in "the bloodiest war in our history":

These calls echoed through our quiet valley and were responded to by many of our best, bravest young men. Less than six months from the firing of the first gun, our young friend gave his name and pledge for a service under the flag of the union; his youthful strength and enthusiasm, his months and years, and as it proved, his life was given for the defence of his country.

Two days before their enlistment on October 13, 1861, Fuller and his friend Nathan Robinson had filled their usual seats in the church choir. "Within twelve months the body of Robinson, labeled 'honor to the brave,' was returned to us for the sad burial service, perhaps the first of the precious lives lost by this parish during the war."

William J. Fuller sent the following letter on February 11, 1862, from Camp Harris in Annapolis, Maryland, to Pastor Pratt:

Dear Sir:
The Soldier has, occasionally, as well as other persons, some leisure time; having a little leisure time this evening, although my tent companions are not very quiet, I will try and write to you as you kindly gave me an invitation too before I left D[orset].

You need not doubt but what I miss quiet Dorset with its religious privileges. When the sabbath comes my mind roves back to the sanctuary where I have spent many happy hours and spend them profitably. There I see God's people gathering to hear his holy word read and explained to them . . .

We are being drilled and fitted for service as fast as possible, although we shall not be well drilled for many months, we expect we shall have to hold ourselves in readiness to be called on as soon as spring comes . . .

Yesterday heavy firing was heard off in the direction of the Potomac. It was said by citizens to be heavier than they heard at the time of the Bull Run Battle.

I hope I am truly thankfull that my health is so good, for it was never better. It now being late, I shall have to close these few broken sentences, you must consider who they are from, and excuse all mistakes.

Yours respectfully,
Wm. J. Fuller

Courtesy of Pete and Charlotte Brooks

A portrait of William Jackson Fuller, who grew up in Dorset and died August 25, 1864, in the Andersonville prison during the Civil War, age 22. The local chapter of the Grand Army of the Republic was named for him.

The Late Nineteenth Century

In the summer of his third year Fuller was captured and sent to Andersonville. Pratt commented: "The unutterable horrors of such a fate you would not wish to hear described in this place. Doubtless it was divine mercy which gave him within two months early release by calling him home to glory."

Another Dorset prisoner at Andersonville lived not only to return home, but to attain the age of ninety-seven. Nathaniel McWayne recalled his Civil War days in a 1920s *Rutland Herald* article, preserved by his great-grandson, Bill McWayne:

I was born in Pawlet, April 17, 1839. I went to Illinois in 1860. That's how I happened to enlist in the 96th Illinois instead of in one of the Vermont regiments.

I was in a few skirmishes, but Chickamauga was my first big battle—and it was battle enough for me. There were 100 men in my company at first. Before we went into Chickamauga we had been reduced by sickness and death to 34. Of those, seven fighting men came out of the battle. The others were all killed or wounded. I got a slight wound but not enough to keep me away from my company.

The night after the battle two companies of us were posted as an advance picket on Missionary Ridge. The Rebels surrounded us, killed a man, and took the rest of us prisoners. We were kept under guard for a day and a night, and then were sent to Richmond, most of the way in cattle cars. There we were kept in a tobacco factory. We were moved from one building to another, and were later sent to Danville. In April we were sent to Andersonville, the worst of all the prisons.

You can't imagine anything so horrible as it was. There were 53,000 prisoners in one enclosure, 13,000 of them died and were buried there. There was never much to

Courtesy of William McWayne

Nathaniel McWayne, a Civil War veteran who survived Andersonville prison. He was the great-grandfather of William McWayne and great-great-grandfather of Milton McWayne, who now operates the McWayne farm north of Dorset village.

eat. I remember three days at a time when we got nothing at all. My first meal in Andersonville was a little cup of corn meal, ground coarse (cobs and all, the boys said). I had a two-quart pail to put it in, without salt, and mix it stiff with a little swamp water. Then I put it on a board, set it in a trench in the ground, and made a little fire in front of it to bake it. That was what we had to eat. Do you wonder that they carried out 25 or 30 dead men daily?

Dorset Historical Society

A family gathering at the Harvey Holley house (now that of Mrs. Dorothy Weston) on Route 30 just north of the Dorset Inn.

Of course this food started the scurvy. Most of the men had it in the mouth. I've seen them pick their teeth out with their fingers. I didn't happen to get it. I had heard that a few vegetables would prevent it. The men in my company put their money together and bought a bushel of potatoes. We paid $25 in good money for them, but they were worth hundreds of dollars to us.

You could buy anything in Andersonville if you had money. The Rebels would bring stuff to sell. They searched the officers and most of the men when they came and took their money away from them. But they didn't think by the looks of me I had any money. When our men didn't have any money the Rebels would trade them food for their clothes or shoes.

Our things were safe because we had hung six men that were caught stealing. That was Captain Wirz's only kind act to us. He gave those men a fair trial. Then he put up a gallows, and turned them over to us. We hung them for an example, and any stuff

The Cody farm about 1890. No longer standing, the house was located across from the J.K. Adams Company on Route 30.

we had was safe after that. It was very quiet in camp after they were gone.

There were always some of the prisoners digging tunnels. If any of the Rebels came in and asked what they were doing, they said they were digging a well. But from that well they'd dig a tunnel that would go way beyond the stockade. Some of them were recaptured and some got away; but very few of them reached home. The bones of most of them bleached in the swamps or forests. Most of the folks down there were ready enough to shoot a Yankee.

Not all of them were cruel, heartless men, though. The morning after I was captured a Rebel soldier said to me: "Have you had any breakfast?" "Not this morning," I told him. He gave me half of his—a big cake of corn bread baked in an iron skillet. It was good corn bread, too—much better than we made for ourselves. He broke it right in two and gave me half of it.

Once before the battle I went two or three miles into the country for peaches. After I'd had all the peaches I wanted I came to a nice house and called there. There were no men at home, but the ladies were very kind. They invited me to dinner—a good dinner, too, and asked me to come again any time I was out that way.

Yes I'm a G.A.R. man. I was commander of our Post for twenty years. I've been a farmer all my life. I sold my farm to my son when I couldn't farm it any more. He's doing fine—keeps fifty cows and had a milking machine. I always had to milk by hand. My daughter lives with me and my other son half a mile south of us.

McWayne's saga was related by Zephine Humphrey, who wrote in 1924 that he was "the youngest and most vigorous man of his age in our Dorset valley." Humphrey also listed the town's commissioned officers: Arnold P. Wait, Charles Field, Gilbert Hart, and William Newel. Warren Dunton enlisted in 1861, rose through ranks to become a captain, and was discharged in 1863 for wounds received at Fredericksburg. After the war he entered the regular army and was brevetted a major. Burns H. Roberts served longer than any Dorset citizen. His activities included Marine Corps adventures in the Southern Pacific Squadron, in which he survived an earthquake and the 1868 tidal wave off Peru.

George Williams, older son of William Williams, who ran the Williams Harness Shop, enlisted in the Civil War, survived, then tried living elsewhere. He went to Lowell, Massachusetts, for a few years but in 1876 came home to join brother Charles as a partner in the Williams store. George stayed with the tannery and harness manufacturing aspect of the business while Charles became a grain dealer. The war veteran of the family, George, who died in 1915, is credited with starting the tradition of Dorset Memorial Day celebrations. It was George's son Herbert who changed the name to H. N. Williams Department Store and branched out into bicycles, sleighs, and wagons.

Augustus Herman Gray, son of Deacon Alonson Gray and grandson of Captain John Gray, may have been the only Vermonter to serve, though involuntarily, with the Confederacy—surely the only Dorseter. He had gone to Salisbury, North Carolina, before the war to open a marble business and was caught in the draft. His daughter, Caroline Rosetta Gray, named for the state of her birth, escaped with her mother near the end of the war by running the blockades, and returned to Dorset.

Augustus Gray's great-grandson, Robert Griffith, age eighty-two in 1988, remembered him as a ninety-year-old with chin whiskers and a twinkle in his blue eyes. One of Gray's best-known traits, Griffith related, was that of expertly eating peas with a knife, a habit not admired by his sister Marcia, a spinster teacher. Toward the end of the war, having not heard from Gray, Marcia and another sister, Ellen, searched for him and learned that this northerner unwillingly conscripted into the Confederacy had been taken prisoner. The sisters arranged for his release but still had to locate him, which they did, and found him lying on a filthy cot in a tent in suffocating heat with other Confederate prisoners. Griffith provided this punch line to the tale:

Marcia stared, unbelieving, at the emaciated wreck of a man as he struggled to a sitting position. "Augustus Herman Gray," she pronounced accusingly. "Can this be you?"

Disease and privation had not dissolved Grandpa Gray's sense of humor. "Just fetch me a plate of peas, Sister," he said, "and a knife. I'll soon relieve you of your doubts."

Caroline Rosetta Gray married Joseph H. Nadeau, one of the few Dorset residents with a French-Canadian name. Nadeau, a native of Crown Point, New York, once aspired to the Catholic priesthood, attended Montreal College, then ran a boarding school in Montreal. He lost three brothers in the Civil War. On a visit to a sister in Benson, Vermont, across Lake Champlain from Crown Point, he met Caroline, then teaching school in Benson. After their marriage they returned to Caroline's home town of East Dorset, where Nadeau farmed, ran a small marble business, superintended a marble mill, and was elected selectman, school director, and town moderator.[11]

Another resident who spent the Civil War years in the South was Robert Griffith's other grandmother, Mary A. Kelley. At the age of sixteen Mary had traveled from Danby to Dardanelle, Arkansas, to visit a married half-sister, Olive Hill Feltus. A letter she wrote home in April 1861, when the war began, indicates that she had absorbed some Confederate feelings: "I think Lincoln ought to be hung. I tremble when I think of what is going to come. Do you think he is right? I know you don't, almost. . . . They say the negroes back in the country are picking out white women for wives. They thought they would be free if Lincoln was elected, but they found out they were mistaken, but they have not quite given up yet. Be sure and write soon and what you think about war and my coming home."

Mary A. Kelley was known as a Quaker Kelley, member of a Quaker family from Rhode Island who settled in Danby.

Documentation has proven elusive, but Dorset profited from the war when ten thousand—some say twenty thousand—headstones for the Gettysburg Battlefield cemetery were ordered from the Upper Prince Quarry, which then became known as the Gettysburg Quarry. Possibly no one wanted to acknowledge a profit motive, for not even Ernest West in his massive study of Dorset quarries mentioned the Gettysburg headstones except in a caption in his 1936 edition. "Gettysburg" does not appear in West's index of quarry names.

Centennial celebrations

The "great event" of the 1870s, according to Zephine Humphrey, was the centennial of Uncle Isaac Farwell, held on July 14, 1879. Farwell was born in Dorset in 1779, a son of John Farwell, who came to town with brothers Isaac and Asa from Mansfield, Connecticut. The centennial, held on a warm, dusty day, attracted more than a thousand, including scores of relatives, who were welcomed by Reverend Pratt and Dr. Joseph Wickham of Burr & Burton Seminary, entertained at a concert led by Simeon P. Cheney, and addressed by Reverend Prentiss. As Humphrey tells it:

Dr. Pratt made an address which we wish we might reproduce, so full of historic interest was it, harking back over one hundred years, indicating the high lights of Uncle Isaac's life. Another song followed, and then many toasts. Dr. Prentiss made a memorable impression by telling a story of his brilliant brother, Sargent Prentiss, who once fainted at the end of an impassioned speech he had been making and was caught in the arms of a companion. "Die, Prentiss, die," this companion shouted. "You'll never have a better chance." "So I say to you, 'Die, Uncle Isaac, die! You'll never have another chance to go out in such a blaze of glory.' "

Uncle Isaac's response to this effusion was laconic:

"Friends and neighbors," he said, rising and speaking in a clear voice, "I rejoice to see so many of you here on this my birthday. I thank you for the honor you have conferred on me by your presence. I was born in the year one thousand seven hundred and seventy-nine, and through the mercy of God I have been spared to see the year one thousand eight hundred and seventy-nine, which makes me one hundred years old today."

The speech was greeted with deafening applause. An outdoor dinner was served, the older people being seated at a table and the younger ones in picnic fashion on the grass.

. . . Uncle Isaac did not take Dr. Prentiss's advice, not he! He even defied it by breaking his leg and recovering perfectly. He lived almost two years longer, going about his business very actively except for occasional spells of feebleness.

Dorset Historical Society

A stereoptican view of the 100th birthday celebration of "Uncle Isaac" Farwell, born in 1779. He lived for two years after this occasion, in what is now the home of Mrs. Beatrice Jackson Humphreys at Church Street and West Road.

Uncle Isaac, who retained his tobacco habit until the end, had lived under all presidents of the U. S. and had voted for or against all but two, voting for the final time in November 1880 for James A. Garfield. In May 1881, "he slipped quietly off to try his luck with an eternity, the swing of which was already more familiar to him than to many people."

Before the century's end more centennials were celebrated. That of Elizabeth Manley "Aunt Betsy" Gray, widow of Paddock Gray, was held in 1891. After friends presented her with a purse on her one hundredth birthday she responded, "I can live a good while now for this house is all mine." Her little house was once used for a tea room. Her obituary said: "Upon all questions of principle she has stood firm and when in her younger days it was customary for every one to take liquor, she advocated total abstinence. She has always been a strong Republican, and today her Democratic neighbors do not dare to talk their doctrine in her presence."

Other centenarians were "Aunt Margaret" Schultz and Sherman Nichols, a Hollow resident who was listed in the Child directory as a "pettifogger and grafter." Those terms seem derisive today but they probably described Nichols as a lawyer who dealt in minor matters such as a notary would perform; he probably also grafted fruit trees. Nichols's centennial was held in 1920.

One of the closest centennials on record was that of Lettie Nichols Baldwin, daughter of Sherman Nichols, and the mother of Ruth Baldwin McWayne. Lettie's funeral was held on her 100th birthday in 1974. A near-centenarian was pioneer descendant William Manley, "a man of remarkable energy, with uncommon power of endurance," who died at ninety-six in 1889. His obituary declared: "Friends had fondly hoped that the deceased would live to complete a full hundred years, but it was not to be, and for the past few months they could but see that he was ripening for heaven."

The Reverend Parsons S. Pratt

The central and most durable personage of the latter nineteenth century, as many references already suggest, was the Reverend Parsons Stuart Pratt, minister of the Congregational church from 1856 to 1896, who lived for another active decade in retirement. Pratt was friend, minister, and mentor to nearly all of Dorset—with preference, of course, to his own parishioners. His ties grew so strong with this community that he compiled genealogies of all families in his congregation. He had discovered early in his career that teaching was not his forte, but he served as Dorset town school superintendent and in 1892 was elected chairman of the Board of Trustees of Burr & Burton Seminary in Manchester, the private-public secondary school that has always served as Dorset's high school.

Pratt kept a journal from the time he was a college sophomore in November 1834, to record events of each day and to give expression to personal and introspective matters. His diaries and genealogies, plus church records, constitute an intensive history of the social, religious, and intellectual life of the Dorset of his era. Pratt's grandson, Alfred Holley Gilbert, used these documents to write his grandfather's biography, which Gilbert published in 1975 at the grand age of ninety-seven.

Born in Sauquoit, New York (near Utica) in 1822, Pratt attended Clinton Academy and was graduated from Hamilton College in 1842. Two years of teaching persuaded him that this would not be his life's work, though it enabled him to earn money to attend Auburn Theological Seminary from which he graduated in 1846. He married Martha Pollard in 1847. On commission from the American Home Missionary Society he preached in Sumptions Prairie, Indiana, and Niles, Michigan. In Niles he met Charles and Fred Field, who were in the Midwest selling Dorset marble—and he left a lasting impression on them. Pratt was ordained a minister at St. Joseph, Michigan, but stayed briefly, returning to New York State because of his wife's health. For seven years he was congregational pastor in Winfield, New York, near Utica. In 1855 the Field brothers invited Pratt to preach for two Sundays in Dorset, then without a pastor. That fall Pratt accepted a unanimous invitation, which he considered a divine call, from the Dorset church. After spending two weeks in town to become acquainted, he fit like a glove.[12]

For Parsons Pratt and Dorset the next half-century was filled with weekly sermons, prayer meetings, Sunday schools, weddings, funerals, and other pastoral activities in a closely knit, church-going community known for its fondness for oyster suppers. Pratt came to town at a time when there was no parsonage, but a home was soon built for him across from the church. He tended his orchard, cared for his cow, cut his own firewood while he was able, and took special pleasure in annual maple-sugar festivities. During the Civil War he left briefly to be an Army chaplain in Philadelphia and Washington.

Pratt and his wife suffered from frequent illnesses, as had been the case with William Jackson, and Pratt often arranged for "supplying the pulpit" in his absence. Dr. Prentiss, Dr. Wickham, and various seminary students filled in.

A highlight of the Pratt era was the church's 1884 centennial, an unforgettable homecoming and reunion. The festivities were attended by Cyrus Hamlin, then president of Middlebury College, who in 1838 had married Henrietta Jackson and quickly departed for Istanbul. Hamlin reminisced about earlier days in Dorset, and he and Wickham vied with each other in their

The Sheldon four-horse team hauls a load of lumber in front of the William Crandall place on Route 30 north of town (now owned by John "Chips" Calloway). Drivers Frank Tarbell and Wilson Reed are perched on springboard seats.

memories of the Reverend William Jackson. Other speakers were clergyman Wright Robbins, a native son, Quincy Blakeley, and Principal Milton Severance of Burr & Burton. A letter was read from Cephas H. Kent, son of the Reverend Dan Kent. Parsons Pratt gave a long speech that recounted the history of Dorset. Simeon P. Cheney directed a large choir, and the congregation joined to sing many familiar hymns.

A recurring church activity centered around sentiment against the use of alcohol. In June 1888 the Congregational church hosted a two-day convention of the Bennington County Temperance Institute. There was a welcome by Mrs. N.E. Snyder, a devotional led by Miss Angie Holley, and a children's program by the Dorset Board of Hope. Papers were presented on parental responsibility, home discipline, cheerful homes, and "Worry Versus Work." Miss Celia Reynolds of Manchester delivered an essay on "How to promote temperance sentiment in our public schools," and an address was heard by Mrs. J.K. Barney, who was National Superintendent of Prison, Jail and Alms House Work.

The fortieth anniversary of Pratt's pastorate was celebrated in 1895, with a speech by Charles B. Kent and many poems and congratulations from the outside world. That year, as longest-serving minister in Vermont, Pratt was presented with an honorary Doctor of Divinity degree by Middlebury College. His wife Martha died in 1897.

When he retired in 1896 and became "pastor emeritus," Pratt was succeeded by the Reverend William Walker from Lunenberg, Massachusetts. Walker did not live up to expectations Pratt had established. He resigned after four years and was succeeded, as the centuries changed, by the Reverend Charles Carhart, a bachelor in his early thirties described as "wide awake, zealous and energetic with glowing dark eyes and a ringing voice."

During his retirement Pratt often filled the pulpit himself. He did not live to see the destruction of the old wooden church by fire on November 24, 1907. Pratt died in 1906 at the home of his daughter Carrie, Mrs. Charles B. Gilbert. As a memorial to Dr. and Mrs. Parsons S. Pratt, parishioners in 1909 installed a memorial Tiffany window over the door of the new church.

Simeon P. Cheney

The Singing Cheneys—four brothers and a sister, Moses, Nathaniel, Simeon, Joseph, and Elizabeth—began giving concerts in 1845. Simeon P. Cheney (1818–90) and his wife Abigail came to Dorset in September 1847 from Sheffield, Vermont, where they lived with his father, Elder Moses Ela Cheney, who pioneered musical conventions and enlivened the musical life of Vermont.

Simeon Cheney's first task in Dorset was to train a church choir for the 1847 installation of the Reverend Cyrus Hudson, a fundamentalist, fire-and-brimstone preacher who filled some of the mid-century gap (1847–53) between pastors Jackson and Pratt.

For the next thirty years Cheney and his family coached, entertained, enthused, and inspired the entire community with the vigor and quality of their musical presentations. Dorset artist Truman Bartlett remembered Cheney as "a public benefactor; no one who ever lived in Dorset deserves to be so lovingly remembered." *Music* magazine once said of Cheney, "His striking personal presence, his fire and limitless power of voice left an impression on audiences never to be forgotten."[13] Charles W. Hughes, a professor of music at Herbert Lehman College who summered in Thetford, wrote a scholarly article about the Cheneys in *Vermont History*.[14]

Cheney first took command of church music by launching a singing class composed of 125 voices. He next formed a choir of sixty members, who filled the chancel and expanded around three sides of the church. He then held singing classes in Manchester, Rupert, and Pawlet, and finally gathered them all together for a massive concert whose renown spread.

About 1850 Cheney built a two-story house near the village, on the edge of what is still called Cheney Woods. He called the place Maple Grove. He introduced the first piano in town and served the first ice cream. Two sons, John Vance Cheney and Albert Baker Cheney, were born in 1851 and 1852; John became a poet, essayist, and librarian of the Newberry Library in Chicago, and Albert became known as the greatest singing son of the singing Cheneys, and a professor of oratory in Boston.

Times were not always auspicious for the Cheneys. In June 1858 Simeon distributed a broadside advertising Maple Grove for sale for twenty-five hundred dollars. He called it "the most beautiful residence in Bennington County . . . truly *romantic* and *substantial*." The poster described the land as a square of about twenty acres, divided into tillage, pasturage, and forest. The advertisement conveys much about the Dorset of 1858 and is reproduced here.[15]

Alas, despite the earnest quality of the prose, the house did not sell, and the Cheneys remained at Maple Grove for many years. In 1879 Simeon and a Boston publisher produced *The American Singing Book From Shore to Shore*, which consisted of "300 pages of a great variety of excellent sacred and secular music old and new." In 1880 he was still listed in the Child directory as "teacher of vocal music."

Cheney later became interested in bird songs and transformed several into

Courtesy of Mr. and Mrs. C. Lee Marsh

FOR SALE.
MAPLE GROVE,

The most beautiful Residence in Bennington Co., can now be purchased of the subscriber, for the nominal price of *Twenty-Five Hundred Dollars*. This place is truly *romantic* and *substantial*. It lies on the cross-road, leading from Dorset Corners to the "West Road," containing about **20** acres in nearly a square form, properly divided into tillage, pasturage and forest.

A very pleasant pond bounds it on the west, on the border of which stands, unrivalled, a young and thrifty orchard, just beginning to bear, that cannot be valued at less than $1000.

The *House* is new, in good style, with ample, high rooms, well arranged in every part, with an excellent dry cellar beneath, containing a good cistern. At the door is a *superb well of Cold Water*, of which if a man drink he *will thirst again*. A barn, that *is* a barn, stands in the rear. They all stand about twelve rods from the road, in the grove, which consists of tall and splendid maples, and affords an abundance of *Sugar, Shade and Fuel.*

The valley running through West Dorset, is as pleasant as "The Vale of Ovoca" *ever* was, and Maple Grove stands about in the center of it *every way*. Indeed, it *seems*, as you stand here and *look*, to be the *center of the World.*

Dorset Corners, which contains two fine Stores, a splendid Hotel, and two respectable Churches, are only quarter of a mile from Maple Grove. Rupert Depot, on the Rutland and Washington R. R., is six miles from it on one side—Manchester Depot, is six miles from it on the other side. Both Depots are two hours from Troy, and six hours from New York.

But the beauties of Maple Grove are not to be shown on a page of paper. Such pages are to be found only on the choicest leaves of *the Book of Nature.* If you have *any* inclination to purchase, just call and see if I tell it right.

Maple Grove, Dorset, Vt., June 30, 1858.   **S. P. CHENEY.**

This description of the property of Simeon Pease Cheney seems like powerful advertising copy. But the place did not sell and he continued to live there. The home is now owned by Mrs. May Foote Lee.

A 1907 view of the Barrows House, converted to an inn by Mr. and Mrs. Experience Barrows, great-grandfather of William G. Barrows, Jr., and his sister Jane B. Whitehead. It was the home of the Reverend William Jackson, minister from 1796-1842, and was built in 1804 by Mrs. Jackson's parents from New Hampshire for their daughter and son-in-law.

musical notation. His studies resulted in a book published in 1892 after he left Dorset, titled *Wood Notes Wild*. Cheney died in Franklin, Massachusetts, May 10, 1890.

The Methodist Church and Jason F. Walker

A Methodist church (designated "M E Ch" on the Beers Atlas map) was once located across from the Dorset Congregational and next door to Parsons Pratt's rectory. It was led by an apparently enlightened clergyman, the Reverend Jason F. Walker.

A religious liberal who chafed "under the narrow tenets of the orthodox church of that day," to quote a biography used by Zephine Humphrey, Walker was convinced that communication with God was impeded by too many doctrinal impediments, and that science was rapidly disproving pet religious convictions and would continue to do so.

Walker provoked dissension wherever he went, and he went many places. Before coming to Dorset he was principal of the Troy Conference Academy at Poultney. He served churches in Johnson and Glens Falls, New York, in Rochester, Minnesota, Chicago, and Colorado Springs. Horace Mann once

A 1988 view of the Barrows House, still an inn.

offered him a thousand dollars to teach in his college at Antioch, Ohio. Ever tuned to his own drummer, Walker sought a home in the Unitarian church and finally was ordained as an Episcopalian in Michigan. At his death in 1880 he was dean of the Cathedral of Topeka, Kansas, and professor of Hebrew there.

Parsons Pratt was not comfortable with Jason Walker. An entry in Pratt's diary in 1856 commented on the use of the Congregational church for the funeral of a Methodist named Farwell. Wrote Pratt:

> *No objection would be made, but for the obnoxious character of Mr. Walker's preaching and it's somewhat difficult to determine just what is duty. Farwell's funeral was attended in our church—I went to the pulpit and made a prayer and read a hymn—Walker preached an hour and a quarter.*

The Dorset Grange

The Dorset Grange was founded in 1870, only three years after the national agrarian Granger movement was founded. The local chapter of the "Patrons of Husbandry" had forty-five charter members, and Frederick F. Gilbert was the first master.

Granges originally served social and education needs but often became heavily political, making the voice of the farmer heard on national issues such as regulation of utilities and railroads and economic injustices in agriculture.

Nearly every family on the west side of Dorset was involved in Grange activities. A leading member of the Dorset Grange was Richard Marston Campbell, who was master fourteen times in thirty years and also served in the state senate.

One Tragedy Presages Another

The nineteenth century came to a close on a tragic note. The town was shocked in 1897 when State Representative Horace Greeley Harwood, who owned a sawmill and gristmill, was killed after he fell onto a moving saw blade. His injured leg was amputated by a doctor but he lived only an hour after the operation. Born in Rupert May 13, 1849, he had lived in Dorset since 1853. He was one of its most prominent citizens, having served as treasurer and director of the Dorset Cheese Association, as justice of the peace, overseer of the poor, auditor, and selectman, in addition to his role as legislator.

Echoes of this unhappy incident would be heard nearly a half century later (see chapter 13) when Horace Greeley Harwood's grandson and namesake perished in World War II.

NOTES

1. Crockett, vol. 3, p. 349; also Edward Conant, *Conant's Vermont* Rutland, Vt.: Tuttle Company, 1925), pp. 252–54.

2. David J. Blow, "The Catholic Parochial Schools of Burlington, 1853–1918," *Vermont History*, summer 1986: p. 149.

3. Rose Burns Koch, "100th Anniversary of the Dedication of Saint Jerome's Church, East Dorset, Vermont," published on the centennial of St. Jerome's Church, August 25, 1974; courtesy of William T. Burns, Sr.

4. Elbridge C. Jacobs, "A Vermont Sketchbook" *Vermont Quarterly*, April 1953. The author acknowledged his debt to Connecticut engineer Charles Rufus Harte who listed Vermont towns that had iron ore, and who claimed that furnaces began in Dorset and Fairfield in 1831. As noted in chapter 6, 184 west side residents protested in 1826 that annexation of the Mt. Tabor Leg would give too much political power to the east side where furnaces were being built, and wood cutters, colliers, ore-diggers, and teamsters were moving in.

5. Victor R. Rolando, "Ironmaking in Vermont 1775–1890," 1980 master's thesis, College of St. Rose, Albany, New York. Rolando also generously provided the writer with his notes on a tour he conducted of ironworks and related sites in Dorset and Mt. Tabor for a meeting of the Northern New England chapter of the Society for Industrial Archeology, May 7, 1983. (Rolando's thesis is available at the VHS in Montpelier.)

6. Richard Sanders Allen, "Furnaces, Forges and Foundries," *Vermont Life*, winter 1956–57. This definitive article demystifies processes by which a blast furnace was charged with loads of charcoal, ore, and limestone to produce "pigs" of iron. To keep a furnace in continual blast, day and night, required twelve-hour shifts; and Allen added, "It has been said that for every ton of iron made, at least a gallon of whiskey was consumed to satisfy workers' great thirst."

The Late Nineteenth Century

7. Alfred Holley Gilbert, "The Iron Industry of North Dorset," paper presented to the Dorset Historical Society February 26, 1969.

8. John C. Huden, *Development of State School Administration in Vermont* (Montpelier, Vt.: Vermont Historical Society, 1944).

9. Edwin L. Bigelow and Nancy H. Otis, *Manchester, Vermont: A Pleasant Land Among the Mountains,* (Manchester, Vt.: Town of Manchester, 1961), pp. 111, 112.

10. Alfred Holley Gilbert, "A History of the Dorset Village Public Library" published by Gilbert in 1965 and "Dedicated to the memory of William Jackson Gilbert and the Small Group of Co-Founders."

11. Data about Joseph H. Nadeau; his mother Caroline; and her father, Augustus Herman Gray, as well as about John Marcellus Griffith, came from the grandson of Nadeau and Griffith, Robert Griffith of Brattleboro, to whom the writer is indebted for his generous correspondence.

12. This discussion of Parsons S. Pratt is based on the biography "Parsons Stuart Pratt, Life and Ministry, 1934–1896" written and published in 1975 by his grandson, Alfred Holley Gilbert.

13. Egbert Swayne, "A Vermont Musical Family," *Music* magazine, date unknown, courtesy of W. S. B. Matthews, ed.

14. Charles W. Hughes, "The Cheneys: A Vermont Singing Family," *Vermont History*, summer 1977, p. 155.

15. Gratitude for the use of Simeon P. Cheney's broadside is expressed to Mr. and Mrs. C. Lee Marsh of Arlington, Vt., whose son Chuck bought an original copy of the poster at a tag sale in California.

10

"Summer People"

Dorset-in-the-mountains
Is quiet, dull and small;
The world has curved around it,
Not touching it at all.
No neon signs; no used-car lots;
No night-clubs, movies, bars—
They light the town at night, I think
With just a moon and stars.
There is nothing much in Dorset—
Small houses, white and neat;
And trees, grown close together,
To edge each winding street;
And mountains everywhere you look;
Air fresh and clear and clean;
A country store, a little church;
A tiny village green.
No progress here, no enterprise—
Yet, strangely, folks will find
When they get home from Dorset
They have left their hearts behind.
                    Abigail Cresson

After the Civil War, "summer people" became a force to be reckoned with, and their influence swelled to great importance in the twentieth century. Starting with "boarding" and then "summering," there was an evolution to the acquisition of farmhouses as part-time residences, then to second homes, and ultimately to a rage for condominiums. "Summer people" is what these visitors were originally called, and many of them later became much more than seasonal residents.

Taverns and inns were operating in Bennington County as early as the mid-1760s, with the Walloomsac House in Old Bennington. Dorset's best-known early inn was that of Cephas Kent on the West Road, built in 1773. It earned state and national prominence because of the four conventions held at Kent's own dwelling house, where ideas were germinated that resulted in Vermont's declaration of independence in 1777. The Dorset Inn, founded in 1796, is Vermont's oldest inn in continuous operation.

On the West Road, other early inns or taverns included Soper's in South Dorset, Manley's, and Farwell's (Bea Jackson Humphreys), plus Jenks's (Lucile Beach) at West Road and Route 30 in East Rupert. These were not designed for "vacationers," a concept unknown in the late 1700s and early 1800s. They were for travelers in a time of primitive transportation, and they also met local needs for socializing and camaraderie by serving food and alcoholic beverages.

Not until the 1850s, when both the Rutland Railroad and Manchester's Equinox House were functioning, did there develop a business for those who sought purely leisurely pursuits. Although taking time off for relaxation was improbable during the Civil War, Mary Todd Lincoln did make two two-week August visits at the Equinox House in 1863 and 1864, and planned to return there with her husband in the summer of 1865.[1] Their Vermont vacation plans were among the least important of matters disrupted by an assassin's bullet that April.

After the war the Equinox House established a series of horse-drawn carriage rides for the amusement of summer visitors. One popular route went to Peru by way of East Dorset and the Mad Tom Road. (A bridge on that road was washed out by a flood in 1906, after which the road was abandoned. One of East Dorset's oldest residents, Miss Jane Leary, cleary remembered, just before her death in 1987 at the age of ninety-nine, when the Mad Tom Road was in active use.)

The Prentisses

Devoting the entire good-weather season of two to four months to restful visitation, or "summering," came about after the Civil War. The beginning of such a phenomenon can seldom be pinpointed, but in this case it seems indisputable: Dorset's reputation as a relaxing and scenic seasonal residence traces to a particular couple, time, and place.

Dorset's first "summer home," built in 1868 by the Reverend and Mrs. George L. Prentiss, is now owned by their descendant, J. Prentiss Whittemore. The house is across from the mill pond, also known as Prentiss Pond, on Church Street. This view dates from the 1880s.

The first "summer people" in Dorset were the Reverend George L. Prentiss and his wife, Elizabeth Payson Prentiss. They were New Yorkers whose regular home was a parsonage on East 35th Street, and Mr. Prentiss had the luxury, as pastor of the Church of the Covenant, of taking the entire summer off. The time was July 1868. The place was Church Street, a short distance west of the wooden Dorset Congregational church that had been rededicated in 1860, and whose congregation had been led since 1856 by Parsons S. Pratt. The two reverends became close friends, and Prentiss often substituted in the pulpit for Pratt, who had recurring spells of ill health.

Elizabeth Prentiss, a writer, recorded her thoughts first about "boarding" and then about "permanent summering" in Dorset. Her best-known book was a sentimental religious work titled *Stepping Heavenward* which, she reported in June 1870, had sold a respectable fourteen thousand copies. Her affectionate feelings for Dorset were also recounted in *The Life and Letters of Elizabeth Prentiss*, published posthumously in 1882 by her widower.

For their first two summers in Dorset, 1866 and 1867, the Prentisses "boarded." Boarding, the short-term rental of rooms including meals, was an important aspect of the local economy that grew to flourishing proportions in the late 1800s and lasted well into the twentieth century. Boarding

The Reverend George L. Prentiss and his friend, the Reverend Parsons S. Pratt.

enabled outsiders to sample the Dorset ambience for a few weeks or months and gave supplementary income to those who owned houses respectable enough to offer lodging. Boarding led to "summering," which often led in turn to the establishment of a second home and to retirement.

When Elizabeth Prentiss first came to town with her husband to rent rooms for the summer, she wrote to a cousin, "We are enchanted with Dorset. We are so near the woods and mountains that we go every day and spend hours wandering about among them."[2]

The Prentisses had taken previous summer retreats in Williamstown, Massachusetts, and comparisons were inevitable. Dorset's virtues were so appealingly superior that Elizabeth hoped nobody else would find the place. She wrote prophetically: "If there is any difference, I think this place even more beautiful than Williamstown; it suits us better as a summer retreat, from its great seclusion. I am, that is we are, mean enough to want to keep it as quiet and secluded as it is now, by not letting people know how nice it is; a very few fashionably dressed people would just spoil it for us."

A few days later she wrote to a friend in Europe:

We are perfectly delighted with Dorset; the sweet seclusion is most soothing, and the house is very pleasant. Mr. and Mrs. F. [Mr. and Mrs. Charles Field] are intelligent, agreeable people, and do all they can to make us comfortable. The mountains are so near that I hear the crows cawing in the trees. We are making pretty things and pressing an unheard-of quantity of ferns. We go to the woods regularly every morning and stay the whole forenoon. In the afternoon we rest, read, write, etc.; sometimes we drive and always after tea George walks with me about two miles . . . I wish you could see my room. Every pretty thing grows here and has come to cheer and beautify it. The woods are everywhere, and as for the views, oh my child!

The Prentisses also passed the summer of 1867 in rented rooms. (The languid term "pass the summer" was favored by Elizabeth, and later by many others.) As summer waned, Dorset's charms intensified, and yet the couple decided that they had grown "rather tired of boarding." Elizabeth wrote to her cousin about an idea that would prove contagious: "We have had our heads full, all summer, of building a little cottage here. We are having a plan made, and have about fixed on a lot. . . . [Dorset] is a lovely spot, and the people are as intelligent as in any other parts of New England."

By August 4, 1868, the project was well under way, and Elizabeth wrote, "Our house proves to be far prettier and more tasteful than I supposed." On August 13 she added: "Our house isn't done, and what fun to watch it grow, to discuss its merits and demerits, to grab every check that comes in from magazines and elsewhere, and turn it into chairs and tables and beds and blankets! . . . Mr. P. is unusually well. His house is the apple of his eye, and he is renewing his youth. Thus far the project has done him a world of good."

In the book he wrote after Elizabeth died, George Prentiss described his wife's state of mind in the summer of 1871: "Early in June, accompanied by the three younger children, she went to Dorset. This change always put her into a glow of pleasurable emotion. Once out of the city, she was like a bird let loose from its cage."

But for all the words they wrote, neither Elizabeth nor George Prentiss contributed much social observation. Her unceasing focus was the serenity and scenery that gave her comfort and pleasure, and the primary concern he expressed was for her happiness. Their writing offers little commentary about the realities of post-Civil-War Dorset, and only a few condescending remarks about the natives. Mr. Prentiss summarized their final decade of idyllic summers together:

For the next ten summers [starting in 1868] the Dorset home was to be her sweet haven of rest from the agitations, cares, and turmoil of New York life. It seemed at the time a venturesome, almost a rash thing, to build it; but when she left it for her home above, the building of the house seemed to have been an inspiration of Providence while contributing greatly to her happiness, it probably added several years to her life. The four months which she passed each season at Dorset were spent largely in the open air, and in such varied and pleasant exercise as exerted the most healthful, soothing influence upon both body and soul. It was just this fruit her husband hoped might by the blessing of Heaven, blossom out of the new home, and in later years he used often to say to her, that if the place should be of a sudden annihilated, he should still feel that it had paid for itself many times over.

Elizabeth finally moved heavenward from her summer residence on August 16, 1878, in her sixtieth year, and Mr. Pratt conducted the funeral. Her widower never disclosed the nature of her illness—the Victorian Age eschewed candor about such matters—but from his account of her lingering months it would seem to have been cancer, for the malaise went on poignantly for several chapters.

Elizabeth Prentiss may have been the first person "mean enough to want to keep Dorset as quiet and secluded as it is now," though that sort of expression became almost an axiom for succeeding summerers. Each person who crosses Dorset's threshold wants, in one way or another, to close the door behind and keep things *just* the way they are.

The Selling of Dorset

An effort to sell Dorset began in the hard times of the 1890s and lasted on and off into the 1920s, mostly by means of three diminutive booklets that extolled the virtues of seasonal residence. The "Dorset, Vermont, as a Summer Home" pamphlets were published by Richard Marston Campbell, who had arrived in town in 1886 at the age of five, a member of one of the earliest "city people" families to settle permanently—and the first in town to install an indoor bathroom.

Campbell wrote a preface for his Dorset-selling pamphlet, included some history, and listed the town's attractions. There were directories of furnished houses and rooms for rent, hotels, boarding houses, livery stables, grocery stores, personal services, and church and physician (one of each).

The first edition, 22 pages long, undated, was printed by H. Stowell of Troy, New York. A clue to the year was a reference to the American victory at the Battle of Bennington in 1777, "at length worthily commemorated by the grand monument recently dedicated in Bennington." That ceremony was in August 1891.

The second 22-page edition, covered with a novelty paper resembling birchbark, bore the imprint of the Tuttle Company of Rutland and was dated April 2, 1900. It included a description of the Dorset Field Club.

Campbell's third booklet, printed by Mirror Printing Co. of Danby, was

A cottage at Emerald Lake in North Dorset, as pictured on a 1908 postal card mailed to Henry G. Stone in Peru, Vermont. Since 1960 Emerald Lake has been a Vermont state park.

dated April 14, 1904. Its 36 pages offered data about the new Manchester, Dorset & Granville Railroad, then "in process of construction." Rail connections were listed for cities throughout the Northeast, the Midwest, and Canada.

These three ambitious booklets constitute a kind of mirror that reflects what Dorset thought about itself at midpoint in its history. Times had been rough during the unstable era between Civil War Reconstruction and the Crash of 1893. Locally the Gay Nineties economy had faltered and there was reason to engage in civic boosterism.

By contrast, the years immediately after the Civil War had been prosperous for Dorset, when much of the rest of Vermont was demoralized by a sluggish economy, worrisome outmigration, manpower depletion, and population stagnation. But Dorset's postwar marble business thrived, and the 1870 census recorded the town's all-time maximum, 2,195. The population in 1860 reached 2,000 for the first time, but by 1890 it would slip to 1,696, then drop in 1900 to 1,477—a severe decline for a town of such stability.

Among the 2,005 Dorset residents counted in the 1880 census, *Child's Bennington County Gazette and Directory* listed 609 heads of household, including 200 engaged in farming and 181 quarriers or marble workers. Most of the

Courtesy of Mrs. James Lynch

In the late 1880s "the Society for Silly Scenes and Solemn Demeanor, Dorset Chapter," took up the fad of barn-back riding. This exercise was appropriate for preparing young people for life in the Victorian age. Note that only males are "riding the ridge." The photo was taken by Henry Prentiss, known for his careful and humorous poses.

marble industry's noise, dust, and commotion took place up in the mountains or near South Dorset at the quarry later known as Norcross-West—out of sight and hearing of residents of the secluded village sometimes known as "Dorset Corners." The villages of South Dorset, North Dorset, and "south village" (of East Dorset) did not figure heavily in the business of appealing to summer people, though East Dorset, with a main highway and railroad, attracted its share.

The "Historical" pages of Campbell's brochures were signed "P.S.P.," which meant Parsons Stuart Pratt, minister of the Dorset church from 1856 to 1896. It is valuable to review Pratt's account, both to savor his writing style and to understand the values he chose to emphasize at the time of his retirement, having served the same church for forty years. Through a veil of patriotism, sentiment, and advanced age, Pratt acknowledged the departure of some of the most able native Dorseters, who found more fertile fields elsewhere yet often returned to "the scenes of their childhood with rapturous delight." He wrote:

The township of Dorset lies on the highest point of valley land midway between New York and Montreal, and here within a stone's throw are the headwaters of both the Hud-

son and St. Lawrence Rivers.

The years of a century and a quarter have passed since it began to emerge from the primeval wilderness; happily there remains enough of the forest to adorn the hills, enrich the valley, and afford a grateful shade to many of our pathways.

The pioneers of civilized life, in 1768, were of the Pilgrim stock, who had first moved up from the Atlantic coast into Central Massachusetts and Connecticut, and thence, after a century's growth, needing more room, pushed up northward into Vermont, and westward into New York.

Victorian-era visitors at the entrance to the Freedley quarry, 1883.

In this natural flow of emigration, there was an eddying play in the sheltered valleys under the shadow of the continuous Green Mountain range on the east, and the rich marble hills of the Taconic range on the west. Just above the junction of two of these valleys, near Manchester, lies the parish of Dorset, on the old track of travel from Bennington to Skeensborough or Whitehall, and Ticonderoga.

Here, in olden time, a few Connecticut families, seeking new fields of enterprise, stuck their stakes and built their cabins.

After a few years of effective toil with ax and plow, occasion was given for taking up musket and knapsack, and in the Revolution they set the brave example which, eighty years later, was nobly followed by the Green Mountain boys in the war for the Union.

The general struggle for Independence being fairly instituted, these and other towns of the New Hampshire grants, seeing the necessity for an organized statehood and the *safeguard of laws made and enforced by the people, proceeded to organize the present State of Vermont. This was effected by the decisive action of two representative conventions on the two sides of the Green Mountains, the first being held at Cephas Kent's tavern in Dorset, in September, 1776 . . . The old site of this tavern is now as attractive for its scenery as it is noted for its history.*

In passing over the two parallel roads of the main valley, or rising into the recesses of the mountains, it is grateful to recall at every old homestead the name of some sturdy pioneer who gave name and character to the locality, or of children who, worthy of their sires and as genuine New Englanders, have found and filled useful spheres in the republic. Of this neighborhood, under the inspiration of these free airs and grand hills, and of these hallowed scenes of patriotic service, there are not a few who, from the author's or artist's studios, from the pulpit or platform, as skilled teachers or effective leaders in the State, the army or the church, have helped notably to make our country strong and true and happy.

Nor do Dorset's true sons and daughters, however successful or honored elsewhere, fail of enthusiastic and perpetual love for the noble heights and dear shades of their native town. Every season brings back some to revisit the scenes of their childhood with rapturous delight. And natives of other states and lands, some of rare gifts and graces, having once penetrated to our quiet valley, are ready to confess "the half had not been told them," and to yield their perpetual allegiance.

An essay by Helen Smith Snyder told about the old Jackson homestead south of the village green, where the Reverend William Jackson, for many years pastor of the Dorset church, resided and from whence his daughter, Henrietta Jackson Hamlin, left "to carry the Good Tidings to heathen lands." It described the durable legend of Henrietta's Elm.

Mrs. Snyder boasted of prominent residents, summer and otherwise, as follows:

The church stands on the street running east and west. Across the way is the Pratt Manse, the home of Rev. P. S. Pratt, D.D., who was, for more than forty years, pastor of the Dorset church.

On the western outskirts of the village we find "The Hemlocks" (Mrs. James Lee) many years the home of the late Simeon Pease Cheney, one of the sweet singers of America, whose bird music made his name famous in the musical world. This is now the summer home of Prof. Albert Baker Cheney of Boston. A little further on is Prentiss pond and the old grist mill. A quarter of a mile beyond stood the old Farwell Inn (Bea Jackson Humphreys), with sign 1777, now Blue Rock Spring cottage and owned by Mr. George F. Kellogg.

During the past few years Dorset has become quite a summer resort. A club-house and several summer homes have been built here. Just west of the church is the summer home of Mr. Allan Bourn, Yonkers, N.Y. The cottage—commanding a fine view of Saddleback and Giant's Arm-chair—with its beautiful lawn, adds much to the beauty of the village (now, much enlarged, the Dorset Colony House). On the opposite side of the road a few rods further to the west is "Kauinfels," the summer home of the late Rev. Dr. Prentiss, whose sainted wife is well known as the author of Stepping Heavenward. *The Prentiss family still own the property and spend the summer months in Dorset.*

A half mile north of the village is another beautiful summer home—that of Miss de Nottbeck of New York City. The house is built on high ground and overlooks valley and mountain for miles.

The road by the Jackson homestead winds eastward into "Dorset Hollow." A charming drive of two miles brings us to "Owl's Head Dairy Farm" (Fred Streeter) owned by Rev. J.H. Potts of Philadelphia, Pa. Two miles further on is "Glen Farm" (Mr. and Mrs. George Wallace) belonging to Rev. S. M. Warren of Boston, Mass., who is making a little Eden of the upper end of the Hollow. Mr. Edwin Child, a New York artist, has a summer cottage (Mrs. Justus DeVries) near "Glen Farm."

A half mile west of the village we come to the "West Road." This was the old State road between Bennington and Burlington and some of the mile-stones are still standing; one opposite Mr. E. Simmons' bears the inscription "XXIX MILES B" [29 miles to Bennington].

About three-fourths of a mile south of "Kellogg's Corner" is "The Maples" (Mr. and Mrs. Arthur Gilbert), a fine residence, built and occupied for a time by the late Rev. Matthew Gates, now the summer home of Prof. George H. Gilbert of Northampton, Mass. Prof. Owen Gates of Andover, Mass., has a summer cottage just north of "The Maples" (now owned by Harold Gates, his son).

A little further south on this road stood the old Kent tavern, where the first "Council of Safety" met. "Westover" (Mr. and Mrs. Raymond Kopituk) the beautiful summer home of Mrs. Harriet Humphrey of New York, was originally the site of the old Kent tavern.

A quarter mile south of Westover stands the old Holley house, and adjacent to it is the "Ethan Allen Spring" (Mr. and Mrs. Warren Crawford).

Past and present associations make this little place attractive to our city friends, and each year brings to the village and neighboring farm houses the familiar faces of those who consider Dorset their summer home. Strangers are cordially welcomed and here find rest and enjoyment.

Roads around Dorset were "in splendid condition for cycling and driving, being hard and smooth," according to Campbell's booklets. His suggested bicycle destinations were "East Rupert Square" through the "dugway," "Kent Lane," and "Armstrong Square." Longer driving routes included Arlington, Manchester (stopping for dinner at the Equinox House), Pawlet, Lake St. Catherine, Peru, and Salem, New York. Points of interest included marble quarries and mountain trails.

A photograph of the Norcross-West marble quarry accompanied John Fisher's description of the town's chief industry:

> *Strange as it may seem, right on the site where Isaac Underhill opened his quarry in 1785 are now in operation the most extensive quarrying interests in the state, owned and operated by the Norcross-West Marble Co., employing more than 200 skilled quarrymen, producing white, light gray and green variegated marble, the latter very much like the famous Italian Cippolino. They have now under contract the New York public library building, the Harvard Medical School building, Jefferson Colbridge House, Boston, Mass., the Phipps House, New York City, besides the interior of several bank buildings, in all amounting to about 800,000 cubic feet.*
>
> *The company has a 16-gang stone mill at Manchester Depot, and in addition have leased the S. F. Prince and Kent & Root mills at South Dorset, which are in operation day and night sawing marble. The mills and quarry are situated on the line of the Manchester, Dorset & Granville Railroad, and the quarry is one and one-half miles from Dorset village. Mr. Spafford H. West, vice president and general manager, and son, Mr. Ernest H. West, secretary of the company, reside in Dorset. They may be found at their office at the quarry and are always pleased to show visitors about their works, where can be seen in operation the latest devices for quarrying marble.*

The Campbell booklets informatively listed boarding houses and furnished rooms. Under "Houses to Rent—Furnished" was a cottage described as one-eighth mile from post office, offering twelve rooms, bathroom, running water, fine views, and shade; its proprietor was identified only as "C.N." Another was that of Mrs. W. R. Dunton, next door to the telephone office and "one minute to postoffice and Club House." She offered twelve rooms thoroughly furnished, with large piazza, large lawn, shade, bathroom, and hot and cold water.

George F. Kellogg advertised his "Blue Rock Spring Cottage, corner Church street and West road, one-half mile from post office; 13 rooms, bathroom, hot and cold water (W.C.) ice house, fine shade and lawn." No prices were listed for houses, but for "Furnished Rooms" rents were given. Mrs. John Fisher on South Main Street offered three rooms, four minutes from post office, for $2 to $3 a week. The number of "minutes from post office" figured heavily in these ads, and prices ranged from $2 to $4 a week, plus board. Others who offered rooms were R. W. Weeks at "Jackson Park" (in

The Dorset Inn, circa 1900, when it was known as the Washington Hotel. The photo shows six sturdy maples and eleven columns.

front of the Barrows House), Mrs. George Weeks, H. B. Kent, E. L. Holley, Mrs. F. D. Graham, and Rollin Sykes, all along Main Street; Mrs. J. H. Sheldon, Mrs. T. Collins, and Mrs. A. B. Roberts, all on Church Street, and Miss Roberts in Dorset Hollow.

The only hotels were the Dorset Inn, which could hold thirty-five, and Barrows House, with accommodations for twenty-five. At the Dorset Inn, rates were $2 a day or $10 to $14 a week. "Table board" was $7 a week. "Special attention given to the table" promised Western meats and delicacies in season. An "N. B." advised: "Modern sanitary improvements." The original booklet listed G. H. Barrows as proprietor of the Dorset Inn, but a rubber stamp corrected it to say that Edwin O. Talbot was now manager.

At the Barrows House, with Experience W. Barrows as proprietor, terms were $10 to $12 a week, with table board an additional $7. N. B.: "Special attention given to the traveling public and driving parties," and livery services were offered.

At nine boarding houses listed, terms ranged from $6 to $8 a week. Mrs. William W. Phelps appealed to bargain hunters with her Woodbine Cottage, two miles north of the village on West Road, for only $4 to $6 a week.

Boarding houses sported fanciful names. Miss Marcia K. Gray advertised her "Outlook Villa" on Main Street as "a home of rest for Christian peo-

The Wade Inn and tennis court, circa 1910. This was later the home of Dr. and Mrs. Donald Bashaw in the 1950s. Marjorie Niles and her sister Elsie made their "Aunt Maria's Cookies" here which sold nationally in the 1950s and 1960s.

ple" and said she could accommodate eighteen at terms of "$7 and upward." One-third mile south of the post office, Mrs. Sarah Connell said her "Sunset Cottage" could take six to eight persons at $6 to $8 a week. A half-mile south of the post office was "Comfort Farm" of Mrs. C.N. Williams, who offered a private livery and accommodations for eight to ten.

Mrs. William Kelley in the Hollow knew how to advertise: "Valley View Farm, in heart of Green Mountains, magnificent views, good, bountiful table, pure spring water, and large rooms. Terms, $6 to $8 per week. Can accommodate 20 people. Best of New York and Boston references. Private livery connected. Two and one-half miles from postoffice. R.F.D. daily."

Other West Road boarding houses were "Maplehurst," owned by Mrs. J. F. Lillie, and Mrs. H. E. Snyder's "Fairview Farm." A note made clear that "boarding houses one mile or more out of the village are in communication twice daily."

Livery stables were those of Baker & Sheldon, J. H. Sheldon, Henry B. Kent, E. W. Barrows, George H. Barrows, and John Fisher. Available from any of these were "single, double, three or four seated carriages for transferring baggage to and from railway station." J. H. Sheldon specified "safe horses for ladies."

Under "Town Directory" there was only one church, the Congregational, with services at 10:45 A.M. and 7:30 P.M.; Christian Endeavor at 6:45 P.M., and Sunday School at 12:15 P.M. The pastor was the Reverend Charles L. Carhart. The physician in 1904 was Dr. F. C. Liddle. The all-important post office, with A. M. Chapman, postmaster, had mails arriving at 9 and 11 A.M. and 5:30 P.M., with outgoing mails at 9:30 A.M., 5:30 P.M. and 6 P.M.

Dorset's self-sufficiency was evident in products and services available not only at commercial establishments but also through ordinary citizens and farmers. J. M. Armstrong (Dorset Alley), G. M. Sykes (Peltier's), and McClaughlin & Tully owned and ran commercial groceries. Each offered something of interest to the affluent. Armstrong's had Equinox champagne and mineral waters, as well as "soda water drawn from a Tuft's Arctic Foundation." Sykes's advertised "Lowney's bon-bons, in one-half and one pound boxes," and McLaughlin & Tully had the best brands of five-cent and ten-cent cigars as well as "bottled mineral waters, ginger ale, root beer, etc., delivered by the case." All three had telephone service.

The Dorset Grist Mill, established in 1876, was "sole agent for Granola, the oldest and best health food in existence," and did custom grinding of corn, oats, feed, middlings, bran, and fine table cornmeal and flour. The A. B. Roberts Store boasted flour, feed, lime, plaster, chicken food, fine clover honey, and maple syrup.

The H. N. Williams Store appealed by renting bicycles by the hour, day, or week, along with mileage books, and also guns and ammunition. William Williams Sons were harness makers, with horse and stable furnishings of all descriptions.

Many residents sold milk, butter, cheese, poultry, vegetables in season, maple syrup and sugar, dry stove wood, and cord wood. F. D. Graham of South Main Street did painting, paper hanging, kalsomining, and interior finishing, with "estimates cheerfully furnished on all grades of work."

Mrs. M. Stannard, Mrs. E. Towsley, Mrs. M.D. Chapman, Mrs. C. A. Towslee, and Mrs. Mary Phelps all took in laundry. "Basket leaves Sykes' store every Wednesday; returns Saturday." Meat carts arrived from Manchester, South Dorset, and Pawlet three times a week in season, and fruit and fish wagons twice a week.

Finally, the 1904 Dorset booklet promoted rail travel to and from Manchester Depot. The fare from the Dorset quarries to Manchester Depot via the Manchester, Dorset and Granville Railroad was 15 cents, and a twice-daily stage ran between those points for 50 cents. To go to Boston via the Rutland Railroad cost $5.50. The fare to New York via Troy boat was $3.08, and by way of New York Central & Hudson River Railroad was $4.73. It cost $3.00 to go to Burlington, $11.23 to Washington, D.C., $18.50 to Chicago.

The Field Club

The first edition of Campbell's brochures ignored the Dorset Field Club, but his 1900 version included it and appealed to visitors' more hedonistic instincts:

> This club was organized in the summer of '96 [sic] by several young men from New York and Troy and became popular at once. The purpose of the club is to furnish amusement, at a small expense to each, for the many summer visitors to Dorset.

Terry Tyler collection.

Woodruff Hall was built in 1896 for the Dorset Field Club, founded in 1886. This picture dates to the 1920s.

The dancing hall is large and roomy, and, with its hard wood floor, laid expressly for dancing, and its ample fire place, is a favorite resort each evening, while from the broad, cool piazzas during the day a magnificent view of the towering mountains and quiet valley may be obtained, in fact the view from the club grounds is one of the finest anywhere in the Green Mountains. The Hall in the club has a stage, piano and shuffleboard, while on the grounds about the house tennis courts and croquet grounds have been laid out, surrounded by velvety lawns.

The club supports and controls the Dorset Golf Links, situate about three minutes walk from the Club House. The natural lay of the land of the Dorset Links makes them at once attractive for Golfing. There are natural bunkers and water hazards, also hills to loft over, and through the long levels one will find a splendid chance to use the "brassy."

Campbell's third edition reassured golfers that no great physical exertion was really required; it described the first "Tee" as just north of the Club House, and the ninth hole was about "seventy-five feet northeast of the Club House porch."

To bolster its reputation as the nation's oldest golf course, the Field Club's centennial history, prepared for publication in 1988, claimed that it was founded in 1886, not "the summer of '96," as Campbell wrote. The following data are condensed from *Dorset Field Club Centennial: The First Hundred Years* by Phebe Ann Lewis and Lawrence Thompson, which in turn, drew heavily upon a history of the club prepared in 1974 by Gilbert G. Sykes.

Competitors for the title of "first" golf course in the nation include some holes laid out in 1884 by a Philadelphia Quaker, Joseph Micklen Fox, on his estate in Foxburg, Pennsylvania, which became a nine-hole course in 1887; a course in Sarasota, Florida, established in 1887, which closed; and the St. Andrews Golf Club, formed in 1887 in Yonkers, New York, and later moved to Hastings-on-Hudson.

Golf was played in Dorset as early as 1881 when Arvin W. Harrington, "assisted by a crowd of thugs, touts and loafers," laid out rough greens centered with tomato cans on Pinnacle Hill. An early course map was dated by Harrington "Monday, Sept. 13, 1886." The late Connie Harrington, widow of Harrington's nephew Roland "Hoke" Harrington, remembered her uncle in 1987 as "the kind of man who made things happen. He was a self-taught artist, too, and a good one."

On that day Harrington laid out a nine-hole course spreading over the pastures of the Edgerton, Edson Holley, and Sykes farms, and the 1886 date is cited to prove the "first in the nation" claim. Original founders of the Dorset Golf Links were listed, giving their winter residences:

Allan Bourne, N.Y., New York Central RR
Richard M. Campbell, Troy, N.Y.
James C. Chapin, Troy, N.Y.
Ransom H. Gillett, Troy, N.Y., lawyer
Arvin Harrington, Troy, N.Y., first president
Joe H. Harrington, Troy, N.Y., lumber
George B. Harrison, Troy, N.Y.
Fred B. Hawley, Troy, N.Y., hardware
S. Frank Holley, New York, N.Y., importer
W.E. Kent, Dorset, Vt., livery
Charles H. Keys, New York, N.Y., department store
O.P. Lipscomb, Troy, N.Y.

George Lewis Prentiss, New York, N.Y., clock manufacturer
Henry S. Woodruff, Dorset, Vt.

Woodruff, who also had a home in Montclair, New Jersey, made a large gift to start a clubhouse fund. So the Dorset Field Club, with clubhouse, tennis court, and croquet ground, formally opened in August 1896. But Henry S. Woodruff died before he ever saw Woodruff Hall, which was named in his memory.

Treasurer J. Frank Holley announced rates as $15 for a family male adult season ticket, $8 for one month, $5 for two weeks, $3 for a week, and 50 cents each day for any time of less than a week. "Ladies and boy minors at one-half the above rates." No game could be played for money in the clubhouse, a rule still in force; and no game of any kind could be played in clubhouse or grounds on Sunday—a rule not still in force. The Dorset Inn and Barrows House introduced guests for a fee.

By 1897 cots were provided for the roomless, and the *Manchester Journal* reported that "all who come once come again and bring others with them."

Ladies of the club held teas, clock-golf, and putting tournaments; bridge, whist, shuffleboard, and dancing were enjoyed during the week. Picnics were held at Hagar's Brook, Lake St. Catherine, and Emerald Lake. The club fielded a baseball team to challenge the Dorset Nine. Saturday night entertainment often featured Ernest H. West, known for his mandolin solos.

In the late 1890s the course was lengthened, so the lineup of holes was as follows:

1.	Bitter Sweet	335 yards
2.	Orchard	307
3.	Elm Tree	221
4.	Hemlock	215
5.	Edgerton's	278
6.	Holley Hill	153
7.	Windhurst	225
8.	Taconic	208
9.	Goats Loose	375
	Total	2,314

Annual matches began in 1901 when the club defeated a team from Bennington's Mt. Anthony Club 11–10, and in 1902 Manchester's Ekwanok defeated the Dorseters 24–2. More ladies tucked up their skirts to play.

In his 1974 history of the club Gilbert "Gib" Sykes told of the first groundskeeper, Grant Matson, "who superbly drained swamps and actually developed the first 'gang mower,' drawn at first by Frank Streeter's team of horses before Henry Ford invented his tractor." The horses wore wide rubber shoes to minimize damage to the turf. Matson stayed with the club from 1904 until Labor Day 1937.

The Fourth of July always began the social season as a day of sport, ending with a dance. Members shared chores such as cleanup, laying tennis tapes, and painting the clubhouse. A second tennis court was added.

In 1910 a challenge to see how many words could be made from the fifteen letters of DORSETFIELDCLUB was won by Miss M. K. Warren in the adult class, with 667 words, and Miss Louisa Reynolds, for those age 16 and under, with 578.

During the teens the first golf pro, "the plump and genial Harry Rawlins," was hired away from the Manchester Hillside Club, part of which later became the Equinox Golf Course. Born of British parents in Bombay, Rawlins was a brother of Horace, first U.S. Open champion.

In 1912 the club hosted the Vermont State Golf Tournament, won by Frederick A. Martin of Ekwanok, and many golf and tennis tournaments followed. Social events included chaperoned hayrides, camping trips, picnics, Monday night auction bridge parties, weekly teas, and evening entertainment. More local residents joined the summer people at the club, and in August 1915, with three permanent cups, the First Annual Invitational Tournament was launched. Results were reported in the *New York Times*: "Archibald G. McIlwaine of Hartford, Conn., all but lost the match to F. T. Clark of Ekwanok . . . He won by a single putt."

In World War I Dorset's Boys Brigade drilled and skirmished on the course under direction of William G. Barrows, Sr. and young Sargent Child. Their maneuvers were "deservedly applauded by a large number of spectators." In March 1918 the Board of Governors reincorporated the club as a nonprofit entity. The year 1919 was a record season, with tournaments and a masquerade party.

During the Depression a financial crisis was averted by officers Ernest H. West, president; E. R. Brumley, vice-president; and Perry Peltier, treasurer, with the assistance of R. Bartlett Arkell of Manchester, Ryland Lockwood, and Barrows. In 1933 the club leased the Vermont Marble Company quarries for swimming but found that supervision was impossible, and the lease was not renewed. In 1936 local boy Charles Kinney was engaged as pro, and in 1937 the first President's Cup Tournament was held.

Playing of golf waned during World War II. The clubhouse was used weekly in July and August for community Red Cross sewing sessions, and parties raised funds for the British-American Ambulance Corps Fund and war relief. The Dorset Home Guard drilled on the golf course, and ladies of the club held a Victory Exchange, with proceeds going to sellers in savings stamps and war bonds. There was no pro or caddymaster during the war.

After the war R. M. Campbell, Mrs. Mark Barbour, Mr. and Mrs. A. W. Harrington, and Perry Peltier were named life members: William G. Barrows, Sr., was added in 1957, Anne Sykes in 1984.

In 1951 the governors installed a small bar for members and guests. Among the first volunteer bartenders was West Road resident Lincoln Isham, Abraham Lincoln's great-grandson. New clubhouse flooring was laid, the old stage was removed, and the Millard estate was purchased so the club might own the fifth and sixth holes and part of the seventh rather than lease them.

Labor Day 1952 ended "the biggest golf season since the club was inaugurated . . . hardly a moment when there was not something scheduled. The new feature was a hole-in-one tournament played on the first hole, floodlighted for the occasion," the *Journal* reported.

In the 1960s there were the usual contests on the Fourth of July and Labor Day, new Pro-Am tournaments, a Flaming Maple event, Grandfathers' and Grandmothers' Tournaments (with a prize of a rocking chair, proceeds going to the Dorset Nursing Association). Carts replaced caddies, then electric carts were introduced, and a storage building was added to shelter them. Consultants from the U.S. Golf Association recommended that the course control Japanese beetles, flies, and "pesky starlings" and install a watering system from Prentiss Brook, a practice putting green, and a turf nursery. Berry Wall raised $700 and he and his sons planted willows, locusts, and colorful mountain ash along the fairways. Tennis star Don Budge visited in 1961.

After a kitchen explosion and fire on October 22, 1968, damaged the clubhouse and burned manager Peter Palmer, major renovations were carried out by architect Fritz Dillmann, engineer Arthur Groves, and builder Dave Beckwith. Among the $40,000 worth of improvements were a larger kitchen and serving facilities. The Carl Parsons Tennis Tournament, an annual doubles competition for men over 40, was established in 1974 in memory of a member who had died a year earlier on the paddle tennis courts. The tournament of July Fourth 1976 was dedicated to Victor Bennett, whose final report as tennis chairman deplored the insufficient number of courts. In 1975 a prize was given in memory of Michael Fay for the winner of the club's Junior Golf Championship. In 1976 the Board of Governors elected the first woman president, Carol E. McNealus.

The Fourth of July 1978 marked the end of annual fireworks displays; deemed unsafe and impractical, they inflicted damage to the course and caused highway congestion. But July Fourth picnics continued, attended by two to three hundred members and guests. And all looked forward to holding the club's one hundredth anniversary party—with fireworks—on July 4, 1986.

The unstoppable Campbell, who sometimes gave his name as Richard M. and sometimes as R. Marston, was still active during the Calvin Coolidge era. His Board of Trade printed one more modest pamphlet, titled "Dorset Among the Mountains Green, Vermont." Officers were William G. Barrows, president, George N. Chambers, vice-president, and Campbell secretary-treasurer and publicity agent. There was a brief directory for vacationers, but as if to excuse its brevity the pamphlet said, "We started to describe it for your benefit. We simply can not do it. YOU will have to come and see this wonderful valley and its more wonderful hills yourself."

Hotels in 1924 were "Ye Dorset Inn" with Miss Amy Ann Lapham as manager, Barrows House, with William G. Barrows as manager, and the Wade Inn, Charles A. Wade, proprietor. Dr. Liddle was still the town physician in 1924 but two churches were acknowledged: the Congregational, with the Reverend William L. Haven, and the Roman Catholic in East Dorset, with the Reverend E. C. Fontaine. The post office had cut service to two mails a day.

Dorset's 1924 attractions were described as follows: "First, the Pure Mountain Air and the Wonderful Scenery; second, the freedom of the social life and its informal simplicity; Artists, Authors, Divines, Bankers, Physicians, Lawyers, Manufacturers, Merchants and Educators are all represented and all unite in singing the praises of Dorset and its wonderful attractions. Like Niagara Falls, it grows on one as one takes in its Natural Beauties."

Four Memorable Women

Zephine Humphrey (1874–1956), author of more than a dozen books, underwent a self-described progression from "boarder" in the village with her mother and sister, to "summer person" who first rented a house and then bought it (still spending winters in New York or New Haven), to permanent resident.

Zephine Humphrey's affinity for Dorset came through inheritance and the desire of her widowed mother to return home.[3] Her mother was Harriette "Hattie" Sykes, a daughter of Hiram Sykes; the family had moved to East Rupert when she was small. Zephine's unusual first name was a feminized version of that of her father, Zephaniah Moore Humphrey, the fifth and youngest son of Heman Humphrey, who was the second president of Amherst College, from 1823 to 1845. Her father was named for the first president of Amherst, Zephaniah Swift Moore, who died unexpectedly in 1823 after founding the college and heading it for only two years.

Harriet Sykes Humphrey was born in Dorset July 5, 1832, and Zephaniah M. Humphrey was born in Amherst on August 30, 1824. They were married April 20, 1853, in Westfield, New York. Because Mr. Humphrey was a Presbyterian clergyman, they moved often. The Humphreys suffered the loss of their first four children, three daughters and a son, before Zephine was born on December 15, 1874, when her mother was forty-three and her father fifty-one. The couple lived in Milwaukee, Chicago, Philadelphia—where Zephine was born—and then Cincinnati, where Humphrey became a professor at Lane Theological Seminary. In Cincinnati, when Zephine was six, her father died of pneumonia. She and her mother and a younger sister moved to Lake Forest, Illinois, where Zephine grew up.

Zephine first saw Dorset at the age of thirteen when they visited an aunt, Rhoda Sykes. In 1893, when she entered Smith College, her mother accompanied her to Northampton and opened a boarding house. On graduating in 1896, Zephine sailed for Europe with her mother and sister, and they stayed two years. Returning to Dorset in 1898, at the time R. M. Campbell was promoting the town through booklets, she found that conditions had changed, and wrote:

> *The village had grown, and had begun to take on a certain modest air of a summer resort. Nothing showy, and all very well; we were glad to have the town prosper.*

Dorset Historical Society

Zephine Humphrey Fahnestock (1874-1956), author of many books including The Story of Dorset *in 1924. Others of her books relating to the town are* Over Against Green Peak *and* The Beloved Community.

We had built a great many imaginary houses in Dorset before we began to turn our attention to an old place which was for sale—house and barn and orchard—outside the village, on the edge of the meadows.

The house was none other than the renovated Cephas Kent inn. They first rented it, then bought it in January 1901. In May they returned to it after a final winter in New Haven and installed a furnace and a bathroom, applied wallpaper and carpeting, built a wide piazza, bought a horse, and devoted much time to gardening. Describing "our Dorset life" in *Recollections of My Mother*, Zephine wrote:

We were often like three children, playing together, experimenting with strange new customs and expedients. For my mother, the garden and orchard and meadow; for my sister [who remains unnamed throughout the book] the broom and dustcloth; for me, the barn and the kitchen; for all of us, the problems and amenities of country social life. Yet, underneath the amusement, there was an ever deepening, widening love which was graver than we suspected. . . . The time was to come when we were to find ourselves fettered beyond all reason by these roots of ours.

They received visitors in the garden at teatime on Fridays during summer, endured their first Dorset winter with its 25-below-zero cold, and closed off all rooms but three to conserve heat. It took a few more seasons to embrace Vermont winters. During the winter of 1903 they took a train to California and the Arizona desert, but on return Zephine wrote: "Personally I found its life irksome and have never been so homesick anywhere as I was there."

They wintered in New York City in a boarding hotel, the Weston, and Mrs. Humphrey considered buying a winter house in New Haven. But they made the cold adjustment and Zephine wrote about it in *Over Against Green Peak*:

Our attitude towards the community changed entirely from the day when we bought the old white house. It was strange how the vision altered at once; we seemed to be looking with different eyes. Before, we had studied the country people as characters, oddities, types, smiling at them, though not unkindly, viewing them at long range; now, on a sudden, they were our people, or rather we were suing to be admitted as their people; love was born in us. I dare say, for their part, their view of us underwent reciprocal alteration. The summer boarder is a strange type to the rustic mind. Not all at once did our neighbors open out the heart of their kindly favor to us; they had need to wait a little and see what manner of people we were, to test our sincerity. That was well. I think we liked them better for their careful reserve.

"Summer People" 215

One of Dorset's most memorable regular "summer people" was Miss Cecelia deNottbeck, sometimes misremembered as "Countess" deNottbeck. She was a great-granddaughter of John Jacob Astor and had no reason to be worried about finances. Her father was John deNottbeck, New York consul general representing Czar Nicholas of Russia. The family was descended from Finnish noblemen.

General deNottbeck died in 1861 after falling from a horse while riding in Central Park; Cecelia, born in 1854, was only seven at the time. Educated in England and France, she read and spoke French, Russian, Finnish, and German as well as English. She could also read her Greek New Testament.

Miss deNottbeck came to Dorset through her affiliation with the First Reformed Episcopal Church in New York and friendship with Bishop Robert L. Rudolph (the father of Robert K. Rudolph), who was then its assistant minister.[4] She and her lifelong friend, Miss Harriet L. Edwards, seeking a place that resembled the English countryside, first boarded at the home of Ada Pratt Sherman, daughter of Parsons S. Pratt. These visitors liked Pratt's preaching, as well as that of Dr. George L. Prentiss, premiere Dorset summer resident who was then pastor of the Princeton Presbyterian Church.

About 1895, after buying the seventy-four-acre farm of Cornelia Viall opposite the Dorset Golf Links (Walter Dane), Miss deNottbeck built her manor house near the knoll known as The Pinnacle, and began acquiring other property. In 1896 she purchased a house and grounds (Mrs. Albert Evans) from A. B. and M. Alta Roberts next to the golf course, prepared the house

Courtesy of Janet Gilbert

A 1910 postcard view of "The Pinnacle," a stone tower located on high ground in Dorset village east of Route 30. It was built for Cecelia deNottbeck on her property, now owned by Robert Keeler.

Charles Gilbert collection

"Persis Sherman and Mrs. Allen," as the photographer identified them, set off for a picnic on a "Dorset day" in 1907, and were photographed by Harriet Gilbert. Choosing a shady spot, they spread their picnic gear under an apple tree and chatted over sandwiches and cookies.

for her coachman, and built a large barn, with stalls for five teams of horses. In 1898 she acquired twenty acres, from the Viall house all the way to Peace Street, the so-called Baker lot. In 1899 she bought from J. H. C. Hodges a house and fifty-four acres on the Hollow Road near the Mettawee, where the Fenton pottery was first located (site of the Miriam Bassett home). And in June 1900, she bought the 241-acre farm of John H. Hilliard in Kirby Hollow, including a magnificent spring. In 1901 she paid $4,000 to lay a pipe to connect the spring with her other houses near Peace Street. She also bought the home of Rollin and Anna M. Sykes and the "Dunton lot" from Allan Bourn. As a residence for her second hired man she purchased the "Barber place" of John H. Sheldon.

These lands were developed into parks, with mowed lawns, shade trees, and gravel paths for carriages. The centerpiece was her Pinnacle tower (now owned by Robert Keeler), built about 1910 to resemble an English ruin. Primarily an ornament, it was also a place of retreat from insects for herself and Miss Edwards, and where the coachman would drive them for picnics. She posted "No Admittance" signs, but sometimes granted written permission—for one day only—to visitors who asked.

In 1919 Miss deNottbeck bought a generator, which Robert K. Rudolph remembered helping to install—and on one occasion he had to clean out the one-cylinder engine after someone poured molasses into it instead of oil. Rudolph penned the following recollection:

It was about that time that Miss deNotteck asked my parents if I could take dinner, Saturdays, at her house, which became a custom for me. . . . Dinner was at eight. The cook placed the food in the butler's pantry where he got it and put the serving dishes in front of Miss deNottbeck. He brought her one of the dishes and took away our dish when that was put before us so that we were never without a plate at our place. When all were served, one of us would say Grace. Conversation would be general and never about anything about the place for the butler to hear. All food was pureed to make it easier to eat. If the final course was ice cream, as it often was, the freezer would be turned by the butler during the afternoon, or one of the other men. It was made of pure cream and very rich and served onto little linen doilies on the dessert plates.

After dinner we would go into the drawing room and Miss deNottbeck would inquire about the progress of any work under way and give her orders about work to be done which I was expected to communicate to the men. . . . Work involved mowing the fields, keeping the paths free of weeds and adding gravel, cutting and trimming trees and moving trees. Miss deNottbeck had a large tree mover: two very large wheels and a pole that could be chained around a tree. In the fall, the tree to be moved would be dug around and the hole where it was to go dug. After freezing, the pole could be backed up against the tree and when pulled down between the horses, it would lift the ball of earth clear for moving. Thus were the paths bordered by shade trees which were kept trimmed to preserve the views.

After we had discussed the work, Miss deNottbeck would ask me to read to her and Miss Edwards. I read many of Dickens' novels and Sir Walter Scott's and other English literature and, gradually, she had me read theology more and more . . . Sometimes a problem could not be solved and I would be asked to seek the answer from my father, to report the next week. . . . At midnight I would excuse myself and walk home through the woods and across the fields.

Mrs. John (Agnes) Musser came to her Dorset home next to the Field Club every summer during the 1920s and 1930s from Philadelphia, driven by her black chauffeur, Percy Dobson. She had a special interest in children and was influential in the village school, which she presented with a Victrola and records so that music appreciation could be taught. Each year she gave prizes, such as a silver star to the fourth grade and a watch to the eighth grade, and rewarded those with best grades, the neatest desk, and the most kindness.

Mrs. Musser, tall, stately, visited the school weekly, always dressed in white, and every Sunday afternoon gathered a group of girls at her home for readings and storytelling. At season's end she would take the group to tea at the Limberlock Lodge in Manchester (now the Golden Toad). She died in 1941. Her granddaughter, Agnes Pearce, still visits each summer.

Another more recent member of the "summer people" colony was Bernadine Barbour Grondahl, who resided north of the Church Street corner on the West Road. In winters she lived in Palm Beach. The wife of Seattle banker and lumber baron Einar Grondahl, who died in 1951, she was remembered by Norma Sheldon Roberts Taft, who worked for her as cook and maid, for her Persian cat and the other cats she raised. One of her longtime employes was Dave Baker of Peace Street. Among the benefactions from her estate were the Manchester Rescue Squad, Putnam Memorial Hospital, Bennington County Humane Society, and Dorset Public Library. She died in 1971 at the age of ninety-three.

Other Summer People

It would be impossible to list all the "summer people" who visited Dorset; even if such an extensive record were available it might constitute a book longer than this one. Yet several more names came to mind when a group whose years reached back were asked to search their memories.

The resulting arbitrary list was headed by the Prentiss family, descendants of Dorset's very first "summer people," who still own the early-Victorian home. Edwin Anderson, who was librarian of the New York Public Library, had a home here with his wife and two daughters. Ruth Taylor was known for her Red Cross work during World War II, then lived here permanently until her death. The Lefevre family are sometimes thought of as summer people (and are mentioned in more detail in chapter 11) though they became permanent residents early on. Others, at random, and with apologies for the many whose names are necessarily omitted, were Mr. and Mrs. H. D. Nims, Mr. and Mrs. James Sykes and family, Mr. and Mrs. Bernard Sykes, Dr. L. Mason Clark, the Frank MacDonald family, Harry and Anne Sheldon, Mr. and Mrs. David Humphreys, Dr. and Mrs. Underhill Moore, Mr. and Mrs. Edwin Codman, Dr. and Mrs. Edwin Goodman, Elizabeth Berryman, Marta Putnam, Susan R. Lord, Anne Geller, Frederika Phillips, Bertha Binkard, Genevieve Wright, Maud Gilmour, Marjorie Davenport, Cordelia deSchweinitz, and Mr. and Mrs. Geoffrey Parsons. Summer residents of North Dorset included Dr. Burnham and family, relatives of Bill W. of Alcoholics Anonymous fame, and Howard Freedley of Marble Hill, East Dorset. Of course there was much overlap between "summer people" and the many arts-oriented visitors and adopted natives who chose to live in Dorset for its scenic values and its culturally vigorous ambience.

More than one summer person came to town the way Howard R. Pfaelzer did. On a summer day in 1925, motoring through Dorset, Pfaelzer was so moved by the beauty of the setting that he changed his day's plan and decided to explore. That decision led to his return the next summer, and soon he purchased a house in the Hollow, and remained until his death in 1944. One of Wallace Fahnestock's stained-glass windows in the Dorset church, where Pfaelzer directed the choir, was dedicated to his memory. His great-nephews and great-great nieces still visit each summer.

East Dorset People

While there was a certain character to the "summer people" phenomenon associated with Dorset village, East Dorset also played an important role in the tourist trade. Because of its location on a more heavily traveled highway, Route 7, and with its station stop on the Rutland Railroad, East Dorset had its share of paying visitors. The inn at the corner of Mad Tom Road (Peru Street) and the old Route 7, known again today as the Wilson House, had been operating since 1852, when it was the Mt. Aeolus Inn.

Dick Cunningham and his sister, Nora Cunningham Gilbert, remembered when their parents, John and Florence, bought the inn in 1925, and when a sign out front each Sunday advertised "chicken dinner 1.50." During Prohibition the inn, about midway between Montreal and New York, became a sort of halfway house for "very rich people on the way to Montreal to drink," Cunningham reports. "The rich people slept in the front rooms and the chauffers slept out back with the family." For heat there was a coal stove in every room.

The inn's association with alcoholic beverages is ironic. In 1933, when Prohibition ended, the Cunningham family opened a bar in the very room where William G. Wilson, the "Bill W." who co-founded Alcoholics Anonymous (with "Dr. Bob"), was born in 1895. When Wilson was born the inn was operating as the Wilson House, run by his grandmother, the Widow Wilson. Bill W. could say with accuracy that he was born in a barroom.[5]

East Dorset's Wilson House has had many owners over the years, and was known briefly as the Barrows House. For a dozen years in the 1970s and early 1980s it stood empty. But in 1987 it was purchased by a Connecticut couple, Ozzie and Sandy Lepper, who restored its rotting sills and its twenty-five rooms and began to take advantage of the unusual word-of-mouth network that surrounds the aura of Bill W. to create a hostelry primarily for those who are guided by Wilson's Twelve Steps.

The story of Bill W. is one of true inspiration. He has become the Dorseter whose name, even though couched in anonymity, is more widely recognized on a national and international level than any other. The jacket of the book *Bill W.* by Robert Thomsen nicely summarizes his life story: "Bill W. grew up in Vermont at the turn of the century, married the beautiful and spirited Lois Burnham, displayed heroism on the battlefields of France, and returned home to a wild ride on the Wall Street roller coaster and a growing dependence on alcohol to clarify confusions. He had nearly succumbed to alcoholic ruin in the postwar years when, in 1935, at age forty, a luminous instant of insight—or miracle—saved him. Eventually he was led to his climactic encounter with Dr. Bob, another alcoholic, and the start of what was to bring new hope to alcoholics—and their families—everywhere and to serve as a prototype for self-help associations for other victims of addiction."

Official State Recognition

The economic impact of "summer people" received state attention in 1931, when the Vermont Commission on Country Life published "A Program for the Future by Two Hundred Vermonters." This panel recommended promoting the conversion of abandoned hill farms suitable for resale as summer homes. Otherwise these properties would only revert to forest, concluded the commission from the depths of the Great Depression and after years of population stagnation.

The commission urged that recreation supplement the state's traditional economic mainstays, agriculture and manufacturing. In addition to abandoned homes, it identified as Vermont assets summer camps, more hard-surfaced roads, the new Long Trail along the crest of Green Mountains from Canada to Massachusetts, bridle paths, cabin resorts and wayside stands, preservation of "our old New England architecture," and the state's natural and unspoiled beauty. Recommendations included better use of the state publicity bureau, formation of a statewide police force, and construction of a scenic highway along the Green Mountains. (The Green Mountain Parkway, after intense controversy, was defeated by state referendum in March 1936.)

Among the "two hundred Vermonters" in 1931 was Zephine Humphrey Fahnestock, who served with fellow authors Sarah Cleghorn of Manchester and Dorothy Canfield Fisher of Arlington on a Committee on Vermont Traditions and Ideals chaired by Arthur Wallace Peach, a Norwich University historian. This panel regarded as Vermont's cultural assets architecture, music, native folk songs and ballads, art, drama, historical material, literature and biography, and conservation of natural beauty. It recommended a study of Vermont poets and poetry and the publication of special books. Under Peach's editorship the committee produced a Green Mountain Series on Vermont prose, verse, biography, and folk songs and ballads.

Charley Wade and the Quabbin Houses

During the Depression the energetic Charles A. Wade (1874–1949), former livery operator, inn owner, and legislator, purchased several houses on sites that were destined to be flooded by rising waters of the Quabbin Reservoir in the Pioneer Valley of Massachusetts, and relocated them a hundred miles away in Dorset. The Quabbin project dammed the Swift River to create a massive reservoir as water supply for Boston and suburbs.

Wade's enterprise served several worthy purposes. Of primary importance were the aesthetic rewards of the so-called Enfield houses that enriched Dorset's architectural character and met the standards of the most fastidious.[6] Building these houses provided employment for Wade and his crew of about thirty-five carpenters, masons, and craftsmen during a time of economic malaise. The endeavour also furthered the goals of house-hunting "summer people."

Wade's personality and ingenuity—he has been described as "colorful," "ebullient" and "rollicking"—added zest to a most creative and enjoyable venture. All involved, whether as carpenter or cook or homeowner, came away with positive and amusing memories.

On August 18, 1971, Arthur W. Gilbert and C. Herbert Simmons delivered an illustrated talk about the Quabbin houses before the Dorset Historical Society; their presentation proved extremely popular and demonstrated widespread interest in the subject. Since then, John A. Kouwenhoven has donated to the historical society a packet of clippings, photos, bills, and letters that document the moving and reconstruction of the house Wade built for his parents, Dr. and Mrs. John B. Kouwenhoven.

All told, within a span of thirteen years, Wade bought about thirty of the Quabbin houses, or parts thereof, assembled at least eight in Dorset, and located others in Woodstock, Vermont, Hingham, Massachusetts, and Staten Island and Croton-on-Hudson, New York.

Several uncanny connections emerged between Dorset and the Quabbin region. Donald Howe's comprehensive *Quabbin: The Lost Valley* utilized photographs taken by Enfield resident Benjamin Harwood, born in 1861. Harwood was a cousin of the North Shire Harwoods, the pioneering family who migrated in 1761 from Hardwick, Massachusetts, to Bennington. One of the Harwood photographs, of a wedding party in Greenwich, shows Dorset resident Ruth Giffin Shroder as a little girl, with a big ribbon in her hair. The name "Enfield" had a Dorset connection, for it derived from that of its most prominent citizen, Robert Field, a legislator, selectman, Bunker Hill veter-

Dorset Historical Society

Charley Wade.

an, and mill owner, who was a cousin of the Dorset Field family. The handsome Robert Field house, built in Enfield in 1777, was moved and reassembled by Charley Wade high up on the flank of Dorset's Mother Myrick Mountain for Mrs. James J. Pocock of Philadelphia; it is now owned by Charles M. Hart.[7]

Wade was neither an architect nor a builder. Many wondered whether he could even read a blueprint. Perhaps he was inspired by the construction in 1929 of the Dorset Playhouse, composed of timbers dismantled from barns in Pawlet and Rupert and rebuilt in the Cheney Woods. He did have experience moving large objects, and had perfected a method of transplanting forty-foot trees for Miss deNottbeck when she wished to create instant forest. Before he went to the Quabbin, Wade moved at least three houses to Dorset from Hebron, New York, about fifteen miles west. Rather than attempting to jack up and move a whole house, he dismantled it, numbered each part, made rough sketches, trucked the components, and reassembled them.

Wade's Quabbin crew included his wife, Agnes, as cook, his brother-in-law, John Parks, as chief carpenter, and craftsmen Lloyd "Stub" Reed, Arch Hazelton, and Ray Parks.[8] During one stint the cook was John Parks's wife Blanche. For a bunkhouse, office, and kitchen they utilized a former Enfield schoolhouse, which later was moved to the Amos Field site near Dorset's West Road. It became a guest house for Susan R. Lord.

The spark for Wade's house-moving adventures was related in a *Christian Science Monitor* article that was reprinted in the *Rutland Herald* in the 1940s. When he operated a livery service, Wade used to drive summer residents around in his horse and carriage to see the scenery. "I used to hear the summer people talking about the beautiful old houses," Wade was quoted.

They would remark on the fine doors, the paneling, the many-paned windows, and the first thing I knew, I was interested, too. Then the automobile came along and put the horses out of business, and I had to look around for something else to do.

About that time I had a lot in the center of the village I wanted to sell, and when a woman came to buy it I told her there was a string attached to that lot—that I always had dreamed of a Colonial house, low and placed well back from the road, settled there.

And she said, "That's odd. I've had the same idea."

The article continued:

Today his blue eyes are bright beneath his shock of white hair when he talks about his work. He can go into a building, sketch the plan of its rooms, main timbers, doors and windows, on the back of an old movie poster, and put the house together again after

The Elsa Bley house on Kent Hill, across from the Dorset Public Library, was moved by Charley Wade from Hebron, New York, in the 1930s.

it has been taken down, shuffled, and carted a hundred-odd miles in a truck. Once you know how the old builders went about things, he says, you can usually figure out just where they would have put any given gun-stock timber or hewn joist.

One rebuilt house, on the lot next to the former Wade Inn, must have had its origin during one of Wade's livery trips to Hebron with Mrs. Agnes Houghton, who became enamored of an abandoned house with a caved-in roof. She hired Wade to dismantle it, move the parts on a truck, and reconstruct it in the location described, low and placed well back from the road. (For many years now the house has been owned and occupied by artist Elsa Bley.) That experience proved so successful that Mrs. Houghton's sister, Mrs. Walter Tyler, employed Wade to haul another house from Hebron; it was placed on the east side of Route 30 north of Church Street (now "The Little Lodge" owned by the Allen Norrises).

Mrs. Tyler's son, Walter, Jr., who wanted a camp, hired Wade to rebuild and relocate in East Rupert an old log blockhouse, said to have been built by the Green Mountain Boys in the 1770s. Much modified, it was later owned by Professor and Mrs. Philip Kissam, and now belongs to Dr. John Shroder. For Bertha Benson, Wade moved and reassembled another Hebron house high up on Barrows Heights. Long the home of Mr. and Mrs. Josiah Allen, it is now owned by Mr. and Mrs. Harry Bloor.

In the fall of 1930, Dr. and Mrs. John B. Kouwenhoven of Yonkers, New

This Enfield house, originally trucked to Dorset and reconstructed for Dr. and Mrs. John B. Kouwenhoven, was purchased in 1987 and moved again to West Union Street in Manchester. The picture shows it under reconstruction in November 1931.

York, began corresponding with the Boston Metropolitan District Water Supply Commission in hopes of acquiring one of the doomed Quabbin houses. They visited the site and selected a house owned by a Wheeler family in the town of New Salem, but it burned before they could pay their $100 for it. The state's agent, C. W. Walker, wrote to Wade, "Come down and find another!" They did, and bought the 30-by-40-foot former Charles Smith house in Enfield for $200 and, to use as a wing, the Arthur Gross house in Prescott, for $50. Dr. Harry W. Titus bought a Quabbin house at the same time.

John A. Kouwenhoven's sister Catharine and his brother-in-law, Lawton M. Patten, visited a ninety-year-old woman, Abby Dow, then residing in Hardwick, who had lived in the Enfield house from 1849 to 1879, and corresponded with her about the house and its moving. The Kouwenhoven house, built on Maple Hill, was considered the most authentically reproduced of all the Enfield houses; in 1987 it was moved again, and is now on Union Street extension in Manchester.

A former Enfield Congregational church chapel was moved to Route 30 near the Dorset Hollow Road and was used as the Dorset post office; later it became the office of Snare Associates Ltd., and is now used by George Wallace and his Dorset Hollow Corporation. Wade's daughter, Laura, still owns it.

Miss Mary Macy commissioned Wade to take a farmhouse from North Dana, a few miles north of Enfield, for reconstruction on the Upper Hollow Road; it later become the home of Captain and Mrs. Mortimer Addoms, and is now that of Michael and Diane Maher.

Just beyond the first bridge to the Hollow, on the site of the old cheese factory, Wade rebuilt an Enfield house for Mrs. Olivia Herbert, later to become known as "Brookhouse," owned by Mrs. Louise Armstrong; it is now owned by Mr. and Mrs. Peter Van Vlaanderen. On Maple Hill, Wade built a Quabbin home for Dr. and Mrs. Henry W. Titus,[9] now belonging to Mrs. June Davis. On Barrows Heights, off the Hollow Road, he built one for the Lloyd Barrick family, later that of Mr. and Mrs. Samuel Wormser, now Mr. and Mrs. James Dreyer. At the summit of Barrows Heights, with an outstanding view, he built a Quabbin house for Mr. and Mrs. Edward Peters; later it was the Edgar T. Salinger house, and now that of the H. L. T. Korens.

Wade's house-moving experiences ended in 1941 when he assembled a house at Route 30 and the Hollow road from several components of other houses he had stored in barns, for his daughter, Laura.

"Summer and Winter People"

Well before World War II the automobile was bringing more and more people into Dorset, lured not only by scenery and serenity but also by the town's hospitable climate for the arts. These new visitors were not necessarily constrained by season. Changing relationships between natives and newcomers were described in an article titled "Summer and Winter People" by John A. Kouwenhoven, an assistant editor of *Harper's Magazine* who was something of a summer person himself, having purchased the Harwood-Rasey farm on Rupert mountain in 1938.

Kouwenhoven sized up the situation and delivered a talk called "Whose Town Is It?" at the Dorset Field Club to benefit the Dorset Village Public Library. The talk not only drew a large crowd but also found its way into the summer 1943 edition of *Yale Review* under the title "Summer and Winter People." This message earned some national attention. An editorial in the *New York Herald-Tribune* on July 11, 1943, suggested: "Every one who has bought a little place in the country in recent years should read [the article] and ponder."

In the article, which used pseudonyms "Summerville" for Dorset and "Barnfield" for Rupert, Kouwenhoven analyzed "a special new kind of summer village" that was "transformed by infiltration." The author found that a social polarity had developed in Summerville, where twelve of the eighteen houses surrounding the village green stood empty and cold all winter, and where most of the church's income was derived from summer people. These developments demoralized the town, the article claimed, as contrasts grew more vivid between hard-working natives and golf-playing, leisure-loving, culture-oriented outsiders.

By 1943, summer residents constituted 20 percent of the town's taxpayers, owned 25 percent of the land, and paid between 40 and 45 percent of the town's taxes, Kouwenhoven wrote. Summerville's tax receipts, moreover, were half again as great as those of its four poorest neighboring towns combined, and between 1918 and 1938 those revenues almost doubled. During the same two decades the cost of maintaining the town's poor was multiplied by six, while in neighboring towns that cost remained level.

The author used 1940 census figures to demonstrate that something was wrong when Summerville's sixty-eight farms had land, buildings, and machinery worth an average of $11,736 each, while the average for Barnfield's eighty farms was only $8,689. Yet it was Barnfield, not Summerville, that gained population since 1920, indicating that Barnfield, where life was organized on a twelve-month basis, was better off economically than Summerville, with its seasonal ebb and flow. "The paradox is that a man who never sees more than a few dollars in Barnfield may be richer than the man in Summerville who gets a substantial cash wage for three or four summer months," Kouwenhoven declared.

A resort town costs far more to maintain than a farm community, the author went on. Summerville's expenses rose 87 percent during the 1930s, while its balance dropped from $1,000 in the black to $12,000 in the red. The same decade, when the main road was blacktopped, saw the greatest influx of summer residents in the town's history: more than twenty new summer homes were built, at an average expenditure of $15,000, or a total of more than $300,000—in addition to substantial investment in remodeled houses.

The author urged that instead of poorly paid part-time listers to appraise properties, expert full-time appraisers should be employed, resulting in a more equitable tax base and thus in increased revenues. He pleaded for understanding: "Here again the necessity for co-operation between the two groups which make up the community cannot be exaggerated. . . . It is only as a democratic unit, composed of individuals who understand and respect one another, that the community can effectively deal with those problems." The author concluded that "the unresolved problems of summer versus winter people will figure largely in Summerville's plans for post-war progress."

The "post-war progress" envisioned in 1943 by writer Kouwenhoven was not really achieved, beyond a continuation of existing trends. Despite some futuristic visions that after World War II everyone would soar about in autogyros or other flying devices, the automobile only increased in popularity. With construction of the Taconic Parkway, and later the Interstate highway system, more and more seasonal residents flocked to Dorset. One of the attractions was skiing, a phenomenon that was difficult to foresee back in the Depression days of the 1930s.

These new relationships were explored during the winter of 1972 by William Gilbert in "A Native Looks at Dorset," a series of four interpretive articles for the *Bennington Banner*. He cited the growing influx of people from prosperous suburbs of New York, Boston, Philadelphia, and elsewhere, and their apparent rush to buy houses in Dorset at inflated prices. He called it "the suburbanization of Dorset" and suggested that it was generating two communities in the same town, two life-styles, and two kinds of economic underpinning—one based on what people produce and the other on what they possess.

Gilbert's interpretation of what was happening to Dorset in the early 1970s tended toward the caustic. He deplored the ways in which local people were "imposed upon" by "the transplants." Of "the shadow community of the skiers" Gilbert wrote:

They are rarely seen. Their cars race up the roads Friday nights in winter to houses carefully concealed. Their cars speed to the mountains Saturday mornings. They jam all available restaurants and bars Saturday nights. On Sunday afternoons they careen southward, passing on curves and hills and risking the lives of man and beast in their determination to return to Stamford, or Larchmont, or Teaneck, in record time.

Their world has almost no connection with the community they live in. In Dorset, this is especially true in recent years, as more and more winter rentals draw skiers to the town. Skiers have virtually only one connection with the town life—they pay either rent or taxes. Their children do not go to school here, the adults do not go to town organizations.

Gilbert continued in this vein, concluding ruefully: "The town has changed completely in character at least three times since I was born here in 1920."

NOTES

1. Edwin L. Bigelow and Nancy H. Otis, *Manchester, Vermont: A Pleasant Land Among the Mountains*, published by the town of Manchester in 1961 to mark the 200th anniversary of the town charter.

2. George L. Prentiss, *The Life & Letters of Elizabeth Prentiss* (Syracuse, N.Y.: Anson D. F. Randolph & Co., 1882) p. 232.

3. Most of the discussion of Zephine Humphrey's family and early life derives from her *Recollections of My Mother*, published in 1912 by Fleming H. Revell Co., New York. The book is an autobiography more of the author than of her mother.

4. Information about Miss Cecelia deNottbeck is based on two recollections: "An Appreciation" by the Reverend Charles Carhart, January 17, 1934, following her death; and an untitled paper by Robert K. Rudolph, dated Dorset, August 22, 1985. Both are on file at the Dorset Historical Society.

5. A fine biography of William G. Wilson titled *Pass It On: The Story of Bill Wilson and How the A.A. Message Reached the World*, was published in 1984 by Alcoholics Anonymous World Services, Inc., New York. The authors are anonymous. Another biography is *Bill W.* by Robert Thomsen, published in 1985 by Harper & Row. A newer book that recounts Wilson's life and the experience of creating a successful self-help organization for alcoholics is *Getting Better: Inside Alcoholics Anonymous*, by *New York Times* writer Nan Robertson, published in 1988 by William Morrow & Company.

6. We say the *so-called* Enfield houses because while many did come from Enfield, there were other Massachusetts municipalities, Dana, Greenwich, and Prescott, that had to be abandoned, and some Dorset houses were moved from those towns also. As a generic term they should be referred to as the "Quabbin houses." Legal work on the Quabbin project began in the 1920s; the four towns were gradually abandoned during the 1930s, and municipal boundaries redrawn; the waters began rising in 1939, but the 415-billion-gallon reservoir was not entirely filled until 1946.

7. From a talk given by Arthur W. Gilbert and C. Herbert Simmons on the Enfield houses, Dorset Historical Society, August 18, 1971.

8. Other workers, based on records kept for the Kouwenhoven house, included Burt and Isaac Harrington, Ely and George Truehart, Bayard Lewis, Frank Tarbell, Frank Lindsey, Van Vermette, Walter Young, Ira Tifft, George Abbott, Burness Kinney, Earl Towsley, William Roberts, William Lanfear, Ed Phillips, and Floyd Reid.

9. Legend has it that once when Mrs. Titus expressed concern that Wade could not read blueprints, her sister assured her, "Don't worry. Charlie has the soul of a poet. Everything will be all right." And it was.

11

The Early Twentieth Century
1900 to 1924

AT THE DAWN of the twentieth century, Dorset was a placid agrarian town on a downward economic slide. The marble industry had stagnated, although conditions would improve for a few memorable years with the contract for Dorset marble as building material for the new New York Public Library. The population in 1900 stood at 1,477, 600 fewer than a mere generation earlier; the number would drop by another 300 after 1920, when the marble business had folded for good. This abrupt decline meant that many houses were for sale—a factor that would prove important in coming years.

In early years of the twentieth century there was no such thing as a real estate agency. Sales of houses were handled by a bank, a businessman, an insurance company, even a funeral home. A few people shared a single telephone line from an office in Manchester, but there was no electricity. Automobiles had yet to replace horses as a primary means of transportation. Most residents lived quietly on self-sufficient farms where they raised vegetables and livestock, frequently selling meat, eggs, and dairy products. Perry Peltier, Mark Fisher, and Albert Roberts produced honey. Nearly everyone made maple syrup and sugar each winter. Many had sizable flocks of chickens, and in 1904 Huntington P. Gilbert and his sister, Anna, began a chicken farm. Their brother, Rufus, specialized in strawberries and raspberries. In the fall of 1906 Hunt P. Gilbert built a grand henhouse that would hold a thousand white leghorns; the elongated building had running water and a

Charles Gilbert collection

Harriet Gilbert, who took this photograph on August 21, 1904, titled it "The Full Load." At right is her nephew Rufus Gilbert. Note Owl's Head in center background.

cement floor. Another large poultry house was built the next spring by the Gilberts' West Road neighbor Eugene Simmons.

The Dorset Inn and Barrows House were doing well, and for a while they had competition from the Wade Inn. In the spring of 1906 the following items, not labeled as advertising, appeared in the *Journal*, offering a glimpse of what the town was like:

> Dorset Inn and its cottages are located in a pretty spot in the Green Mountain state where the scenery is ideal. The hotel is open from May until November and no more delightful spot can be found to spend a short or long vacation. It is homelike and the house is fitted up in a manner that brings an idea of comfort at the first sight. There the golf player can enjoy his favorite game in surrounds that are filled with all the beauties that nature can bestow and the fisherman can find good sport in many a pleasant sylvan spot. A. W. Curry is proprietor, and a letter to him will bring a prompt reply, giving rates and other information.
>
> The Barrows House, one of the most popular hotels among the mountains, is enjoying a very successful season. It is within a short walking distance of the Casino, and there is a good livery in connection. The proprietor, E. W. Barrows, is one of the best known hotel men in Vermont, and is perfectly cognizant with the details of the business.

The Wade Inn, halfway between the other two inns, and across from the present post office, was started in 1914 by Charley Wade. The popular Wade, famed for his salvaging of houses from the Quabbin Reservation, was elected to the legislature in 1921. Zephine Humphrey raved about him: "His enterprise and initiative, his good cheer and courage, his brilliant self-development make Dorset proud of him . . . He is one of the wholesome, tonic influences of our valley."

In East Dorset, the Wilson House (formerly known as the Barrows House; not to be confused with the Barrows House in Dorset village) was also being operated as an inn. For a few years before and after 1900, the Widow Wilson, who ran it, was joined there by her son, Gilman Barrows Wilson, his wife, Emily Griffith Wilson, and their children, William Griffith Wilson, born in the Wilson House in 1895, and Dorothy Brewster Wilson, born in 1898.

Dorothy Wilson later described East Dorset at the turn of the century as a village of "about twenty homes on two main streets with marble sidewalks and many beautiful trees, mostly sugar maples. There were two general stores, two marble mills, a cheese factory, a blacksmith shop, and a cobbler shop; also a public school and two churches."[1]

As the promotional brochures of R. M. Campbell testified, Dorset residents were pleased to offer summer boarding to strangers, both for the extra income and for welcome sources of contact with the outside world. It was fortunate for those who remained in town that Dorset exhibited other special qualities—of scenery, serenity, friendliness, integrity, heritage, and a receptivity to the arts—that appealed to outsiders who were eager to visit or even settle down, and thus to make their own contributions to a sparse economy.

The Lefevres

Important components of the experience of visiting Dorset included lengthy summer visits, the marble industry, artistic outlets, and, to use the modern term, gentrification. The family of Edwin Lefevre, Sr., embodied all of these. Urbane and internationalist, the Lefevres welcomed the relief Dorset provided from urban pressures, and they saw in the rustic countryside opportunities for health, peace, culture, beauty, even livelihood.

The family purchased a solid marble house—one of only four or five in Dorset—from a marble entrepreneur in a town best known for its marble industry. For the next twenty years, they enlarged and upgraded the premises to an elaborate extent. In 1920 Edwin organized Dorset's first electric light company, selling shares of stock. After the Lefevres became year-round resi-

The Early Twentieth Century

Photo by Agnes Pearce in Terry Tyler collection

Looking east toward "Cheese Factory Bridge" that crosses the Mettawee River at the entrance to Dorset Hollow. Barns in foreground are on the site of an early Fenton pottery; building in background was probably the cheese factory. Road at left leads to Kirby Hollow.

dents in 1917 they exercised considerable influence over community and state affairs.

Edwin Lefevre, Sr., first saw Dorset in the summer of 1907 as a guest of the artist Lorenzo Hatch. The visit was prompted because his little son Eddie, aged five, was considered "peeked and puny" and a doctor had recommended that he be taken away to the mountains. Another son, Reid, aged two and a half, seemed more robust.

Edwin Lefevre, Sr., could boast of exotic connections. Born in 1871 in Colon, Canal Zone, then a province of Colombia, he was a son of George Edwin Henry Harding Lefevre and Emilia de la Ossa Lefevre. His father, an American, was Panama agent for the Pacific Mail Steamship Company and had been a naval officer during the Civil War. His maternal grandfather was chief justice of the Panama Supreme Court and his uncle, Dr. Manuel Amador y Guerrero, became the first president of Panama in 1904. (Lefevre's brother, Ernest, also served as a Panamanian president in 1910.) Dr. Amador headed a faction that successfully brought about the secession of Panama from Colombia, a development desired by the United States and its president, Theodore Roosevelt, who wished to dig a canal across the isthmus.

In the 1890s Lefevre became a reporter for the *Mining and Engineering Jour-*

nal, moved to the *New York Sun*, then specialized in financial writing for the *New York Commercial Advertiser*. In 1902 he married Martha Moore, a native of Brooklyn, who worked for Dow-Jones Publishing Company. Having followed his father's advice to study mining engineering at Lehigh, Lefevre then pursued his own inclinations as financial writer and novelist. He became the financial editor of *Harper's Weekly* and began to be regarded as an authority on Wall Street. He wrote for the magazines *The Iron Age, McClure's, Cosmopolitan*, and *Everybody's*, then settled exclusively with the *Saturday Evening Post*, specializing in articles on antiques and activities of Wall Street. By 1907, living in the Westchester suburb of Bronxville, he had published three novels about the world of finance.

In the course of seeking a mountain climate beneficial to young Eddie's health, the Lefevre family took the train to Manchester Depot, and proceeded by stage to Dorset. Edwin liked Dorset, and met with Ernest H. West to look at some places for sale. There were houses available with intriguing views, including one at Crane's Knoll on the West Road that appealed to Martha. They began to inspect a farm somewhere near an old whitewashed stone house on the West Road. As Edwin "Eddie" Lefevre, Jr., recalled from the perspective of 1987, a formidable thunderstorm suddenly erupted and halted their quest. Martha Lefevre, fearful of the storm, insisted that they buy the nearby stone house, which she thought could withstand any kind of weather. It was available, and West happened to own it.

The origins of the West Road marble house were not precisely known but it had vague associations with hardship; some thought it might have been a town poor farm. Its original owners were Manleys, and a previous owner, William Corey, an Irish immigrant farmer and sometime marble polisher, had died in 1904. Corey's widow was unable to keep the place going and so early in 1907 she sold in distress to West.

In 1907 the blocks of marble—finished neatly but not polished—that compose this house were mostly covered with a whitewash, which was weathering away. The blocks had been placed with precision so that the house measured exactly 30 by 40 feet. Edwin saw possibilities in the place and on May 11, 1908, he bought it.

The Lefevres' summers grew more lengthy, lasting from May to November. As the doctor had predicted, little Eddie thrived in the mountain air. He made fast friends with Lorenzo Hatch's son Harrison. Because his livelihood depended on telephone messages, and he found it unacceptable to share a twenty-four-party line, one of Lefevre's first moves was to cause the service to be split into two lines, along West and East roads.

Lefevre engaged New York architect Eugene J. Lang to add a one-story

The Manley-Lefevre-Dickenson house on West Road, as it looks today. The original marble section at left was built about 1812.

kitchen wing; in 1910 the house was expanded again. Onto the new wing was added something Dorset had never seen before, an indoor marble swimming pool, complete with dressing room. Meanwhile, in 1909, because of his connections with Panama, Lefevre accepted an appointment as that nation's ambassador to Spain, Italy, and France. Before he left, Lefevre had a electric powerhouse built on a hill behind the house so the place could be electrified, the first Dorset house to be so. The powerhouse contained a generator, storage batteries, and tools. He then took his family abroad, and the boys were placed in private schools. On returning, he decided that Dorset's native marble should be used to replicate some elaborate formal gardens he had admired in northern Italy.

Among Lefevre's New York friends was Charles Downing Lay, a landscape architect experienced in designing estates and municipal parks. Lay was landscape architect for the New York City Parks Department, working in the tradition of Frederick Law Olmstead. The firm of Lay, Hubbard & Wheeling launched the quarterly *Landscape Architecture*, with Lay as its editor and manager from 1910 to 1921.

Starting in 1913, Lefevre commissioned Lay to design some formal Italian gardens next to the marble dwelling. The gardens grew during 1914, and in 1915 a marble teahouse was built, followed in 1916 by a marble pergola, from which there was a fine view of Mt. Aeolus. Most of the marble consisted of leftover blocks Lefevre purchased locally for $50, which he regarded as a bargain. The project halted during World War I, when Lay was a planner for the U.S. military. A few years later Lay would write a book, *The Freedom of the City*—a misleading title, for he meant the freedoms made available to those who flee the confinements of the city—describing palatial grounds he had designed in Greenwich, Connecticut, as well as the elegant estate he had created in Dorset.

During the war Lefevre gave up the house in Bronxville. When he and Martha traveled to New York from Dorset they stayed at the Seymour Hotel, and he remained a member of the prestigious Century Club. By 1920 the genial Lefevre knew everybody in Dorset. He set about organizing the Dorset Electric Light Company, urging acquaintances to buy stock, with a minimum purchase of $100. He had some financial help from the Samuel Insull interests, then investing extensively in public utilities. The system covered Dorset village, South Dorset, the Hollow, and the West Road. The charge was the maximum allowed by law, a hefty 18 cents per kilowatt hour. Eddie Lefevre, then about to enter Williams College, remembered with amusement years later that his father's business methods were "probably illegal," because each customer was required to purchase stock. But if the corporation was dubious it was also congenial; Eddie also recalled that the incorporators assembled each Sunday afternoon for cocktails.

After four or five years Lefevre sold all the stock for $200 a share, dou-

Photo from Mary Nichols in the Terry Tyler collection

Jerry Legare operating a drill rig he made about 1910 for digging water wells. He was the father of Mrs. Charles "Tuck" Nichols.

bling the investors' money. The equipment was acquired by Central Vermont Public Service Corporation as its Dorset substation.

In 1925—the year he published his last novel, *The Making of a Stockbroker*—Lefevre began a major two-year renovation. A marble second story was added over the kitchen wing and pool; there were no active quarries in Dorset and the marble had to be hauled, like coals to Newcastle, from Rutland or Proctor. The addition included a large upstairs studio-living room patterned after architecture Lefevre admired in Seville. Its two-foot-thick marble walls made the room extremely quiet, and he used it as his writing studio. Its distinctive windows were surrounded by decorative tiles he had brought with him from Spain in 1912, produced in Spain by Dutch tile makers imported during the sixteenth century. They are of the Delft blue that marked the Dutch work of that era, though the scenes depicted are Spanish. On the walls were hung antique Spanish paintings.

Eddie wrote about his father at this time: "Dad . . . was making good money with his writings and he found the labor costs in Dorset very reasonable. The rate was set by what they paid at the quarry, which was $1.25 for a ten-hour day, 7 A.M. to 5:30 P.M., with a half hour off for lunch. A carpenter could get twice that or 25 cents per hour. So Dad felt that all work being done was a good investment for the future."[2]

In the 1920s Lefevre became a partner of Ernest West in the Dorset Orchard Company, which Eddie operated for a few years. He remembered the venture as profitable; a bushel of apples costing 35 cents to produce sold at

Terry Tyler collection

Brothers Edwin and Reid Lefevre with their friend Libus West (daughter of Ernest H. West), outfitted for a costume party, circa 1930.

Photo by Bertha M. Pratt in Charles Gilbert collection

A Gilbert family Fourth of July outing in 1901.

a retail stand on Route 30 for $3.50. The business was sold to Carleton G. Howe, who later sold it to the architect Henry van Loon, who built a large apple-storage facility.

Edwin Lefevre, Sr., collected early American flasks, bottles, and furniture, and was at work on a book of Americana when he died at the age of seventy-three on February 22, 1943. Martha lived until 1960. Meanwhile, Reid, born in 1904, followed his brother to Williams College, then attended the University of Vermont. He pursued a dual career as carnival operator and colorful Vermont political figure. The gregarious Reid belonged to the Elks, the Masons, the Shriners, the Rotary Club, the Equinox Club, and the Bennington Club; he served on the boards of the Boy Scouts of America and the Dorset Players. By 1964 King Reid's traveling carnival was the largest in New England. He was a governor of the National Showmen's Association and a director of the Showmen's League of America.

In 1947 Reid Lefevre became Manchester's representative to the Vermont House. He later served in the Senate, and rose to positions of state leadership. In all, he served twenty-one years in the legislature. On one famous occasion he brought his carnival into the House of Representatives, an event that was photographed for *Life* magazine. As a political personality Lefevre

Real horsepower was used to thresh oats at the Charles Gilbert farm on West Road in 1909.

was known for his elegant vocabulary, his camaraderie, and his girth, and he was in demand as a master of ceremonies. He died unexpectedly in 1968 in Portland, Maine, attending a convention of carnival exhibitors.

The marble house, grounds, and 114 acres of land were sold in 1977 by Mr. and Mrs. Edwin Lefevre, Jr., who moved to smaller quarters off the Morse Hill Road. A marble connection remained, for the buyer was Proctor Trust Company, a subsidiary of the Proctor Bank. In 1983 the bank sold the property to David B. Dickenson, a real estate attorney from Boca Raton, Florida, and his wife, Katharine, active in historic preservation work. On June 14, 1984, by order of Mr. and Mrs. Lefevre, a "most important auction" of family antiques and Americana was conducted under a large tent on the lawn.

Apple Orchards

About 1912, after the New York Public Library job was completed and the Norcross-West quarry was finished, Ernest H. West again changed careers, and went into the apple business. He began with a small orchard that had been planted years earlier by his maternal grandfather, George Holley.

West, born in 1874 in Dorset, attended Burr & Burton Seminary, graduated from UVM with a civil engineering degree, then worked in New York City designing and building the subway system. But spending time in dank urban tunnels did not agree with him, he discovered, and he returned to the

Photo by A.L. Bowen, courtesy of Ada Rumney

Herbert and Isabelle Williams in front of their home (on Route 30) in 1904, perhaps on their way to church. Henrietta's Elm can be seen at right.

family's marble business. Although he played a vital role in Dorset marble (a role fixed in time because of his research and writing about marble) Ernest West was also associated with apples for more than forty years. In the early days he entertained visions of the Dorset Valley as one vast bouquet of apple orchards, aromatic when in blossom each spring, ablaze with color in fall.

West's interest in orchards was enhanced by the development of the MacIntosh, considered almost the perfect apple because it would bear annually, tasted great as an eating apple, baked nicely, stored well, and looked beautiful. West set out about eight thousand trees and, assisted for a time by the Edwin Lefevres, father and son, between 1914 and 1916 created what became the Dorset Orchard. West's enthusiasm was contagious, and an apple rush developed. Soon more trees were planted by J.B. Milliken and Carleton Howe along south-facing slopes east of Morse Hill Road. The Gilberts set out trees on West Road, and other orchards were started by Frank Overton, the deSchweinitz family, Dr. and Mrs. Goodman, the Corbins, and the Parsons. In all, between thirty-five and forty thousand trees were planted. At first they were placed in 20-by-20-foot squares, and when mature they were opened up to 40-by-40-foot spacing.[3]

The Early Twentieth Century 241

The clever sign reads "E. E. Kent Horseshoeing and Jobbing" in this photo taken about 1920, when the business was operated by Elmer E. Kent. It was formerly the Fred Seymour blacksmith shop, located on the Dorset Hollow Road.

Visions of profit glittered. If there were eight to ten thousand mature trees and if each tree could be expected to produce thirty bushels of fruit, then an annual crop of as many as three hundred thousand bushels might be contemplated. Sales at $2.50 each multiplied out to a yearly gross of as much as $750,000—big money for a small town in pre-Depression days. The future appeared rosy, until a series of catastrophes conspired gradually to deflate these bubbles.

First came the Depression, when it was difficult to sell anything to those who had little cash. Hard-pressed people spent more time in their kitchens, preparing and preserving, to make their dollars go further. Then came widespread use of electricity to power refrigerators and freezers, meaning that competing fruits could be marketed and sold anywhere. Too, with hundreds of acres under cultivation, orchard owners felt oppressed by both town taxes and bank loans.

Later, as the Depression economy shifted toward war preparedness, better jobs became available and it was impossible to attract persons willing to work seasonally to climb ladders, and pick and grade apples. As was the case with Dorset marble, which suffered from competition with better quality material found in Proctor and West Rutland, so it was with apples. Orchards

This picture of Dr. Frederick C. Liddle, for many years Dorset's physician, was taken by Harriet Gilbert on July 28, 1910. A native of Salem, New York, Dr. Liddle earned his M.D. at the University of Vermont, settled in town in 1887, and retired in 1942.

could be managed more easily and profitably in the warm, flat Champlain Valley towns of Orwell and Shoreham than on high, rocky slopes in Dorset.

In the 1930s the Dorset Orchard Company built a packing house and cold-storage plant out of old stone walls and parts of a barn and established truck routes for a radius of about thirty miles in each direction, selling to independent stores and homes. Hank van Loon recalled amusing situations, such as the time foreman Art Van Orman, who handled the sales route, came in to report, "I don't know what you will think of this. I sold all the apples I had on the truck but I didn't get all cash. I've got two hooked rugs and a crate of chickens, but I guess we can get rid of them some way." Another time an old woman in Salem took a box of apples but refused to pay until she had tried them. When the driver called later for payment, she produced a hot apple pie and gave him and the helper a big slice.

"How is it?" she asked.

"It's great," said the startled salesmen.

"Well then I'll pay you," she said.

In spite of negotiations to form a cooperative, roadside stands, other attempts to capitalize on apples, and valiant efforts to keep going during World

The Early Twentieth Century

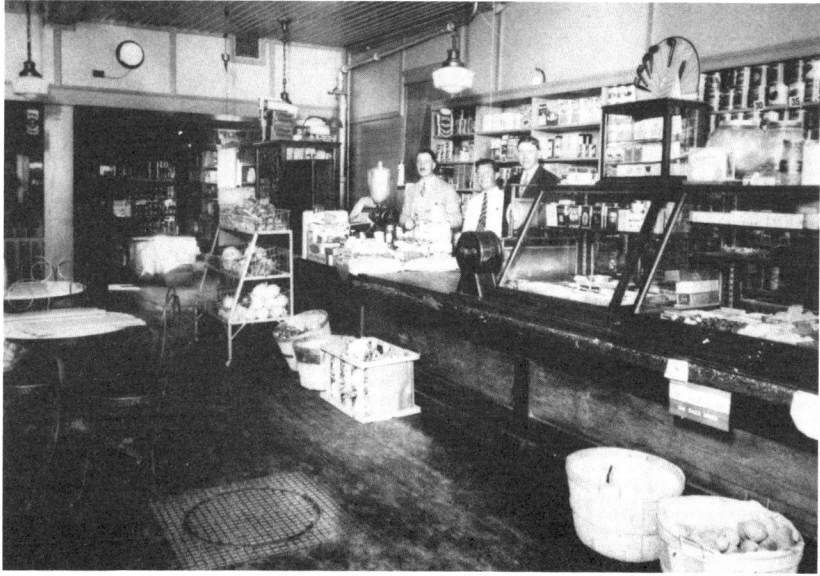

The interior of Peltier and Tifft's store in 1932. Clerk Charles Allen is flanked by owners Perry M. Peltier, left, and Kimball Tifft. Note the ice cream tables and chairs, ready for summer treats.

War II, the business succumbed after 1946 to other pressures on orchard acreage. The stone-and-barn-beam storage house of the Dorset Orchard Company was converted into a house.

Roads, Automobiles, and Telephones

Perhaps because horizons were expanding so rapidly, a certain residual insularity persisted as the age of automobiles was launched. Symbolically, one of the new century's first legislative acts was a 1902 law granting Dorset the right to elect two road commissioners at town meeting and authorizing selectmen to divide the town into two highway districts. The dividing line, as before, would be "as near the bar of the mountain that divides said town as possible."

The poor condition of roads became a target of Si Clone's invective in the *Manchester Journal*. "A move is afoot to indict the road commissioner on account of the almost impassible road," he wrote in April 1906. His other gratuituous comments included: "What little mud the road machine scraped into the road this spring has gone to New York via the Battenkill in the flood

Gathering maple sap in a wooden tub.

of Sunday," and "There is talk of getting larger wheels for the road machine so it will go over the big rocks in the road."

Some of the first automobiles were remembered in 1989 by one of the oldest natives of East Dorset, Robert Griffith of Brattleboro. Griffith lived next door to George Roberts, whose mother was of Japanese ancestry. Roberts bought a 1913 Ford, became a good mechanic, then operated a garage in Manchester Center. Griffith had other auto memories:

Henry Stone had a Willys-Knight and he too was a good mechanic. Dr. John Cochrane, scientific man that he was, drove an air-cooled Franklin at 15 mph down to the Manchester library and back. My father [Jack Griffith] had a Briscoe Eight. Cliff Copping had a Hudson Super Six. He removed the cushion, so that he could sit low in the seat while driving, with his left elbow draped over the door. Cliff was training at Camp Devens when he was among the first casualties of the first influenza epidemic. A squad of soldiers came down from Fort Ethan Allen to give him a military funeral.

Ernest Whitney had a chain-drive Metz. The chain broke frequently. My Uncle Bill Griffith had a Buick roadster. George Freedley had a Buick touring car.

Dr. Clark Burnham, Brooklyn, N.Y., gynecologist, at his summer place up on North Dorset Pond [he called it Emerald Waters, and the Burnham property is now the Emerald

James Beebe boiling sap in his evaporator, about 1940. This East Dorset farm is now owned by Jack Frost.

Lake State Park], had a number of big cars, a Pierce Arrow, a Peerless. In his later years he drove a Buick roadster with the top down. On a Sunday morning he would drive to Manchester to get a newspaper, and I've seen him on his way back, the newspaper spread over the steering wheel, reading as he sped along, only occasionally glancing at the road. At that time Route 7 was hardly more than two ruts with grass growing between.

Before the automobile became firmly established, various proposals for railroads were considered—other than the Manchester, Dorset & Granville described in chapter 8. In January 1911 a charter was granted to the Mettawee Railroad, and ground was even broken in December of that year, for a line between Dorset and Lake St. Catherine. In the same year, the same group organized the Taconic Valley Railroad Company and proposed a railroad line between Dorset and Bennington through Manchester, Arlington, Shaftsbury, and Glastenbury. Even though these proposals were said to be backed by the New York, New Haven & Hartford, they came to naught. Nor did anything result from a charter sought in 1912 by the Rutland Railroad for a rail line between Wilmington and Manchester by way of Somerset, Stratton, and Sunderland.

The H. N. Williams Department Store, showing owner William Williams chatting with customers, circa 1940. The white clapboard addition was Mrs. Agnes Musser's garage, moved to this site from Church Street about 1902. Note the bicycle built for two, available for rent.

The *Manchester Journal* commented wryly:

Governor [John A.] Mead has signed the Taconic Valley Railroad bill . . . and now there are charters enough for roads through this valley to make Manchester as central a point as Chicago—if all the chartered roads are put through.[4]

Reporting that the 1903 Dorset town meeting had voted "wet"—that sales of liquor would be permitted—Si Clone commented in his column, "Many are disappointed but now it is adopted we hope it will be given a fair trial and then we can see which method is best for the community." Two weeks later the first arrest was made: "An Italian workman in the quarry of Norcross & West was arrested for the illegal sale of liquor," Si wrote. "A small riot followed, where the same was drank, resulting in the seller's arrest. Justice Fisher was the court, who fined violator of the law $1.00. The fine being paid, the Italian resumed his work." The unlucky immigrant was not identified by name.

There was a good deal of parochialism and prejudice in Si's columns, notably about the "Dagos," the Italian workmen employed in the quarries; he used that derogatory term freely in his writing. Si once asked, "Did you ever see 200 Dagos drink 30 barrels of beer in 30 minutes? They can do it." In

The interior of the Williams Department Store, taken in the 1960s, showing Ada Williams Rumney, the owner, with Henry McWayne, now deceased.

May 1903 he reported that an Italian was suspected in the murder of Fred West in Peru, and added: "I tell you, this scum of the old world is getting too strong for us. They will usurp our freedom and cause a reign of terror."

Another group of Italians, who worked on the railroad section gang, lived in East Dorset in a "carhouse," a caboose transformed into a dwelling.

The Church Fire

At 6 A.M. on the Fourth of July 1907 a choir sang out from the tower of the old Dorset Congregational church. Wrote Si Clone, "This is a pleasant feature of Independence Day and has been practiced for several years." Then he added, "A wish has been expressed that the bell will not be so loudly rung at midnight as on some previous occasions."

But that episode ended a tradition, because on November 24, the Sunday before Thanksgiving that year, the beloved church was destroyed by fire. Zephine Humphrey wrote: "A disaster befell the community which few of us can even now remember without tightened throats." Dr. Liddle's barking dog alerted people to the fire about 5 A.M. The village had no fire department, no hose, and no central water system. The blaze was fought in vain by bucket brigade. "It was awful, and I guess there was not a dry eye in that crowd as the old bell went down and crashed into the furnace."

The Congregational Church of Dorset and East Rupert, in a photo taken a year before it burned on November 24, 1907.

Reverend Charles Carhart took charge immediately, held church services in the school hall, and accepted the challenge of raising funds for a new building by announcing that he would donate $400, his own salary until the next July 1.

After much disagreement among parishioners about a proper design for a new building, architect Jordan Greene of New York, a summer visitor, won applause with a plan he presented in May 1909 that would resemble the old church in general lines, but made of marble instead of wood. The Norcross-West Company, still quarrying for the New York Public Library job, offered to provide material, and Orlando W. Norcross got the contract. The firm gave marble that was already quarried and waiting in Manchester to be delivered, and contributed a good deal of labor.

A ceremony was held at the cornerstone laying in July 1909 that included a memorable poem read by Dr. George Holley Gilbert. In August 1910 the new marble church was formally dedicated.

Predictably, the community rallied after the crisis to remedy the pressing need for a fire department. A good turnout of citizens authorized legal steps to be taken, according to a history of the Dorset Fire District No. 1 by its first secretary, J.H. Sheldon. Members named to the original fire district prudential committee were John M. Armstrong, Austin W. Phelan, and Charles N. Williams.

Voters incorporated the district on July 11, 1911. An option was secured by Dr. Liddle for rights to waters of Kellogg Spring, a reservoir was constructed above the Tom Warren farm off West Road, water was piped to the village, and hydrants were installed that are still in use today.

According to Sheldon's account, back in 1872 the Reverend George L. Prentiss had wanted to form a fire company and offered to pay half the cost of bringing the waters of Kellogg Spring to the village. But residents were unwilling to pay the other half and the matter was dropped. Perhaps it was just as well, Sheldon recounted, because the tiny water pipe Prentiss proposed would not have met even the needs of 1912.

The Vermont legislature in 1912 created Dorset Fire District Number 1, with authority to build reservoirs and aqueducts, dig up public streets, levy taxes, and issue bonds. But a lawyer advised that the money needed to acquire land, build a reservoir, and lay pipes would have exceeded what the Grand List would warrant and so, Sheldon wrote, "we looked elsewhere and Mr. J.[ames] B. Wilbur [of Manchester] loaned us $8,650 with some personal endorsements." Wilbur called in the loan two years later "which proved to be for our benefit as we had been paying him 6 percent interest." Then Ernest H. West and his mother, Augusta, came to the rescue by lending the district $11,000 at 5 percent with a note dated August 25, 1915. Receipts from taxes and water rents steadily reduced the debt until another $1,000 was bor-

Photo by Bertha M. Pratt in Terry Tyler collection

The interior of the old Dorset church; the chairs and pulpit were rescued from the 1907 fire and are still in use.

Photo by Harriet Gilbert in Charles Gilbert collection

Installation of the cornerstone of the new marble church took place during formal ceremonies on August 20, 1909. A highlight was a poem read by Dr. George Holley Gilbert. Note the array of fashionable women's hats in foreground.

Terry Tyler collection

The Dorset Church (United Church of Dorset and East Rupert), centerpiece of the village, in a 1940 photo.

rowed to build a West Road extension.

When Sheldon resigned as secretary in 1927, feeling that "it's time for a younger man to take [my] place," the books showed a debt of $4,700 and cash balance of $500.

The first fire equipment consisted only of hand-drawn hose carts. Resources were slowly expanded, with a second reservoir and, about 1927, the first fire truck (which Ernest G. Edgerton, the chief from 1952 to 1972, recalled had no windshield). A 275-gallon pumper was added in 1935, a 500-gallon pumper in 1959, a 750-gallon pumper in 1972, and a 1,250-gallon pumper in 1988.

Genuine General Stores

Griffith's General Store in East Dorset was managed by John Kelley "Jack" Griffith after the death in 1912 of his father, John Marcellus "Marley" Griffith, who had returned home from California. Jack Griffith's son Robert, wrote a recollection of the store for this book:

> Griffith's Store had as comprehensive a stock as you could imagine. Drugs, candies, cheese, canned goods, footwear, ladies' undergarments, and men's, dress material, buttons, thread, horsewhips, firearms, ammunition, traps, brooms, garden tools, nuts, bolts, screws and nails. As you went downstairs, you were aware of the combined odors from barrels of kerosene, molasses and vinegar. Upstairs, among other items, horse blankets, stoves and stovepipes.
>
> There was a barrel of coffee beans in the back room, and a giant grinder. You had your choice of black tea, green tea, or mixed. My grandfather owned three houses next south of the store. The nearest served as a storehouse, and the other two were rented.
>
> My father, Jack Griffith . . . was an all-round sportsman. He played golf, tennis, baseball, football, and he was an expert fly fisherman. Never a November came but

Courtesy of Howard Bowen

G.H. Brophy's store in East Dorset on Mad Tom Road, as it appeared in a postcard photo in the early 1920s. The store burned on March 24, 1926.

we had a big buck hanging from the oak tree in our back yard. He had my brother and me boxing when we were seven or eight years old.

For deer hunting season my father displayed in the store every year a chart recording the local kill. Here you found the name of the hunter, caliber of rifle, weight of the deer and number of antler points, location of the event, distance of the shot, and finally, the hunter's rating as liar. Traditionally, the more truthful hunters were rated as outrageous liars, while those less respectful of the truth were praised for their modesty and veracity. . . .

Courtesy of John Sweeney

After the 1926 fire Gilbert Brophy purchased the former Griffith store (right) opposite Mt. Aeolus Inn, now Wilson House. Later his son Howard took over the store. The building briefly housed the East Dorset post office and in the 1960s served as the village library.

There was another equally versatile general store [which also housed the post office] in town. The sign over the door read: H. A. & G. H. Brophy. Harvey Brophy was a Civil War veteran. The store burned down about 1924. At the time Griffith's store had been bought by Barney Rosen, a peddler, who left it in charge of his two daughters, Flo and Rose, while he continued his peddling in the horse and wagon tradition. Later on Howard Brophy, grandson and son of H. A. and G. H., respectively, bought the store and operated it for some time.

The Science Club

The idea for a get-together of those interested in the workings of natural science was that of Dr. George Holley Gilbert. A first meeting of twelve charter members of the Dorset Science Club was held

The Early Twentieth Century 253

February 10, 1915 in Dr. Gilbert's West Road home. Original officers were Dr. Gilbert as president, Miss Anna Gilbert, vice president, Ernest H. West, secretary, and Wallace Fahnestock as treasurer.

Zephine Humphrey, who was there, wrote later: "The enterprise was modest. None of us knew very much about natural science, few of us had acquired even a scientific habit of mind. But the essence of science is modesty; and since we appreciated the humor of our attempts to discuss obscure

Photo from Ed Leary in the Terry Tyler collection

Downtown East Dorset in 1914 featured the Rutland railroad station that housed a ticket office and freight depot. Trains took milk, mail, passengers, and blocks of marble south to New York and north to Montreal. In the 1920s there were several trains a day including the "midnight sleeper" and the "Green Mountain Flyer."

matters, we were in a fair way to grow, which we did, vigorously. When spring brought our summer colony back, the membership of the Club was more than doubled."

For the next several years the Science Club obtained distinguished speakers from the University of Vermont, Middlebury, Dartmouth, and even the Rockefeller Foundation. A telescope was purchased to study the heavens, and members climbed surrounding peaks, christened Jackson Peak, blazed a series of hiking trails, and built a camp overlooking a commanding view.

By 1928 the Science Club's focus had shifted fully toward a passion for the nearby out-of-doors. Never in the town's history were its own mountainous environs so deeply appreciated. The club published a map of the trails and a diminutive thirty-two-page booklet, "The Dorset Trail," with a

Ready to score: the Dorset baseball team, circa 1910, probably pictured on Edgerton's field behind the Field Club. Identifiable in front row, seated, are Dan Blackmer, Fred Sheldon, and Ernest Edgerton, Sr. Known players in back row at right are John Nichols, Albert Harwood, and Burr Phillips.

descriptive essay by Dr. Gilbert and a series of black and white photographs by Carl T. Ramsey of surrounding vistas and mountain scenes. The introduction summarized matters this way:

> It is proverbial that men are enamored of what is far away in place or time—touched as those things usually are with the agreeable light of fancy or romantic legend—while they fail to appreciate the beauty and the excellency that are near, even beside their own doors and on the path where they daily walk. This is perhaps one reason why our Dorset scenery has been underrated by us whose homes are in the midst of it. Equinox in Manchester and Haystack in Pawlet, not to mention mountains more remote, were well known among us many years before anyone had taken the trouble to climb Dorset Mountain, or even to ascertain which one of our mountains properly bears this name. It is well to see the White Mountains and the Adirondacks and the Canadian Rockies but certainly it is not well to slight the precious things of our own environment.

The booklet discloses that the state erected a wooden tower on the summit of Dorset Mountain in the summer of 1922. But the tower did not last out the winter of 1923–24. Even so, the club cleared part of the mountaintop, which offered the following "great panorama" that locates Dorset visually in the midst of an extraordinary New England context:

> *We see the Green Mountains as far as Mansfield, the White Mountains and the Catskills on a few rare days. The Presidential Range is on a line about midway between Killington and Ascutney, and the Catskills are visible through the Sandgate Notch. Greylock in the Berkshires can be identified by its tower. On any fair day we get the entire sweep of the Adirondacks from their southern limit to Whiteface. The Otter Creek valley from Danby to Pittsford is spread out before us. We see Ascutney on the Connecticut and the Bennington Monument against the background of Mount Anthony. The south end of Lake Champlain is visible and with a glass the steamers may be seen. [Visible from Dorset with binoculars, steam-driven passenger ferries plied Lake Champlain between Vermont and New York.] These items will suggest the extent and variety of the great panorama.*

Mrs. Emily H. Terry, sister of Professor Hitchcock, who christened Mt. Aeolus, became the first woman to climb to the summit of Dorset Mountain. She was especially enthusiastic about the ferns that grew on Dorset's mountains, and she donated her carefully mounted and labeled collection to the library.

World War I

The name most closely associated with World War I is that of John J. McBride, a twenty-eight-year-old native of Dorset who worked as an accountant for his father's soapstone company in Virginia until he enlisted in "the war to end all wars." As a member of the 107th Infantry, 27th Division, McBride lost his life on September 29, 1918, in France at Willow Trench, during the Battle of Hindenburg. He was cited for bravery by both the French and American governments, and was buried at Bony Aisne, France.

McBride's name was immortalized when fifteen veterans of the war met in a room above Peltier's Market on January 7, 1930, to organize an American Legion Post. The original members of the post, all World War I veterans, were Roland R. Harrington, commander; George W. McBride, vice commander; David J. Wyman, historian and adjutant; Perry M. Peltier, finance officer; Walter E. Jones and George G. Abbott, executive committee; Henry M. Gilbert, chaplain; Paul E. White, sargeant-at-arms; and John L. Tully, Walter J. Koch, Clarence Blackmer, Burton Blackmer, Albert E. Knowles, Carleton G. Howe, William T. Burns, and Alfred A. Seymour. The

John M. Armstrong's store on Route 30 across from the Dorset Inn had a windmill for pumping water. At the turn of the century this was one of three stores in Dorset village. In the 1920s it was owned by Burr D. Phillips, who resided in the addition at right. Today the building serves as shops and apartments.

subsequent history of the post, including its change of name to the McBride-Harwood Post, is detailed in chapter 13.

In all, fifty-six Dorset lads saw active duty. Other fatalities besides McBride were Clifford J. Copping and Richard Lee; George B. Dunbar was seriously injured. William G. Wilson of East Dorset, later to be known as "Bill W." who co-founded Alcoholics Anonymous, reportedly displayed heroism on the battlefields of France. Several residents worked for the YMCA, among them Theophile Comba, who taught at Camp Meade, and Charles L. Lee, who served in France. Another who went overseas, as a YMCA secretary, was Reverend MacIntyre, minister of the East Dorset and Danby Congregational churches. On the home front, women knitted afghans and other garments, and a local Red Cross chapter provided bandages, sweaters, socks, and other supplies.

Stuart P. Sherman

Stuart P. Sherman (1881–1926) was a grandson of Parsons S. Pratt and therefore a son of Dorset, though he was born in Iowa and lived in town but briefly. At the time of his untimely death he was one of the na-

The Early Twentieth Century

Miss Sims was the teacher of these West Road School pupils in 1926. In front row are George West, Charlotte Gilbert, William Gilbert, Charles Gilbert, and Carl Nichols. Center: Patty DeSchweinitz, Huntington Gilbert, Sykes Gilbert, Jean Nichols, Janet Gilbert, Lewis DeSchweinitz, and Stuart Gilbert. Back row: Lorraine Nichols, Beatrice Nichols, Miss Sims, and Stan Towsley, and Howard Nichols.

tion's most distinguished literary figures, having taught English at the University of Illinois for twenty years, and been literary editor of the *New York Herald-Tribune*.

A son of John Sherman and the former Ada M. Pratt, Stuart was raised in the Midwest, California, and Arizona. He lost his father as a youth and his mother returned to Dorset in 1896, the year her father, Parsons Pratt, retired. Stuart graduated from Williams College in 1903, earned a graduate degree in literature from Harvard, and joined the faculty of the University of Illinois where he chaired the English department. His teaching was so popular that when it became known that he was considering an offer to teach at Yale, thousands of Illinois students protested his leaving; he stayed. He also rejected an offer from progressive educator Alexander Meiklejohn to teach at Amherst.

In 1924 Sherman became literary editor of the *New York Herald-Tribune*. The literary world was stunned when, on August 21, 1926, he died while swimming to shore on Lake Michigan after his canoe overturned. The *Herald-Tribune* published a six-page tribute that included encomium from such national figures as Mark Van Doren, Carl Van Doren, Joseph Wood Krutch,

Allen Nevins, Sinclair Lewis, and H. L. Mencken. Even the competing *New York Times* editorialized: "He was not merely a critic, but that rare compound, a man of ample knowledge and also of the impulse and ability to express himself. Mr. Sherman was one of the few surviving great readers." When a two-volume *Life and Letters of Stuart P. Sherman* by was published in 1929 it included a sixty-page bibliography of Sherman's own works—verses, books, critical essays, book reviews, articles. His widow, the former Ruth Mears, a native of Williamstown, endowed a faculty chair at Williams in his memory.

In his own diary Sherman mentioned that early in his life he had mined gold in California and nearly died of thirst in the Arizona desert, and that during visits to the Dorset mountains of his mother's family he had developed his "taste for the wild."[5]

Robert R. R. Brooks

By the 1920s postmarble Dorset was at a low ebb. The town in that era has been described in most candid terms by Robert R. R. Brooks, who remembers, as a lad of about 11, living in South Dorset in 1920.[6] He was a son of James Brooks, headmaster of Burr & Burton Seminary from 1908 to 1920. Although the BBS headmaster was provided with a fine house, the Brooks family—father and mother and six children from infancy to age thirteen—bought a farm on what is now Kelleher Road, south of Morse Hill Road. They lived there several summers, and for some reason Brooks still could not explain as he recalled it in 1986, his father decided to live there for the entire year of 1920. (He looked back on the decision as "most injudicious.")

Robert "Triple R" Brooks went on to become an economist, the dean of Williams College, author of a history of Williamstown, and a shrewd observer of life. His South Dorset in 1920 was a depressed and isolated settlement abandoned, he said, by most people of initiative. The quarries had closed and farming provided the only employment. By bicycle, Brooks peddled cottage cheese his mother made, and in summers they would pick and sell strawberries, gooseberries, black and yellow raspberries. On his route were the Dorset Inn, Barrows House, and some private residences, mostly of summer people in the village.

Brooks attended the South Dorset School, which had grades 1 through 4 in one room, 5 through 8 in the other, and a two-hole outhouse out back. One teacher was Kate Kelleher, "a wonderful teacher, patient and stern [who] did a very good job of maintaining order and teaching the kids." (Mrs. Kelleher died in 1989 after observing her 100th birthday.)

"On my side," he remembers, "I had Miss Stewart, who was a Scottish

Pupils at the East Dorset School in 1919. Front row: Dorothy Cunningham, Nora Cunningham, Richard Dunn, Richard Cunningham, Emerson Whitney, Wilbur Bowen, Howard Brophy, Cecil Twyne, and unknown. Second row: Two unknowns, Anna Whalon, Alice Brock, Peggy Whalen, Marion Warner, Jessie Brophy, teacher Mrs. Whitney. Third row: Sherman Towslee, Myrtle Brophy, Mary Cooper, Dick Brophy, D. B. Stone, and Bob Brock. Fourth row: Tom Dunn, George Haley, Jack Cunningham, unknown, Elizabeth Sheridan, Lois Brophy, and Agnes Sheridan. Top row: unknown, Beatrice Twyne, Grace Foster, unknown, and Ed Beauregard.

woman, with still a little burr. She was the same kind of person, a wonderful person, stern, and kept a good discipline, was very thorough and very insistent." He recalled that one classmate, Regina Cody, daughter of the postmistress, later became the dean of Bennett Junior College, but that few of the youngsters went on to Burr & Burton or other education after grammar school.

That winter Brooks's father and older sister Rosa commuted the five miles to BBS every day by sleigh:

There were times when the snow was right up to the horse's belly. There was no plowing and the sleigh had to flounder through that for half a mile out to the road where at least there would be some packed-down snow. Then he drove from there to Burr & Burton Seminary where he would have to put the horse in the barn, unhook it, and he went to work. And then at night they hitched up again and came back. It was crazy because he had this big handsome [headmaster's] house right there next to the school.

The fall term of the Dorset Village School, 1920, with Miss Mary Leary as teacher. Front row, Henry Hulsberg, Dunning Harwood, Dolly Park, Ada Williams, Dorothy Eastman, Jane Barrows, Margaret Patterson, and Ruth Hulett. Middle row: Barbara Hulsberg, Moses Sheldon, unknown, William Park, Horace Eastman, and Helen Andrews. Top row: Cecil Taft, Edna Wade, Frances West, Henry Park, teacher Leary.

Brooks recalls that living in South Dorset involved a "small orbit," and he did not get around much except for trips to Manchester; he only climbed Green Peak once. He also remembers: that many "dry holes" were drilled at the marble quarries because the quality was so poor; that the Dorset village green has changed little except for the value of its houses; that his father used to hire Peter and Merritt Wideawake to help build fences around their farm; that the only good soil for farming was the "bottom land" along the Mettawee valley; and that except for "jack jumpers" made of barrel staves, he never knew about controlled skiing until the 1930s.

Zephine Humphrey's *Story of Dorset* sums up the essence of the town in 1924 this way:

For the last twenty years, Dorset's destiny has been more and more clearly defined as that of a summer resort, and for the last ten years her development along this line has been rapid. She is fully awake to the situation and is lending herself to it with en-

The Early Twentieth Century 261

The upper grades at the Dorset Village School in the fall of 1920, with Miss Grace Hammond, teacher. Front row: William Williams, Ada Weeks, Betty Tharp, Olive Dern, Marion Hulett, Ted Harwood. Middle row: Francis Norcross, Floyd Eastman, Jim McBride, Aaron Taft, George McWayne, and Russell Parks. Back row: Henry McWayne, Charles Harwood, Laura Wade, Ruth Andrews, and Beatrice Kinnie.

thusiasm. . . . *Building lots are for sale everywhere, and hardly a year passes that some old homestead is not bought and made over into a summer home. . . . From the first of May, when the populous tide sets our way, to the first of November, when it ebbs again, our valley is quick with human life and activity.*

So far, we have been singularly fortunate in the character of the people who have come to sojourn with us. They are largely professional or artistic folk, clergymen, physicians, teachers, writers, painters, musicians, widely intelligent and glad to give us of their best. Moreover, their tastes are simple, inclining them rather to adopt our quiet ways than introduce urban elaborations of custom and dress. They help us in all departments of our common life, contributing generously to the church and schools, to the upkeep of our roads, to our local charities. Apparently they want to make our interests theirs.[7]

The year 1924 seemed to be an important turning point. Though the town was basically depressed, its chief industry moribund, signs of what the future would bring were already clearly seen. The comfortable old gray goose was about to start laying some golden eggs.

262   Dorset

The town road scraper, pictured in front of the Frank Streeter home about 1913, was powered by a six-horse team. The crew consists of Perham Phillips, Ernest Tifft, Frank Streeter, and Silas Streeter (seated).

NOTES

1. *Pass It On: The Story of Bill Wilson and How the A.A. Message Reached the World*, p. 18.
2. From the undated manuscript of a reminiscence of his father by Edwin Lefevre, Jr., delivered before the Dorset Historical Society.
3. Much of this discussion of apple orchards derives from a paper by Henry B. van Loon delivered before the Dorset Historical Society on August 26, 1977.
4. Bigelow & Otis, p. 93.
5. Gratitude is expressed to Nora C. Gilbert for the use of her collection of the works of Stuart Sherman.
6. Robert R. R. Brooks's recollections of the Dorset of 1920 were tape-recorded by the writer October 30, 1986.
7. Humphrey, *The Story of Dorset*, p. 282.

12

The Arts and the Artists

JUST AS significantly as its economy, heritage, scenery, and climate, the arts have defined Dorset's image and reputation. Both the visual and the performing arts have been a continually invigorating, mind-expanding, and even profitable force. Dorset's visual artists include some painters of international renown as well as an impressive number of amateurs inspired to take up brush and palette, and many in between. Performing arts are represented notably by the Dorset Theatre Festival, Dorset Players, and the Svetlova Dance Center. Several writers have made Dorset their base either full time or seasonally, and the craft is practised by playwrights at the Colony House for Writers. The scope of Dorset's artistic creativity has covered, as well, the stencil artistry of Jessica Bond and Adele Bishop, and the low-relief marble carvings of Ernest H. West. An atmosphere of esthetic appreciation has also been established by Egidio Moresi, Gertie Bickel, and many other antiques dealers.

According to both Alfred H. Gilbert and Robert McIntyre, the organization of painters traces to 1904, when an exhibition of several Dorset artists was held at the Field Club to benefit the library. Artists included Bryson Burroughs (later curator of paintings at the Metropolitan Museum in New York), Edwin B. Child, Lorenzo Hatch, Carrie Holley, Walter Shirlaw, Harold Warren, Frederick Ballard Williams, and Mary E. Winch of Toronto. The next year another exhibit was held at Lorenzo Hatch's studio, with Child, Shirlaw, Holley, Frederick Crane, and John Lillie as exhibitors. These were among the earliest joint showings of art in town, after which interest seemed to wane.

Artist-members of the Southern Vermont Artists Inc. pose for a group portrait about 1948. Front row, from left: Elsa Bley, Beatrice Jackson Humphreys, Dean Fausett, Edith Dulles Snare, Wallace W. Fahnestock, and Clay Bartlett. Back row: Robert G. McIntyre, Bernadine Custer, Mary Powers, Herbert Meyer, Harriet "Tarzan" deSanchez, and Felicia Meyer Marsh. Nine of these were Dorset residents.

McIntyre credits Mrs. Huntington Bigelow with stimulating in the early 1920s a permanent renewal of interest in the exhibiting of works of regional artists. In the summer of 1922 "The Dorset Artists" was the name of a show of works by W. R. Leigh, Edwin B. Child, Wallace W. Fahnestock, John Lillie, and Herbert Meyer, at the old Dorset Village School. By 1926 their number had expanded to seventeen and they exhibited in the Burr & Burton Seminary gymnasium. Another show was held in the Equinox Pavilion at the invitation of Mrs. George Orvis, owner of the Equinox House.

Continued interest prompted the incorporation in 1933 of Southern Vermont Artists, Inc. After a pause during World War II, membership and interest grew to the point where, in 1950, purchase was made for $25,000 of the grand Manchester estate, Yester House, of Gertrude Devine Webster, along with 375 acres on the eastern flank of Mt. Equinox. The Southern Vermont Art Center, as it is now called, continues to emphasize the visual arts; but since the addition, in 1956, of a performing-arts pavilion, SVAC has offered a strong program in music, film, and other cultural events. SVAC's 1989 sixtieth-anniversary, 132-page catalogue lists 1,500 artist-members, whose media range from traditional oil and watercolor to sculpture and photography.

The original "Dorset Artist" members from 1922 to 1933, as recorded by SVAC, were: Edwin B. Child, Francis Dixon, Wallace W. Fahnestock, John Lillie, Herbert Meyer, Mary S. Powers, W. Hurd Lawrence, Laura S. Hollister, H. E. Schnakenberg, F. F. Vanderhoef, P. Beckwith, Horace Brown, Cordelia deSchweinitz, Franklin W. Orvis, Florence C. Powers, Mrs. S. J. Randall, Della Shull, Albert Smith, Jay H. Connaway, Gertrude H. Grant, E. Lillian Reitzenstein, and Jesse Whitsit. Most were serious artists; not all actually resided in Dorset. New artist members were added each year by invitation.

The formation of the Dorset Players in 1926 served to focus the region's attention each summer on the pleasures and challenges of drama, at first on a community-amateur level and then on a professional basis. For many years the Caravaners, succeeded by the Dorset Theatre Festival, with its affiliated Dorset Colony House for Writers, have made the town an important nucleus of creative activity.

Any list of "Dorset artists" will fail from someone's point of view, whether through erroneous omission or unjustified inclusion. For example, Reginald Marsh, nationally known master of the sketched female form, was connected with Dorset primarily because of his wife Felicia and her parents, Herbert and Anne Meyer (all artists). But those who remember Marsh, who summered in town between 1940 and his death in 1954, knew that he felt more comfortable in the urban settings his sketches depict and that he did not always appreciate Dorset's charms. "Too many trees," he complained.

Courtesy of Louise B. Connaway

Jay Connaway, N.A., famed for his marinescapes and Vermont landscapes, returned to Vermont to paint in 1947 after living for seventeen years on Monhegan Island, Maine, and rented in Dorset Hollow before moving to Pawlet. He and his painting students were a familiar sight during the 1960s. This photograph was taken by Manchester photographer Clara Sipprell.

"Dock in Winter," one of Jay Connaway's many Monhegan Island paintings.

Dorset can also claim Jay Connaway (1893–1970), a distinguished National Academy marine and landscape painter who lived in town for a few years in the 1940s before establishing a permanent home in Rupert. Having studied at the Art Students League and the Ecole des Beaux Arts in Paris, Connaway, with his wife Louise, a pianist, and their daughter Leonebel, lived a sort of self-imposed exile between 1930 and 1947, year round, on Monhegan Island, off the coast of Maine. While Louise served as the island's teacher and nurse, Jay concentrated on marine scenes and made an intense study of the infinite moods of the sea.

When they first returned to Dorset after World War II, the Connaways stayed at Ern Roberts' boarding house in the Hollow. Later they crossed the paths of two earlier artists, residing for a time in the former home of Lorenzo Hatch, across from the cemetery, then in the Edwin B. Child house, in the Hollow.

Artist Beatrice Jackson Humphreys related an anecdote about visiting the Connaways while they were enduring the cold barns that Child had remodeled. Connaway took David Humphreys out to see his studio. Humphreys remarked on the low temperature and wondered how Jay could work with oils there. Characteristically, Connaway replied, "Chum, I like to paint cold."

Connaway taught for many years at the Southern Vermont Art Center and exhibited in its galleries from 1950 on. He was an SVAC trustee for fifteen years and influential on its art committee. A major posthumous retrospective showing of his works was held at SVAC in 1970.

Dorset was much more briefly the residence of the late watercolorist Ogden Pleissner, before he moved to Pawlet and later to Manchester.

One of Dorset's prominent patrons of the arts was Lincoln Isham, great-grandson of Abraham Lincoln. A Manchester resident starting in 1904, the year Hildene was built by his grandfather, Robert Todd Lincoln, Isham lived in Dorset from 1927 until his death in 1971, usually spending winters in New York with his wife, Leahalma, who died in 1960. Isham was an incorporator of Southern Vermont Artists and active on its music committee. A member of the Ekwanok Country Club and the Dorset Field Club, he was known for his philanthropy, having donated the observatory, biology laboratory building, and Isham Library at Burr & Burton Seminary; he gave his Lincolniana to the Smithsonian and Library of Congress.

Robert G. McIntyre, a prominent authority on nineteenth-century art, resided on Kent Hill from his retirement in 1953 until his death in 1965, at the age of seventy-nine. A nephew of William Macbeth, who founded the Macbeth Gallery in New York City, McIntyre operated the gallery from 1940 until 1953. He was among founders of SVAC as well as the Dorset Corn Exchange.

Edgar Salinger (1887–1971), resident of Barrows Heights, was a patron of the arts, an amateur cellist, and a trustee and honorary trustee of SVAC, active on its music committee. A collector of American and Asian art, he was devoted to chamber music and the opera. He was an uncle of President Kennedy's press secretary, Pierre Salinger.

An air of artistic distinctiveness was created by Egidio L. Moresi, an antiques dealer who catered to a particular clientele. Between the early 1920s and late 1960s, "Egidio's Shop" on the Lower Hollow Road specialized in rare Whieldon pottery, Chinese export, eighteenth-century paintings, and one-of-a-kind objects. Born near in Italy in 1890, Moresi came to Dorset as a summer visitor in 1920 and liked it so well that he did not return to close his Venice apartment for five years. Then he made frequent buying trips to Europe before World War II.

A Compendium of Dorset Artists

The town's earliest recognized visual artist was Buell Moore, born in 1806, the youngest son of Grove Moore, a lawyer, judge, and justice of the peace from East Rupert. Buell began to paint at an early age and was known as talented and high-spirited; some of his childhood pranks are described in Humphrey's *Story of Dorset.* Moore went to Boston to study in the studio of John Quidor, a renowned portrait painter, then moved to the area of Troy and Albany, New York, and became a successful portrait painter himself. In 1855 he went to Europe to paint.

Humphrey relates an amusing episode in which Moore returned to Dorset in 1869, bought an old mill by Prentiss Pond, outfitted it with knitting machinery, and made stockings. The enterprise was picturesque but not a business success, for the stockings "were of all shapes and sizes, hardly two of a kind to make a pair, and had so many dropped stitches that in the end they had to be sold or given away for mops." When anything went wrong, Moore was said to pound the machinery; when things went well he would pace the floor, reading *Paradise Lost* aloud to his workers. He moved to Rhinebeck, New York, where he died in 1878.

Truman D. Bartlett, born in 1836 in the Hollow, was a portraitist and monumental sculptor who gained his first work experience lettering tombstones in the marble finishing shop of Charles Fields. In 1855 Bartlett went to Mansfield, Massachusetts, to work as an apprentice in a marble mill where he again lettered tombstones. After jobs in New York, Ohio, and Connecticut, he went to Europe in 1867 with his wife Mary Ann White and son Paul. He worked and studied in Rome and Paris and became a prominent sculptor.

In 1877 Bartlett was engaged, with Boston architect J. Phillip Rinn, to design a monument to celebrate the centennial of the Battle of Bennington. Their suggestion for a one-hundred-foot column that resembled the Vendome monument in Paris was widely publicized but ultimately rejected.[1] The successful design was an obelisque three hundred feet high, designed solely by Rinn.

Bartlett exhibited at the National Academy of Design in New York, and for many years taught modeling at the Massachusetts Institute of Technology. Son Paul Bartlett also became a sculptor, and designed several statues that were incorporated into the New York Public Library, whose building material came from the Norcross-West quarry.

Several nineteenth-century landscapists are known to have been attracted to Dorset, though few details about them survive. One was Charles Heyde, who in 1852 sent a letter to his mother-in-law, Louisa Whitman, about the grand views near his new home in North Dorset. The whole scene, he said, was so closed in by mountains that one had to look straight up to see the sky: "Nothing could be more solemn and sublime than the effect of these mountains whose tops are amid the clouds the shadows of which rest upon their

Painting in Terry Tyler collection; photo by Stetson Fletcher

A painting by Dorset native John Lillie of winter logging by oxen.

surfaces."[2] It is tempting to speculate that the unknown artist who painted an 1860-era landscape of North Dorset might have been Heyde.

Walter Shirlaw was a Scotsman, born in 1838, who came to the United States at the age of two. He became an engraver but abandoned that work in favor of painting, spent much time in Dorset, and was a member of the National Academy of Design. He was said to be influential in sparking John Lillie's artistic interest. Shirlaw died in 1910. About 1944 the Brooklyn Museum held an exhibit of his works, including several Dorset landscapes.[3]

Frederick Crane, born in Bloomfield, New Jersey, in 1847, was known as a painter of mountain scenery and for a while owned a house and barn on the Dorset West Road. At the St. Louis Exposition of 1904 he was awarded a bronze medal for meritorious work. He died in New York in 1915.

John Lillie (1867–1942), Dorset's best-known native artist, remained in town throughout his life, though his fame spread far. He was born in 1867 in a house near the so-called Ethan Allen Spring on the West Road, near where his father was born. The house no longer stands, and its site is now a cellar hole. Lillie, a farmer, mason, and builder as well as self-made artist, lived to see his paintings in the permanent collections of the Metropolitan Museum in New York, the Corcoran Gallery in Washington, and the Carnegie Institute in Pittsburgh.[4]

Lillie attended the West Road district school until he was twelve and became a "helper" for neighbors and relatives. At sixteen he developed an interest in carpentry and carried with him a book, *Use of the Square*. "His life," wrote Rose Lindley Kent, "was a record of long seasons of faithful duties, of deeds cheerfully administered, temptations resisted, and of unfailing friendliness to the last round."

Lillie's studio became a meeting place for summer people, including notable artists and authors. His first painting, made with a shaving brush on a wooden panel, hung in his carriage house along with the canvases of summer boarders. In his paintings he admitted to using four brushes of various sizes, but he preferred a flat bristle brush about an inch and a half wide.

Lillie became president of the Vermont Guild of Manchester, and was among founders of SVAC. He exhibited in prominent galleries, and his works were selected in 1938 by Homer St. Gaudens from a group representing twenty-seven nations to tour the country with the Carnegie International circuit. Just before his death Rose Kent described Lillie: "At seventy-five, he was erect; his step firm; his manner courtly. He maintained his splendid mental powers, his sound judgment and his intimate knowledge of world affairs. His pleasing address, fine bearing and cordial manner won him friends in great numbers."

Lorenzo Hatch (1856–1914), a contemporary of Lillie's, had different origins, talents, and horizons. He came to be known as one of the world's finest

Terry Tyler collection

A 1939 painting by Claude Dern of John Lillie (1867-1942), self-taught artist, farmer, mason, and carpenter, who was introduced to painting by an artist who boarded at his home, Walter Shirlaw.

engravers. Born in 1856 in Hartford, New York, he arrived in Dorset in the 1870s with his mother, Frances Elizabeth Sheldon Hatch. His father, William Crandall Hatch, a sculptor, had recently died, and the widow bought a modest house across from the Maple Hill Cemetery in which to raise her son and two daughters, Elizabeth and Martha. At fourteen, Hatch was apprenticed to a watchmaker in Salem, New York, a Mr. Whitcomb, whose wife suggested that he try some engraving tools, then was startled by his abilities.

At sixteen, Hatch made a copper-plate engraving of the head of George Washington, which two years later came to the attention of George B. McCartee, chief of the U.S. Bureau of Engraving and Printing, who was vacationing in Dorset. The youngster was encouraged to go to Washington, where at eighteen he became the youngest apprentice in McCartee's bureau. He executed a portrait of Ulysses S. Grant that was used on five-dollar silver certificates and an engraving of Lincoln that appeared on the five-dollar bill.

In 1888 Hatch went to Chicago to work for the Western Bank Note and Engraving Company, then to New York for the American Bank Note Company, where he did an engraving of President James Garfield. In the 1890s he took up watercolor, held an exhibition, and received his first critical acclaim. He also studied portraiture and landscape with Robert Henri. He often returned to Dorset, where he painted in a small studio behind his mother's house, still standing today, and formed a small summer art colony.

Photo by Chet Ringheiser from Southern Vermont Artists Inc.

A portrait of Lorenzo Hatch's mother, Mrs. William Hatch, painted by her son. It is in the permanent collection of the Southern Vermont Art Center.

In 1907 Lorenzo Hatch painted this view of Mt. Aeolus and Owl's Head, showing apple trees in blossom and foliage creeping up in the mountain. Far better known as an engraver, Hatch did few oil paintings.

Courtesy of Bennington Museum; photo by Tyler Resch

The interior of Lorenzo Hatch's studio, a house across from Maple Hill Cemetery now owned by Mr. and Mrs. John A. Fennie. Among paintings on the wall is one of Henrietta's Elm.

Hatch's engravings, many of which illustrate allegorical themes, earned greater critical acceptance than his paintings.

In 1894 Hatch married Grace Harrison, whom he met at the Chicago World's Fair, where she was performing as a pianist. She was a great-granddaughter of President William Henry Harrison. Their son, Harrison Hatch, was born in 1902. In the summer of 1908 Hatch received a visitor in Dorset, a Chinese official who told him that the Chinese government needed engravers for its new bureau of printing. He was recommended by the U.S. Treasury Department and authorized to travel to China, accompanied by an associate, William A. Grant.

Hatch hesitated, anxious about journeying so far because of his mother's failing health. It was also speculated that he knew of his own serious condition, Bright's disease (chronic nephritis) and perhaps thought that the job would best provide for his wife and son. On reaching Honolulu he learned that the Chinese dowager empress and emperor were dying, to be succeeded on the throne by their three-year-old son. But Hatch carried out his six-year contract with the Chinese, and was joined by his wife, who gave concerts for the American legation in Peking.

His mother died in 1913, and the next year, while working on a portrait of Yuan shih K'ai, first president of China, Hatch succumbed to kidney disease. His body was returned to Dorset in a sealed lead casket, accompanied by two Chinese officials who never took their eyes off it until its burial in

Maple Hill Cemetery. The behavior of his guards gave rise to speculation that he might have been murdered, but the rumor was denied by family friends who attended his final illness.

Grace Hatch and Harrison returned to the States and resided winters in California and summers in Dorset. Harrison died of strep throat in 1929 while on a bicycle tour of Europe. The widow sold Lorenzo's 1906 oil portrait of his mother to Delnoce Hopkins, daughter of his colleague William Grant. In 1967 Mrs. Hopkins donated it to SVAC, where it remains in the permanent collection. A 1906 portrait by Hatch of his wife and a 1907 oil, a spring scene of Mt. Aeolus and Owl's Head, are in the Bennington Museum's collection.

Hatch's sister Elizabeth became the wife of Albert Baker Cheney (1852–1948), a pianist, baritone, and teacher at the Boston College of Oratory, whose father was Dorset choirmaster Simeon P. Cheney.

Closely linked to Dorset, though not a native, Edwin Burrage Child (1868–1937) first stayed with John Lillie and was among painters who encouraged Lillie to take up brush and canvas. The son of a Baptist minister, Jonathan Bush Child, Child grew up in parishes his father held in Governeur, New York, Pawtucket, Rhode Island, and Ludlow, Vermont. In Dorset he sang in the church choir. At Amherst College he illustrated college publications, did charcoal drawings, and sold some landscapes. At the Art Students League he studied with John LaFarge, then sold illustrations to *Scrib-*

Courtesy of the Bennington Museum

Edwin B. Child in his Dorset Hollow studio, now the home of Mary DeVries. The painting on the wall is that of his children Katherine and Sargent.

ner's, Harper's, McClure's, and *Appleton's* magazines.

In 1894 Child married Anna Sykes of Dorset. For their honeymoon they traveled by horse and carriage to the Bromley House in Peru. They moved to Long Island, then to West 90th Street in Manhattan, then to Washington Square. After 1908 Child concentrated on portraits and landscapes. Among his portraits were those of Senator Dwight W. Morrow, educator John Dewey, Governor Wilbur Cross of Connecticut, and U.S. House Speaker Henry T. Rainey. At the St. Louis Exposition of 1904 Child earned a medal for his landscapes, and had a solo exhibit in 1930 at the National Gallery in Washington.

Child's 1933 portrait of Noah Webster is reproduced in nearly all Webster dictionaries. To achieve a likeness he visited a Webster granddaughter in Massachusetts who was said to resemble the subject. She had a trunk of Webster's possessions from which Child selected a plum-colored coat and lace jacket with which to adorn the portrait. Once he was invited to paint a portrait of President Franklin D. Roosevelt and was leaving for Washington when a telegram arrived announcing that Roosevelt's mother had changed her mind and commissioned another artist.

Child spent his last decade in Dorset Hollow where he had remodeled two barns, one for a studio and the other a residence. He also remodeled a colonial-design house in the village, once the tavern of Captain John Gray, built about 1800. It was presented in 1928 to the community by his wife's brother, Bernard G. Sykes (1869–1944), and became the Dorset Village Public Library.

Courtesy of Mr. and Mrs. Duncan Ogden; photo by Tyler Resch

Edwin B. Child painted this scene of a blasting operation at a marble quarry. It accompanied an article Child wrote for Scribner's Magazine *in 1905 titled "The Marble Mountains."*

This Dorset Hollow maple sugaring scene was painted by Wallace W. Fahnestock about 1930. The subjects were identified in 1978 by Emma Payne Roberts, who said the man near the saphouse was her father, Frank Streeter; at right was her brother Fred, and the person in the foreground was her uncle, "French" Wilkins. The horses were "Kit" and "Star."

The Childs' daughter, Katherine, was its librarian from 1937 to 1966. In 1936, a year before his death, Child went West to paint Yosemite and the San Bernadino Mountains, and lived in a cabin owned by his Aunt Hattie.

Wallace Weir Fahnestock (1877–1962), a protege of John LaFarge, was commissioned by Zephine Humphrey to execute a stained-glass window in the Dorset Church as a memorial to her mother, Harriet Sykes Humphrey. The window depicts the Sykes garden, with Mt. Aeolus in the background. In 1914 Fahnestock and his patron were married, and lived in the West Road home that had belonged to Mrs. Humphrey. About 1928 the Fahnestocks built a smaller house on the Lower Hollow Road and named it "Chrysalis" (now the home of Mr. and Mrs. Frederic Taylor).

Fahnestock was born in Harrisburg, Pennsylvania, in 1877 and attended

The Arts and the Artists

Wallace W. Fahnestock (1876-1962) designed four of the Dorset church's stained-glass windows. He was a protege of John LaFarge, who had worked with the Tiffany studios.

The Harriette Sykes Humphrey memorial church window, designed by her son-in-law Wallace Fahnestock in 1914. It depicts her garden at the foot of Nichols Hill looking east toward Mt. Aeolus.

public schools of Cleveland, the Case School of Applied Science, and the Art Students League. Intending to become an architect, he studied three years at the Cleveland Art School. An early connection with Dorset occurred in New York where he was a fellow art student of Herbert Meyer. Fahnestock went to Boston to work in advertising, then began painting murals. Little has been written of his life, but a chatty 1930 *Rutland Herald* article personalized him and his work as follows:

> There is a decided charm to Wallace Fahnestock's pictures. A quality of warmth even in his winter scenes which are never cold or colorless. But it is perhaps for his paintings which contain groups of flowers that he is best noted.... He has been able to "do" flowers and retain their full color and grace without a suggestion of stiffness or unnatural position.... But there is nothing "arty" about the man himself.
>
> He discusses his pictures, yes, but not with the Greenwich Village type of conversation which leaves one gasping for breath and wondering if they are looking as dumbfounded and ignorant as they feel.

And neither does he dress or look the part of the artist; no flowing locks or ties or other affectations. Nine times out of ten one might think that he was ready for a hike, fishing trip, or round of golf, to judge by his conventional dress.

And in Dorset no one would think of calling him anything but Wallace. That's a characteristic of the neighborly nature of Dorset, and of course he is interested in everything from the Dorset Players, in which he is a moving spirit, to the Congregational church where he is a willing and efficient worker. He is a member of the Salmagundi Club in New York, the Paint and Play Club of New Haven, and the Connecticut Academy of Hartford.

Fahnestock's wife once said of him, "He hopes to have made a better art of living than he has a living from art."

After living in Paris fourteen years, David and Beatrice Jackson Humphreys fled the Nazis in 1940 and chose to settle in Dorset for its scenic attributes. From the Sykes sisters they rented a home they later bought, the former Farwell Tavern at Church Street and West Road.

David Humphreys was born in 1901 in Morristown, New Jersey, and studied with artists in Woodstock, New York, New York City, Provincetown, and Paris. He was known as a sensitive landscapist whose works won much acclaim. He was treasurer of SVAC for a decade, served on its art committee, and was an honorary trustee until his death in 1970.

Born in London, Beatrice "Bea" Jackson was educated at the Colorossi Academy in Paris, the Art Students League, and Grand Central Art School in New York. She and her husband painted landscapes in Europe and North Africa between 1927 and 1940, and exhibited regularly. Her first show was in Paris and she exhibited there and in New York and Hartford. Her awards include the Leon Lehrer Memorial Prize in the 1973 Allied Artists of America Annual Exhibition. She has been active with SVAC for many years, chaired its art committee, and served as a trustee.

A master of the miniature, Arthur Jones grew up on Nichols Hill, first worked as a gardener, and received instruction from Ada Lillie Davis, daughter of John Lillie. As a student at Burr & Burton in 1948, his work was shown by the Southern Vermont Artists. His first solo show was on the Dorset Green on a Sunday afternoon in August 1952. From that experience his stature grew, and his work has been exhibited in galleries throughout New England. He is known not only for the tiny scale of some of his landscapes but also for his mastery of exquisite detail.

A Reginald Marsh painting.

Reginald Marsh was born in 1898 in Paris, in an apartment over the Cafe du Dome, a popular rendezvouz for artists and writers. His father, Frederick Dana Marsh, was a painter and muralist. At Yale, Marsh was art editor of *The Record*, and developed a lifelong devotion to New York. He worked as a staff artist for the *New York Daily News* and contributed drawings to *The New Yorker*. He made large backdrops for the Greenwich Village Follies and was a founder of the stage designers' union. He traveled widely and made seven extended trips to Europe, including Moscow and Leningrad.

Best known for his watercolors and sketches of the female form and the New York scene (often combined), Marsh also illustrated books and taught at the Art Students League. In the Depression he was commissioned by the Works Project Administration to execute murals in the New York Customs House and the post office in Washington.

Marsh died unexpectedly of a heart attack on July 3, 1954, at the age of fifty-six. He was honored by a retrospective in 1964 at the Museum of Modern Art titled "The Burlesque, the Beach, and the Bowery." In 1965, SVAC, where he had exhibited summers since 1940, held an exhibit of Marsh's watercolors and drawings, and a major show was staged there in 1989.

Dorset

Photo by Robert Terrill, courtesy of *Vermont Life*.

Herbert Meyer and his wife "Nan" at right pose with their daughter Felicia and her husband Reginald Marsh—all four of them artists. The painting is a Reginald Marsh.

Herbert Meyer, born in New York in 1882, became one of the best known of the Dorset artists who founded SVAC. He received education and inspiration in Europe and training at the Art Students League. He was a member of the National Academy. His works, notably evocative scenes of Vermont in all seasons, were handled by the Macbeth Gallery and are in many private museums and collections, including the Metropolitan. He succumbed in 1960 to injuries received in a Nichols Hill Road auto accident two years earlier that also had proved fatal to his wife. A memorial exhibition of Meyer's works was held at SVAC in 1963. Some of his works may be seen in the Fleming Museum in Burlington.

Anne Norton Meyer, known as Nan, was born in Connecticut and studied commercial art at the Pratt Institute. She was working for a New York advertising firm when she met Meyer and they were married in 1907, after which they made several lengthy trips to Europe. She was best known for her paintings of nature, especially flowers. She was a prominent SVAC exhibitor until her untimely death in June 1958.

Felicia Meyer was born in Brooklyn in 1913. Since childhood she had been a West Road summer resident with her parents, and remained so after her marriage to Marsh. She painted many landscapes of Dorset. She served as a trustee of SVAC and was an active painter whose works are in several private collections. She died at her home in New York in 1978.

A resident of Nichols Hill Road since 1945, muralist and portraitist William Dean Fausett discovered when he came to Dorset that he was descended from Captain John Fassett Bennington, leader in 1764 of the first militia of Green Mountain Boys, and from Captain William Dean, an early settler of Windsor when Vermont was known as the New Hampshire Grants. He lives in a house part of which he claims was the dwelling of Cephas Kent where the Dorset Conventions were held in 1775 and 1776. Fausett was born in Price, Utah, on July 4, 1913.

Fausett has been president of the National Society of Mural Painters, and has painted many scenes depicting events of the American Revolution and the drafting of the Constitution. Some were done for the Bicentennial in 1976 and others to commemorate the two hundredth anniversary of the Constitution in 1987. Among his many portraits is one of Anna Mary Robertson "Grandma" Moses on her hundredth birthday. In 1969 he executed a series of eight paintings that depicted aspects of the Powell expedition of 1869 that explored unmapped regions of the American West.

Educated at the Art Students League and the Beaux Arts Institute of Design, Fausett first exhibited at the Colorado Springs Fine Arts Center in 1936, toured Europe in 1935 and 1937, and began painting in Vermont in 1939. He received several Guggenheim fellowships. Before moving to Dorset he resided in Old Bennington, where he did a landscape titled *The Green Mountains* that won a Carnegie international award. His works have been purchased by the Metropolitan Museum, the Whitney Museum of American Art, and the Museum of Modern Art.

Following a visit in 1939, James Ashley returned to Dorset after the war to paint. Known for representational landscapes, he exhibited at the Macbeth and Grand Central galleries in New York and Cowie Galleries in Los Angeles. From 1953 to 1959 he was the director of SVAC, where he was remembered for his closeness to benefactress Louise Ryalls Arkell, for whom the SVAC performing-arts pavilion is named. In 1959 Ashley sold his Peace Street home and returned to California. He died in 1985.

Claude Dern, a native of France, came to the United States in 1929 and studied at the Art Students League and Grand Central Art School with George Bridgeman, Ivan Olinsky, and Alpheus Cole. He first exhibited at SVAC in 1934 and had a solo show there in 1971, and his paintings were again exhibited there in 1976.

Dern taught at the Newark School of Fine and Industrial Art in New Jersey, then conducted his own art school in Maplewood, New Jersey. His paintings, mostly landscapes, are in private collections as well as those of the Bennington Museum, the Vermont State House, and the American Embassy in Paris. Among subjects of his portraits were Reid Lefevre and John Lillie. Dern's memberships have included Allied Artists of America, Salamagundi Club, National Arts Club, Vermont Artists Guild, American Veterans Society of Artists, and life membership in the Art Students League.

Carl T. Ramsey of "Swampacres," also described in chapter 13, should be mentioned here for his paintings of orchids, notable for their accuracy because of his botanical expertise. He was also an accomplished photographer.

Norman B. Wright (1901–1971) another SVAC founder, studied in Chicago and France and taught drawing and painting at the National Academy of Art in Chicago, where he was also dean. An art collector, he chaired the SVAC art committee and was long active as a trustee.

Elsa Bley, a native of New York, settled in Dorset in 1945 and now lives in a house Charlie Wade moved from Hebron, New York, and rebuilt across from the village green. She too studied at the Art Students League and the Grand Central School of Art, and with such prominent painters as George Luks and John Sloan; she studied for three summers in Europe with Henry B. Snell. She left a successful school of art which she had established in 1934 in Scarsdale to devote more time to her painting, but once in Vermont began classes for children and adults, and taught and exhibited at SVAC for more than twenty years. Among her exhibits and solo shows have been those at the American and Washington Watercolor societies, the New York Watercolor Club, and the National Association of Women Artists.

Cleade Enders, a native of Utica, New York, studied at the Munson-Williams-Proctor Institute there, at the Pennsylvania Academy of Fine Arts, the Barnes Foundation, and the Art Students League. He has lived and worked in Dorset for many years. In 1988 he and Anthony Holberton-Wood, a former executive director of SVAC, opened the T/C Gallery on the Lane Road.

Known for his realist landscapes, Enders has twice earned Tiffany Foundation awards, and has exhibited at the Boston Museum of Fine Arts, the Museum of Modern Art in New York, and the National Academy of Design and Corcoran Gallery in Washington.

A resident in the Green Peak Orchard, the late Sigrun Taylor drew artistic inspiration from her Swedish heritage and its folk traditions of trolls, elves, and ancient gods. She was a life member of the Art Students League and exhibited often at SVAC, where a solo show was held in 1987.

Sculptor Richard Erdman, born in Princeton, New Jersey, in 1952, grew up in East Dorset and graduated from UVM with a degree in art education. Inspired by the heritage of marble in East Dorset and by sculptor Jane B. Armstrong, his interest led him to study in Florence and Carrara, Italy. Among other places, his work has been shown at SVAC, the Stratton Arts Festival, the Hopkins Center, the Byck Gallery in Louisville, Kentucky, the Four Winds Gallery, the Peel Gallery, and the University of Vermont.

Jane B. Armstrong is one of Dorset's newest artists, though she resided and worked in nearby Manchester for many years. By moving in 1988 to a home and studio on Dorset Hill Road, near the old Freedley quarry, she demonstrated her affinity for the material in which she works. Her specialty is carving appealing animal forms from marble, and she encourages an philosophy of "please touch."

A former journalist, Armstrong became a student of Jose deCreeft and John Hovannes at the Art Students League in 1964. Since 1969 she has had thirty-seven museum or university solo shows. Among nearly forty awards from national juried exhibitions in New York, she won a Gold Medal of Honor in 1986 from the Knickerbocker Artists, a national art society.[5]

The Dorset Players

In April 1927 a three-act play, *39 East*, was presented in the Dorset Town Hall to benefit the PTA. The production was inspired by Dr. and Mrs. Edwin Goodman, summer residents and devotees of the arts. Enthusiasm about the play was so strong that it led to the creation of the Dorset Players, with Dr. Goodman as first president.[6]

Other founding officers included many familiar names: Mr. and Mrs. Wallace W. Fahnestock, Mr. and Mrs. Frederick Gilbert, Mrs. Huntington Gilbert, Mr. and Mrs. Rufus Gilbert, Mr. and Mrs. Joseph Harrington, Mr. and Mrs. Carleton G. Howe, Mr. and Mrs. Ernest H. West, Edwin Lefevre, Jr., Egidio Moresi, Howard Pfaelzer, Mrs. Ryland Lockwood, Miss Evalyn Paxon, Mrs. Alan deSchweinitz, and Miss Elizabeth West.

Because the town hall had its limitations, May Goodman purchased three acres of Cheney Woods located along the road and donated it to the Players in September 1927 in anticipation of some sort of building. Proceeds from

Drama was an enthusiastic pastime in East Dorset in the summer of 1932 when "Henry's Wedding" was presented under the direction of Helen Thornton of Jonesboro, Arkansas. The stage was in the East Dorset school's meeting room (See note 9 on page 291).

plays presented in those first two years in Dorset, Manchester, Pawlet, and Proctor, along with donations, totaled $2,000, enough to prompt Ernest West to offer a barn he owned on Rupert Mountain to build a playhouse on the Cheney Woods land. Material from another barn was added, a $9,000 mortgage was obtained from the Factory Point National Bank, and the hardy Players began to assemble the building in the snows of January 1929.

The playhouse was designed to give the audiences a rustic effect, with weathered barnboards facing the interior, and old one-foot-square, hand-hewn beams. The total cost of the building was $10,600. The premiere performance was *Sun Up*, a three-act play by Lula Vollmer, which opened on July 2, 1929. Dr. Goodman was again the director, and the cast included May Goodman, Ernest and Helen West, Frederick Gilbert, Wallace Fahnestock, Joseph Harrington, Carleton Howe, Hawley Fitch, and Hiram Jones. That winter *Sun Up* went on tour to Bennington and Burlington.

During their first five years, the Dorset Players produced many three-act plays as well as a tournament of one-acts, and the mortgage was reduced to $2,500. But the Depression and economic conditions took their toll, and in the summer of 1935, when one production failed to get off the ground, the Players called on counterparts in Proctor to fill out the season. Summer seasons of 1936, 1937, and 1938 were unsuccessful financially, and in March 1939, with the death of Dr. Goodman, the Players lost their driving force. A one-act tournament scheduled for that summer was canceled, though it was held for the last time in 1940. Paul Stephenson of the Brattleboro Drama Festival was engaged to produce plays in 1939 and 1940, but attendance was poor; a better season was held in 1941 as war clouds loomed. Except for one more production of *Sun Up* in September 1943 the theater remained dark throughout World War II. The building was used for dances, card parties, and other wartime benefits for the Red Cross and other groups.

The Players revived somewhat in 1945 with William G. Barrows, Sr., as president, and Stephenson returned for two summers. But attendance remained sluggish, a new $2,000 mortgage was necessary, and the last two shows of the 1947 season were called off.

In 1948 John Herrick wrote a musical especially for the Players. Titled *Green Mountain Grit: The Mystery of Lord Howe's Diamond*, it was a musical melodrama of the American Revolution, set in Dorset in the era of the New Hampshire Grants, relating how the Green Mountain Boys took Fort Ticonderoga. Directed by May Goodman, it was well received, and some of the old enthusiasm was restored. Elected Players president in the fall of 1948, Herrick set out to fill a summer schedule for 1949. Among groups he contacted was the Caravan Theatre of Westchester County, New York, which put on a program of three one-acts that March. An agreement was reached by which the Players would produce a summer season of plays with the Caravan Theatre as the acting group.

Under the direction of Fred Carmichael and Patricia Wynn Rose, and in the early years Dee Stemph, the Caravaners' productions took firm hold, and their first summer of plays was extended to include Labor Day weekend. The seeds of success, finally planted, germinated and flourished for the next twenty-seven summers. Miss Rose became Mrs. Carmichael, Susan Richardson became business manager, and Judith "J. P." Murray joined the team as scene designer.

In 1953 the first of many original plays by Carmichael, *The Green Snowman*, was produced. Many of the Dorset-originated plays that followed were purchased by the Samuel French organization and produced all over the globe. In 1954 the Caravaners launched a fall season that continued for ten years. In November 1954 Fred Kennedy, the newly elected Players president, carried into the audience a tray bearing the twenty-five-year mortgage. To applause and cheers, Martha Lefevre held the document while May Goodman set it afire. Kennedy also vowed that from that moment on, all minutes of Players meetings would be kept on file—a detail overlooked in the past.[7]

During the 1950s the Caravan Theatre produced two plays by Dorset resident Warren Murray (husband of "J. P."), *Death and Taxes* and *Proposals at Geneva*. In 1954 Fred and Pat Carmichael rented the theater building outright, increased the number of performances, oversaw many physical improvements, and continued to play a major role in the cultural life of the town. Mrs. Einar Grondahl, known as Aunty Bee, helped finance a Green Room that was used to display the work of some Dorset artists; it later became the Stage Right Gallery. In 1964 a thorough renovation took place, including an urgently needed lighting-control system. Another Warren Murray play, *Dear Miss Peabody*, was produced in 1970.

Photo from Ernest H. West in Terry Tyler collection

The Dorset Playhouse under construction in the winter of 1929. Two barns, donated by Ernest H. West, were reconstructed on land given by Dr. and Mrs. Ned Goodman. The barnboards were reversed to reveal their weathered side to the audience.

For the twenty-seventh and final Caravan season, the plan was to produce only one play, Fred Carmichael's well-received *Last of the Class*. And Pat Carmichael agreed to direct the venerable *Green Mountain Grit*, which played to full houses for six nights. The Players presented a repeat performance of *Harvey*, and an outside group was engaged.

In June 1976, another creative couple, John Nassivera and Jill Charles, who had participated in the Caravan Theatre for several years and were encouraged by the Carmichaels, rented the playhouse for the summer and produced plays briefly under the name of Harlequin, Ltd. In 1979 the name was changed to the Dorset Summer Theatre Festival, organized as a nonprofit corporation.

In the past decade the Dorset Theater Festival has produced plays for increasingly sophisticated and well-informed audiences who have grown to expect to make an effort, mentally as well as physically, to attend good theater in an age of easy television and cinema. Nassivera sees Dorset, especially with the continuing presence of important playwrights at the Colony House, as part of a creative movement that includes Off-Broadway and regional theater. In 1988 the Vermont Council on the Arts tended to confirm his aspirations when it termed Dorset "the best theater in Vermont."

Photo by Stetson Fletcher

The Dorset Playhouse today, located on Cheney Road near Dorset village.

Svetlova Dance Center

Since 1965 Dorset's artistic ambience has been diversified by the existence of the Svetlova Dance Center, located near the Dorset Field Club in a large house on ample grounds, formerly the home of the Durand family. Founded by Marina Svetlova, dancer, teacher, choreographer, and former prima ballerina with the Metropolitan Opera Company, the dance center each summer attracts some sixty students, mostly girls, aged eight to eighteen.

During the academic year Svetlova is a professor at Indiana University in Bloomington, where she has developed a prestigious ballet department. She runs the four-week dance center in Dorset with her husband, Theodor Haig, a concert pianist and student of Claudio Arrau. Haig is general manager of the center and teaches music. A staff of professional dancers forms the faculty, and several former students return each year as counselors.

Svetlova began life as Yvette von Hartman, the daughter of White Russian parents who fled the 1917 Revolution and then endured Nazi occupation of France. After the war, inspired by her teacher, Vera Trefilova, she adopted a Russian name (Svetlova means "sweet love") and launched a career in dance that took her, among many other places, to Australia with the original Ballet Russe de Monte Carlo, to Jacob's Pillow in the Berkshires, and to the coronation celebration for the queen of England.

Starting in 1959, Svetlova taught ballet for five seasons at SVAC, then decided to open her own summer school. Although it is listed under advertisements for "camps" in the *Sunday New York Times Magazine*, the Svetlova Dance Center considers itself not a camp but one of the nation's premiere summer schools of dance. In addition to a curriculum in classical ballet, the school teaches jazz, flamenco, aquatic ballet, and modern dance. Other offerings are tennis, swimming in a large pool, drama, crafts, instruction in French and Russian, and piano. Every few days the students go to see professional ballet at the Saratoga Performing Arts Center or Jacob's Pillow.

In an interview, Svetlova once summed up her approach this way: "Papa Shawn taught me at Jacob's Pillow that all forms of dance are important. . . . We run school the European way: work three days, next off—here we all go to Saratoga to see the New York City Ballet Thursdays—work two days and then Sunday free to hike or swim or dream; it is free studio time also."

Photo by Stetson Fletcher

The entrance sign to the Svetlova Dance Center is in keeping with the unusual architecture of the building itself.

Writers and Musicians

Most of Dorset's artistic focus has been on painting and drama. The best known musicians in the recent past were violinist Carol Glenn and her husband, pianist Eugene List, who lived on the Dorset Hill Road. Margaret Meachem, long known for her musicianship, has been composing electronic music.

Several writers have made the town their base, notably novelist Moira Pearce, magazine writers Geoff Norman and Lionel Atwill, and mystery writer Judson Phillips. William C. Heinz, now retired, was a war correspondent and then sports columnist for the *New York Sun* until it folded in 1950. Among his three novels and six sports-related books was a novel called *MASH* (without the asterisks), written in collaboration with H. Richard Hornberger, which was the precursor of the television series. Heinz won the E. P. Dutton Award five times for a best magazine sports article. Another retired journalist is Gordon Harrison, who wrote for the *Springfield Union* and *Detroit News*.

A writer who has made a strong mark on Dorset is Richard M. Ketchum. After serving in World War II aboard a Navy subchaser, Ketchum came to town and worked at the Orvis Company in Manchester. A Yale graduate, he was with the U.S. Information Agency and in 1956 joined the American Heritage Publishing Co., where he became editor of the books division. Among his books are *The Battle for Bunker Hill* in 1962 and *The World of George Washington* in 1974. Ketchum and his wife Barbara always retained their Dorset ties, and in 1974 became permanent residents when Ketchum and William Blair of Guilford, former publisher of *Harper's*, launched *Blair & Ketchum's Country Journal*. The magazine had its editorial offices in Manchester for more than a decade.

Other Art Forms

One of the most influential figures in the production of Dorset marble, and who researched and recorded the only detailed history of this industry, also used marble as his favored art medium. In 1949 Harper & Brothers published *Handcrafts of New England* by Allen H. Eaton, describing the low-relief marble carvings which Ernest H. West, in his retirement, liked to make as gifts for friends and neighbors.

Eaton also wrote about Dorothy Howe, wife of Carleton G. Howe, who then was raising sheep in Pawlet. She liked to encourage the West Roaders, "an organized group of knitters who take deep pride in their skill and who help her in working up the yarn from her sheep's wool into a variety of sweat-

A rare art form, the building of an enduring stone wall. John Prouty and Floyd Wade were photographed in the 1960s as they rebuilt Harold Gates's West Road wall.

ers, suits for women, socks, mittens, and a few examples of bed coverings."

Dorset is known for a nucleus of interest in wall stenciling. Although there were only two houses in Dorset with early stenciled walls, the Dorset Inn and Barrows House, Jessica Bond, wife of Eugene A. Bond, made it her business to search elsewhere for stenciled designs done years ago by itinerant artists. Through careful study of this art, she identified the work of twenty-three different stencilers around New England, and assembled a book on the subject.[8] She was a charter member of the Historical Society of Early American Decoration.

Taking these esthetics a step further, Adele Bishop incorporated a business in Manchester to offer for sale various pre-cut designs of stencils, along with special paints and brushes so that people could place their own stencils on walls, over mantels, along ceiling beams, on floors, or even on textiles. From these two women and their pursuit of a vanished art, Dorset gained a certain reputation from devotees of decorative early Americana.

The Arts and the Artists

NOTES

1. John Spargo, *The Bennington Battle Monument: Its Story and Its Meaning* (Rutland, Vt.: Tuttle Company, 1925), p. 97.
2. Andrea Rebek, "The Selling of Vermont: From Agriculture to Tourism, 1860–1910," *Vermont History* vol. 44 (winter 1976), p. 17.
3. These sketchy accounts of the Dorset connections of Walter Shirlaw and Frederick Crane are from Robert McIntyre's paper on Dorset artists presented to the historical society on March 19, 1964.
4. Rose Lindley Kent, "John Lillie," *Vermonter Magazine*, vol. 47 (December 1942), p. 152. Bassett 4052.
5. Other artists affiliated in some way with Dorset, either as residents, as summer visitors, or through having painted its scenery, are here compiled from lists provided by SVAC and by McIntyre, and others knowledgeable about the arts scene: Charlotte Brooks, Kent Crane, Ada Lillie Davis, John Lillie Davis, Harriet deSanchez, Cordelia C. deSchweinitz, Guy Pene Dubois, Lea Ehrich, Frederick Gilbert, Huntington P. Gilbert, Janet Gilbert, Kay Hamlin, George Hughes, C. Alton Kent, Rose L. Kent, Pam Marron, James Montague, William Newman, George Noyes, Tom Parsons, Russell Parks, Allan B. Sheldon, Barbara Sheldon, Marcella Sheldon, Carl Tremper, Bernice West, and Dorothy Vietor.
6. Warren Murray, arr., "The Dorset Playhouse," a pamphlet published in 1979 by the Dorset Historical Society to commemorate the fiftieth anniversary of the Dorset Players.
7. Past presidents of the Dorset Players, listed alphabetically for the fiftieth anniversary, have been Betty Adams, William Barrows, Sr., Clay Bartlett, Eugene Bond, William Cruikshank, Claude Dern, Lynne Evans, Rhys Evans, Ernest Edgerton, Dr. Edward Goodman, John Herrick, Carleton Howe, Arthur Jones, Fred Kennedy, T. Wylie Kinney, Edwin Lefevre, Jr., Jack Spafford, Charles Schubert, Craig Wheaton-Smith, and Alfred Yates.
8. Jessica Bond tells an amusing anecdote about Ray Bushee, for many years Dorset's independent-minded taxi driver. Wanting to go to Cavendish, where she had heard about a wall stencil she wished to inspect, Mrs. Bond, recovering from surgery and not wanting to drive herself, called Bushee for a ride.
Said she, "What are you doing between noon and five this afternoon?"
Replied Bushee, "I have to take a woman to the doctor's at two o'clock."
"Well I guess you can't drive me to Cavendish, then."
"I'll call you back."
Bushee called back in a few minutes: "It's okay. I can take you to Cavendish."
"But what about the woman who had a doctor's appointment at two P.M.?"
"I called the doctor and canceled the appointment for her."
They drove to Cavendish, located the house on "Twenty Mile Stream," surrounded by snow that seemed ten feet high. But the wall was in such bad condition and so dirty, and the stenciling so faded, that its pattern could not be determined. Mrs. Bond hoped that the doctor's appointment had not been an emergency.
9. Members of the cast include: Back Row, from left, John Cunningham, Clarence Button, Richard Brophy, James Kelley, Frank Merrow, Paul Landon, Wallace Brock, Lynn Baker, Ray Swan, Arthur Brophy, Frank Eggleston, Robert L. Anderson, John Dalton, Ray Joslin. Next Row, from left, Nellie Brock, Jennie Griffith, Elida Wade, Lawrence Wade, Albert Hitchcock, Julia Merrow, Ida Leary, Nellie Baker, Elizabeth Kelley, Edw. Eggleston, Gladys Lang, Eva Burns, Gertrude Tully, Clara McDevitt, Pearl Merrow. Sitting, from left, Edw. Bowen, Oliver Harris, Maynard Grout, Nora Cunningham, Francis McBride, Wm. A. Griffith, Anna Abbott, Burton Snow, Anna Whalon, Maurice Nugent, Ann Sherlock, Alice Brock, Frank Read. Front Row, from left, Eleanor Deveneau, Virginia Abbott, Leona Leary, Florence Wade, Velma Jackson, Eleanor Welch, Josephine Welch, Shirley Welch, Doris Bowen, Sarah McDaniels, Theresa Landon.

13

Since 1924

DORSET WAS in rough shape in 1924. The marble industry was dead. Town population approached its lowest point, half that of the prosperous era of 1870 and 1880, when the census exceeded 2,000. By 1920 the number dropped to 1,326 and in 1930 the bottom was reached, 1,119. This level would be frozen for forty years. For two consecutive censuses Dorset's population stayed precisely the same: in 1950 and again in 1960 an even 1,150.[1]

The year 1924 was the first full year of the presidency of Vermont-born Calvin Coolidge. But the national prosperity that appeared to surround Coolidge did not always include Vermont, which earned the reputation of a backwater of rural isolation—roads dusty or else mired in mud, children barefoot, one-room district schools of variable quality, hardscrabble agriculture, houses for sale. In 1924 there were only nine miles of paved highway in the state, between Montpelier and Barre, recalls John A. Kouwenhoven, who first came to Vermont in that year.

The year 1924 marked the end of School Supervisory Union District 38, composed of Dorset, Manchester, and Sunderland, with Harry B. Dickinson, superintendent. The next year Dorset became part of the so-called Bennington North District in combination with Manchester, Pawlet, Rupert, and Sunderland, with B. P. Hamlin as superintendent. In 1926 Edwin L. Bigelow was named superintendent, a position he kept for the next thirty-one years. In 1935 the school union was joined by Sandgate, Danby, and Mt. Tabor, and its name was changed to the Bennington-Rutland District because three of its towns are in Rutland County.

Dorset may have been at a low ebb in the mid-1920s, but there still remained a carefree aspect to the summer season, epitomized by the two-page weekly newspaper *The Dorset Docket*, "published every Saturday during the summer" at five cents a copy, or one dollar for the season. John Mason Bigelow's editorials promoted the idea of a Dorset orchestra and concert hall as well as an auditorium for the Dorset Players. The little paper often recounted the histories of some older houses. One article described the building of the Prentiss place in 1868, and mentioned the Prentisses' youngest son Henry, who was born in Switzerland but grew to manhood in Dorset. The article told how Henry, then elderly, had selected his wife, Lila, daughter of Mr. and Mrs. John Parkinson Roberts, who was "the rosiest girl in the bunch of young folks who climbed Equinox."

One issue of the *Docket* contained the obituary of Dr. Thomas William Salmon (1876–1927), who had resided next to the Dorset church. He was described as "a wise physician and able counsellor, who in state and national service developed and introduced modern methods for the guidance of the mentally normal as also for the mentally affected . . . a sympathetic physician who attacked the problem of the patient and his family with a broad social interest and with the attitude of an advisory friend."

Among advertisers in 1927 were the Brown Teapot, the Green Gate Tea Room, and Clarence Blackmer's jitney service, which urged the reader to "visit Dorset's points of interest in a Hudson car."

The Depression

Most older residents share a common recollection upon looking back on the Great Depression. They bear no tales of impoverishment and despair, but remember the early 1930s as a time of self-sufficiency when people went about their business frugally, but not in hardship.

"We didn't have anything to start with. So we didn't notice anything was missing," says Ruth Baldwin McWayne, descendant of original settler Benjamin Baldwin. Her family had pigs, cows, and chickens. Her father, Joseph Baldwin, made butter which he peddled around town, often trading it for other commodities.

Nora Cunningham Gilbert remembered Depression-era tramps getting off the train in East Dorset. Her mother, Florence Cunningham, who ran the Mt. Aeolus Inn, would always feed them if they did some work, such as splitting wood. But she made them sit outside on the front porch to eat.

Ernest G. Edgerton, who attended Burr & Burton during the Depression, said that people considered themselves lucky if they could find work for 75 cents to a dollar a day. He did some work for his father, Ernest H. Edgerton, but did not much like farm work. By 1942 Edgerton had joined his fa-

Harvesting ice in the 1930s on South Village Pond (also called Deming Pond) at the foot of Morse Hill Road, involved this motorized saw to cut the ice into blocks. In foreground are Harold Snow and Rene Nolet, with Irving Jones or Art Van Orman at rear. The photo dates to about 1937.

ther in the operation of the Edgerton Sawmill, north of the village on the Mettawee. (By 1965 the Edgerton mill, with a crew of six, was cutting 1.25 million board feet of lumber annually. But the mill was closed about 1969, then leased to Pete Cobb, who ran it for a couple of years and bought it. Cobb sold to Hal Wilkins who updated the mill, ran it a few more years, then sold it to Bear Paw Lumber, which still operates it.)

There were strong memories of cutting ice during winters in the early 1930s, an activity that waned as electric refrigeration came into use. Edgerton cut ice on Prentiss Pond for Clarence Blackmer's ice barn, where the ice was insulated by sawdust. The rest of the year Blackmer peddled the ice blocks.

Rene Nolet of the Mad Tom Road, who came to East Dorset in 1925, has vivid memories, as well as photographs, of cutting ice on Deming Pond for the East Dorset Creamery (located where the firehouse is now), and for Mt. Aeolus Inn. He recalls that the ice was cut by a thirty-inch circular sawblade installed on a 1924 four-cylinder Chevrolet engine. On a good cold morning this rig cut as many as 1,500 cakes of ice measuring 20 by 30 by about 12 inches. Nolet worked for the creamery from 1931 to 1936, then took a job driving a milk tanker truck between East Dorset and New York City. (Nolet is well known in beekeeping circles and the honey he produces is in demand for its clear, clean qualities.)

The creamery's ice harvest would take two to three weeks, depending on weather. Its ice house had thick walls, and the cakes of ice were insulated by hemlock and spruce sawdust from the Swezey sawmill. The ice was chopped to refrigerate milk in bulk tanks, Nolet recalls. The East Dorset Creamery never did convert to mechanical refrigeration; it was bought out by Borden's, then abandoned. Part of the building later became the firehouse.

After ice cutting ended, Nolet says, there was often little work until sugaring began, usually in late February. The operating sugarhouses he remembers in East Dorset included the Egglestons, Walter Beebe's, Henry Stone's, Baker's, and Reed's. Nolet was paid $4 a day for ice cutting or for sugaring—both hard work.

Dorset was unusually exempt from the excesses associated with the Depression. Town reports reveal few recipients of largesse from the overseer of the poor. Nearly everyone lived on a farm and had fruits, vegetables, livestock, dairy products, chickens. For those not on a farm neighborliness was the rule, and there was often enough to share. The economy thrived not on cash but on barter. Summer business suffered, but everyone made do and had few complaints.

It can be debated whether the paving of highways was Depression makework or whether this improvement coincided with growing popularity of the automobile. In any case, Route 7 was fixed in concrete during 1929 and 1930, and most of Route 30 received its blacktopping in 1938. That year the Barrows House was heavily damaged by a fire, which spared its facade.

One Depression-age benefit to the town is the long, low, unusually wide stone wall in South Dorset along Route 30 in front of the homes of William T. Burns, Sr., and his son William T., Jr. It was started by Bill Burns, Sr., in 1921, but was completed as a Depression-time project by Burns and his brother Jim, who returned home from Florida after the banks failed. Having little else to do, they concentrated on clearing rocks from the fields and created this handsome wall.

Depression or no, there was time for some sport, and the East Dorset Athletic Club fielded a baseball team that played in Benedict Meadow. They held meetings at the Mt. Aeolus Inn, and raised money to buy uniforms.

Toward 1940, the economy of war-preparedness lured many to remunerative factory jobs elsewhere.

World War II

Everyday life in small-town Dorset, Vermont, during World War II was chronicled in the January 1944 issue of *Harper's* magazine by an article that focused on Paul White's gas station, on Route 30 across from the Barrows House. It was not easy being in the garage business during the war, author John A. Kouwenhoven wrote, because gas was rationed and deliveries were infrequent. In good times White had sold 31,000 gallons a year, but in war years that quantity dwindled to 8,000. Nor was there much profit margin. To quote the article:

> *You make four cents on each gallon you sell, which may seem like pretty good profit, but isn't when you think of the time it takes to check the battery, the oil, the tires, and to perform all the rest of the special services you have to provide. It's all right if there's nothing else to do, but when you have overhauling or repair jobs on hand and have to take twenty minutes out to sell five gallons of gas (gross profit twenty cents), it doesn't pay.*
>
> *"If in good times a fellow could have the same business in repairs and service and not sell gas," Paul tells me, "he'd be better off." But of course you have to sell gas or people don't patronize your place.*

Kouwenhoven described other wartime vignettes: scrap drives, boarded-up tourist cabins and camps, unoccupied summer homes with uncut lawns, government red tape, paperwork, ration books. It was hard to find people to do odd jobs or farm labor. The men had either gone off to war or taken jobs at machine-tool factories in Springfield, at the Portsmouth naval shipyard, or plants far away in Los Angeles or Seattle.

Paul White was a solid citizen. Besides running the garage and caretaking for summer homes owned by those who could not get to Vermont during the war, he was a selectman, town meeting moderator, member of the ration board, chairman of the Fire District Prudential Committee, and commander of the American Legion post that met upstairs over his garage. A World War I veteran, White had grown up in Bennington, worked at a collar-manufacturing plant there, and learned to drive while working as a mechanic at Bennington Garage. He was hired as a mechanic-chauffeur by a wealthy family who had a farm in Dorset Hollow. He moved to Dorset when he resumed his chauffeur's job after the war in 1919. In 1928 he opened the garage, and in 1936 married his Bennington sweetheart, Mary Peabody.

In all, more than 80 Dorset men went off to war. That was not as many as the 140 who served in the Civil War, but now the population was half as big. Joe Brophy of East Dorset, who had joined the navy before the war, went down with the *Arizona* at Pearl Harbor on December 7, 1941.

In 1942 Dorset exceeded its $2,000 quota for the Red Cross War Relief drive. Committee chairman Miriam Tifft reported a total of $2,064.33, of which almost half, $1,005, came from summer residents. In that year too, Dorset as well as most other Bennington County towns voted "wet" at town meeting, favoring sales of "malt and vinous" as well as "spiritous" beverages. Each town voted on those questions every year.

Pastor Arthur P. Colburn resigned on July 8, 1942, to accept a call to serve as an army chaplain. Church deacons voted not to accept the resignation but to offer him a leave of absence. The committee to act with the deacons to supply the pulpit in Colburn's absence was composed of Howard R. Pfaelzer, Dr. W. D. McDonald, and Kimball O. Tifft.

Among many heart-breaking losses of the war for Dorset was that of Pilot Officer Horace Greeley Harwood. Born in 1920 in Trenton, New Jersey, he was a son of Sam Harwood and grandson and namesake of the town representative who lost his life in a sawmill accident in 1897. Harwood graduated from Burr & Burton in 1938 and went to war, intending to be a flyer. An injury from a teenage prank kept him out of the U.S. forces, so he joined the Royal Canadian Air Force. He was shot down over England on September 7, 1942, while piloting a Spitfire, the hottest British fighter plane of the war.

Harwood kept a diary between February 19, 1942, and the day he was lost, nearly seven months later. It recounts much war action as well as his purchase of a motorcycle so he could visit an English girl, Joan Ramsay, whom he intended to marry. A copy of the diary, provided by his younger brother James K. Harwood of Lewiston, Maine, has been turned over to the Dorset Historical Society.

The newspapers were full of items like the following, from the *Manchester Journal* in 1942:

A Hail-and-Farewell party will be given at the Playhouse Friday evening to honor five young men who will leave for Camp Devens on November 5. They are John N. Stannard, Roy W. Casey, Berniss Taft, Neil Hartwell and Edward McDevitt, who passed their final examinations last week. Charles Jones is already listed for the navy and Raymond Stannard will also enlist for service in the U.S. army.

Dorset dedicated its World War II Honor Roll on the Fourth of July 1943 with ceremonies around the Green. The Reverend John Theodore said a prayer for the eighty-four men who had left to serve in the armed forces. Speakers were Robert Warner and William G. Barrows, Sr.

The McBride-Harwood American Legion Post

The name Harwood was added to that of McBride, the World War I hero, to form a new combined name for the Dorset American Legion Post. When Mr. and Mrs. Raymond Bushee bought the former gas

The Dorset Sportsman's Club in Kirby Hollow, built by members and friends in 1972-73 on land given by Paul and Leona McWayne.

station of Paul White in 1961, the Legion met for a time in the basement playroom of Mr. and Mrs. Terry Tyler, then bought the old one-room North District Schoolhouse for its meetings, and charter member Albert Knowles paid off its mortgage. In 1973 the Legion post, whose members also belonged to the Dorset Sportsmen's Club, built their community hall and club rooms in Kirby Hollow.

The post has contributed many services and activities to the community, including planning annual Memorial Day ceremonies and placing flags on the graves of veterans of all wars. The old flags are burned at the Legion post quarters each Veterans' Day. In 1985 the post donated $3,000 for permanent bronze markers for each grave. Post membership began in the 1930s with sixteen, then grew to eighty-two, but more recently has had an active core of about ten.

A woman's auxiliary operated from 1947 until about 1962, took part in Memorial Day services, and held an annual Memorial Day dinner in the church vestry for all veterans and their families, preceded by a service in the church that included a salute to the dead and the sounding of taps. "It is a poignant sound on a bright May day to hear the taps echo through the mountains, and to remember the men who gave their lives for freedom," concludes the post's written history.

The Dorset Sportsmen's Club formed in June 1967 with thirty members, an outgrowth of an earlier group that met at Paul White's garage. First officers were Edward Tarbell, president, Dudley Griffis, vice president, and Joseph Harrington, secretary-treasurer. By late summer 1967 the club had released more than two thousand half-grown pheasants, a number matched by the state. Other activities included fishing derbies and hunter-safety courses. In 1973 the club built its quarters in Kirby Hollow on land donated by Paul and Leona McWayne. Labor came from volunteers from Dorset and surrounding towns. Dances, turkey shoots, and other fundraisers were held to finance the building and activities.

The Sportsmen's clubhouse has been used as a meeting place by Boy Scouts and a snowmobile club, as classrooms for the Long Trail and Equinox schools, and for auctions, dances, and wedding receptions.

The East Dorset Fire District

In 1943 a group met in East Dorset to recognize that the Manchester Fire Department should no longer be expected to cover for a community more than five miles away. Walter Read, Sr., in an account written for this book, recalled that funds were raised through dances, card parties, bake sales, and lawn parties to equip the new department. The first East Dorset fire chief was Ed Eggleston, then Howard Brophy, then Read.

A previous attempt at organizing East Dorset fire protection had produced one old Cadillac with a front-mount pump and about 250 feet of hose. "The car was unusable but the pump and hose was thought worth using," Read said, and so a Model B Ford pickup was obtained and had the pump installed on it, and the vehicle was housed at the town shed.

The men practiced on this rig but at a major fire it was discovered that the pump shaft was damaged and could not lift water. A 500-gallon-per-minute unit mounted on a trailer was obtained from the Boston Civil Defense office. Another fund drive enabled the unit to be purchased, and it was housed in a building offered by Byron Bowen. The pumper arrived by rail but because of war shortages it lacked tires. Surplus CD hose was obtained, and an East Road fire rallied support for the fledgling fire department.

The old Vermont Milk and Cream property, site of the present firehouse, was purchased for a token amount, and on January 12, 1948, selectmen authorized creation of the East Dorset Fire District No. 1. When Will Whalon's water supply dried up later that year, the organization was expanded to include a water district. In 1950 a new reservoir was built, financed by the North Bennington bank. Volunteers dug trenches for the pipes. A four-wheel-drive army car to tow the trailer-pumper and carry extra hose was also purchased, and in 1951 came a vote to build a 40 by 22-foot firehouse, completed for $2,500.

Practicing with the East Dorset Fire Department's equipment in 1943. From left: Buster Read, Wilbur Weber, Walter Young, and Walter Read. Holding nozzles are Leland Beebe and Byron Bowen.

A four-wheel-drive Air Force crash truck with 250-gallon tank and power takeoff became the first unit to carry water to a fire. The 1954 annual meeting approved enrollment in the Vermont State Firefighters' Association. The 1955 meeting initiated a street-lighting program for East Dorset and the South Village.

In 1963 the East Dorset water company paid off its reservoir construction loan. In 1980 the reservoir was enlarged again, and the water district now serves some seventy families. The larger fire district covers all territory in the eastern half of town, the border being the "height of land" on Mt. Aeolus.

The J. K. Adams Company

In 1941 Josiah K. Adams, a native of San Francisco, quit his job as a Wall Street stockbroker and came to Dorset, near where his son and daughter were attending college at Dartmouth and Bennington. In a garage opposite the Maple Hill Cemetery, after his discharge from the service in 1945, his entrepreneurial instincts prompted him to start making wooden toys, fish floats, and lures. His first successful product was the "speedy

Josiah K. Adams, original owner of the J. K. Adams Company, with Malcolm E. Cooper, owner since 1959. This photo was taken after the 1962 fire.

racer," a pull-toy made by the thousands. Adams pleased townspeople by declining a tax exemption at the 1945 town meeting.

In 1947 Adams moved operations into a former Manchester ice house at the now-familiar pine-shaded site on Route 30. Within a decade four additions were built for machinery and operations, box kilns, and lumber storage. Products expanded to fun racks, work benches, and lawn chairs. Not until 1951, after the arrival of Malcolm E. Cooper as a partner, did the firm produce its well-known wooden platters and chopping blocks. Cooper, who met Adams by chance in a parking lot and who had experience as an industrial engineer with legal training, has been the dominant figure at the plant ever since.

All the wood used—maple, beech, oak, cherry, and birch—came from Vermont. It was dried by oil-fired kilns which took it up to 180 degrees, reducing the moisture content from 55 percent down to 7 or 8 percent.

J. K. Adams employees came mostly from Dorset, Pawlet, and Manchester, and the products found successful outlets in gift and sport shops, department stores, and industrial firms. The business thrived and established itself as one of Dorset's few industries.

On the evening of April 13, 1962, Kathe Parks sounded the alarm that the J. K. Adams factory was on fire. The cause of the fire was never known for sure, but it was thought perhaps to have started in the spray room. The blaze spread rapidly and engulfed the building. After only brief hesitation,

An interior of the J. K. Adams plant in 1988 shows Malcolm Cooper, Jr., leaning on a planer, Ken McKeighan stacking blocks, and Charles Lake at a molder.

Cooper began plans to rebuild, with himself as architect and contractor. He made a virtue of adversity by designing a more efficient plant made of fire-resistant steel, with the same space, 25,000 square feet, as the old grown-like-Topsy series of wooden buildings.

The new plant was square with high ceilings, well lighted, protected by a sprinkler system with a 15,000-gallon tank supplied by a 300,000-gallon reservoir. There was a humidifying system and a dual-purpose dust collector—both to stabilize the woods and to improve the working environment—which returned warm air to the plant to save fuel in winter. Machinery was salvaged from the old plant and reconditioned. The new building also sported a showroom fronting the road, attracting tourists and visitors to its "Ver-magic" line of products.

"My dream," Cooper once said, "is to make just one item, maybe clothes-pins, and make them by the millions." Each product requires different jigs, materials, employee direction, and markets, and a single product would simplify all of that. But that ideal was not to be the case, for J. K. Adams continued to expand its offerings—T-square heads, architect's rods, engineering levels, and ruler bases for other firms to finish. In 1953 the company introduced its popular trencher trays for the carving of roasts or fowl, with

To passersby on Route 30 this is the familiar J. K. Adams Company as it looks in 1989.

a grooved trap for juices; and Paddy Whacker boards, "fine for cutting, serving (and domestic tranquility)."

In recent years Malcolm Cooper has been joined by his son Malcolm, Jr., as vice-president for manufacturing.

Unity Achieved: The Elementary School

In this town of diverse topography and scattered settlements, the massive mountain in its midst has both provoked division and suggested unity ever since the earliest days. School districting has been a continuing problem. How many districts to have? How much local control? How big should each district be? Where to draw boundaries? School districts had grown in number until after the Civil War, when they reached an unmanageable fourteen, then declined in 1870 toward an ultimate goal of a single town-wide school district.

The final act of consolidation was not achieved until 1958, when the last two districts, East Dorset and Dorset village, merged and agreed to build a single elementary school. After many meetings and designs, the vote authorizing the school was a solid 219–152. The location, chosen by a site committee of representative citizens, was a compromise—partway up that mountain on the Morse Hill Road. The eleven-acre parcel, on a foothill of the

Courtesy of Beatrice N. McWayne

The Dorset Village School in 1938-39, the last year Beatrice Nichols McWayne taught there. Front row: Allen Blackmer, Betty Jean Streeter (Clayton), Jean Parks (Towsley), Lloyd Casey, Gene Vermette, Gordon Kinney, Rosecille Hart, Bobby Harrington. Second row: Phyllis Kinnie (Booth), Ann Salmon, Dick Casey, Bob West, Gertrude Taft, Millie Bovey (O'Leary). Next to top: Robert Kent, Nellie Baker, Evangeline Vermette, Edna Baker, Robert Streeter, Shirley Blackmer. Top row: Ellis Vermette, Edwin Kinnie, Harriet Bovey, Chris Morris, Mrs. McWayne, Jane Park (Beebe), Mary Casey.

Courtesy of Ruth Shroder

Students at the Dorset Village School in 1943-44 with their teacher, Nan Bradder (Leach). Front row: Jack Shroder, Malcolm Jones, Gladys Tifft, Louise Moffit, Edmund Taft, Francis McLaughlin, Laura Twyne, Johnny Gilbert. Second row: Elaine Humphreys, Woodburn Tifft, Nadine Hart, Carl Jones, Bobby Parks, Kay Galusha, Jackie Nichols, Lottie Twyne. Back row: Chester Phillips, Susan Hart, Morris Tobin, Byron Hazleton.

Since 1924

Courtesy of Pauline Beebe Johnson

Students at the East Dorset School in 1936. Front row: Earl Bowen, Ann Marie Brophy, Jim Whalen, Ruth Stone, Pauline Bebee, Leonard Merrow. Second row: Larry Jack Whalen, Bernard Lillie, Harold Beebe, Worth Bowen, Richard Lang, Bill Leary, Alvah Beckley. Third row: Charlotte Lang, Kenneth Clayton, unknown, Olive McDonald. Fourth row: Winnie Beckley, Florence Devenow, Shirley Granger, Donald Leary, Loren Butler. Top row: unknown, Doris Slavin, Flora May Bowen, unknown, Henry Gallagher.

Courtesy of Joseph Nadeau

The East Dorset South Village School about 1923. Front row: Evelyn Grout, Marion Warner, teacher Gert Tulley, Rebecca Read, Catherine Warner. Back row: Maynard Grout, Billy Warner, Walt Read, John Rowell, Joseph Nadeau.

distinctively round Owl's Head, was acquired from Dan Wade for $3,500.

The new eight-room school of modern design was completed in February 1960, when 187 pupils entered. Designed by architects Helmer & Cole of Woodstock, it was completed at a cost of $189,000. Mrs. Helen Mach, who had been a teaching principal in the old village school, was the first principal.

Voters of the unified Dorset School District were not profligate with their tax money. In March 1965 they conclusively rejected an appropriation of $7,300 to start a kindergarten.

In 1962 the eighty-seven-year-old Dorset Village School was razed, its bell carefully saved. The site became that of the new post office, where an open house was held in June 1963, with Boy Scouts raising the first flag. The staff consisted of Morris Depew, postmaster, Roy Casey of South Dorset as rural carrier, Frances Monroe as clerk, and Mrs. Leland Hazelton starting her eighth year as "substitute."

In 1963 the State Board of Education and Governor Philip Hoff toured the eight-town supervisory union of Superintendent Robert B. Vail. Part of the motive was to promote the governor's ill-fated proposal to divide all Vermont into twelve regional school districts. Another reason was to investigate Vail's complaints about the inadequacy of some of his schools, notably Sunderland's four one-roomers. The Dorset Elementary School was held up as a model for quality education.

A six-by-three-foot mural by Wallace W. Fahnestock depicting maple sugaring in the Hollow was presented to the Dorset Elementary School in April 1964 by Margaret Lockwood, his sister. Fahnestock, who died in 1962, was an original member of the Dorset PTA.

The Dorset school, designed for 200 students, had been expanded by a two-room addition and a kindergarten. But by 1986, although enrollment was 175, the school board explained that more space was needed for the ever-expanding curriculum and programs such as physical education, music, and manual arts. Another reason for concern, James Lengel, deputy state commissioner of education, told the town, was that while most Vermont towns had grown at a rate of 10 percent in the 1970–80 decade, Dorset grew at 27 percent. This proved to be a rate not borne out by the school population.

A new 15,828-square-foot addition was proposed, architect Fred Keil of Waterbury was engaged to draw plans, and throughout 1987 board member Cynthia Marion and others campaigned tirelessly for the project. After a series of public hearings, a bond issue for $997,000 was approved on November 3 by a vote of 371–253 (about 46 percent of the electorate). Total estimated cost of the new facilities was $1,425,000, and state aid of

This was the Junior Ski Program of the Dorset Elementary School in 1964. Back row, from left: Roberta Tarbell, Marchen T. Skinner, Edward Ferenc, Ted Bennett. Upper middle: Doug Beebe, Karen Weber, Margaret Skinner, Millie Clough, Marjorie Edgerton, William Gilbert, Elisabeth Gilbert (Sturges), Richard Wilkins. Lower middle: Mary Hope Glover, Anita Rosencrantz, Ann Tarbell, Toni Rosencrantz. Bottom row: Cynthia Tarbell, Malcolm Cooper, Helen Warren, Barbara Towsley, Geoffrey Chapman, Larry Parker, Peter Chapman.

$427,000 brought the town's cost to just under $1 million. A local contractor, Jack Heaton of Wooden Indian, then won the contract to build it.

Winds of Change in the Sixties

Some might say that in the 1960s Dorset came to life and entered the twentieth century. Others contend that this decade saw the character of the town begin to change, and old values of neighborliness and altruism begin to erode. Whatever the point of view, there would be little disagreement that the 1960s was a time of change: many new people, new institutions, new technologies, different trends in land use, housing, sources of income, and life-styles.

The old style of community trust was demonstrated one morning in the 1950s when Fred Carmichael, producer of the summer Caravan Theatre, came into Gilbert's Hardware and asked Nora Gilbert about her supply of

Gilbert's Hardware Store on Meadow Lane, established in 1947 by David and Nora Gilbert.

candles. As she started to go look, he laughed, then explained. The previous night the electricity had gone off during a performance and Carmichael, knowing that the store's back door was never locked, had dashed over to help himself to an armful of candles so the play could go on.

Through all the changes there have remained the Dorset rummage sales, sponsored by the Women's Fellowship of the United Church of Dorset and East Rupert. These semiannual events serve to recycle clothing back into the community. They raise about $9,000 a year to benefit groups such as the Church World Services, Dorset Nursing Association, Rescue Squad, and Planned Parenthood.

The Corn Exchange

A phenomenon of the early 1960s that reflected the new Dorset character was the Corn Exchange. This informal weekly luncheon gathering for retired men at the Dorset Inn has grown to such an extent that membership is now limited to forty. The waiting list has given it an air of exclusivity.

The name "Corn Exchange" was first suggested by J. K. (Joe) Adams. The group began in the early 1960s, when Eugene A. Bond and Robert McIntyre found themselves at a cocktail party discussing how much they disliked cocktail parties. Their predilection led to a weekly discussion meeting in the

Bonds' kitchen. The room was lined with six rocking chairs, occupied by Adams, Bond, McIntyre, Codman Hislop, Herbert Meyer, and the Reverend Herbert Perry, who all agreed to discuss one subject at a time. They then rotated houses. After McIntyre died and Perry left town, the discussion group evolved into a luncheon with additional participants. The one-subject rule has evolved too, though there are often invited speakers. Women have reportedly attempted to break into membership, but thus far no innovations in that area have been tolerated.

Dorset in Print

To the outside world, Dorset remained one of Vermont's best-kept secrets. Much local news tended to consist of the familiar who's-visiting-whom or who-has-returned-from-where items. There was also the occasional travelogue article, such as one by resident Judson Phillips in *Ford Times*.

But changes of the early 1960s began to be chronicled more substantively in pages of the daily *Bennington Banner* by its Dorset correspondent, Marchen T. Skinner. These included in-depth articles about public issues, news of the selectmen, the town manager, the school board, and other public agencies. She also focused on the people who were shaping developments of the 1960s, and sometimes she delved into the past. Compiled in several scrapbooks, her writings constitute a vivid journal of a changing town (and were consulted frequently for this chapter).

Another chronicler of Dorset, who tended to emphasize its folklore and

Photo by Nancy Otis

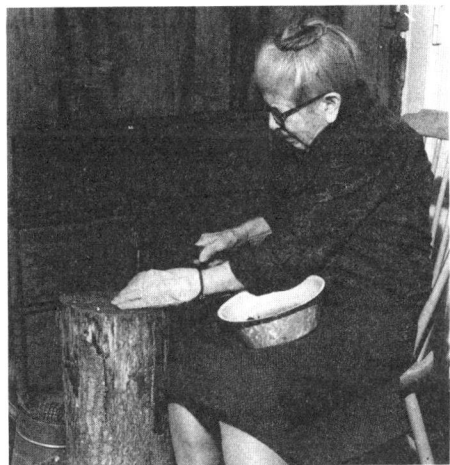

Miss Anna Gilbert at her favorite maple stump cracking butternuts for her maple sugar candy. She lived in the north half of the Rufus Gilbert house on West Road.

eccentricities, was Allan Sheldon (1904–85), a native son and free spirit who returned to town in the late 1960s and wrote weekly "contributions to the Dorset atmosphere" for Marshall Peck's *Vermont News Guide* of Manchester. One of those stories, which conveys both ambience and intonation, has been related by Sheldon's nephew, Peter Salmon:

> *My grandmother used to buy fresh fruit from John Jones who drove down Danby Mountain and around to people's kitchen doors in an old gray horse-drawn wagon. One day he offered her some plums. "Why Mr. Jones, they look sour," she said. He looked her square in the eye and said, in a more gravelly voice, "Misus S'elden, you say those plums be sour. I was up t'the store yesterday. Johnny Reid was in there. Wanted to buy him a basket of them plums. I sold it to him, went over t'other store. 'Bout half hour I come back; Johnny had 'et all them plums, wanted to git him another basket. Naow, Mrs. S'elden, if them plums was sour, I guess he'd a knowed it!"*

This yarn was also adapted as one of *his* stories by the late poet Walter Hard, Sr., of Manchester.

Emerald Lake State Park

Among the first physical changes during the sixties was the opening of Emerald Lake State Park in North Dorset. The Forests and Parks Department trucked in sand to create a beach, developed a picnic area, and created camping grounds to cater to both local people and tourists along Route 7. The park soon expanded from 34 camp sites to 105, and by 1965 the adjoining section of Route 7 was widened and divided, and trees that formerly lined the highway were removed. The result is a scenic view that combines Green and Taconic mountains, the lake and its island, the railroad paralleling the road, and a dramatic roadside outcropping of limestone.

Attendance at Emerald Lake in the first season of 1960 totaled 3,802 day uses and 3,621 camper days; by 1987 those figures were 22,714 and 20,893.[2] The development of Emerald Lake was part of Vermont's "beckoning country" campaign in the late 1950s and early 1960s, which included many new state parks. By the end of the decade Vermont stopped beckoning and Act 250 began to apply some brakes—at least it imposed a series of standard criteria—on developments.

Emerald Lake (once known as Dorset Pond), the largest body of water in town, with about sixty acres, was among lands purchased in 1918 by Robert Alfred Shaw, a wealthy New Yorker. Shaw leased the lake from the state, which has jurisdiction over all bodies of water of more than twenty acres. By 1921 Shaw had accumulated several parcels and incorporated them as "North Dorset Farms," with Fred Harwood as supervisor. During the 1930s this farm had a fine herd of Guernseys and shipped milk south by train.

Each winter Harwood and his crew cut ice from the lake, and in early spring boiled maple sap into syrup and sugar. Every Monday, when owner Shaw was not in residence, Harwood placed a well-iced container of fresh ice cream on the night train—bound for Shaw's New York City breakfast table.

After World War II Shaw drew up ambitious plans for an endowed recreational area surrounding the lake. By that time few trains were running, except for an occasional freight that did not even stop. North Dorset Farms ceased operations. Shaw's death in the early 1950s put an end to all the plans, and in 1957 the state bought a thousand acres from his estate for $62,000. Half was developed as state park, and the other half became state forest. Shaw's main house, which he had moved from town, became the ranger's residence. His three-car garage was turned into quarters for seasonal help, and an octagonal building that was Shaw's library and dining room remained familiar to campers until it was vandalized, then demolished, in 1969.

The park's first ranger was Bill Eagan, and he was succeeded by Albro Ramey, then Bruce Brown. Since 1975 the ranger has been Edward Eno.

Town Business, and a Town Manager

In May 1960 the town of Dorset, after several years of deficit budgets, engaged its first town manager, John W. Browne. A town meeting vote in 1959 authorized a committee to look into the possibility of hiring a professional manager. The committee was headed by J. Frank Burke and included Howard G. Brophy, Malcolm Cooper, Leon Edgerton, and Henry Stone.

"Town business is getting out of hand. It's just too much for the old system," Stone explained. "We have to have some head in order to succeed.... Now I'm as conservative as anyone but I saw that it was impossible to go on."

Besides a creeping deficit that reached $18,000 in 1959, there was need for central record keeping and an overall look at expenses and revenues. Manager Browne, an engineer, came from a similar post in Cavendish. He began to acquire road machinery, altered seventy-four culverts, and widened several roads.

A town audit in 1963 showed improved finances. About $40,000 in new equipment had been purchased, efficient use of which cut costs. But Browne resigned unexpectedly in February 1964 after the discovery of a deficit of $36,034. Selectmen had no comment for the news media as they went about advertising for a successor. At town meeting that year, nonetheless, voters agreed by a resounding margin of 284–98 to continue the manager form of government.

In April 1964 selectmen voted to hire one of their own, Selectman James H. Beebe, sixty-six, as town manager. In 1970 Beebe, an East Dorset farmer, chose to step down and persuaded another selectman, Vernon Squiers, a barber, to succeed him as manager. Squiers agreed, resigned as selectman, was appointed manager, and remained so in 1989. Through his efforts the town has built up an inventory of $370,500 worth of equipment and a fund of nearly $200,000 to assure its continuance. He has managed to hold the town's adjusted general fund tax rate steady for twenty years.

The Dorset Historical Society

In September 1963 papers were filed with the secretary of state to incorporate the Dorset Historical Society as a nonprofit venture to discover and collect material that will help establish or illustrate a history of the town, to provide for preservation of relevant materials, and to disseminate historical information. Signatories were Alfred Holley Gilbert, president, William G. Barrows, first vice president, Eugene A. Bond, second vice president, Emma Stannard, secretary, and Terry Tyler, treasurer. On the first board of directors were Mrs. Harold Boswell, Leon Edgerton, Charles Smith, Miss Marjorie Niles, and Mrs. Ford Shroder.[3]

Trustees of the village library made an upstairs room available, furniture was donated, and a desk belonging to the Reverend William Jackson was given by Mrs. Einar L. Grondahl.

Eugene A. Bond, who began summering in Dorset in 1940 and retired there in 1955 from the telephone company, became the second president. Bond's retirement was an active one, for he also became president of the Dorset Players, and was elected in 1960 to a term as town representative in Montpelier.

In 1973 the historical society marked its tenth anniversary with a brochure that boasted an impressive number of speakers and local topics explored. Many of the papers accumulated in the society's files have been utilized for this book. Presidents since the late Alfred H. Gilbert's term ended in 1965 had been, besides Bond, William F. Gilbert, Terry Tyler, Warren Murray, and Arthur W. Gilbert. Presidents since 1973 have been Don Kellogg, Terry Tyler, Henry A. G. "Geoff" Chapman, and Elisabeth Sturges. At first a museum was established next to Peltier's store, and a pamphlet was published about the marble quarries. Paid membership, at five dollars each, in 1973 totaled 150.

In 1976, coincident with the national bicentennial, the society's museum and headquarters moved into the former firehouse next to the post office. The museum's location is central but its lack of a heating system enables it to open only during good weather. One of the key figures in the society, Arthur W. Gilbert, was its curator for a long time. Gilbert returned to his native town after retiring in the mid-1960s as assistant superintendent in charge of instruction for the Kansas City schools, a system he served since 1926. He is a graduate of the West Road District School, Burr & Burton Seminary (1917), and Dartmouth (1921). As curator, Gilbert was followed in recent years by William Manley, a descendant of one of the founding families.

In 1978 the Kent Neighborhood Historic District was entered on the National Register of Historic Places. These two hundred acres near West Road and Nichols Hill are associated with the Cephas Kent Inn and dwelling house, where the Dorset Conventions were held in 1775 and 1776. The nomination has been a subject of controversy because of the contention of artist Dean Fausett that a portion of his house was the actual location of the Dorset Conventions (see footnote 2, chapter 5).

In 1985 the society announced that the National Park Service had designated a specified area as "Dorset Village Historic District" and placed it on the National Register. A key paragraph of the designation was:

The Dorset Village Historic District holds primary significance for retaining the distinctive architectural characteristics of a late 18th-to early 20th-century rural Vermont village. While most of its buildings constitute vernacular expressions of their styles, the Congregational Church exhibits a more fully developed Late Gothic Revival style un-

Courtesy of Constance Harrington McGuffin

Connie Harrington (1899-1988), shown here at the age of 17 or 18, was Dorset's unofficial historian.

common in Vermont. The church is built of locally quarried marble, thereby representing (along with the village's unusual marble sidewalks) the industry that dominated Dorset township during the 19th century. Dorset village lies within an exceptionally scenic landscape of the pastoral Mettawee valley flanked by the forested and abrupt slopes of the Taconic Mountains. . . . Dorset lacks entirely the usual types of contemporary intrusions; indeed, two buildings that originally contained automobile repair shops have been converted to residences.

The historical society provided half the funding for this project, with the other half from the Vermont Division of Historic Preservation. The efforts of Bob Cushman were credited with guiding the project to completion.

Some Dorset Personalities
Dr. F.C. Liddle, Dr. John Cochrane

In September 1945, a month after World War II ended, so did the life of one of Dorset's revered citizens, Dr. Frederick C. Liddle. Not long before that, Dr. Liddle was honored upon his retirement by about five hundred residents. Dr. E. H. Goodman wrote a poem for the occasion that included these lines:

> *How can one count hours of serving*
> *Infinite as the heavenly sphered?*
> *Steadfast, loyal, true, unswerving,*
> *Through all these forty years! . . .*
>
> *Fortunate that man, Dr. Liddle,*
> *Who, through grave, has met with you!*
> *Never truer friend or neighbor,*
> *Nor physician half so true!*
>
> *Blest be the day you saw this valley*
> *Forty years ago! Two score!*
> *Well! May we save our Vale! Vale!*
> *For yet two score and more!*

Dr. Liddle was born in Shushan, New York, in 1861, and moved to Dorset to practice medicine in 1886. For years he was the town's only physician, and is still thought of fondly by older residents, some of whom remember his discreet deep-voiced query, "And how about the bowels?"

Dr. Liddle also served as honorary president of the Dorset Church, the Memorial Library, and the Maple Hill Cemetery Association. In that cemetery he lies buried between his two wives, Gertrude Holley (1859–1911) and Emily Louise Sykes (1865–1951).

As the town's doctor he was preceded by Dr. Charles S. Harwood (1833–1902), a homeopathic physician who took medical training at Cincinnati College. Harwood was the father of rural mail carrier Elmer Harwood and an uncle of Dr. Clifford Harwood of Manchester.

Dr. Liddle was succeeded by, among others, doctors Donald Bashaw, Gerald McGuiness, Arthur Gillette, Elizabeth Byrnes, and John Mackey. When Dr. Byrnes, the wife of Claude Dern, retired in December 1971, a celebration in her honor at the elementary school was attended by some three hundred people. The town has not had a general practitioner since Dr. Mackey left, in 1975.

The early-twentieth-century physician best remembered in East Dorset was Dr. John Cochrane, a descendant of Green Mountain Boy Robert Cochran (spelled without the final *e*) of Rupert. Dr. Cochrane was termed "an important character in East Dorset" by Robert Griffith, who had these recollections of the doctor: "[He was] tall, spare, had a great mane of white hair, horn-rimmed eye-glasses, the barest shadow of a moustache. He smoked Lucky Strikes in a long cigarette holder, spoke in a grave, formal voice. He was friendly in an abrupt, professional manner; he had kindly, inquiring brown eyes. Nobody ever addressed him as 'Doc.' He dressed impeccably in tasteful tweeds."

Henry G. Stone

Born in East Rupert in 1886, Henry G. Stone lived in Peru for a dozen years, then moved to East Dorset to drive a team of horses for Ed Harwood for $26 a month plus board. Then, because he was courting the woman who became his wife, he accepted a $2 a month raise and agreed to stay. He never left. In that time he attended Burr & Burton, became a life insurance agent, farmed, quarried, and held almost every town office.

Stone was a lister (appraiser) for nearly twenty years, served on the first five-man board of selectmen, was a legislator, school director, and justice of the peace, and chaired the Prudential Committee of the East Dorset Water Company. He was also active in church work. Stone died in January 1974 at the age of 87. His son, Guy Stone, carried on his tradition in local government as moderator and selectman for many years.

Mark Whalon

East Dorset's Mark Whalon had many talents, but was best known as rural mail carrier and poet. He and his familiar 1935 Plymouth received national publicity in the January 18, 1943, *Life* magazine with a spread of photographs by Alfred Eisenstadt. He was shown in a coonskin cap making postal rounds—much of it wartime V-mail—on a wintry day when the temperature dove to 35 below zero.

Whalon said he decided to become a mailman at the age of thirty-nine after "unsuccessfully trying cheese-making, cow doctoring, mush-rat trappin' and water-witchin'." His war duties included helping with scrap drives and selling war stamps and bonds. One of Whalon's books, published by the Stephen Daye Press of Brattleboro, was *Rural Free Delivery*, which sold for $1.75. In it he said, "I've delivered mail by ox team and bobsled . . . horseback and snowshoes, and I'm strong of the opinion that the best thing about a Vermont winter is its end. And I means the last end, not the front end."

In 1933 the Tuttle Company of Rutland published *Rural Peace*, a book of his poems that included some charming line drawings by Marion Adams. Many of the verses had first appeared in his column "Peregrinations" in the *Rutland Herald*.

Wrote *Herald* editor Howard L. Hindley in the introduction, "Mark Whalon is one of the Vermont poets who have helped to make 'Peregrinations' a department of verse and comment that seems to gather new friends and daily readers as the months and years pass. In the name of two hundred old friends and colleagues, who from time to time have appeared in Mark's company, I welcome *Rural Peace* as an Opus of Vermont and a permanent contribution to our steadily richening store of native literature."

Whalon's poetry is starkly evocative of the Vermont experience. Here are three stanzas from the book's title poem:

> *Did you ever go out to the cattle barn*
> *On a stormy winter day*
> *When it blowed and snowed and drifted so*
> *You scarce could find your way?*
> *You reached the door and you yanked the bar*
> *As the storm around you swirled,*
> *You stumbled in and found yourself*
> *In the midst of another world!*
> *Just the click and creak of the stanchions*
> *And the sound of munching hay;*
> *What a harbor of peace and quiet content*
> *In the midst of a stormy day. . . .*

Since 1924

Mark Whalon, the East Dorset rural mail carrier and poet, pictured in 1950 with his faithful 1935 Plymouth.

> Did you ever sit out on the porch alone
>   On a summer Sunday night,
> When the hayin's done and the oats begun
>   And the crop all comin' right?
> You tried to think and to plan ahead
>   But somehow your mind would stray,
> The magic night and the fire-fly's light
>   Kept leading your thoughts away.
> Your thoughts it seems all turned to dreams
>   But none of those dreams were bad;
> A king you reign in a kingdom sane
>   In the midst of a world gone mad. . . .
>
> If none of these things you've ever done
>   You never will read this through,
> I'm sure you'd find it so profound
>   It wouldn't appeal to you.
> If you don't know what I'm drivin' at
>   Nor what I'm trying to do
> It don't make a mite of difference,—
>   I wa'nt a-talkin' to you.
> I wrote this for the folks I know
>   Who live the life I've led,
> Who can build their song as they read along
>   With the things I might have said.

Rena Chapman

The following recollection of Rena Chapman, reprinted from a June 1962 issue of the *Bennington Banner*, was written by Dorset correspondent Marchen T. Skinner.

If only poor Rena Chapman—and everyone always called her that—could see her flowers, blue and pink lupin, oriental poppies, lilacs and iris, a-blooming wildly in her yard on the Hollow Road.

They bloom near the spot where her weathered, weary house stood.

Can't you remember Rena, hoe in hand, dressed in knicker pants, limp blue sweater and odd hat, hovering over her flowers or pumping water from the ancient pump?

Seeing her trudge home from the village on a wintry day with her gallon of kerosene for her lamp—she refused to have electricity because it would have meant replacing a white birch with a pole—made one admire her sturdy independence. She had probably traded her homemade jams of wild berries picked in summer for the kerosene.

Refusing help from neighbors or a home with relatives, she lived aloofness. No smoke from her chimney one day a few years back gave the clue. Rena was found dead in her rocking chair. Her property was bought and her house razed. Now only the lupin bloom in memory and the lilacs mark her door.

Rena Chapman's house stood in a field, now empty, next to Bertha Lyons' home on the Dorest Hollow Road.

Carl T. Ramsey

A weekly column made its debut in the *Bennington Banner* in May 1964, named for its author, Carl T. Ramsey, "The Sage of Swampacres." Ramsey was a naturalist, orchidologist, photographer, poet, and artist, who with his wife Edith lived in a modest house near the wetlands, which he called Swampacres, between West Road and Route 30. He had drifted away from his original vocation as an engineer for Ingersoll-Rand and for Mack trucks.

Ramsey was the author of *The Odyssey of the Orchids*, a two-volume work that contained 350 prints, and several other books, *Between Chores*, *The Story of the 22-Acre Swampacres Sanctuary*, *Vermont Mountain Poems*, and *Orchid Models*, a study of pollen mass structure.

In an article on Vermont native orchids in the summer 1958 *Vermont Life* magazine, Ramsey wrote of his love for Dorset and for the orchid:

Over three decades of orchid interest preceded my coming to Dorset, whose enchanting hills and streams drew me like a magnet. Imagine spending a decade hunting for the Queen Lady's Slipper Cypripedium reginae, *ultimately seeing it by the thou-*

sands in New Jersey, and bringing a plant to Dorset on our honeymoon in 1918, only to find that neighbors had seen it almost within a stone's throw of our backyard. Here in 1934 we established our 22-acre wild orchid sanctuary, Swampacres.

His first newspaper column concluded:

The velvety call of the bluebird and the thundering of the ruffed grouse were once common in the Dorset Valley as elsewhere. But something tragic occurred within the past decade that was covered so dramatically by Rachel Carson in Silent Spring.

The spraying of vegetables and herbage, as we so tragically experienced, is still to be remembered and should be a caution for stopping this common practice. Not only baby birds, but deer and many other different animals who live in a cycle of food relationship have been affected by this insidious insecticide battle.

It is a great satisfaction to the conservationist, as I have observed in our refuge, that the grouse, woodcock, and a few other species seem to be coming back. But of special note is the disappearance of the hermit thrush, our state bird. We have not had these birds in our woods for a half dozen years.

Ramsey continued his column of curmudgeonry until he died in March 1968, at the age of eighty-six. Edith's death followed. Their daughter, Margaret Meachem, after a career as teacher and musician, recently moved back to their homestead at Swampacres, now a wildlife sanctuary.

Helen Bryan

An activist resident of Dorset in the 1950s and 1960s was Helen Bryan, who brought home the true meaning of "McCarthyism." Miss Bryan, a 1917 graduate of Wellesley, served time in the federal penitentiary for women at Alderson, West Virginia, where she was sentenced for contempt of Congress for refusing to cooperate with the House Un-American Activities Committee about her work on behalf of Spanish refugees from the Franco regime. She wrote *Inside*, published by the Houghton Mifflin Company of Boston in 1953. The book brings warm understanding to the plight and daily routine of women in a federal prison, or as she put it, "the tediousness, timelessness and heartbreak that was Alderson."

Edith Dulles Snare

In her forty-five years in town, Edith Snare left the imprint of her good taste and imagination by buying, occupying, and remodeling at least a dozen houses. Born in 1897, she was a cousin of John Foster Dulles, secretary of state under Eisenhower. Arriving in town in 1941, she began

"Bill W.," co-founder with "Dr. Bob" of Alcoholics Anonymous. Aldous Huxley called Wilson "the greatest social architect of our times."

The grave of "Bill W." in the East Dorset South Village Cemetery has become something of a tourist attraction. This flower arrangement on his gravestone, one of many placed there each year, bears a card reading, "Thank you for nine years of sobriety." Beside Wilson's grave is that of his wife, Lois Burnham Wilson, 1891-1988.

to raise Angora rabbits, taught at the Hollow School, then worked at the J. K. Adams Company.

In 1942 she was elected a member of the Southern Vermont Artists, where she had a long association. As its executive director in the late 1940s, she was instrumental with Richard M. Ketchum and Dean Fausett in raising funds to purchase the Webster estate on the slopes of Mt. Equinox for permanent SVAC headquarters. She also ran an art store in Manchester with Thomas Dibble and architect Fritz Dillmann.

In 1965 Edith Snare was among founders of the Dorset Nursing Association, became its first vice-president, and remained active in its operations. In 1960, with Brenda Parsons, she founded one of the town's first real estate offices, now Snare Associates.

Edith Snare died in April 1985, and memorial services were conducted by Robert Green of the Danby Mountain Road, a former Episcopal priest. At those services there was such a warm outpouring of fond memories about her that they were gathered up and published as a booklet.

Since 1924

The Wilson House, the home of East Dorset's William G. Wilson, as it looked in 1988 after extensive renovations by owner Ozzie Lepper. For many years this was the Mt. Aeolus Inn, known as a stopping place halfway between New York and Montreal.

Carleton G. Howe

Carleton G. Howe, ninety-one as this book is published, has been a versatile fellow—farmer, orchardist, politician, and patron of the arts. He was born in Cannon City, Colorado, in 1898, and came to town in 1920 after graduating from the University of Illinois and receiving a law degree from the University of Chicago, then serving in the navy during World War I. His father, Warren Howe, a doctor, in 1915 purchased the then-twelve-hundred-acre Glen Farm from the Warren family because his children liked it and because "Dorset Hollow attracted him no end."

When Howe ran Glen Farm as a dairy farm with horses, he recalls, it was an especially rugged place in winter. The road was kept open by packing down the snow rather than plowing it. The farm's water wheel generated direct-current electricity until the penstock was washed out by a flood in the 1920s; after that a gasoline engine generated power. Howe recollects cutting ice in Prentiss Pond and storing two-hundred-pound blocks for use by householders in the village.

Howe was among founders of the Dorset Players and remembers when its building was created from beams of two old barns. He was also active in the early Dorset Artists and Southern Vermont Art Center. In the early 1940s, Howe and his second wife, Dorothy, lived in North Rupert (where she had the first wire hay baler in the Mettawee Valley).

Apple picking in 1935 at Ernest H. West's orchard on the West Road.

In the late 1940s and early 1950s Howe operated the Dorset Orchard off Route 30, growing mostly MacIntoshes, Cortlands, and Northern Spies. In addition to having a roadside stand selling apples and cider, the orchard also made shipments to England. For a time Howe also had the Green Peak Orchard above East Dorset.

Howe was elected to the Vermont House from Dorset in 1945, and to the Senate in 1946, 1948, 1950, 1952, 1954, and 1956. He is the last Dorset resident to serve as a Bennington County senator, and was a member of that body far longer than anyone else from the town. Since 1960 he has resided in Manchester.

Roland Palmedo

Roland Palmedo (1895–1977), one of the best-known figures in the history of eastern skiing, lived for more than thirty years in a house he converted on Dorset Hill Road next to the old Catholic cemetery. When he bought the place in 1938 it was abandoned, and he understood that it had been a tavern that served the former Irish community near the Freedley quarry. He settled in East Dorset to be near his friend Fred Pabst, the founder of Bromley.

Inside the walls of this house, some of which he paneled with old wood-

Sorting and grading apples in 1931 at Ernest West's orchard.

en skis, Palmedo founded the National Ski Patrol and the Eastern Ski Areas Association, and hosted many Olympic ski contenders. He was a founder of the Mt. Mansfield Corporation and the Mad River Glen ski area.

Palmedo was a prolific author of books and articles about kayaking as well as skiing. He helped organize the annual whitewater kayak races on the West River in Jamaica. Palmedo's daughter, Elizabeth Palmedo Spier, occupied his house for a time and now his granddaughter, Scout, and her husband, Matt Proft, reside there with their children.

Carl Parsons

A former professor of zoology at the University of Vermont, Carl Parsons (1914–73) operated the sixty-acre Mad Tom Orchards in East Dorset for several years in the 1950s and 1960s in harmony with principles articulated by Rachel Carson in *Silent Spring*. "You don't want to kill all the insects or the balance of nature is upset," he said.

Parsons was interviewed in 1962 during a successful apple season, when his expected crop was 26,000 bushels of Cortlands and Delicious apples, in contrast to his previous season of 12,000 bushels. Because local labor was unavailable, 1962 was the first time he had to hire migrant labors to do the picking.

Apple pickers at the Rufus Gilbert packing barn, behind the Gilbert home on the West Road. In this picture, among others, are Hattie and Jim Fisher, Ruth Gilbert, Bessie West, Rufus and Ethel Gilbert.

An entomologist, Parsons was a specialist in the study of insects, so he enjoyed the task of attempting to fine-tune his modified program of spraying in keeping with nature's balance.

His apples were sold at Parsons's Mad Tom Shop on Route 7 just south of the Dorset line, among many other markets. The year 1962 was also when his wife, Harriet, launched Mad Tom Books, a shop for paperbacks that offered, at the outset, four thousand titles.

"Save Dorset Hollow!"

In the summer of 1965, Helen and Kuhrt Wieneke were not aware that Camp Wynakee was in its twelfth and final season. This farm, majestically located at the head of Dorset Hollow, was first tilled in 1829 by Experience Barrows, held briefly by other families, then run by the Howe family as Glen Farm. At Camp Wynakee, children scampered over scenic acreage, played in the Mettawee, rode horses, and posed for pictures on the old waterwheel. The camp's name was pronounced the same as that of the owners but spelled as if it were of Indian origin.

Wieneke was a former professor of physical education at Ursinus College in Pennsylvania, and his wife was headmistress of Kimberton, a private elementary school. They ran the summer camp with a practical philosophy—to teach children to focus on wise and constructive use of their leisure time. Helen Wieneke once told an interviewer: "Every child, no matter how well adjusted or appreciated at home, should have one experience in a resident camp away from parents and home before the age of 12. It's a primary ground for democracy." The program balanced work and play, activity and rest, and offered swimming, horseback riding, tent making, and puppet shows.

By 1965, idyllic Camp Wynakee proved too valuable as real estate to justify its existence. That November the Wienekes received an offer they could not refuse and sold the place, nine hundred acres of it. They consolidated operations at a 250-acre site in Benson where they had another summer camp. In contrast to the frigid Mettawee, a welcome feature at Benson was the warm water of Lake Champlain. The Wienekes were paid "a handsome sum" at a time when they faced the prospect of indebtedness for a needed swimming pool.

The buyers were Mr. and Mrs. Frederick Tetzlaff of Wyncote, Pennsylvania, who declared their intention to use the place for "summer and weekend vacations for the present." But gossip soon spread about more grandiose plans, fueled by reports that gauges were being placed on the mountainsides to measure snow and rainfall. There was substance to the rumors because Tetzlaff and others, including Manchester real estate brokers George Breen and Thomas Martin, with Manchester logger Christopher Swezey, were quietly assembling the components of a massive new ski resort. It would cover 3,000 acres of mountain land of the Swezey Lumber Company, with about 500 acres spilling over the mountains toward Emerald Lake. Its crown jewel was former Camp Wynakee, with its extensive frontage on the Upper and Lower Hollow roads and along the Mettawee.

Backers of this project did not enhance their public relations by remaining elusive. News of the ski proposal was leveraged out of Tetzlaff by the *Bennington Banner*'s Dorset correspondent Marchen Skinner, from her strategic residence near the intersection of Upper and Lower Hollow roads. The developers finally decided to hold a community party on October 8, 1965, to announce plans publicly.

Their model revealed designs for four base lodges, numerous ski trails, an eighteen-hole golf course, two swimming pools, tennis courts, a 250-room resort hotel, a night club, and extensive residential developments connected by a network of new roads. Dorset Hollow would attract an estimated three thousand cars every weekend. A statement boasted: "Dorset Hollow will serve an estimated population of twenty-four million persons within a 200-mile radius of the area. The skier market in this area is presently increasing at the rate of approximately 16 percent annually."

It gradually dawned on Dorset what massive impact this project would have. One almost minor aspect that offended many was a proposal to make

Dorset

Glen Farm in Dorset Hollow, about 1906. First settled as a farm by Experience Barrows in the 1830s, it was later owned by the Warren family, then the Howes; it became "Camp Wynakee" in the 1950s. In the mid-1960s this site was proposed for a major ski area, then became headquarters of the Dorset Hollow Corporation. The elegant stone wall in this photo, as with all stone walls in the Hollow, was built by Israel Streeter.

traffic one way, going out by the Lower road and returning by the Upper—all blacktopped. "How am I supposed to get to my house, by backing up?" asked Marchen Skinner. Jack Hubbard took one look at the model and exclaimed, "You're using half my mountain!" The planners had mistakenly located a ski lift on a slope he owned.

Dorseters also chortled because the mountains that surround the Hollow are notorious for their scanty snow cover. They recalled that Fred Pabst had learned the hard way in the early 1930s when he installed a tow in East Dorset and suffered four winters of sparse snowfalls.

To fight this scheme, "Save Dorset Hollow" bumper stickers began to appear, courtesy of William G. Barrows, Jr. Influential letters to the editor were written to newspapers. Then, on top of faulty planning and public relations, inadequate research, and flawed financing, the principals set to squabbling among themselves. Tetzlaff took his partners to court, claiming that they had not lived up to their contract.

By 1966, amid heavy public opposition, the ski development collapsed.

Photo by Stetson Fletcher

A familiar landmark is this waterwheel and power shed built in 1927 for Glen Farm at the head of Dorset Hollow. The overshot waterwheel generated electricity for the house and farm when it was owned by Dr. Warren Howe, father of Carleton G. Howe.

It was a fortuitous time for one George L. Wallace to enter the picture. Wallace, a Yale graduate in civil engineering, and management consultant from Wilton, Connecticut, was driven out to the Hollow by Edith August of Snare Real Estate Associates. She suggested to him that this attractive property probably would be coming on the market.

Negotiations proceeded. Wallace spoke of a new concept for "limited development," and Mrs. August introduced him to the owners of some nearby tracts. As Wallace recollects, his line of thinking was: "It's going to be on the market. Why don't we get a group together and buy it, control the development, develop it in a limited way but in keeping with the character of the area, sensitive to environmental considerations at a time when Dorset had no town plan and no zoning bylaws . . . I told them from the start that it wasn't going to be a real money maker, but I thought that over a long period of time we'd come out all right."[4]

The new group called itself the Dorset Hollow Corporation and included, among others, Hollow landowners Fayette and Mildred Dunn, Larry and Betty King, and Justus and Mary DeVries, with residents Edwin Lefevre and Ray Foote. Their initial concept was for no more than fifty homesites on the

900 acres, with at least 300 acres kept in a conservation preserve. The scale was then altered to forty homes and 400 conserved acres, including a thirty-acre wildlife preserve between the two Hollow roads and two thousand protected feet along the Mettawee. Of those numbers, by 1988 only two dozen parcels of land had been sold and only a dozen houses built, with three summer cottages renovated for year-round use.

The Dorset Hollow Corporation, located where Camp Wynakee was, has expanded its sights to be concerned with all properties in the Hollow, and to influence their development, as Wallace puts it, "in a responsible and committed way instead of just trying to maximize the dollar return."

Zoning and Planning

In March 1960 a town meeting first authorized selectmen to appoint a zoning feasibility study committee. It was headed by J. K. Adams, and it reported a year later that zoning should indeed be considered. But it was not until October 1965, after the threat to Dorset Hollow and other forms of Sixties growth had become apparent, that a town meeting authorized a more serious approach toward a zoning ordinance.

Selectman J. Ford Shroder was named to chair a committee, along with town representative William T. Burns, Sr., Beatrice Nichols McWayne, and selectmen Robert Dressler and James W. Lee II; it was later chaired by Leon Edgerton. State officials told Dorset that of Vermont's 246 towns, ninety were working on zoning laws and that sixty towns already had them in place.

By December 1966 a proposed ordinance was ready to submit to a series of public hearings. It divided the town into two zones, village and rural. Agricultural uses would be allowed anywhere, and trailers would be allowed in the rural district if they met requirements for single-family homes.

The rationale made it sound as if the ordinance could solve all future problems. The law was designed "to provide residents of Dorset with the means of considering, reviewing, and controlling any proposed new uses of land and buildings, in order to promote Dorset's general health, safety, and welfare, to preserve and perpetuate its character, charm, and natural beauty, to protect the value of its property, and to prevent overcrowding."

Two public hearings were called, then two more. Dorset folks seemed to take zoning calmly at first, and made a few suggestions. But still water ran deep, and some rough times were in store for those who saw zoning as a necessary way to control inevitable growth. First put to a vote in June 1967, zoning was defeated 227–189. Two years later, in June 1969, a two-year interim zoning ordinance was adopted; and it was not until long after that had expired, in March 1973, that a successful vote, 292–242, was finally taken on comprehensive bylaws. Zoning then withstood an attempt to rescind by a strong vote of 436–233 in May 1973.

The interim zoning plan, as well as the more permanent zoning bylaws, had been prepared by the Planning Commission that was appointed in 1969 under the chairmanship of Mrs. Russell Fenn. The Planning Commission also developed a land-use plan that was adopted by selectmen. Commission members attended weekly meetings as well as workshops and study courses, and took advantage of membership in the Bennington County Regional Commission shortly after that agency was formed.

In 1987 a new comprehensive town plan was adopted, along with the creation of a Dorset Village Design District that coincided with the Dorset Village Historic District. A subcommittee study of valuable agricultural land, chaired by Barbara Ketchum, resulted in a formal Land Evaluation and Site Assessment Plan for the town that included a mapping of recharge areas for twenty-two important springs and significant wetlands. Also in 1987, selectmen accepted a series of regulations to insure the orderly and environmentally appropriate subdivision of land; these were endorsed by a town meeting vote in July 1989.

Other Milestones Not Mentioned Elsewhere

★ 1926—Perry M. Peltier and Kimball O. Tifft enter into a partnership in the operation of the Peltier & Tifft general store. The relationship lasts until 1955, when Tifft sells his half of the business; Peltier retains ownership of the building.

★ 1927—The Reverend R. Hawley Fitch becomes pastor of the Dorset Congregational church, devoting much attention to church music and to the formation of youth groups.

★ 1927—Residents join a large cast to celebrate the sesquicentennial of the Battle of Bennington with a production of *The Pin Peddler*, centered around local incidents that took place before the battle.

★ 1927—A major November flood devastates many Vermont communities but most of Dorset is spared. The Mad Tom goes on a rampage, washes out the railroad tracks near Morse Hill Road; milk cannot be shipped by train for several days and is either dumped or fed to pigs.

★ 1928—Bernard G. Sykes purchases the former Gray's Tavern building from Fred Manley and donates it to the Dorset Village Public Library Association as a memorial to his parents, Gilbert M. and Lydia Greenleaf Sykes. Artist Edwin B. Child, his brother-in-law, supervises remodeling. At June 20 dedication ceremonies a historical paper is read by Louise Sykes Liddle. The library opens with 5,300 volumes, capacity for 12,000, and no indebt-

330　　　　　　　　　Dorset

Photo by Marshall Brooks, courtesy of Pauline Stewart

Right:
George Streeter, Jr., fiddles and George Kelly plays the guitar, in this joyful scene of square dancing on the second floor of the Dorset Village School in 1943. In foreground are Pauline and Albert Stewart, Merrill West, Emma Aldrich, and Charlotte Parks; in back are Nan Bradder Leach, Cliff Tarbell and Tom Warren.

Far right:
Street dancing on the village green in front of the Peltier and Tifft store in the summer of 1944. Jim Leach and Judy Sheldon are in the center, surrounded by Ellis Vermette, top left, Martha Howe Gogel, Dorothy Howe, George Sheldon, and Marjorie Leach.

edness. Benefactor Sykes, born in Dorset in 1869, has been associated with the Locomobile Company; in 1903 he opened the first automobile store on Michigan Avenue in Chicago.

★ 1932—The Reverend Harry Foot succeeds Fitch as pastor of the Congregational church, in time to help celebrate the church's 150th anniversary in 1934; Foot leaves in 1935, succeeded for three years by the Reverend Ernest F. Edmunds.

★ 1937—Miss Katherine Child, daughter of Edwin B. Child, becomes Dorset librarian, succeeding Miss Sally Clarke. One of her first initiatives is to solicit selectmen for support from the town. She asks for $400, gets $200, of which $50 is turned over to the struggling library in East Dorset.

★ 1939—Bob Warner and Dave Parsons canoe from Dorset, along the Battenkill and Hudson rivers, all the way to New York City and receive official greetings from Grover Whalen at the New York World's Fair; their picture is published in the *Herald-Tribune*.

★ 1941—"The Green Mountain Shop" opens in Dorset village, featuring light meals, antiques, and gasoline. Owners are Russell and Kathe Parks. (Parks, an artist whose works were admired by his friend "Grandma" Moses, went on to be Dorset's representative for three terms in the Vermont House. He died in 1975 and Mrs. Parks closed the shop in 1977.)

★ 1947—Lloyd McGuffin takes over the operation of the Dorset telephone exchange from his father, Harry, who had run it since 1932.

★ 1947—A raging October forest fire sweeps two hundred acres of dry timber on Netop Mountain, sending up clouds of white smoke visible from as far away as Rutland. James Beebe, town and federal fire warden, says the

Photo by Marshall Brooks, courtesy of Caroline Durand Brooks

cause was uncertain—maybe a careless smoker or a clandestine hunter. The woods have been closed to hunting by Governor Ernest Gibson because of dry conditions. The scar on Netop will remain visible for decades.

★ 1947—Sisters Elsie and Marjorie Niles launch a most successful business making "Aunt Maria's Cookies" (pronounced Ma-RYE-a) that lasts more than twenty years and puts Dorset on the map of international cookiedom. Their sugar cookies earn praise in Clementine Paddleford's prestigious food column in the *New York Herald Tribune*. Shipments of cookie tins overpower the local post office as they are sent to friends, college students, and commercial outlets all over the nation.[5]

★ 1947—Nora and Dave Gilbert open Gilbert's Hardware on Meadow Lane, featuring a full line of building hardware, paints, and garden supplies, and also—thanks to the advice of artist Jay Connaway—extensive art supplies. The Gilberts, who live next door, accommodate sportsmen at all hours by issuing hunting and fishing licenses. (The business was sold in 1965 to Peg and Bert Harrington, who continued it for fourteen years; it changed hands several times, then closed in 1988. The building now houses Mr. and Mrs. Edward Modlish's plumbing and heating business.)

★ 1952—Upon the death of Mrs. F. C. Liddle, the Dorset Library receives a substantial bequest from the estate of Dr. and Mrs. Liddle. Other generous contributions come to the library from Mrs. Bernadine Grondahl and Mrs. W. H. Calfee.

★ 1954—Mrs. Frances Scott takes over the operation of the Dorset telephone exchange from Lloyd McGuffin, who has been transferred to another department.

Courtesy of H. N. Williams Department Store

West View Farm on Route 30, was a boarding house between 1917 and 1953, where Henry and Lavinia Harwood could feed thirty-five, with rooms in both the house and an annex. The annex was moved across the road and became a home for John and Emma Stannard. After 1953 Pete and Betty Abbott continued to take overnight guests until 1973. The same building today is the restaurant Village Auberge, owned by Helmut Stein.

★ 1957—*Vermont Life* magazine publishes a series of photographs of new Vermont architecture, including the James Parton house on the Cross Road, built in 1945–46 on the site of the old Prince marble mill. Parton was the creator of *American Heritage* magazine.

★ 1957—The Reverend William Chace, Jr., becomes pastor of the Dorset Congregational church, succeeding the Reverend Herbert B. Perry, Jr. Chace presides at ceremonies marking the 175th church anniversary.

★ 1959—Hartford Woolens opens a mill outlet in the old North Dorset Schoolhouse (later to become an antiques shop). Across Route 7 is the old North Dorset Depot, operated by Paul Connors. The depot was moved closer to the highway, after passenger trains stopped running, to serve the automobile by becoming a gas station.

★ 1962—Concerns over health-care needs prompt Nora Gilbert and Kathe Parks to call a meeting attended by seventy-seven persons that results in formation of the Dorset Nursing Association. Under guidance of Dr. Elizabeth Byrnes, Ellen McCooey, R.N., and Nelle Williams, medical social worker, with Sydney J. Meachem, legal advisor, the DNA is incorporated in 1963, but does not begin operations until August 1, 1966. Then, with support by a federal grant of $4,492 and community contributions, an office is opened at the elementary school, with Nora Gilbert as secretary. Services include home nursing, a school health program, and home-health instruction, with plans for dental, eye, and pediatric clinics in the fall. Admiral R. B. Tompkins, president, announces that registered nurses will be Mrs. McCooey and Mrs. Margaret Stiles. In the following twenty years the staff grows to twelve, with many new services, and the association becomes one of the town's most active and useful organizations. Other presidents have been W. Lawrence King, Rosann Foote, Sandy Baldwin, Joy Green, Dennis Burden, Margaret Bennett, Paul McCully, Patricia Bourhill, and Kevin O'Toole.

* 1962—In June the Dorset Inn marks its twenty-fifth anniversary under the management of Fred O. Whittemore. Built in 1796, the inn has had eight previous owners. Whittemore discovered the inn while employed by the Treadway chain in Middlebury, and bought it in 1938 from Miss Amy Lapham, owner and manager for two decades.

* 1962—Signs of overcrowding: postmaster Morris Depew complains of inadequate space at the post office due to the arrival of seventy new families since he came in 1954, and to the growth of J. K. Adams Company and the Aunt Maria's Cookies business. A newspaper feature quotes Anna Gilbert recalling how she got her mail at Gilbert Sykes's store (Peltier's) during Republican regimes and at John Armstrong's store (Don McWayne's West Side Grocery) when Democrats were in power. The postal boxes, she said, were moved by wheelbarrow; the postmasters did not usually follow.

* 1963—Governor Philip Hoff speaks at the Dorset Inn at an annual meet-

Courtesy of Lloyd McGuffin

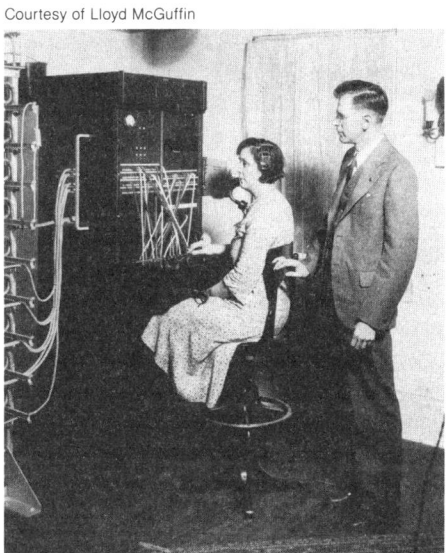

The switchboard of the Dorset telephone office when it was opened in May 1932. Ready to respond with "Number please" is Aileen McGuffin, while her husband Harry stands at the ready. The office was in their home next to Peltier's store.

Courtesy of the Bennington Banner

Dorset's Blood Bank gives its share, circa 1965, in a photo designed to demonstrate different blood types. Back row, from left: Rev. Robert Dana, Emma Stannard, Ruth Schroder, Barbara Reed, Edwin Kinnie. Front row: Elisabeth Gilbert (Sturges), Joyce Miller Tarbell, Morris Depew, Joseph King, Charlotte Stannard Brooks.

ing of Vermont Hotel-Motel Association. He appeals to legislators to enact statewide zoning to prepare for greater interest in Vermont from the tremendous influx of new people expected to arrive in the state by the year 2000. At this time Dorset has no zoning ordinance. It is the third time the statewide association has met at the inn.

★ 1963—*The Dorset Weekly,* published by elementary school pupil Thomas Cooper, makes its debut with the motto "All the News That I Can Print." The mimeographed periodical produces two dozen issues, boasts numerous correspondents and contributors. A sample editorial: "Money is a very good thing to have and you get almost anything with it. But almost as fast as you get it, it's gone. It just burns a hole in your pocket. You also can collect money. I collect pennies and have one that goes back as far as 1909." (Cooper is now the editor of *Horticulture* magazine.)

★ 1963—The end of an era that began in 1932 is marked with conversion of Dorset's operator-handled telephones to the dial system, and the retirement of Frances Scott and her switchboard. Her personal approach to the job has endeared her to many, as town babysitter, sleuth, and watchdog. Rife are the tales of small-town cognizance, such as the time a Kent Hill resident called her friend in the village with no success, but the operator said, "No luck, she isn't home. But try again in a minute. I see her walking by the office. She will be home soon." Other part-time operators affected are Mrs. Edward Ference, Mrs. Orla Reed, Mrs. Ray Parks, Mrs. Chester Phillips, Mrs. Gordon Mooney, and Mrs. Scott's daughter, Mrs. Charles Matteson. Codman Hislop pens a verse inscribed on a silver tray:

> *For Mrs. Scott, our mistress of the phone*
> *Whose voice, alas, is now the dial tone;*
> *Whose patience our impatience put at ease,*
> *This tray from us who'll miss her 'number please.' "*

★ 1964—Mrs. Einar Grondahl endows the Manchester Rescue Squad, which also serves Dorset, with $100,000.

★ 1964—Announcement is made of the sale of 1,100-acre Saddleback Farm to Richard and Barbara Ketchum of Bronxville, New York. The Kirby Hollow farm, most of which is woodland, has been owned since the early 1930s by S. S. Yates of Englewood, New Jersey, who has raised a prize herd of Guernseys, managed for seven years by Merwin Wells of Peace Street. The Ketchums lived in Dorset from 1946 to 1951, when he took a position with the U.S. Information Agency. He is now editor of the book division of American Heritage in New York.

★ 1964—The Reverend Robert Dana is welcomed in September as new pastor of the United Church of Dorset and East Rupert. A native of St. Johnsbury, Dana is a graduate of UVM and the Andover-Newton Theological Seminary.

Photo by Calvin Skinner

Rufus Lake was a familiar personage in South Dorset in the 1960s. He is shown here with his little friend, "Red" Monahan's daughter. "Rufe" lived in a house along Route 30 and traded horses and good fellowship with all he met.

* 1964—The East Dorset Library, which has struggled for survival, reopens in new quarters provided by Mr. and Mrs. Philip B. Harrigan. Anna Whalon Pelsue is librarian. The Dorset Library donates $100 as well as services and books.

* 1964—An interesting race for town representative pits two native sons. The Republican incumbent (who ran on both tickets in 1962) is William T. Burns, Sr. A UVM engineering graduate, Burns retired as vice-president of Kings County Lighting Company in Brooklyn, and returned to his native South Dorset in 1959. He is a charter member of the McBride-Harwood Legion Post. The Democratic challenger is Sargent B. Child, born in the Hollow, a son of Mr. and Mrs. Edwin B. Child. A graduate of Amherst, he holds a master's from Columbia, taught at Deerfield, served in the army and with the USIA. Burns wins handily.

* 1965—A dispersal sale is held of eighty-seven head of Guernseys at Saddleback Farms, not one of which is bought by a Dorset resident. The number of dairy herds in town is reduced to a mere six or seven.

* 1965—Reapportionment of the Vermont House of Representatives and the reduction of its number from 246 to 150 means that Dorset is combined with Manchester, Peru, Landgrove, and Winhall in a two-member legislative district. (Representative William T. Burns, Sr., who served two terms under the one-member-per-town system, will be elected to two more terms under the new district system.)

* 1966—The town authorizes demolition of the old East Dorset schoolhouse, built in 1874. Howard Brophy and his son Harvey take the job for the salvage.

* 1966—William Gilbert publishes a map of pen-and-ink drawings of 105 Dorset houses still standing that are more then a century old. Data were provided by his aunt, Anna Gilbert, and the map is dedicated to the memory of Ernest H. West, orchardist and quarry owner. Also shown are churches, major quarries, stores, inns, and historic sites.

* 1966—Katherine Child, librarian since 1937, dies, and is succeeded by Emma Stannard.

* 1966—The community Christmas party on December 20 marks a fifty-year tradition with a children's event at the Playhouse. It includes a magic show by Philip Moore, songs with Robert McFall on the accordion, MC Terry Tyler, soft drinks, an appearance by Santa Claus, and a community tree. The custom began, Anna Gilbert says, in 1913 or 1914, when Elma Pratt started giving homemade gifts to children under a large tree on the village green. The outdoor party proved too chilly and moved into the church, then to the Playhouse. A fund left in the early 1900s by Will Holley to buy gifts

for children is being handled by the Dorset Players and Dorset Fire District.

★ 1967—At its ninety-seventh annual meeting the Dorset Village Library announces receipt of a $10,000 gift in memory of Mr. and Mrs. Robert McIntyre, donated by their family. The couple were long-time residents, first summers, then in retirement. McIntyre was director of the MacBeth Gallery in New York and an authority on nineteenth-century art. Library book circulation for 1966 was reported at 8,777, an increase of 1,700.

★ 1967—Mrs. Elisabeth Gilbert buys a tiny but distinctive Greek-Revival building in Wallingford, dating to 1848 and once the law office of Judge Button, and moves it to the West Road near the Rufus Gilbert residence, to be used as a guest house.

★ 1967—A 150-acre wildfowl sanctuary is formed by Mr. and Mrs. Henry Van Loon. It is a nonprofit organization involving about twelve owners of wetlands between the Lane Road and the South Dorset Crossroad.

★ 1968—*Life* magazine calls it "one of the great finds of the present century" when Dr. Codman Hislop of Dorset, a professor of history at Union College, identifies some fifty-one letters from George Washington among a box of family papers he had been asked to look over by John L. Hawkes, also of Dorset. The papers include the first news to Washington of Benedict Arnold's treason, and letters from Alexander Hamilton, Benjamin Franklin, and John Adams. The documents relate to the military career of Major General Alexander McDougall and had been passed down in the family. Hawkes said that until now he has been unable to find a historian willing to look over the collection of letters of the founding fathers.

★ 1968—The town mourns the death of Rose Lindley Kent, ninety-five, who made national headlines when she entered the Mrs. America contest at the age of ninety. She was the widow of Clifton Kent, a descendant of Cephas Kent. She had been a teacher, and was the last townwide school superintendent before the Bennington-Rutland Supervisory District. She was also an assistant town clerk, painter, and writer, the town's *Banner* correspondent, ran for the legislature, and raised two sons.

★ 1968—The horror of the Vietnam war hits home with news of the deaths of Dorset native Allan Wilkins and resident Robert Ransom, Jr. Wilkins's funeral is attended by an overflow crowd at the Congregational church.

Lieutenant Ransom, aged twenty-three, was wounded by a mine while leading his unit on night ambush patrol near Quang Ngai, and died eight days later. Among his letters home, which were published, he wrote: "There is not a man over here that wants to see this war go on any longer. This is not to say that anybody shrinks from doing a job. But everyone is as confused as I as to exactly what, if anything, we're accomplishing."

A modern photo of the Dorset Public Library, which in 1928 found its permanent home in the former Bernard G. Sykes residence. Before that it was the home of William Manley and his son Fred. The building was originally the tavern of Captain John Gray about 1800.

Ransom was buried with full honors in Maple Hill Cemetery.

* 1968—The new minister of the Congregational church, the Reverend Hal C. Miller, III, with his wife Judy and son Todd, age 1, are welcomed at a reception given by the deaconesses, attended by more than a hundred. Miller, from Barre, is a graduate of Hartford Theological Seminary.

* 1970—The Dorset Village Public Library celebrates its hundredth anniversary on July 9 with a tea and an exhibit of quill drawings by Dean Fausett.

* 1971—The Dorset Fire Department launches a drive, chaired by Edwin Lefevre, Jr., to raise $40,250 to buy a new truck and build a better firehouse. The department's older truck is thirty-six years old—sixteen years older than the maximum age permitted by fire insurance rates—and its newer one is twelve years old and "grossly inadequate." Lefevre suggests that each homeowner make a two-year pledge, based on a percentage of insured value of one's house.

* 1971—A *New York* magazine article describes the recent filming at the Dorset Inn of a scene in *Portnoy's Complaint*. Filmmakers took over the Inn, jammed the village green with sound trucks, spread webs of wiring and cables and lights, lost money to a rainstorm, all to re-create one scene in which

Portnoy, played by Richard Benjamin, and the Monkey, by Karen Black, register at the inn pretending to be married. Dorset is described as "now inhabited by a few hard-pressed, heavily taxed natives and a large number of retired tycoons from the Middle West who think the natives are quaint. In Dorset, money buys time, and the time chosen is about 1925."

★ 1972—Ernest G. Edgerton retires after twenty years as Dorset fire chief, and the department, having raised about $50,000 by auctions and donations to its fund drive, buys a new 1972 Ford pumper with a 600-gallon tank, and builds a new firehouse on the east side of Route 30 near Williams Department Store.

★ 1972—A *New York Times* article features Barrows House owners James W. Lee II and his wife Betty, who arrived in 1961 from Darien, Connecticut, as "year-round summer people." The lighthearted article is headlined, "He Says His Cooking Gets Worse Each Day—But Don't Believe It." Lee, chairman of Dorset selectmen, ran a public-relations firm in Grosse Point, Michigan, then Darien. Barrows House prices are $3 for lunch, $5.50 for a regular dinner, and $6 for steak or beef.

★ 1972—Rene Nolet of East Dorset is elected president of the Vermont Beekeepers Association.

★ 1974—The March town meeting endorses a resolution to the Vermont congressional delegation urging that "corruption and abuse of power" at top levels of government be brought to an immediate end. The vote is influenced by the still-brewing Watergate scandal, to be climaxed by President Nixon's resignation in August.

★ 1974—Dorset gets its first bank when a branch of the Factory Point Bank of Manchester opens on Church Street on June 10.

★ 1974—In July, Dorset becomes the first town in the county to receive its award as a National Bicentennial Community, with a bicentennial flag. Former representative Eugene A. Bond chairs a celebration on the village green, with a Boy Scout honor guard, invocation by the Reverend Lester Tufts of the East Dorset Congregational Church, and organ prelude by Joe Stannard. Speaker Sandy Smith, a Burr & Burton sophomore, says that history does not flow in predetermined channels but is "a broad stream of culture fed by many tributaries" and carves its own course. Arthur W. Gilbert discloses plans for 1976 celebrations.

★ 1976—The private Long Trail School opens in rented quarters of the Sportsmen's Club at Kirby Hollow for twelve high-school-age students and three and a half teachers, including Headmaster David D. Wilson. The independent, coeducational day school says its mission is to provide "a stimulating and enriching college-oriented curriculum in a warm, family-like at-

In 1968 Paul and Leona McWayne won the Outstanding Conservation Award of the Bennington County Soil and Water Conservation District. In 1989 the McWaynes' was one of only two remaining dairy farms in Dorset.

mosphere." (In 1989 enrollment is forty, the faculty numbers seven in addition to Headmaster Wilson, with a board of ten trustees; annual tuition is $8,500, though there is a generous scholarship program.)

★ 1977—Perry M. Peltier, age eighty-one, sells his venerable general store to Jay and Terri Hathaway, and decides to retire. Hathaway, researching the store for the historical society, from its origins in 1816 as Blackmer & Holley, offers this affectionate portrait of Peltier:

Perry was an extremely well-liked gentleman known mostly for his crisp, white shirt, necktie, and a large cigar. He was rarely seen without his cigar and, as I was told the other day, all his aprons were ripped in the middle of the bib so that he could put his apron on over his head and not take his cigar out of his mouth.

Ed Molloy [for many years a clerk at the store] remembers Perry Peltier: he paid good bonuses, he gave no vacations, he relaxed in winter, he never argued.

I think that most all of us who knew him can remember that Perry's ground beef was famous, not only for its freshness and quality, but also for its garnishing of cigar ashes—which isn't far off from the truth as reflected in the 1976 Town Report which was dedicated to him. His picture shows him bending over his cutting board, cigar dangling over a huge piece of meat. He was a wonderful man who never had a great deal to say, but when he spoke, it wasn't forgotten.

★ 1978—The new McIntyre Gallery of the Dorset Village Public Library

Photo by Stetson Fletcher

The McWayne barns and silos along Route 30 north accommodated 46 milkers and 50 young stock of Holsteins when this picture was taken in 1988. Paul McWayne's son Milton has been running the farm since his father's death. Milton is a great-great grandson of Nathaniel McWayne, one of Dorset's best-known Civil War veterans.

is dedicated with an exhibition of the paintings of Elsa Bley.

★ 1979—Perry Peltier dies at the age of eighty-four, only weeks after the death of his wife, the former Exina Markey.

★ 1983—Dinah Voorhis succeeds Emma Stannard as librarian of the Dorset Village Public Library.

★ 1984—The United Church of Dorset and East Rupert celebrates its bicentennial with special ceremonies and the publication of a book of its history.

★ 1986—When obituaries appear of Sherman Adams, the flinty counselor to President Eisenhower, many Dorseters are surprised by newspaper accounts that claim Adams was born in 1899 in East Dorset. The reports are untrue; Adams was really born in East Dover, where his father was a minister.

★ 1986—The 3,230-foot mountain that towers over Dorset is authoritatively designated "Mt. Aeolus." Research to substantiate the official name is provided by Harold Grout, native of East Dorset, who vowed to end the confusion by which the mountain is also known variously as Green Peak or Dorset Mountain. Grout circulated a petition and sent it to Governor Madeleine M. Kunin, who turned it over to the Board of Libraries which made the decision.

★ 1987—Dorset Selectmen vote 3–2 for a moratorium on multiple housing and commercial development. Selectmen in favor are chairman Bill Mahlmann, Peter Sturges, and David Wilson; opposed are Warren Crawford and Jim Faszholz. "We want manageable growth," said Sturges, "and the time to do something is here and now." Said Richard Ketchum, who initiated a petition for the halt to building, "I am encouraged and delighted. I hate to see the town divided. We had representatives of every kind of person in town sign the petition."

★ 1989—Development rights and perpetual conservation restrictions on two hundred acres of Saddleback Farm in Kirby Hollow are donated by Richard and Barbara Ketchum to the Vermont Land Trust of Woodstock, making a total of 710 Saddleback acres covered by restrictions. This land can be used for agriculture, forestry, education and noncommercial recreation, but not for residential, commercial, or industrial purposes.

★ 1989—North Shire Probate Judge Ellen H. Maloney, Dorset resident and an attorney in Pawlet, is appointed a Superior Court judge by Governor Kunin, the first woman in Vermont to be named to that position.

NOTES

1. "Since 1924" becomes an important demarcation because, among several other reasons, that was the year Zephine Humphrey's *Story of Dorset* was published. Until now, hers was the only book-length history of the town. This chapter, intended to bring matters up to date, has been assisted by the recollections of many older residents, some thirty-five of whom were interviewed.

2. Information about Emerald Lake State Park was provided by Rodney A. Barber, assistant director of the state lands division, Vermont Department of Forests, Parks and Recreation, who was involved in building the East Dorset park. Barber also contributed a detailed history prepared by former ranger Bruce Brown, and an archaeological study, copies of which have been deposited with the Dorset Historical Society. Brown's work includes recollections from Mrs. Fred Harwood, widow of the supervisor of "North Dorset Farms." State parks created during the "Beckoning Country" era included, besides Emerald Lake, Woodford, Molly Stark, Lake Carmi, Groton, Grand Isle, North Hero, Silver Lake, Thetford, Bomoseen, St. Catherine, and Branbury.

3. Charter members of the Dorset Historical Society were Rita W. Barbour, Jessica H. and Eugene A. Bond, Mary Burnett Burke, Mollie J. Cushman, Gertrude G. Drury, Edith C. Finlay, Alfred H. Gilbert, Anna Elizabeth Gilbert, Frederick F. Gilbert, George Holley Gilbert, Ruth W. Gilbert, Elsie E. Niles, Marjorie L. Niles, Harold C. O'Neal, Mildred O'Neal, Marian L. Schumacher, Ruth Shroder, Marchen T. Skinner, and Emma Stannard.

4. From an interview by the writer with George M. Wallace.

5. Here, published with permission of Elsie Niles and Herbert Schachinger, is the recipe of sisters Marjorie and Elsie Niles:

Aunt Maria's Sugar Cookies
(Recipe makes 360 cookies)
6 cups flour
4 cups sugar
2 tablespoons almond or whatever flavor you like
2 teaspoons salt
4 large eggs
1 pound shortening (Crisco, margerine, butter, etc.)
optional: 2 teaspoons baking powder

Put shortening in mixing bowl. Add ¼ of sugar at a time. Be sure to get out lumps and bumps. Add eggs, slightly beaten. Add flour in small amounts and mix in. Then add almond flavoring. If you wish, you can add the 2 teaspoons baking powder.

Shape dough into small balls and press with cookie press (the Niles sisters used a floral-shaped glass). Bake in 375 oven on cookie sheet: 10 minutes for electric oven, 5 minutes for gas oven.

14

A Final Word: Cemeteries

THE CEMETERY is one of the most serene and beautiful places in town, and suddenly Walt Whitman is here with us, for the lilacs—the flower he linked forever to the Civil War—are in bloom and their fragrance is everywhere. By now only the muffled tap of one drum breaks the silence and then there is no sound, no movement except the slow flapping of flags in the breeze while the minister says a prayer and a soldier lays a wreath on a grave. Someone calls the honor guard to attention and to order arms; there is the crack of rifles and then, from high on the hill, a bugler concealed somewhere in the ancient maples sounds taps. In this tiny cemetery lie the dead of all our country's wars, and somehow they are all comrades when those clear, heartbreaking notes float on the air, bidding them all "Go to sleep, go to sleep."

Richard M. Ketchum[1]

A few words should be recorded about the final resting places of so many of those who figured in this history of an important Vermont town. In addition to the three largest and best-known cemeteries, Maple Hill, East Dorset, and St. Jerome's, there are more than a dozen others, mostly in remote, oft-forgotten locations.

All cemeteries are equalizers of social, financial, and other categories, but there are qualities about Dorset's pre-eminent burial ground that convey a more particular sense of equality among its occupants. A visitor entering the Maple Hill Cemetery will be awed not only by its beauty and serenity but by its sense of oneness. This is a place where all trivial distinctions among people have vanished. Here, every soul has been accepted with the purest kind of dignity and equanimity.

A Final Word: Cemeteries

Between the highway and an old road that once curved westward, toward the front of the Barrows House, stand the very oldest stones, dating to 1772, only four years after the first settlers arrived. Except for that fact, newer and older sections of this cemetery are relatively intermixed. Gravesites are located along a series of rising terraces on the side of a cedar-shaded hill above a tomb where caskets were once placed in winter awaiting spring burial. Near the tomb a dignified marker commemorates the veterans of all wars.

Of the six pioneering settlers of the town, Felix Powell, Isaac Lacy, John Manley, Jr., Abraham Underhill, Benjamin Baldwin, and George Page, three lie here in eternal rest: Underhill, who died in 1796, Baldwin, in 1830, and Manley, in 1816. Powell is believed to have been buried with several others near the West Road and Route 30, where no traces of a cemetery remain.

The oldest Maple Hill stone is that of settler Benjamin Baldwin's nine-month-old son Benjamin, Jr., who died on September 6, 1772. The inscription on his stone, its imaginative spelling now blurred by time, reads:

> NB. he was the first
> That was beuryd
> In this yard.

In a 1969 paper on the restoration, art, and history of Dorset burying grounds, Arthur W. Gilbert told about the beloved but austere village physician, Dr. F.C. Liddle, who once criticized stonecutter "Yank" Tully for mis-

Courtesy of Nora Gilbert

The spelling is primitive but the meaning is clear. This Maple Hill Cemetery gravestone of Benjamin Baldwin, who died in 1772, aged nine months and four days, reads, "NB he was the first that was beuryd in this yard."

spelling the name "Gertrude" on a headstone he had ordered. Offended, Tully retorted, "There are more of your mistakes in this place, Doctor, than there are of mine."

Throughout the Maple Hill cemetery are the graves of other early settlers and their families and descendants—Cephas Kent, Captain John Gray, Stephen Martindale—along with the familiar names of Baldwin, Gilbert, Farwell, Barrows, Pratt, Field, Dunton, Sykes, Paddock, Manley, Prentiss, Kent, Edgerton, Harwood, Williams, McWayne, and many others known to all hereabouts.

Though the cemetery was expanded once in 1865 and again in 1919, it is now virtually filled. Its 6.6 acres contain 350 eight-grave plots, and its population exceeds that of the town's highest-ever census, 2,195, that of 1870.

Almost all of the gravestones here are of the native material, marble, though some granite stones date to a time since the closing of the marble quarries. The pioneering families had no way of knowing that toward the end of the twentieth century marble would be subject to deterioration from manmade acid rain. But perhaps the Dorset marble that was used for headstones was of a special quality, or perhaps it has been protectively shaded by so many maple and cedar trees, for many headstones here have not eroded as badly as marble memorials elsewhere.

Dorset's largest cemetery is located at Maple Hill because the first church was located here, though no trace of a foundation can be seen and graves have been placed without regard to the original building site. That first meetinghouse, a log church that because of its draughtiness came to be known as "the Lord's barn," was built about 1773 under the direction of Cephas Kent and John Manley, and was moved in 1797 or 1798 to the north side of Church Street. It was destroyed by fire during a violent storm in January 1832, and then a decision was made to locate a new church across the street, where after another fire, in 1907, its marble successor stands. The cemetery stayed where it was.

The East Dorset Community Cemetery, next largest burial ground, offers a beauty and dignity of its own, surrounded by a rough retaining wall made of marble slabs, with a black iron gate, and shaded by a few sugar maples. Though more than ninety percent of all Vermont cemeteries face west, this one faces east toward the massive Green Mountains.

A gravesite here that often attracts tourists is that of East Dorset native William G. Wilson (1895-1971), the "Bill W." who co-founded Alcoholics Anonymous. In places where AA meets, among other helpful literature a simple blue brochure offers directions to his grave. When this writer visited the site, someone had taped carefully to the stone of William G. Wilson a single

A Final Word: Cemeteries

Among several cemeteries scattered throughout Dorset is this private burial plot of the Armstrong family on Upper Hollow Road. A stone memorializes Jonathan Armstrong 1791-1828.

wooden toothpick—an enigmatic personal memento symbolizing something important to someone who had been helped.

The number of cemeteries in town depends on whose study you read, or how you count. The late Alfred H. Gilbert, a founder of the Dorset Historical Society who worked on cemetery research in the early 1960s with his sister Anna and town manager James Beebe, concluded that there were eleven. In his paper presented to the historical society in 1969, Arthur W. Gilbert listed fifteen. Maple Hill and the East Dorset Community are the largest and most all-inclusive, while smaller burial sites are revered mostly for their historic or family associations.

According to Anna Gilbert, who cited reliable oral tradition, the first burial place in town was where Felix Powell was believed to be interred in South Dorset at the southwest corner of the intersection of West Road and Route 30. On the east side of town another early burial ground, now obliterated, was said by Arthur Gilbert to have been near the Deming-Viall-Benedict house at the foot of Morse Hill Road.

The only cemetery in Dorset Hollow, restored in recent times, holds the remains of Jonathan Armstrong and his family, dating to Revolutionary days. It is located on the Upper Hollow Road. Arthur Gilbert wrote of it: "Obviously the Armstrongs originally established a proper cemetery, with elaborately carved headstones, and initialed footstones. It may even be more than just coincidence that the designs on three of the markers are related. On the one for Abigail, Jonathan's wife, are both the urn and the weeping willow, in the conventional pattern. On the son's stone the urn is predominant; on the grandson's only the willow appears."

Off the Danby Mountain Road, near the town line and protected by a wire fence, lies the Hazelton cemetery, so called for its most prominent stone. This was dedicated to the memory of Hyram H. Hazelton of the 7th Vermont Volunteers, Company D, who died at the age of twenty-three in 1862 in the service of the Union while in Louisiana. Other fieldstone markers bear no legible inscriptions, though one carries a date of 1791. Also buried here were Eseck and Eunice Blackmer.

In North Dorset, south of Emerald Lake State Park on the west side of Route 7, is the grave of pioneer Zachariah Curtis, who died in 1805 at the age of eighty-nine. Curiously, north of the park other members of the Curtis family are buried near the grave of Welcome Allen. Off the Bowen Hill Road two obscure burial grounds hold the mortal remains of the Gifford and Bowen families.

Dorset Historical Society

Zachariah Curtis's grave is located in this small cemetery north of Harold Beebe's farm on Route 7. Curtis came to town in 1769, the second year of settlement, sired twenty-five children, and died in 1805.

A Final Word: Cemeteries

Courtesy of the Bennington Banner

A few graves are still found in the old Catholic cemetery near the Freedley quarry on Dorset Hill Road; others were moved to the new cemetery at St. Jerome's church in East Dorset village.

Several more cemeteries are located north of the Morse Hill Road along the road that once led to the Freedley quarry, now known as Dorset Hill Road. As one goes north there is a burial plot of the McDonald family, then another of the Collson family, and then the old Dorset Hill Cemetery, so called, with graves of some of the first Irish immigrants, who came to escape the potato famines of the 1840s and to work in the quarries or on the railroad. Several stones record the Irish counties and parishes of origin of the deceased. Under a weatherbeaten wooden cross the remains of "unknown soldiers" of the immigration lie in unmarked graves. Among those interred in this old Catholic cemetery is Edward Bowers, born in Ireland in 1792, who marched off to fight in the Civil War when he was seventy years old.

In East Dorset, the cemetery of St. Jerome's Church was established directly north of the church in 1868, the year its first resident pastor, the Reverend Thomas J. Gaffney, arrived and bought land for the new Catholic church. To initiate this cemetery, some graves were disinterred from the old Dorset

Dorset

The Dorset Color Guard at a Loyalty Day parade, circa 1960. From left are George McWayne, Peter Brooks, Dick Stannard, Robert Burns, and James Stannard, squadron leader.

Hill Cemetery and moved. Formal dedication was held a decade later, in 1878, when the Right Reverend Louis deGoesbriand, first bishop of the Burlington diocese, preached a sermon and presided over the installation of a cross. The first official burial at St. Jerome's was that of Patrick Kelly, who died March 23, 1878.

The Morse cemetery is near the height of land and south of Morse Hill Road. One of its oldest stones is that of John Morse, who died in 1827, aged sixty-two. Others include Chapmans, Bardslees, Wades, a Beers, and a McGuigan; the most recent stone is dated 1875. Here next to the graves of his two infant daughters one finds the marble marker of Bennet Bardslee, on which a cautionary inscription exclaims, almost as clearly as the day in 1839 when it was carved:

> *All you that read with little care,*
> *Who walk away and leave me here:*
> *Do not forget that you must die,*
> *And be entomb [sic] as well as I.*

A Final Word: Cemeteries 351

Scrutinizing a town's cemeteries yields important understanding of its people over many years. Gravestones tell stories that can be inferred and are rarely related in history books. They tell of hard times, of incurable sicknesses and plagues, fatal accidents, and the heartbreak and helplessness that accompany the death of children. Clues can be assembled from the tombstones' locations, materials, artistry, inscriptions, and maintenance.

While many remote cemeteries in Vermont towns become forgotten and overgrown, Dorset's are tended more carefully than many thanks to a $10,000 trust established by John J. Flynn, formerly of East Dorset, upon his death in 1940. Income from the fund, administered by the Chittenden Trust Company, helps maintain "the neglected and uncared-for cemeteries" throughout the town. Flynn himself was buried in St. Jerome's Cemetery.

NOTES

1. Richard M. Ketchum, *Second Cutting* (New York: the Viking Press), 1981, p. 111.

The Schoolhouses
A Pictorial Portfolio

THE BEERS ATLAS MAP of 1869 (see back endpaper) depicted school districts at the time of their maximum proliferation. Dorset's first school opened on the West Road in 1785, and by 1800 several more districts had been created. Schools continued to be located in neighborhoods where children could walk to and from home. When a new cluster of population developed, a school was built to serve those children.

Very gradually, state legislation was enacted that moved toward more centralization and more standards. The era of 1827 to 1870 was called "the period of slow development" by John C. Huden, a former state education commissioner and school historian. Nothing was done until after the Civil War to end the archaic system of a multiplicity of separate school districts in each town.

Dorset was typical of towns divided into an excessive number of school districts. The 1869 map indicates that the total number was fourteen, but it showed only twelve (districts eleven and thirteen do not exist on the map). The Beers Atlas maps showed each district in a color. It was perhaps a coincidence that 1869, the year the Beers Atlas was published, was the last year in which no state action was taken on school districts. In 1870 the legislature authorized towns to abolish districts and to establish townwide school systems. The townwide system was then mandated in 1892, which meant a single town superintendent.

Still, many school districts persisted until transportation improved sufficiently to carry children farther from their homes. Not until the 1920s did Dorset really begin to relinquish its district schools. Then it was not until 1958 that the town voted for consolidation, and in 1960 voters authorized construction of an eight-room elementary school on the compromise location of Morse Hill Road—about halfway between the last two districts to merge, East Dorset and Dorset village. The new school cost $189,000, was located on eleven acres of land, and initially served 187 pupils.

What is remarkable is that so many of the old district school buildings still exist and are converted to so many useful purposes. Their designs, with the suggestion of a belfry or a large expanse of windows, often gives away their original function long after they have been converted to shops or private homes.

The district numbers listed with the photographs correspond to those on the Beers Atlas.

Photo by Harriet Gilbert in Charles Gilbert collection

West Road School. *(District No. 1)* This one-room school, pictured in 1910, was built in 1834 and moved in 1859 to its present site, purchased from Jubah Kent for $18. The building replaced the earlier school built in 1785 and located on West Road either opposite the Cephas Kent inn or a half mile north near Gilbert Brook. This school was discontinued in 1941, its nine remaining pupils transferred to the Dorset Village School. The building was sold to Guy Stone in 1949 for $1,100. Present owners are Mr. and Mrs. James McClure.

The Schoolhouses

North District School. *(District No. 2)* Located on Route 30 a mile north of the village, this building was in operation in 1856, and discontinued in 1948 when the Dorset Village School was remodeled. It was reopened in 1953, then closed permanently when the central Dorset Elementary School was completed. This school had electricity but lacked running water and relied on chemical toilets. It was heated by a pot-bellied stove. In 1961 the McBride-Harwood American Legion Post purchased the building from the estate of Ernest Edgerton, Sr., and later sold it. The present owner is Mary McKhann.

Photo by John Hawkes

Dorset Hollow School. *(District No. 3)* Located on the Lower Hollow Road across from the Harlan Coolidge farm, this building had been moved from a site on land that connects the Upper and Lower Hollow roads. Miss Emily Allyn purchased it after its ten students transferred to the Dorset Village School in 1945. Zephine Humphrey wrote in The Story of Dorset that at one time there were ninety students ranging in age from 2 to 20 in this building. The present owner is David Zirak.

Photo by John Hawkes

South Dorset School. *(District No. 4)* Built in 1910 on Route 30 by Frank Norton, grandfather of Charlotte Brooks, this building replaced one that had burned the previous year. There were two classrooms on the first floor, a meeting room with a stage on the second. The school closed in 1948 when students were moved to the Dorset Village School. The present owner is Mrs. Dorothy Jones, who uses the first floor as an antique shop. The picture was taken in 1988.

Photo by Stetson Fletcher

Morse Hill School. *(District No. 5) Located on Morse Hill at the corner of Overlook Road, this school was probably built about 1867 on land given by John McDevitt, grandfather of Ellen Gallagher. It closed in 1922, and its pupils were sent by horse and wagon to the East Dorset Village School. The town sold the building in 1933.*

Photo by John Hawkes

Photo by A.L. Sowen

East Dorset Village School. *(District No. 6) Built in 1874, this school had two rooms downstairs and a town hall upstairs. It replaced a one-room school that was sold to Ira Cochran for $300 and moved to its present site on Pleasant Street. The East Dorset School measured 32 by 52 feet and cost $5,020.17 to build. It was razed in 1966 by Howard Brophy who told a Town Meeting, "I'll tear it down for free, because I hated it so." He sold the lumber to Terry Tyler for six cents a board foot. Tyler, in turn, built his three-car garage out of it. The school was used by all East Dorset students until the new Dorset Elementary School opened on Morse Hill Road in 1960. It was used for town offices until the new town office was built in 1965.*

Photo by Marshall Brooks, courtesy of Helen Mach

Dorset Village School   *(District No. 7)   This was built in 1875 to replace an 1837 school. This school, like the East Dorset School, had two classrooms downstairs and a meeting hall upstairs. It was remodeled to convert the second floor to two classrooms in 1948, when North District and South Dorset children were transferred here to complete west-side consolidation of eight schools. The school closed in 1960 and was razed in 1962. Its marble doorstep is owned by Mr. and Mrs. Calvin Skinner. (The earlier 1837 school was converted to a blacksmith shop and is now known as "The Forge," located on the Hollow Road and owned by Dr. Elizabeth Vivienne-Smith.) The picture dates to 1944.*

Dorset Hill School. *(District No. 8) Located about two miles in on the Dorset Hill Road, this one-room school was sold in 1929 after the quarries had closed. It is still recognizable as a school in this 1988 picture.*

Photo by Marchen Skinner

Steam Mill, or Wheelerville School. *(District No. 9) This was its appearance in the 1880s when Howard Bowen's father William A. Bowen attended it. The school was on Bowen Hill Road, past the Country Lane Motel, next to the Mt. Tabor Leg Road. It was later moved to North Dorset and used as a barn but burned in the 1970s.*

Courtesy of Howard Bowen

Danby Mountain Road School. *(District No. 10) There is no known photo, and no school remains today, but Mrs. Lettie Baldwin, mother of Chester Baldwin, recalled a schoolhouse in 1892 on the east side of the road. The Beers Atlas does not show a school located in this district in 1869.*

Upper Hollow School. *(District No. 11) No building remains today, and only legend has it that a District No. 11 school was located near "Glen Farm," now owned by George Wallace and home of the Dorset Hollow Corporation. The Beers Atlas shows no school near this location and in fact shows no District 11, though the map has a 12 and a 14.*

The Schoolhouses

Photo by John Hawkes

North Dorset School. *(District No. 12)* *One of the most conspicuous old schools today because it is an antique shop on Route 7, this one-roomer was built in 1843 and remained in use until 1939 when pupils were transferred to East Dorset Village School. As a school it was never electrified. The building was purchased in 1949 by Ernest Edgerton, Sr., for $1,500.*

District No. 13 School. *No building remains today, and there is no photo, but District No. 1 (West Road) records in 1859 mention a meeting with District No. 13 to combine schools. The Beers Atlas shows no District No. 13, though a tiny neighborhood at the north end of the West Road is shown as part of a Rupert school district.*

South Village School, East Dorset. *(District No. 14) Built on land bought by the town in 1852, this school operated until 1930 when pupils were sent to East Dorset Village. It was sold to Paul Leary of Manchester for $300, and is now owned by Trudy Myers.*

Photo by John Hawkes

Dorset Elementary School. *"The new school," built on Morse Hill Road and opened in February 1960, completed the centralization of all fourteen districts. It was built on eleven acres bought from Dan Wade for $3,500 in 1958. This photo dates to 1965. "Dorset has conquered the mountain that divided it, through its children," said the chairman of the state board of education at the dedication in 1960. Kindergarten and more library space were added in the early 1970s, and a 1987 bond issue for $1.5 million was passed to finance an extensive addition.*

Courtesy of *Bennington Banner*

Epilogue

The past is gone.
Gone are the proprietors of the 1760s who with gleams in their eyes speculated in seemingly inexhaustible quantities of virgin land. Gone are the settlers and first families who migrated to these new lands amid hardships but armed with hope. Gone are the shepherds and farmers who cleared that land for their beasts and in so doing laid bare the mountains. Gone are sympathizers of the Green Mountain Boys who drove off the Yorkers and helped establish a "separate district" that would be named for the green mountains in their midst. Gone are the quarriers who fled the Irish potato famine and came to labor beneath the soil for marble. Gone too are the Victorian summer visitors who boarded with farm families, hiked the trails, picnicked under maple trees, gathered for evening discussion groups, and on Sundays relaxed in green rockers to digest generous chicken dinners with fixin's and homemade ice cream. Those who really liked the town often bought a little place of their own.

People still come to Dorset. The drawing cards are many: tennis and golf, theater and art, restaurants and lounges, four diverse seasons of scenic beauty, sylvan hideaways. There remains a strong heritage of acceptance of outsiders, of those sympathetic to culture and the arts. Since 1868, when first "summer person" Elizabeth Payson Prentiss discovered the place and wanted to keep its charms a secret, accessibility has been eased greatly by real estate agents, nationwide advertising networks, professional promoters and developers.

It is easy to say that times have changed but not always easy to accept many of those changes. The milk trucks have gone the way of the iceman. Only two dairy herds are left in Dorset. It is hardly possible to find a fresh-laid egg in town. Cement mixers, gravel haulers, and trucks carting loads of instant grass thunder along dirt roads that evolved more than a century ago for horse-drawn wagons. Owners of former farmland who want to keep it open must hire someone to clear unwanted vegetation, and it's not always easy to find that someone to do it when they want.

Does it matter that condominiums rise from pastures which for decades yielded hay for cattle, horses, and sheep? Is it a problem that television "dishes" sprout from cornfields like mutant mushrooms? Look mountainward and what you are likely to see, aside from a diminished number of songbirds (victims of environmental degradation), are distant slated roofs peeking through the treetops, or skylights glinting in the sun. Dorset's once-proud apple orchards still bloom each spring, but not for the gorgeous McIntosh apples harvested in October; they bloom for second-home owners who paid plenty for the view.

The future lies ahead.

It is tempting for those who appreciate the heritage and traditions of the past to wallow in cynicism about the future. So many aspects of the old "quality of life" are changing, so rapidly. Dorset's approximately 38 square miles of meadows, valleys, swamps, rivers, and mountains are evolving inexorably into a kind of post-modern suburbia.

But there will always be choices to be made, new crossroads where basic decisions take place. To help shape those decisions, on a national level one can join forces with groups like Greenpeace, the Sierra Club, or the Natural Resources Defense Council. Statewide, one can keep in touch the Nature Conservancy, or even the Vermont Historical Society, and with many offices of state government—the Housing and Land Conservation Trust Fund and the new Council of Regional Commissions, to name but two. Locally, for those who wish to perpetuate venerable values, it is possible to support—in addition to the Dorset Historical Society, of course—the Vermont Natural Resources Council, or the Mettawee Land Trust, or the new Dorset Citizens for Responsible Growth, become involved with the Dorset Planning Commission, watch cases before the regional Act 250 Commission, or attend meetings of the Bennington County Regional Commission and follow its implementation of Act 200, the state law designed to control growth. One person can make a difference.

The choices are ours.

Appendices

Dorset

State Legislators from Dorset

It should be noted that after 1966 the State of Vermont was reapportioned and Dorset was grouped with Manchester, Winhall, and Peru. This area is now known as Bennington-Rutland No. 2 District and elects two representatives every two years. The first two representatives were Reid Lefevre of Manchester and Norman Fair of Winhall.

State Senators*

1846-1847	Heman Morse	1931-1932	Richard Marston Campbell
1859, 1860	Laurel B. Armstrong	1947-1948	Carleton G. Howe
1865, 1866	Ira Cochran	1949-1950	Carleton G. Howe
1880-1881	Gilbert M. Sykes	1951-1952	Carleton G. Howe
1882-1883	George M. Viall	1953-1954	Carleton G. Howe
1884-1885	John Curtis	1955-1956	Carleton G. Howe
1902-1903	Moses Sheldon	1957-1958	Carleton G. Howe

State Representatives

Dates when each representative served are shown in the left hand column. Where available, birth and death dates follow a representative's name.

1778 (March)	Cephas Kent (1725-1809)	1794	Stephen Martindale (1766-1845)
1778 (Oct.)	Abraham Underhill (1730-1796)	1795	John Shumway
1779	John Strong (1738-1816)	1796	Jonathan Armstrong
1780-1781	Abraham Underhill, John Strong	1797-1799	John Shumway
		1800	Jonathan Armstrong
1782	Benjamin Baldwin (1743-1830)	1801-1802	Stephen Martindale
	John Strong	1803-1804	John Shumway
		1805-1806	Samuel Collins (1763-1813)
1783	John Shumway (1735-1829)	1807	John Shumway
	Timothy Brown	1808-1811	Samuel Collins
1784	Benjamin Baldwin, Abraham Underhill	1812-1814	Benjamin Deming
		1815-1822	John Underhill (1772-1846)
1785	John Shumway	1823-1824	Reuben H. Blackmer (1793-1866)
1786	John Gray (1750-1814)		
1787	John Shumway	1825	Johnson Marsh
1788	William Dunton (1755-1840)	1826	Reuben H. Blackmer
1789	John Shumway	1827	John Cochran (1777-1841)
1790	William Dunton	1828	Stephen Martindale
1791-1792	John Shumway	1829	John Cochran
1793	Jonathan Armstrong (1743-1826)		

* Compiled from *Principal Civil Officers of Vermont from 1777 to 1918*, edited by John M. Comstock. D. Gregory Sanford of the Vermont State Archives provided information concerning Senators who served from 1931 to 1958.

Appendix

1830-1831	Azel Morse (1799-1856)	1896-1897	Horace G. Harwood (1849-1897)
1832-1833	Sylvanus Sykes (1775-1840)	1898-1899	William E. Tully (1859-1925)
1834-1835	Paddock Gray (1793-1858)	1900-1901	Henry B. Kendall (1846-1930)
1836-1837	Robert Bloomer (1800-1862)		
1838	Abiel Blanchard	1902-1903	James M. Beebe (1857)
1839	Chauncey Green (1801-1876)	1904-1905	George M. Viall (1849-1912)
1840	Heman Morse (1802-1862)	1906-1907	James M. Beebe
1841-1843	William S. Martindale (1782-1866)	1908-1909	Frederick G. Stone (1867)
1844	None	1910-1911	George M. Viall
1845	None	1912-1914	Jeremiah C. Flynn (1859-1949)
1846	None		
1847-1848	James Curtis (1807-1853)	1915-1916	Nathaniel McWayne (1839-1935)
1849	Jarvis Andrus (1790-1874)		
1850-1851	Daniel G. Williams (1808-1868)	1917-1918	Michael F. Kelly (1872)
		1919-1920	James M. Beebe (1857)
1852-1853	Marcus B. Roberts (1799-1870)	1921-1922	Charles Augustus Wade (1874-1949)
1854-1855	George W. Farwell (1813-1893)	1923-1924	Jerry C. Flynn (Jeremiah?) (1858-1940)
1856	George B. Holley (1812-1869)	1925-1926	William Proctor McWayne (1873-1952)
1857-1858	Ira Cochran (1810-1894)	1927-1928	Richard Marston Campbell (1861-1931)
1859	Charles Field (1824-1886)		
1860-1861	John W. Batchelder (1825)	1929-1930	Herbert N. Williams (1875-1937)
1862-1863	Henry B. Kent (1827-1906)		
1864-1865	Welcome Allen (1811-)	1931-1932	Walter H. Beebe (1895-1970)
1866	Augustine B. Armstrong (1817-1890)	1933-1934	Frederick Field Gilbert (1893-1962)
1867-1868	Gilbert M. Sykes (1834)	1935-1936	Thomas Henry Burns (1894-1957)
1869	William H. Bebee (1822-1904)	1937-1938	Henry Farwell Harwood (1881)
1870-1871	William A. Tyrel (1833-1890)	1939-1940	Henry G. Stone (1886-1974)
1872-1873	William H. Bebee	1941-1942	Howard G. Brophy (1911)
1874-1875	Duane L. Kent (1827-1882)	1943-1944	Robert Warner (1905)
1876-1877	George W. Farwell	1945-1946	Carleton G. Howe (1898)
1878-1879	Isaac Barrows (1820-1894)	1947-1948	Robert Warner
1880-1881	Orren E. Whitney (1833-1907)	1949-1950	Leland P. Beebe (1920)
		1951-1956	Russell Parks (1906-1975)
1882-1883	Dwight Sykes (1837-1905)	1957-1958	Frederick Whittemore (1904)
1884-1885	Moses Sheldon (1850)	1959-1960	Claude Dern (1906)
1886-1887	Geoge M. Viall (1849-1912)	1961-1962	Eugene Ayres Bond (1899)
1888-1889	John L. Cochran (1846-1906)	1963-1966	William Thomas Burns (1899)
1890-1891	John E. Buffam (1838-1914)		
1892-1893	Albert B. Roberts (1850)		
1894-1895	Andrew J. Loveland (1857-1915)		

Dorset

Courtesy of Allen Farnum

William Gilbert Barrows, town moderator for thirty years. This photo is dated September 18, 1928.

Photo by Marchen Skinner

Henry Stone, longtime East Dorset resident who held town offices for many years and played a major role in improvements to the East Dorset water system.

Town Officials

Selectmen

Cephas Kent	1774-1776, 1782, 1783
John Manley	1774, 1779
Asa Baldwin	1774, 1775
Abram Underhill	1775-1779
Augustin Underhill	1776, 1780, 1781, 1784
Ephraim Reynolds	1777
John Manley, Jr.	1777, 1778
Asahel Harmon	1778, 1780-1783, 1785-1788
Ebenezer Morse	1779
Zachariah Curtis	1780
Richard Dunning	1780, 1790
John Gray	1780, 1811, 1813, 1815, 1817, 1818
Isaac Farwell	1781
Benjamin Baldwin	1782-1787, 1800-1806
Eli Deming	1784, 1785
John Matteson	1786
John French	1787, 1788
Jonathan Armstrong	1788-1789, 1794, 1796-1808
Eleazer Baldwin	1789
William Underhill	1789
Stephen Martindale	1790, 1793, 1809, 1810, 1812
Seth Smith	1790
(Missing)	1791 and 1792
John Shumway	1794, 1799
Missing	1795
Samuel Collins	1796-1798
Price Beardsley	1796-1798, 1800-1806
Titus Sykes	1799, 1808
Benjamin Matteson	1799
Noah Morse	1799
Benjamin Deming	1807-1810, 1812, 1813
John Vail	1807, 1809, 1810
E. Farwell	1818
Israel Sikes	1817, 1818
John Underhill	1810-1813, 1815
Sylvanus Sykes	1824-1829
Joseph Morse	1824-1825
Horatio Sykes	1824-1826
Joseph Leach	1826
John Chapman	1827-1832

Appendix

Courtesy Sister Anthony Marie Leary

Ed Leary, East Dorset station agent for the Rutland Railroad, was a selectman for many years from the 1930s through the 1950s.

Photo by Marchen Skinner

Russell Parks, who depended on crutches for many years, kept busy as artist, garage operator, restaurateur, caretaker, and legislator. He also had special talents as fisherman, antiques dealer and Yankee trader.

Photo by Nancy H. Otis

Guy Stone, East Dorset contractor and son of Henry Stone, was town moderator and selectman for many years.

Paddock Gray	1827, 1829	Chauncey G. Borland	
Samuel Merick	1828		1847, 1848
Juba Kent	1830, 1831	Wm. S. Martindale	1847, 1848
Benjamin Ames	1830-1833, 1846-1848	James A. Hodge	1849
		I. N. Sykes (Sikes)	1850-1851, 1853
Experience Barrows	1832, 1833, 1837, 1844	Hiram S. Sowle	1852
		John Curtis	1853, 1876
Alvin Gray	1833-1836, 1838-1840	Nelson J. Sanford	1854, 1871-1872
		John Petty	1854
Heman Morse	1834, 1855-1857	George W. Farwell	1858, 1859, 1862, 1865, 1866, 1873-1874
Lyman Sykes	1834-1836		
William Bebee	1835, 1836		
Daniel G. Williams	1837, 1838, 1850-1852	W. A. Martindale	1858, 1859, 1864
		A. B. Armstrong	1860, 1861
Cyrus Armstrong	1837	John W. Batchelder	1860-1864
Zalman Barnum	1838-1840	W. H. Bebee	1858, 1863, 1865-1866, 1871-1872, 1875, 1877-1878
James Curtis	1839-1842, 1849		
David Baldwin	1841		
James T. Wilson	1841-1843, 1853-1857, 1859	Charles Baldwin	1865-1866, 1877
		William D. Clemons	1867-1868
Anson Gray	1842, 1843	James B. Wood	1867-1868
Josiah Daton (Dayton)	1843	Azariah Hilliard	1867-1869
Jarvis Andrews	1844, 1845	F. G. Harwood	1869-1870
John T. Griffith	1844	Oliver B. Gilbert	1869-1870
William J. Soper	1845	H. A. Williams	1870-1871, 1873-1876
Norton Sikes (Sykes)	1845-1846, 1860, 1861, 1864	J. L. Cochran	1872, 1873
		J. M. Griffith	1874
Harvey Holley	1846, 1849-1852, 1855-1857, 1862-1863	E. J. Sanford	1875
		H. G. Harwood	1876-1877

Dorset

The Dorset town office building, East Dorset, 1988.

Dwight Sykes	1878	William E. Tully	1895-1902
Nathaniel McWayne	1878	H. B. Kendall	1895-1908
William D. Ames	1879-1880	A. L. Bowen	1903-1904
James Codey	1879	Michael F. Kelly	1905-1943
Martin Sheridan	1879-1885, 1889-1891	John Fisher	1905
G. M. Sykes	1880, 1886	F. G. Stone	1906-1909, 1924, 1926
Isaac Barrows	1881-1883		
J. E. Buffum	1881-1885, 1888-1891	Ed. Griffith	1909
George H. Williams	1884-1885	J. H. Nadeau	1910-1913, 1916-1926
B. A. Rogers	1886-1887	Dighton Lee	1910, 1911
Edward Young	1886	A. J. Loveland	1914-1916
W. C. Landon	1887	S. F. Holley	1918-1920, 1923, 1924
Michael Connel	1887		
John Sheldon	1888	J. C. Flynn	1926-1931
Robert Carney	1888-1889	R. R. Harrington	1927-1933
Charles N. Williams	1890-1891	F. J. Harwood	1932-1940
E. M. Torrey	1892-1893	Byrne Harwood	1933-1938 (died)
Patrick McDevitt	1892-1893, 1894	John H. Stannard	1944-1948 (resigned)
Martin Sheldon	1890	Ed Molloy	1949-1950
A. B. Roberts	1892-1893, 1904-1907, 1912-1917	Walter B. Read	1947-1950
		Paul White	Appointed 1938-1960
G. F. Griffith	1894	Edward J. Leary	1941-1946, 1951, 1961 (appointed)
W. Clemons	1894		
Sherman Nichols	1895-1903	James P. Stannard	1951-1953
		Guy Stone	1952, 1964-1969

Photo by Stetson Fletcher

The East Dorset Firehouse (District No. 2), located on old Route 7, was built in 1951 on the site of a former cheese factory and later enlarged.

Lloyd McGuffin	1953-1956	Nathaniel (Terry)	
Harold Beebe	1954-1961 (resigned)	Tyler	1974-1977, 1980,
Harlan Coolidge	1957-1966		1985
Frank Burke	1960, 1961	Robert Sheridan	1974-1976
Henry G. Stone	1960, 1961 (resigned)	George Ludlam	Appointed 1974-1978
	1970-1973 (appointed)	Morris Depew	1975-1977
Josiah K. Adams	1961	Karen Bovey	1976-1979 (1st
Robert Dressler	Appointed 1961-1970		woman Selectman)
John Ford Shroder	1961-1964	Howard Steere	1977-1980
Harold Boswell	Appointed 1961-1962	Col. Henry A.	
Russell Parks	1962, 1963,	Chapman	1978-1980
	1967-1970	Robert D. Thum	1978-1983, 1986
James Beebe	1963, 1964 (resigned	Dave Richards	1979, 1982
	to be Town Manager)	William Mahlmann	1981-1989
David Gilbert	1964	Robert Wells Brown	1981-1984
Calvin C. Skinner	1965-1973	William Calfee	1983, 1984
Paul McWayne	1965-1966	Charles Steward	1983, 1984
William G.		Peter Sturges	1984-1989
Barrows, Jr.	1967, 1968	Warren Crawford	1985-1989
James Lee II	1969-1974	James Faszholz	1986-1988
Vernon Squiers	1969	Dave Wilson	1987-1989
Byron Bowen	1971-1973 (resigned)	John Ezell	1989
John P. Stannard	1971-1975, 1981,		
	1982		
Roger Rumney	1973 (resigned)		

In August 1970, the Dorset volunteer firemen in front of the old firehouse, now the historical society building. Sitting: Raymond Bushee, Chief Ernest Edgerton, Harry Sheldon, Pete Wyman. Back row: Morris Depew, Calvin Skinner, Vernon Squiers, Richard Jones, Eugene Vermette, Chip Hirth, Tim Sheldon, Leland "Shorty" Hazelton, Steven Hazelton, Berton Harrington.

Moderators

Cephas Kent	1774-1776	Stephen Martindale	1826
Isaac Reynolds	1777	John Cochran,	
Ebenezer Morse,		Stephen Martindale,	
Capt. Abraham		Hiram Walkes	1827
Underhill	1778	John Cochran	1828
Col. John Strong	1779	Gordon Southworth	1829
Cephas Kent	1780	Gordon Southworth	1830
John Strong and		Reuben H.	
Cephas Kent (1783)	1781-1782-1783	Blackmer	1831
Benjamin Baldwin	1784	Paddock Gray	1832-1835
John Shumway	1785	Gordon Southworth,	
Benjamin Baldwin	1786	Paddock Gray	1836
William Dunton	1787	Alvin Gray, David	
Benjamin Baldwin	1788-1790	Moore	1837
Zadock Huggins	1791	Royal Sargeants	1838, 1839
(Missing)	1792-1796	John Landon	1840
Benjamin Baldwin	1797, 1798	Israel N. Sikes	1841
Stephen Martindale		Asa Baldwin	1842
(also)	1798	Chauncey Green	1843, 1844
Stephen Martindale	1799, 1800	James Curtis	1845
Benjamin Baldwin	1801-1809	Augustine	
(Missing)	1810-1824	Armstrong	1846
Stephen Martindale	1825	James Curtis	1847

Photo by Stetson Fletcher

A 1988 picture of Dorset Volunteer Fire Department No. 1, located next to H. N. Williams Department Store on Route 30. The fire station was built in 1972 after a major fund drive.

Chauncey Green	1848	A. L. Bowen	1887
Royal Sargeants	1849	H. G. Harwood	1888, 1889
Jasper Viall	1850, 1851	W. H. Bebee	1890-1892
Israel N. Sykes	1850	Charles B. Kent	1893-1897
Royal Sargeants	1852	J. M. Armstrong	1898
Jasper Viall	1853	Charles B. Kent	1899-1907
Royal Sargeants,		Austin W. Phelon	1908-1912
Alex. Bliss	1854	J. M. Bebee	1913, 1914
Joseph Viall	1855	Austin W. Phelon	1915-1917
Joseph Viall	1856	J. M. Bebee	1918
George W. Farwell,		Oliver B. Gilbert	1919
Israel N. Sykes	1857	J.M. Bebee	1920
George W. Farwell	1858	William G.	
George Batcheldor	1874	Barrows	1921-1937
(Missing)	1859-1873	Paul White	1938
A. B. Armstrong	1875, 1876	William G. Barrows	1939-1943
W. H. Bebee	1877	Paul White	1944-1960
A. B. Armstrong	1878, 1879	Guy Stone	1961-1969
John L. Batchelder	1880	Sydney J. Meachem	1970-1978
J. E. Buffum	1881	Nathaniel (Terry)	
Isaac Barrows	1882, 1883	Tyler	1979-1980
J. M. Armstrong	1884	Rhys Evans	1981-
A. B. Armstrong	1885, 1886		

Treasurers

Cephas Kent	1778-1782	Clifton P. Kent	1913-1919
Isaac Farwell	1783-1798	O. B. Gilbert	Dec. 17, 1919-1920
Samuel Collins	1799-1809	William F. McDevitt	1921-1927
Peleg Smith	1810-1826	Perry M. Peltier	1928-1955
Robert Bloomer	1827	David Gilbert	1956-1960
Azel Morse	1828-1834	Ada Towslee	1960-1966
Hemen Morse	1835-1857, 1859-1861	Margaret J. Harrington	1967-1979
Byron Sargeant	1858	Robert Ross	1980-1982, 1986-1988
John W. Batchelder	1862-1864		
S. F. Holley	1865	Warren Crawford	1983-1984
J. G. Viall	1866-1872	James Gilbert	1985
G. M. Sykes	1873	Karen Bovey	1988
George W. Farwell	1874-1878	Nancy Rubadeau	1989-
George M. Viall	1879-1912 (33 years)		

Town Clerks

Asa Baldwin	1774-1775	I. G. Viall	1866-1872
Nathan Manley	1776-1784	George W. Farwell	1873-1878
John Shumway	1785-1796	George M. Viall	1879-1912 (died July 20, 1912)
William Dunton	1797		
John Shumway	1798-1814	Lucy E. Viall	Aug. 1, 1912-1916
John Underhill	1815-1826	William J. Whalon	1916-1918
Azel Morse	1827-1834	Anna A. Sherlock	1918-1946
Heman Morse	1835-1857	Janice M. Stone	1947-1955
Byron Sargeant	1858	Helen E. O'Donavan	1956-1981
Heman Morse	1859-1861	Margaret Phillips Burden	1982
John W. Batchelder	1862-1864		
S. F. Holley	1865	Denise M. Hebert	1983-

* These records of town officials were compiled from: (1) Town records; (2) Town reports contained in the collection of Nathaniel (Terry) Tyler; and (3) *History of Bennington County*, edited by Lewis Cass Aldrich, published by D. Mason & Co., Syracuse, New York, 1889.

Appendix

Postmasters and Rural Mail Carriers

Postmasters

(Dorset Post Office)

Name	Date Appointed	Name	Date Appointed
Zachary Booth	03/31/1806	Albert O. Chapman	06/16/1897
Paddock Gray	02/28/1824	Austin W. Phelon	07/16/1914
James A. Hodge	01/31/1829	Alfred A. Seymour*	10/31/1916
Return M. Underhill	09/23/1845	Albert B. Roberts	01/13/1917
Clark Gray	05/15/1849	William M. Batchelder	02/16/1922
Homer Gray	03/25/1851	Smith M. Matson	06/18/1934
Byron Sargeant	09/16/1853	Morris W. Depew*	03/04/1954
Samuel R. Wiley	07/26/1861	Morris W. DePew	08/02/1954
Gilbert M. Sykes	12/23/1862	Francis W. Monroe**	10/31/1969
Martin J. Blakely	10/07/1880	Francis W. Monroe	03/20/1971
Gilbert M. Sykes	02/12/1883	Clarence M. Ross Jr.**	09/27/1974
John M. Armstrong	08/14/1885	Clarence M. Ross Jr.	02/01/1975
Gilbert M. Sykes	06/24/1889	Carol A. Niles**	07/31/1987
John M. Armstrong	03/31/1893	Marilyn B. Kinney	11/21/1987

*Acting Postmaster
**Officer-in-Charge

(East Dorset Post Office)

Name	Date Appointed	Name	Date Appointed
Johnson Marsh	02/02/1826	Miss Sadie M. Sherlock	07/16/1914
David E. Deming	03/29/1832	Stuart R. Sheedy*	06/30/1948
M. B. Roberts	05/30/1833	Stuart R. Sheedy	04/01/1949
Daniel G. Williams	09/29/1852	Miss Anna J. Gormley*	10/31/1951
M. B. Roberts	08/13/1853	Frank D. Eggleston*	03/27/1953
Flynn D. Ames	09/22/1853	Frank D. Eggleston	03/25/1954
William H. Bebee	06/29/1857	James B. Shields*	11/01/1968
George Marsh	04/13/1861	James B. Shields	04/03/1971
John W. Batchelder	02/27/1862	Ruby Tufts**	08/10/1979
Stephen Grout	12/16/1864	Albert R. Lawrence	01/26/1980
John E. Buffum	07/20/1885	Theresa B. Harrington**	03/18/1983
Stephen Grout	05/10/1889	Marilyn B. Kinney	05/14/1983
John L. Cochran	11/17/1899	Donald S. Wyman**	11/23/1987
Gardner F. Griffith	06/28/1905	Peter J. LeFurgy	04/09/1988

*Acting Postmaster
**Officer-in-Charge

(South Dorset Post Office)

Name	Date Appointed	Name	Date Appointed
Thomas D. Manl(e)y	04/07/1847	David Richardson	12/07/1855
David Richardson	03/20/1850	Norman H. Matteson	12/14/1861
William J. Soper	03/24/1852	Mrs. Maria H. Matteson	09/11/1865
Elhanan W. Howe	06/19/1854	Nelson J. Sanford	01/09/1871

Courtesy of Doris Depew

The present Dorset Village Post Office, built in 1963 on the site of the old Dorset Village School, which was razed when the townwide elementary school was built in 1960. From left: Clerk Emma Stannard; Leland Hazelton, husband of clerk Hilda Hazelton; rural carrier Roy Casey; Elizabeth Monroe, wife of clerk (later postmaster) Francis Monroe, Doris Depew, wife of Postmaster Morris Depew.

Terry Tyler collection

The Dorset Village Post Office, circa 1930, located on Route 30 where Russell and Kathe Parks later kept store, now the Dorset Framery.

Courtesy of Inez Beebe

This former marble company building at the foot of Mad Tom Road became the East Dorset Post Office.

Photo by Stetson Fletcher

The East Dorset Post Office as it looked in 1988, with a new dormer.

Dorset

The versatile Smith Matson, postmaster and fiddler for square dances at the Dorset Playhouse stage. Circa 1945.

Name	Date Appointed	Name	Date Appointed
Nathan W. Sanford	11/27/1874	Mrs. Helen Wyman	04/12/1927
Samuel E. Moore	09/27/1880	Mrs. Gertrude F. Molloy	11/14/1929
James Codey	10/27/1884	Mrs. Marilyn B. Kinney*	06/30/1970
Margaret Codey	04/08/1904	Mrs. Marilyn B. Kinney	07/31/1971
Clara M. McDevitt	12/12/1916		

Post office temporarily closed June 10, 1983; discontinued June 20, 1986; mail to Dorset, Vermont.

* Officer-in-Charge

Rural Mail Carriers

(Dorset Route #1, Established October 1, 1902)

Elmer D. Harwood	October 1, 1902-April 30, 1946
James K. Harwood	May 1, 1946-February 14, 1948
Roy William Casey	February 16, 1948-July 1, 1977
William McFall	July 2, 1977-

(Dorset Route #2, Established November 19, 1988)

Richard Reiman	November 19, 1988-

East Dorset Route #1, Established November 1, 1907

Ernest L. Whitney	November 1, 1907-December 31, 1923
Leo J. Abbott	January 2, 1924-March 31, 1926
Frank D. Eggleston	April 1, 1926-May 15, 1926
John Mark Whalon	May 17, 1926-June 30, 1948
Anna Whalon Ackert	July 1, 1948-September 23, 1950
William Kelleher Whalon	September 25, 1950
	(Separation date not available)

The Post Office Department was unable to locate any rural carrier service out of South Dorset.

Photo by Harriet Gilbert in Charles Gilbert collection

Elmer Harwood, rural carrier for Dorset from 1902 to 1946, was pictured delivering mail in 1908 at the Charles Gilbert farm on West Road.

Photo by John Hawkes, courtesy of Dorset Historical Society

Elmer Harwood was always called "Doc" by his wife Emma; they are pictured on their fiftieth wedding anniversary in 1959. Of their seven children, four went into medicine.

Dorset Veterans

Revolutionary War
Buried in Dorset, Maple Hill Cemetery

Name	Date of Death	Name	Date of Death
Armstrong, Jonathan	1826	Kellogg, Titus, Capt.	1831
Baldwin, Asa, Lt.	1806	Kent, Alexander, Cpl.	1813
Blackmer, Eseck	1843	Kent, Cephas	1809
Bloomer, Reuben	1824	Kent, John	1849
Bromley, Josiah, 2nd Lt.	1823	Manley, John	1803
Dimock, Ichabod	1795	Manley, John Jr.	1816
Dunning, Richard, Lt.	1810	Manley, William, Cpl.	1835
Dunton, Thomas	1791	Martindale, Stephen	1845
Farwell, Asa	1815	Paddock, Prince	1833
Farwell, Isaac, Lt.	1833	Sargeant, John, Capt.	1827
Fuller, Noah, Capt.	1846	Sargeant, John, M.D.	1843
Gray, John, Capt.	1814	Shumway, John, Capt.	1829
Gray, Luke B.	1814	Sykes, Titus	1811
Hodge, James	1792	Underhill, Abraham, Capt.	1796
Holley, Justus	1849	Underhill, Isaac, Capt.	1805
Jones, Hemen	1864	Viall, Nathan	1846

Buried in North Dorset Cemetery

Allen, Welcome

Buried in East Dorset, South Village Cemetery

Marsh, William (a Tory)

War of 1812
Buried in Quarry Road Cemetery

Bowers, Edward

Civil War
Buried in Dorset, Maple Hill Cemetery

Name	Date of Death	Name	Date of Death
Aldrich, H. H.	1880	Dunton, Warren, Maj.	1902
Baker, Aaron H.	1921	Farwell, Edgar	1876
Baker, George W.	1906	Farwell, Philo B., Cpl.	
Barber, Benjamin	1918	Field, Charles	1886
Barlow, Wescott G.	1890	Fisher, John	1917
Brooks, Joseph	1895	Fisher, Bela	1864
Brooks, Seymour	1886	Fuller, William J.	1861
Byant, Edgar	1865	Goldsmith, Fletcher B.	
Crandall, Albert		Gray, Charles H.	1870
Crandall, Willard	1915	Gray, Charles P.	1866
Dunton, Henry	1865	Gray, Riley	1875

Appendix

Name	Date of Death	Name	Date of Death
Harrington, Elisha	1870	Roberts, Burns	1875
Harrington, Hiram H.		Roberts, Stephen D.	1900
Haskins, Merritt B.	1874	Robinson, James	1916
Hazelton, Ichabod	1870	Robinson, Nathan	1862
Hazelton, Wright	1917	Smith, Marquis D.	1864
Hopkins, Oscar		Stannard, Curtis	1911
Hill, Horace S.	1864	Stannard, William H.	
Ladd, Alfred		Sykes, Asaph Kirk	1894
Ladd, Wilson	1893	Sykes, Dwight	1905
Lake, Alan	1861	Tifft, James	1924
Lathrop, Asa		Tifft, Moses	1908
Lee, Dighton		Tobin, William	1913
Martindale, William, Major	1866	Wade, Charles H.	1871
McWayne, Nathaniel	1935	Ware, George	1914
McWayne, Sylvanus	1909	Weeks, William C.	1908
Nichols, Ezra	1899	Wescott, Barlow G.	1890
Nichols, Horace	1865	Wilkins, John R.	1909
Nichols, Walter	1864	Williams, George H.	1915
Peck, Medad	1865	Wood, Myron	1905
Potter, Keyes	1914	Wyman, Abel T.	
Reed, James			

Buried in Dorset, Danby Mountain Cemetery

Hazelton, Hyram   1862*

*Died in New Orleans, Co.B. Vt. Infantry vol.

Buried in East Dorset, St. Jerome's Chuch Cemetery

Berry, Peter
Bowen, John
Bowers, James
Burns, James
Connell, John
Cooney, Bernard
Daley, Daniel

Joyce, John
Gaherty, Peter
Horan, Edward
Horan, John
Leary, John
McDonald, John
Moore, Patrick

Mylott, Andrew
Moore, William
Planky, Philip
Sears, Alexander
Sheridan, James
Stone, Edward
Stone, Louis

Buried in East Dorset, South Village Cemetery

Barrows, Waldo
Brophy, Harvey
Brooks, Martin
Edgerton, Peleg
Gardener, Henry

Griffith, Gardner
Jacobs, Francis
Kent, Duane
Luther, Charles
Roberts, Bennomi

Sexton, Edgar
Streeter, Albert
Tier, Norman
Tier, S. W.

Buried in Quarry Road Cemetery

Hanlon, Michael

Note: Vermont sent more men per capita to the Civil War then any other State in the Union

Dorset

Buried in Dorset, Maple Hill Cemetery

Dunn, Thomas   Dunton, Sam W.   McWayne, Charles D.

Buried in East Dorset, South Village Cemetery

Rich, Frank

The following lists include only veterans who entered the service from Dorset.

World War I

Abbey, Raymond
Abbott, Leo J.
Applin, William F.
Beebe, Thomas E.
Belland, David L.
Benedict, Frank W.
Brophy, Elijah T.
Brophy, Victor L.
Burns, William T.
Cody, George L.
Colvin, Lewis F.
Condon, Edward H.
Condon, George
Cooledge, Harlan F.
Cooney, Walter J.
Copping, Clifford J.*
Dunbar, George B.
Dunbar, Millard**
Eggleston, William C.
Gilbert, Arthur W.
Gilbert, Jr., George H.
Gilbert, Henry Minor
Gilbert, Wilfred C.

Griffith, Thomas H.
Harrington, Roland R.
Jones, Walter E.
Kelley, Edward C.
Kendall, George E.
King, Louis P.
Lanfear, William H.
Lawler, Joseph E.
Leary, Edward J.
Leary, John S.
Lee, Richard S.*
Loveland, Lawrence R.**
Macomber, Otis R.
Manley, Ernest C.
McBride, George W.
McBride, John J.*
McCormack, Henry T.
McDonald, John
McLaughlin, Thomas J.
McNamara, William J.*
Nichols, Walter J.
Norcross, Fred C.
Peltier, Perry M.

Phillips, James
Phillips, Joseph E.
Potter, Edward G.
Potter, John J.
Ramsey, Ulysess G.
Reed, John C.
Roberts, Lester K.
Rowell, William H.
Saunders, Robert W.
Seymour, Alfred A.
Stone, Edwin L.
Sweeney, John H.
Tully, Frank A.
Tully, John L.
Wade, Daniel N.**
Whalon, Cornelius D.
Whalon, John M.
White, Jesse E.
White, Paul E.
White, William B.
Wilson, William G.
Woodard, Herbert E.
Wyman, David J.

*Died in service
**Wounded

World War II

Adams, Josiah K.
Ameden, Richard
Baker, Rufus J.
Barrows, Jr., William G.
Beebe, Willson H.
Besselievre, Arthur H.
Blackmer, Benjamin A.**
Bowen, Wilbur C.
Brophy, Milton S.
Burke, Claude E.
Burns, Robert W.
Carpenter, Frank W.
Casey, Roy
Clayton, Kenneth E.
Colbourn, Arthur P.
Cole, Arthur P.
Colvin, Cecil C.

Colvin, Leo L.
Connors, George H.
Connors, Robert C.
Depew, Morris W.
Dern, Claude
Dorr, Reginald F.
Dorr, Silas E.
Drew, Claude
Edgerton, Leon B.
Eggleston, Frank D.
Fairman, Charles
Gallagher, John P.
Gaudette, William H.
Giddings, Frederick D.
Gilbert, Charles B.
Gilbert, David
Gilbert, Frank W.

Gilbert, Huntington K.
Gilbert, Rufus Sykes
Gilbert, Stuart K.
Gilbert, William F.
Gilbert, William P.
Grout, Raymond E.
Hanlon, Jr., Michael O.
Harrington, Joseph H.
Harrington, Louis E.
Harwood, Donald H.
Harwood, H. Greeley*
Harwood, James K.
Harwood, Jr., Samuel F.
Hazelton, Arden L.
Jones, Charles E.
Jones, Harold V.

*Enlisted from Canada

Appendix

Courtesy of Francis McBride

John J. McBride, the Dorset-born soldier who lost his life in the World War I Battle of Hindenburg on September 29, 1918, at the age of 28. His name was honored by the American Legion post.

Courtesy of James Harwood, Sr.

Royal Canadian Air Force Pilot Officer Horace Greeley Harwood, born in 1920, died September 7, 1942, while flying a World War II Spitfire from Exmouth, England. In his honor the Dorset Legion Post No. 44 incorporated his name in its title, the McBride-Harwood Post.

Jones, Irving L.
Jones, Jr., Walter E.
Joslin, Fay E.
Joslin, Warren A.***
Kelleher, John L.
Kelleher, Phillip M.**
Kelley, Jr., John**
Kelly, James J.**
Kent, Elmer*
King, Thomas C.
Kinnie, Robert J.
Lindsey, Frank R.
McBride, Francis A.
McDevitt, Edward J.
McGuffin, Lloyd H.B.
McVicker, Jr., Robert J.
McWayne, George E.
Merrow, Donald J.
Merrow, George E.
Merrow, Raymond P.
Messenger, Albert L.
Miller, James R.**
Moffitt, Cyrus E.
Nichols, Clarence B.
Nolet, George E.
Nolet, Victor W.

O'Neil, Ralph S.
Packard, Beulah W.
Park, Raymond J.
Park, William V.
Parks, Duane H.
Parks, Edward L.**
Parsons, David T.
Phillips, Ernest E.
Read, James W.
Reed, Sherman E.
Reynolds, Lyman F.
Reynolds, Ralph A.
Reynolds, Willaim F.
Riley, Christopher S.
Roberts, Dennis S.
Roberts, William H.
Scott, Winfield G.
Shores, Ralph D.
Slavin, James E.**
Snare, William D.
Stannard, Henry C.
Stannard, James P.
Stannard, John N.
Stannard, Raymond C.
Stannard, Richard N.

Stevens, Cecil W.
Stone, Guy S.
Streeter, George A.
Streeter, Howard F.
Sweeney, John R.
Taft, Bernice D.
Tifft, Roy E.
Tobin, Harold P.
Towsley, Charles B.
Towsley, Stanley H.
Van Orman, Arthur W.
Vermette, Ellis, L.
Wade, Paul D.
Wade, Philip A.
Wade, Walter L.*
Warren, Byrne A.
Warren, Franklin K.**
Weber, Wilbur R.
West, George E.
West, Walter H.
Whalon, James D.
Whalon, Lawrence J.
Whalon, William K.
Wyman, David T.
Wyman, Hiram F.

*Died in service **Wounded ***Killed in action

Dorset

Korean War

Allen, Josiah, Jr.
Baker, David C.
Baker, Gardner C.
Blackmer, Allen F.
Bovey, Loyerston A.
Brock, Jr., Robert H.
Brophy, Jr., Robert D.
Burke, Jr., Owen F.
Coulter, Laverne L.
Currier, Richard D.
Dressler, Jr., Robert C.
Dumas, Paul E.
Dunn, Jr., Thomas P.
Glens, Thomas P.
Hall, Stanley F. KIA
Harwood, Samuel F.
Hawley, Charles F.C.
Hazelton, Leland A.
Jones, Arthur G.
Jones, Sidney H.
King, Joseph E.
Kinnie, Gordon G.
Molloy, Patricia
Mason, Louis J.
McIntyre, Warren J.
Merrow, Joseph E.
Miller, George J.
Miller, Robert C.
Moffitt, Harold E.
Molloy, Jr., Edward L.
Nichols, Kenneth J.
Parsons, III, Geoffrey
Patch, Don Ivan
Payne, William C.
Phillips, Robert W.
Piper, Kathryn A.
Sheldon, Harry C.
Slavin, Clarence K.
Snow, Jr., Harold W.
Squires, Frank F.
Stannard, Raymond C.
Stannard, Richard N.
Streeter, Robert
Streeter, Howard F.
Tarbell, Edward B.
Tifft, Delmar E.
Tifft, Vernon O.
Tobin, Harold P.
Vermette, Ellis L.
Vermette, Eugene O.
West, Merrill W.N.
West, Robert D.
Yates, Alfred J.

Vietnam War

Baldwin, Carl Michael
Beauregard, Morris Alec
Bowen, Carroll Byron
Bowen, Jack Richard
Burke, Jr., Claude Edward
Burke, Patricia Ann
  See: Viault, Patricia A.
Burke, Thomas Owen
Carpenter, Judson Larry
Casey, Scott Lincoln
Cepela, Richard Vincent
Chapman, Daniel William
Chapman, Henry Alan
Chapman, Philp Xavier
Clough, Hiland Elwin
Cook, Jr., Alfred
Coolidge, John Harlan
Dean, Lewis Lyman
Dean, Lyman Erl
Depew, Jill Joyce
Dern, Claude Garrett
Deyo, Michael Lee
Eaton, Jr., Roger Jesse
Gaiotti, Densmore Anthony
Glover, Jr., Robert Walker
Gunther, Edward James
Harney, Jr., William John
Holmberg, Simon Axel
Jones, Richard Irving
Lake, Arnold George
Lake, George Arnold
Leonard, Peter Thatcher
Mattison, Richard Almon
McFall, Jr., Robert Muir
McFall, William James
Merrow, Adolore Adolph
Merrow, James Alphonse
Nelson, Jr., Howard Sheldon
O'Donovan, Howard Martin
Palmer, Douglas Reginald
Park, Robert Alan
Parker, Leo Vernon
Payne, Francis George*
Read, Roland Charles
Read, Thomas Wayne
Reed, Teresa Ann
Rosencrantz, Eric John
Rubadeau, Jr., George Clarence
Rumney, Thomas Norton
Slavin, Douglas Robert
Smith, Richard Harvey
Sprague, Joseph Lee
Stannard, William Henry
Taft, Bradley Aaron
Towsley, Donald James
Viault, Patricia A.
  See: Burke, Patricia A.
Wallace, Donald George
Wilkins, Allan Francis*
Zecher, Douglas Stanford

*Died in service

Many veterans claimed Dorset as their home of record at the time they entered military service, however, the mailing address of the official records may list one town while the veteran may have resided in another.

Appendix

Population Statistics

Year	Dorset	Bennington County	Vermont
1791	958	12,254	85,539
1800	1,286	14,617	154,465
1810	1,294	15,893	217,895
1820	1,359	16,125	235,966
1830	1,507	17,470	280,652
1840	1,432	16,872	291,948
1850	1,700	18,589	314,120
1860	2,090	19,436	315,098
1870	2,195	21,325	330,551
1880	2,005	21,945	332,286
1890	1,696	20,448	332,422
1900	1,477	21,705	343,641
1910	1,492	21,378	355,956
1920	1,326	21,577	352,428
1930	1,119	21,655	360,000
1940	1,128	22,286	359,000
1950	1,150	24,115	378,000
1960	1,150	25,088	390,000
1970	1,293	29,282	444,000
1980	1,648	33,345	511,456

Dorset's population for the years 1792–1880 was compiled from Child's *Bennington County Gazeteer*; state population statistics to 1920 were compiled from Conant's *Vermont*, seventh edition, Tuttle Company, Rutland, 1925.

Dorset

Bibliography

Books

Aldrich, Lewis Cass. *History of Bennington County, Vermont.* Syracuse, N.Y.: D. Mason & Co., 1889. Contains a lengthy history of Dorset written by its then-legislator, George Viall of East Dorset, which is mostly a copy, errors and all, of a history by Laurel B. Armstrong in *Hemenway's Gazetteer* of 1868.

Alexander, Edward P. *A Revolutionary Conservative: James Duane of New York.* New York: Columbia University Press, 1938. A biography of a prominent New York lawyer and land speculator, one of the proprietors of Princetown, the New York town that covered Vermont's Battenkill Valley (including parts of Manchester, Dorset, Arlington, and Sunderland) in 1765. Duane and Colonel Walter Rutherford toured Princetown three years before Dorset was settled. Contains map of New York patents of Princetown, Eugene, and Chatham, overlying settled towns already chartered by Benning Wentworth.

Anonymous. *Pass It On: The Story of Bill Wilson and how the A.A. Message Reached the World.* New York: Alcoholics Anonymous World Services, Inc., 1984. A most readable biography of East Dorset's "Bill W." Includes much about his family and upbringing in East Dorset.

Austin, Aleine. *Matthew Lyon: 'New Man' of the Democratic Revolution—1749-1822.* University Park, Penna.: Pennsylvania State University Press, 1981. A fine biography of a Green Mountain Boy who belonged to Seth Warner's regiment, saw service at Ticonderoga, Hubbardton, St. Johns, member of John Fassett's company after July 1777, served in Congress, was jailed for violating Alien and Sedition Laws. Lyon represented Wallingford at third Dorset Convention, July 24, 1776, and voted for resolution to form New Hampshire Grants into "a separate district." He was clerk of first statewide Court of Confiscation, 1778.

Batchelder, Ira K., a history of Peru, Vermont, the formal title of which is *Reunion Celebration Together with an Historical Sketch of Peru, Bennington County, Vermont, and Its Inhabitants from the First Settlement of the Town.* Brattleboro: Phoenix Job Print, E. L. Hildreth Co., 1891. This is the only published history of Dorset's neighbor to the east. It has an incomplete account of how the Mt. Tabor Leg originated. Description of life in days of earliest settlers.

Beers, F.W. *Atlas of Bennington County, Vermont.* New York: F. W. Beers, A. D. Ellis and G. G. Soule, 1869. A classic reference work of the post-Civil War era because of the detailed data supplied by its maps of each town and village in the county, showing who lived where, locations of school districts, mountains, railroads, businesses, mines, quarries.

Benton, C., and Barry, S.F. *A Statistical View of the Number of Sheep.* Boston: Folsom, Wells, and Thurston, 1837. A rare volume containing statistics about numbers of sheep throughout northeast in 1836.

Bigelow, Edwin L. and Otis, Nancy H. *Manchester, Vermont: A Pleasant Land Among the Mountains.* Privately published in 1961. The most recent town history of Dorset's close neighbor. A good index and orientation by subject make this a useful reference.

Caverly, A.M. *History of the town of Pittsford, Vt.* Rutland: The Tuttle Co., 1872. Relevant only for reference to Felix Powell, alleged first settler of Dorset, of Burlington, and possibly of Pittsford. Caverly's data on Powell conflict with those of Crockett.

Child, Hamilton. *Gazetteer and Business Directory of Bennington County, Vt. for 1880-81.* Syracuse, N.Y.: 1880. One of a series of Child directories, valuable for histories of each town and lists of residents and business people, cross-referenced; lists of county officials, post offices, town clerks, justices of the peace, populations, social organizations.

Crockett, Walter Hill. *History of Vermont.* New York: The Century History Co., 1921. This five-volume series is a standard Vermont history reference, chronologically arranged. If you want to know who was elected to which office in what year, by what margin, and what the issues were, Crockett is indispensable.

Dean, Leon W. *The Admission of Vermont into the Union*. Montpelier: Vermont Historical Society, 1941. Prelude to Dorset Conventions, with thesis that inhabitants living west of Green Mountains were more adventuresome, free-thinking, irrepressible than those on east side; describes how seeds planted at Dorset in January 1776 flowered in declaration of statehood on January 16, 1777.

Doyle, William. *The Vermont Political Tradition*. Barre: Northlight Studio Press, 1984. Interesting interpretive political history, with useful appendices that include a state chronology, state constitution, and lists of governors, congressmen, and senators.

Federal Writers' Project, Works Progress Administration for State of Vermont. *Vermont: A Guide to the Green Mountain State*. Boston: Houghton Mifflin Co., 1937. Depression-era guidebook descriptions as part of the American Guide Series.

Graham, John A. *A Descriptive Sketch of the Present State of Vermont*. London: 1797 (reprinted in 1987 by Vermont Heritage Press, Rutland, with an interpretive introduction by Noel Perrin). Graham, the first practicing lawyer in Rutland, was a "half dandy, half humbug, yet with talent enough to attain notoriety in England and eminence in New York." Graham offers a town-by-town itinerary of Vermont of 1790s.

Graffagnino, J. Kevin. *The Shaping of Vermont: From the Wilderness to the Centennial, 1749-1887*. Rutland: Vermont Heritage Press, 1983. A cartographic reference work. Included is the 1779 "chorographical" map of the province of New York by Claude Joseph Sauthier that depicts a peculiar conglomeration of townships and patents granted in Vermont by governors of both New York and New Hampshire.

Hall, Benjamin H. *History of Eastern Vermont*. New York: D. Appleton & Co., 1858. Author was unrelated to Hiland Hall, and his pro-New York interpretation was greatly disliked by Hiland Hall. Valuable for background and aftermath of Dorset Conventions.

Hall, Hiland. *The History of Vermont from its Discovery to its Admission into the Union in 1791*. Albany, N.Y.: Joel Munsell, 1868. A resourceful history of Vermont, though obsessed with bias in favor of hardworking settlers of New Hampshire Grants and against greedy, tyrannical Yorker politicians and land speculators. Includes full account of Dorset Conventions, appendices with biographies of central figures on both sides of the border, many relevant documents.

Harris, Brice. *Charles Sackville, Sixth Earl of Dorset: Patron and Poet of the Restoration*. Urbana, Ill.: University of Illinois Press, 1940. Background on the nobleman for whom Dorset was named by Benning Wentworth, and how the name *Dorset* became synonymous with artistic patronage in fifteenth-century England.

Haviland, William A., and Power, Marjory W. *The Original Vermonters: Native Inhabitants Past & Present*. Hanover, N.H. and London, England: University Press of New England, 1981. Strong on Abenakis in northwestern Vermont but weak on Indians in southern Vermont.

Hemenway, Abby Maria. *Vermont Quarterly Gazetteer*. Burlington: published by author. Bennington County II, October 1861, with histories of all towns. Dorset's is by Laurel B. Armstrong, an early trustee of Vermont Historical Society; brief biographies of early settlers.

Hibbard, George S. *Rupert, Vt.: Historical and Descriptive*. Rutland: The Tuttle Company, 1899. Detailed early history of neighboring town, with emphasis on brief biographies.

Hitchcock, Edward. *Preliminary Report on the Geology of Vermont*. Montpelier: E.P. Walton, 1859. The author, a professor of geology at Amherst College, concludes that " . . . we think we have discovered the reason why Vermont so excels all the other New England States in the agricultural capabilities of its soil. It is the existence, in almost all of her rocks, of lime in such a state that natural processes bring it out in just about the quantity needed by vegetation . . . "

Hollister, Heil. *Pawlet for One Hundred Years*. Albany, N.Y.: J. Munsell, 1867. A thorough history of Pawlet; relevant to Dorset in many respects, with accounts of the winter of great severity of 1780-81, destitution caused by a short crop season in 1789, the great drought in 1805, the "year of famine" of 1816, a grasshopper infestation of 1826. Other relevant subjects are the temperance movement, deer, railroads, popularity of baseball.

Huden, John C. *Development of State School Administration in Vermont.* Montpelier: Vermont Historical Society, 1944. A helpful summary of public education in Vermont, divided into eras starting with "period of no organization, 1724-1777," then more and more involvement by towns and state; a chapter on the investigation of 1913-14 by the Carnegie Foundation for Advancement of Teaching, and its aftermath.

Humphrey, Zephine. *Over Against Green Peak.* New York: Henry Holt & Co., 1908. One of her earliest books.

———.*Recollections of My Mother.* Old Tappan, N.J.: Fleming H. Revell Co., 1912. This details Dorset origins of the author's mother, born Harriette Sykes in Dorset, July 5, 1832; how the family lived in Chicago, Philadelphia, Cincinnati, Lake Forest, and New Haven, yet was always magnetized by thoughts of returning to Dorset, which they did after death of Zephine Humphrey's father, Zephaniah Humphrey, and after her graduation from Smith College in 1896. Insight into "summer people" at turn of century. The book also constitutes a biography of the author before her marriage to Wallace W. Fahnestock.

———.*The Story of Dorset.* Rutland: Tuttle Company, 1924. Written in collaboration with Elizabeth Sykes Lee, with "occasional drawings" by Katherine Field White. This is the only published history of Dorset other than those that appear in *Hemenway, Child's, Aldrich,* and 1896 GAR booklet. It is indispensable and mostly factual, where facts are provided; it is also written in the author's own chatty, sentimental, and informal style—adroit but often unspecific.

———.*Chrysalis.* New York: E. P. Dutton, 1928. A charming description of the decision by the author and her husband to give up their large home on West Road and build a smaller one on Lower Hollow Road.

———.*The Beloved Community.* New York: E. P. Dutton, 1930. This is a sequel to *The Story of Dorset,* but more sentimental in tone and outlook. It was written thirty years after Humphrey and her mother first settled in town as summer residents. An especially appealing chapter is titled "On Writing a Town History."

Jellison, Charles A. *Ethan Allen, Frontier Rebel.* Syracuse, N.Y.: Syracuse University Press, 1969 (reprinted in 1983). In addition to being an excellent biography of Vermont's homespun hero, this offers a felicitous account of the situation on "the Grants" in the 1770s that prompted, first, Benning Wentworth to charter so many towns, and second, Ethan Allen to become so aggressively involved in fending off Yorkers, paving the way for Vermont independence.

Jones, Matt Bushnell. *Vermont in the Making, 1750-1777.* Cambridge, Mass.: Harvard University Press, 1939. A solid scholarly study of disputes among New York, New Hampshire, and Great Britain over jurisdiction of today's Vermont. Some detailed accounts of petitions and correspondence between colonies and authorities in London. Good discussion of Dorset conventions. Includes as appendices diaries of 1765 visit to yet-unsettled Dorset by James Duane and Walter Rutherford, proprietors of Princetown.

Ketchum, Richard M. *Second Cutting.* New York: Viking Press, 1981. A collection of charming and urbane "Letter from the Country" columns that appeared in the first few years of *Country Journal* magazine, co-founded and edited by Ketchum. Several essays pertain to life in Dorset.

Lawrence, Margarette Woods. *Light on the Dark River* subtitled *Memorials of Mrs. Henrietta A. L. Hamlin, Missionary in Turkey.* Boston: Ticknor, Reed & Fields, 1854. This biography of Henrietta Jackson Hamlin, daughter of Rev. William Jackson, was written by a friend grieved by her premature death at thirty-nine in 1850. It is a fine if sentimental biography of an early 19th-century resident of Dorset that sheds light on many aspects of town and church. Explains origins of the legend of Henrietta's Elm.

Ludlum, David. *Social Ferment in Vermont 1791-1850.* New York, Columbia University Press, 1939 (reprinted by Vermont Historical Society, 1969). An important study of such transitory phenomena as anti-masonry, anti-slavery, religious revivals, temperance, utopianism.

Meeks, Harold A. *Time and Change in Vermont: A Human Geography*. Chester, Conn.: The Globe Pequot Press, 1986. A fine history of Vermont's pioneer days, highways, boundaries, agriculture, and railroading, contrasted with changes in modern manufacturing, recreation, and agriculture; written by a professor of geography at UVM.

———. *Vermont's Land and Resources*. Shelburne, Vt.: The New England Press, 1987. A sequel to the above that covers natural landscape, glaciers, water, geology, minerals, weather, floods, energy, vegetation, woods, soils, land-use legislation.

Newton, Earle W. *The Vermont Story: A History of the People of the Green Mountain State 1749-1949*. Montpelier: Vermont Historical Society, 1949. Somewhat outdated but a readable and simplified survey of the state's history.

Nye, Mary Greene, ed. *State Papers of Vermont. Volume VI: Sequestration, Confiscation and Sale of Estates*. Montpelier: Vermont Secretary of State, 1941. Legal documents about confiscation of properties of those who remained loyal to the British in Vermont at outbreak of American Revolution. The idea for confiscation was Ira Allen's, suggested when Burgoyne's troops were pressing down from Canada and Vermont had no treasury. Documents tell of several Tories from Dorset: Enoch and Ephriam Mallary, Israel and Price Bardslee, Colonel William Marsh.

———. *State Papers of Vermont. Volume VII: New York Land Patents 1688-1786, Covering Land Now Included in the State of Vermont*. Montpelier: Vermont Secretary of State, 1947. Details the sequence of events that began with Governor Wentworth's 1749 query to Governor Clinton about the location of their common boundary, actions and disputes that followed. Not so interpretive as Matt Jones, more statistically oriented.

Pearce, Moira. *A Sunset Touch*. New York: Charles Scribner's Sons, 1960. A novel by a summer resident that takes an irreverent look at "a small mountain town filled with rustic natives, rich summer people and the comfortably well-off who have retired there to finish out their lives," to quote a review in the *New York Herald-Tribune*.

Perkins, Rev. Nathan. *A Narrative of a Tour Through the State of Vermont from April 27 to June 12, 1789*. Woodstock, Vt.: Elm Tree Press, 1930. A classic for its descriptive candor about rugged conditions encountered by the author on his horseback tour of Vermont in spring 1789.

Prentiss, George L. *The Life and Letters of Elizabeth Prentiss*. New York: Anson D. F. Randolph & Co., 1882. Documents the motives behind construction of the first "summer cottage" in Dorset, the Prentiss house on Church Street. Elizabeth Payson Prentiss (1818-1878) was wife of Rev. George L. Prentiss, friend of Rev. Cyrus Hamlin and Rev. Parsons S. Pratt.

Proctor, Redfield, ed. *Records of Conventions in the New Hampshire Grants for the Independence of Vermont, 1776-1777*. Washington, D.C.: Vermont Historical Society, 1904. Facsimile reproductions from manuscripts in Library of Congress of documents, in Jonas Fay's handwriting, pertaining to Dorset Conventions; interpretive background.

Slade, William, Jr. *Vermont State Papers*. Middlebury: 1823. Compiled and published by Secretary of State William Slade, later a congressman and governor. Provides documents of convocations that preceded Dorset Conventions as well as the conventions themselves.

Spargo, John. *Potters and Potteries of Vermont*. New York: Dover Publications, 1972 (reprint of a 1926 volume published by Houghton Mifflin and Antiques Incorporated). Sketchy on details of Fenton potteries in Dorset but thorough on their later work in Bennington.

Stevens, Marcia and Malcolm. *Against the Devil's Current: The Life and Times of Cyrus Hamlin*. Lanham, Md.: University Press of America, 1988. The first biography of Hamlin, husband of Henrietta Jackson, later a pioneer in Near East missionary and educational efforts, then president of Middlebury College. Covers the Jackson family and Jackson era in Dorset.

Stilwell, Lewis D. *Migration from Vermont*. Montpelier, Vt.: Vermont Historical Society, Proceedings, 1937 (reprinted in book form by E.L. Hildreth & Co., Brattleboro, 1937). A classic study of the massive emigration from Vermont between the Revolution and Civil War. Includes town maps that graphically illustrate how population changed.

Swift, Esther M. *Vermont Place Names*. Brattleboro: Stephen Greene Press, 1977. Background on reasons for the naming of townships (and other places); many can be traced to transparent motives of Benning Wentworth to solidify his relations with those who held prestige or power in London.

Thomsen, Robert. *Bill W.* New York: Harper & Row, 1975. A 1985 edition was published to mark 50th anniversary of 1935 meeting between East Dorset's Bill W. and Dr. Bob that launched Alcoholics Anonymous.

Two Hundred Vermonters. *Rural Vermont: A Program for the Future*. Burlington: The Vermont Commission on Country Life, 1931. Analyzes and expresses ambivalence about the value of "summer people" from a viewpoint of the early Depression. Commission member from Dorset was Zephine Humphrey.

Van de Water, Frederic F. *Reluctant Republic*. New York: John Day Company, 1941. A lively if conjectural account of the era of Vermont's independence, including a colorful chapter, "His Excellency the Realtor," that tells how Benning Wentworth chartered dozens of townships in the "New Hampshire Grants" without authorization—the same towns we live in today.

Walton, E. P., ed. *Records of the Council of Safety and Governor and Council of the State of Vermont, Vol. 1*. Montpelier: Secretary of State's Office, 1873. Official records of Dorset Conventions and other proceedings during formative years of the republic of Vermont.

Williams, Samuel. *The National and Civil History of Vermont*. Walpole, N.H.: Isaiah Thomas and David Carlisle, Jr., 1794. The first history of the state, written by a clergyman who also founded the *Rutland Herald*.

Williamson, Chilton. *Vermont in Quandary, 1763-1825*. Montpelier: Vermont Historical Society, 1949. The title tells it all. The book includes the "Chorographical Map of the Province of New York" by Claude Joseph Sauthier, 1779, showing Dorset squeezed between "Derby" and "Chatham."

Wood, Frederic J. *The Turnpikes of New England*. Boston: Marshall Jones Co, 1919. A source book on early turnpikes, but sketchy about the Mt. Tabor Turnpike of 1804. In 1815, certain exemptions from toll were established, and on November 15, 1826, the Dorset Turnpike corporation was allowed to surrender all of its road "south of Demings' saw-mill in Dorset" to its northerly end in Danby.

Articles, Booklets, Theses

Allen, Richard Sanders. "Furnaces, Forges, and Foundries," in *Vermont Life*, winter 1956-57. Describes iron mining and processing in 19th-century Vermont, says the best-preserved blast furnace stack in Vermont is that at East Dorset.

———.Notes dated July 28, 1986 on the North and East Dorset iron business, in possession of Mr. and Mrs. Dennis Conroy, owners of the remains of the East Dorset blast furnace that was built in either 1846 or 1849.

Baker, Charles L. "The Dorset Players Inc.," in *Vermonter* magazine, Vol. 35, July, 1930, p. 170. Bassett 4038. A factual article on the Players' origins in the 1920s.

Campbell, G. Murray. "Manchester, Dorset & Granville Railroad Company." A mimeographed history of the MD&G written in 1951 by a Manchester resident who was a vice president of the Baltimore & Ohio Railroad. Available from Manchester or Dorset historical societies. Originally published *Manchester Journal*, October 25, 1951.

Child, Edwin B. "The Marble Mountains," an article with illustrations by the author, originally published in *Scribner's Magazine*, Vol. XXXVII, No. 5, May 1905, and reprinted in *Tales of Old New England* published by Castle Books, Inc. of Secaucus, N.J., in 1986. This is an important and vibrant first-person account of the sweaty realities of work inside Dorset marble quarries. Artist Edwin Child reveals his skills as a writer as well as an illustrator.

Dorset Bicentennial Committee with Charles Neave. "A History of the United Congregational Church of Dorset and East Rupert, Vermont, 1784-1984." A 56-page bicentennial booklet.

Appendix 389

Dorset Historical Society. "Dorset's Marble Mountain," a booklet published in 1972 that summarizes research of Ernest West and Arthur Gilbert on the town's marble industry.

Gilbert, Alfred Holley. "A History of the Dorset Village Public Library." Published in 1965. A 55-page history of this community institution that began as the Dorset Book Club in 1870 and ended up in a handsome building that was once a tavern.

———."The Fenton Potteries," in *Vermont History* Vol. 34, No. 4, October 1966, p. 268. Results of the author's pioneering studies of the important origins of the work of Christopher W. Fenton.

———."Parsons Stuart Pratt: Life and Ministry , 1834-1896." Published by the author when he was ninety-seven years old in 1975. A 41-page biography of the extraordinary minister of the Dorset church who compiled genealogies of the families of all his parishioners.

Gilbert, George Holley. "The Dorset Trail," published by the Dorset Science Club, 1928, with photos by Carl T. Ramsey. A descriptive appreciation of Dorset's trails and scenic views. The accompanying photographs are excellent.

Hathaway, Jay. "Peltier's Market." A published talk by the owner of Peltier's store, given before the Dorset Historical Society in October, 1981, tracing the store back to 1816.

Hilliard, John R. "One Hundred and Fifty Years," in *Vermonter* magazine, Vol. 39, November, 1934, p. 259. Bassett 4048. A 150-year history of the Dorset church.

Hislop, Codman. "The Coinage of Vermont 1785-1788," in *Rare Coin Review*, April-May 1984, Vol. 51, pp. 11-13. Published by Bowers & Merina Galleries, Inc., Wolfeboro, New Hampshire.

Kent, Rose Lindley. "John Lillie," in *Vermonter* magazine, Vol. 47, December, 1942, p. 152. Bassett 4052. A good biography, including the verbatim account of "John's own story."

Koier, Louise. "Dorset's Wooden Dollars," in *Vermont Life*, winter 1956-57, p. 56. Background on history and operations of J.K. Adams Company.

Kouwenhoven, John A. "Summer and Winter People," *Yale Review*, Summer 1943, p. 742-759. Astute observations of social and economic problems involved in the "summer people" phenomenon, in which Dorset is "Summerville" and Rupert is "Barnfield."

———."He Runs a Garage," *Harper's Magazine*, January, 1944, p. 175-182. The author, then assistant editor at *Harper's*, profiled Paul White, Dorset selectman and operator of a garage, and described everyday impact of World War II experience.

Lee, Elizabeth Sykes. "Dorset, in Vermont," in *Vermonter* magazine, April, 1908, Vol. 13, p. 116. Bassett 4053. A miscellaneous assortment—call it a checklist, perhaps—of historical tidbits about the town.

Marsh, Edward Sprague. "Justice Strong's Book of Records," in *Vermonter* magazine, Vol. 28, October, 1928, p. 163. Bassett 4055. Tidbits from Dorset Justice of the Peace John Strong's "Book of Records for Crimenals and Delinquents" of 1779-81.

Northshire Senior Center, "City Pups and True Mules: Personal Reflections of Yesterday," a booklet of recollections of the old-timers of 1981, including from Dorset Mildred O'Neal and Carleton G. Howe.

Ramsey, Carl T. "Vermont Mountain Poems," privately published, 1959, by this naturalist whose talents and expertise included those of artist, environmentalist, ornithologist, botanist, and writer.

———."Vermont Native Orchids," in *Vermont Life*, Summer, 1958, p. 2. In addition to details on orchids, this tells of the author's establishment in 1934 of "Swampacres."

Rolando, Victor R. "Ironmaking in Vermont: 1775-1890," a master's thesis for the College of St. Rose, Albany, N.Y., 1980. Good descriptions of 19th-century iron-making process, a blast furnace versus a forge or a bloomery, etc., but sketchy on Dorset's iron. In manuscript collection of VHS library, Montpelier.

———."Tour of ironworks-related sites in Dorset and Mt. Tabor, Vermont," a paper prepared for the Northern New England Chapter, Society for Industrial Archaeology, spring meeting, May 7, 1983. Somewhat more Dorset detail than in Rolando's thesis. Available from VHS library, Montpelier.

Taplin, Winn. "The Vermont Problem in the Continental Congress and in Interstate Relations, 1776-1787." Unpublished doctoral thesis, University of Michigan, 1955. Places Dorset Conventions in a context of national importance because "the Vermont problem" created there remained divisive for Continental Congress throughout the American Revolution. Available in manuscript collection of VHS library, Montpelier.

Watkins, Lura Woodside. "Vermont Stoneware Potteries," a chapter from *Early New England Potters and Their Wares*, published by Archon Books, 1968. Mentions early Fenton potteries.

West, Ernest H. Monograph on marble, formally titled *A report on the general history of the marble industry in Dorset and Danby in which thirty-five quarries and prospects are considered, with especial emphasis on the historical side*. Prepared in 1921 and revised in 1936; copies are available at Dorset Historical Society. Ernest H. West was the son of Spafford H. West, who with Orland W. Norcross reopened the old Main Valley quarry in 1901 after it had been abandoned for twenty-five years.

Williams, Norman, Jr., et al. *Vermont Townscape*, published by the Center for Urban Policy Research at Rutgers, the State University of New Jersey, 1987. Dorset is among thirty towns selected for this study of Vermont townscapes.

Wilson, Harold F. "Population Trends in Northwestern New England, 1790-1930," in *New England Quarterly* Vol. 7, 1934. Analyzes early agriculture in Vermont and New Hampshire for four phases dating from 1820s to 1930s.

Wickham, Joseph D. "A Discourse delivered at Dorset, Vt., at the Funeral of Rev. William Jackson, D.D." The text of a funeral oration delivered October 18, 1842, by the principal of Burr Seminary, constituting an obituary-biography of the pastor of Dorset's church for forty-eight years. Available at VHS library, Montpelier.

Appendix
Sponsors

The Dorset History Book Committee would like to thank the following people and/or organizations for their financial support without which this book could not have been published.

Adsit, Mr. & Mrs. W.B.
August, Mrs. Robert F.
Bartlett, Mr. Clay S.
Brown, Mr. & Mrs. Thatcher M. III
Buechner, Mr. & Mrs. Frederick
Chapman, Col. Henry A.G.
Chittenden Bank
Clark, Mr. & Mrs. William H.
Cooper, Mr. Malcolm E.
Cornwall, Mr. Joseph C.
Crawford, Mr. & Mrs. Warren
Cross, Mr. & Mrs. Henry B., Jr.
Davis, Mr. & Mrs. Peter D.
DeVries, Mrs. Justus
Dickenson, Mr. David B.
Dole, Mr. Jeremy
Dorset Historical Society
Dorset, Town of (Revenue Sharing)
Eichel, Mr. Charles R.
Elliott, Mr. & Mrs. Harry
Factory Point National Bank
First Vermont Bank & Trust Co.
Hislop, Mr. Codman
Howe, Mr. Carleton G.
Humphreys, Mrs. David
Jones, Mrs. Dorothy R.
Jones, Dr. Wyatt C.
Keeler, Mr. & Mrs.Robert T.
Ketchum, Mr. & Mrs. Richard
King, Mr. & Mrs. William
Koren, Mr. & Mrs. H.L.T.
Kouwenhoven, Mr. John A.
Lee, Mr. & Mrs. James W. II
Lefevre, Mr. Edwin
Lewisohn, Mrs. Walter
Lyons, Mrs. Basil
May, Mrs. Barbara V.
McLaren, Mrs. Richard K.
Meder, Dr. and Mrs. Albert
Melton, Mr. Andrew J. Jr.
Merchants Bank, The
Miles, Mr. Richard K. Jr.
Miller, Mr. & Mrs. Elam
Moritz, Mr. Charles W.
Mulliken, Mr. John
Owers, Mrs. James
Pearce, Miss Agnes
Pearson, Mr. & Mrs. Edwin J.
Plimpton, Mr. Harold
Schomp, Mrs. A.L., Jr.
W.H. Shaw Insurance Agency, Inc.
Shroder, Mr. & Mrs. J. Ford
Skinner, Mr. & Mrs. Calvin C.
Smith, Mrs. Robert M.
Speir, Mr. & Mrs. Dean
Stollenwerck, Mr. & Mrs. S.C.
Sturges, Mr. & Mrs. Peter
Swinarton, Mr. & Mrs. Robert
Taylor, Mr. Frederic F.
Thompson, Mr. & Mrs. Norman III
Thum, Mr. Robert D.
Van Vlaanderen, Mr. & Mrs. Peter
Wall, Mr. & Mrs. Berry
Warner, Mr. & Mrs. Beverly W.
Whalen, Mr. & Mrs. Kenneth J.
Whitehead, Mr. & Mrs. Joseph
Wormser, Mrs. Samuel

Index

Abbott, George C., 255
Able, Lois, 155
Adams, J.K., 300, 301, 308, 309
Albee, Addison, 94
Albee, Eleazer, 94
Albee, James, 94
Albee, William, 94
Alger, Asa, 40, 48
Allen, Ebenezer, 74
Allen, Ethan, 33, 34, 47, 51, 72, 73, 74, 76, 77, 82
Allen, Florenz R., 159
Allen, Heman, 74, 76, 77, 78, 82, 84
Allen, Ira, 44, 54, 63, 74, 76, 81, 101
Allen, Josiah, 224
Allen, Samuel, 105
Allen, Welcome, 110, 159, 161, 348
Ames, Benjamin, 115
Ames, Plyn D., 156
Ames, William, 53
Ames, William D., 142, 162
Armstrong, A.W., 206
Armstrong, Abigail, 348
Armstrong, Augustin B., 161
Armstrong, Jane B., 283
Armstrong, John M., 206, 249
Armstrong, Jonathan, 52, 60, 103, 347, 348
Armstrong, Laurel B., 53, 57, 109, 111, 161, 164
Armstrong, Susan F., 166
Arnold, Benedict, 47, 73, 74, 337
Atwill, Lionel, 289
August, Edith, 327
Aunt Maria's Cookies, 331, 334
Avery, Samuel, 44

Babit, Joy, 103
Bagley, Francis, 103
Baker, (Family), 295
Baker & Sheldon Livery, 205
Baker, Dave, 218
Baker, Merrill T., 162
Baker, Remember, 34, 72
Baldwin House (Asa), 67
Baldwin, (Family), 46, 51, 346
Baldwin, Asa, 45, 46, 54, 56, 57, 60, 61, 105, 123, 164
Baldwin, Benjamin, 44, 45, 47, 60, 64, 103, 293, 345
Baldwin, Benjamin, II, 46

Baldwin, Benjamin, Jr., 46, 345
Baldwin, Charles, 165, 175
Baldwin, Chloe, 57
Baldwin, Elisha, 45
Baldwin, Henry, 172
Baldwin, Joseph, 293
Baldwin, Lettie Nichols, 183
Baldwin, Sandy, 334
Baldwin, Silas, 45
Baldwin, Susanna (Jackson), 175
Baldwin, Thomas, 45
Barber, Rev. Daniel, 60
Barbour, Mrs. Mark, 211
Bardslee, (Family), 350
Bardslee, Bennet, 350
Bardslee, Hannah, 57
Bardslee, Israel, 56, 57
Bardslee, Price, 53, 56, 57, 103
Barnes, W.F., 141
"Barnfield," 226
Barnum, Barabas, 74
Barrick, Lloyd, 226
Barrows House, 120, 164, 204, 209, 212, 220, 231, 232, 258, 290, 295, 296, 339, 345
Barrows, (Family), 51, 346
Barrows, Experience, E.W., 100, 101, 116, 204, 205, 231, 324
Barrows, George H., 204, 205
Barrows, Milutus, 155
Barrows, Philetus, 161
Barrows, William G. Jr., 312, 326
Barrows, William, Sr., 210, 211, 212, 285, 297
Bartlett, Buckley F., 123, 124
Bartlett, Joel, 123, 124
Bartlett, Paul, 268
Bartlett, Truman D., 186, 268
Bashaw, Dr. Donald, 315
Bassett, Miriam, 217
Bat Cave (Mt. Aeolus), 10, 11
Battenkill River, 12, 16, 18, 21, 22, 36, 37, 107, 143, 330
Battle of Bennington, 45, 52, 53, 74, 83, 197, 329
Bebee, Rev. Mr., 58
Beckwith, Dave, 211
Beckwith, P., 265
Beebe, James, 14, 312, 330, 347
Beebe, Walter, 295
Bennington, 25, 32, 35, 37, 38, 39, 45, 48, 49, 50, 52, 57, 60, 67, 70, 72, 83, 93, 100, 103, 111, 124, 131, 158, 159, 164, 188, 197, 200, 202, 222, 284

Appendix

Benson, Bertha, 224
Bickel, Gertrude L., 263
Bigelow, Edwin L., 292
Bigelow, John Mason, 293
Bigelow, Mrs. Huntington, 264
Bigelow, Reuben, 91, 93, 98
Bishop, Adele, 263, 290
Blackmer, Burton, 255
Blackmer, Clarence, 255, 294
Blackmer, Dr. Jonathan, 103
Blackmer, Eseck and Eunice, 348
Blackmer, Norman, 109
Blackmer, Reuben H., 88, 89, 96, 98
Blakeley, Quincy, 185
Blakely, Jellis, 74
Bley, Elsa, 223, 282, 341
Bloomer Quarry, 142
Bloomer, (Family), 48, 51
Bloomer, Reuben, 47, 48, 100, 130
Bloomer, Reuben II, 48, 155
Bloor, Harry, 224
Boardman, Daniel, 103
Bogart, Hendrick, 40
Bogart, John, 40
Bond, Eugene A., 290, 308, 309, 312, 339
Bond, Jessica, 263, 290
Bongheart, John, 40
Boorn, Jesse & Stephen, 124, 125
Booth, Josiah, 132
Bostwick, Deacon Israel, 49, 59
Boswell, Mrs. Harold, 312
Bourhill, Pat, 334
Bourn, Allan, 202, 217
Bowen, (Family), 157, 348
Bowen Hill Road, 348
Bowen, Andrus L., 168
Bowen, Byron, 299
Bowen, Oliver, 171
Bowers, Edward, 350
Bowker, Joseph, 55, 77, 80, 81, 82
Boyle, Father J.J., 157
Bradley, Joseph, 60
Brayton, Thomas, 80
Breakenridge, (Brackenridge) James, 49, 50, 72, 76
Bromley, 89, 90, 91, 106, 322
Bromley, Elizabeth, 106
Brooks, Robert R.R., 258, 260
Brooks, Rosa, 259
Brophy Store, 252
Brophy, Harvey, 252, 336
Brophy, Howard, 252, 299, 311, 336
Brophy, Joe, 296
Brown, Bruce, 311
Brown, Horace, 265

Brown, Silvanus, 72
Browne, John W., 311
Brownson, Gideon, 74
Bryan, Helen, 319
Buffum, Caleb, 87, 94, 96, 97, 98
Buffum, Paris, 160
Bulkeley, Solomon, 174
Bullis, Charles, 61
Burden, Dennis, 334
Burnham, Lois, 220
Burns, (Family), 157
Burns, Jim, 295
Burns, William T., Jr., 295
Burns, William T., Sr., 157, 255, 295, 336
Burr & Manley's Store, 168
Burr Philip's Store, 67
Burroughs, Bryson, 263
Bushee, Raymond, 297
Butterfield's Inn, 91
Byrnes, Dr. Elizabeth, 315, 332

Calfee, Mrs. W.H., 331
Callahan, (Family), 157
Camp Wynakee, 324, 325, 326, 328
Campbell, Richard Marston, 190, 197, 212, 213, 232
Caprin, Mrs. A.D., 161
Caravan Theatre, 285, 286, 307
Carhart, Rev. Charles, 186, 206, 248
Carmichael, Fred & Patricia, 285, 286, 307, 308
Carney, (Family), 157
Casey, (Family), 157
Casey, Roy, 297, 306
Cephas Kent Inn, 51, 65, 71, 201, 202, 214, 313
Chace, Rev. William, Jr., 332
Chambers, George N., 212
Chapman, (Family), 350
Chapman House, 173
Chapman, A.M., 206
Chapman, Henry A.G., 312
Chapman, John, 97, 138
Chapman, Mrs. M.D., 206
Chapman, Rena, 318
Charles, Jill, 286
Cheney, Abigail, 186
Cheney, Albert Baker, 187, 201, 274
Cheney, Elder Moses Ela, 186
Cheney, Elizabeth, 186, 274
Cheney, John Vance, 187
Cheney, Simeon P., 181, 185-188, 201
Child, Hamilton B., 3

Child, Edwin Burrage, 263, 264, 265, 266, 274, 275, 276, 329, 330, 336
Child, Katherine, 276, 330, 336
Child, Sargent, 210, 336
Childs, (Family), 51
Chipman, John, 74
Chipman, Lemuel, 64
Chipman, Nathaniel, 64, 67, 107
Chittenden, Thomas, 54, 82, 101
Church Street, 48, 59, 65, 194, 203, 204, 224, 278
Claghorn, James, 74
Clark, Jeremiah, 75
Clark, Nathan, 72, 73
Clarke, Sally, 330
Cleghorn, Sarah, 221
Cleveland, Job, 111
Clone, Si, 168, 243, 246, 247
Cobb, Pete, 294
Cochran, John, 115, 126
Cochran, Robert, 34, 72, 73, 315
Cochrane, Dr. John, 244, 315
Cockburn, Will, 5, 41
Cody, (Family), 157
Cody, Regina, 259
Colburn, Arthur P., 297
Colden, Alexander, 141
Colden, Cadwallader, 33, 34, 35, 36, 41
Collins, (Family), 157
Collins, Mrs. T., 204
Collins, Samuel, 105
Collins, Zerubabel, 131
Collson, (Family), 350
Colvin, Russell, 124
Comba, Theophile, 171, 256
Committee of Safety, 52, 54
Comstock Landing, 135, 136
Condon, (Family), 157
Connaway, Jay H., 265, 331
Connaway, Louise, 266
Connell, (Family), 157
Connell, Mrs. Sarah, 205
Connors, Paul, 332
Conroy, Dennis, 158
Continental Congress, 71, 73, 74, 76, 77, 78, 80, 81, 82, 83, 84
Conyne, Casparus, Jr., 40
Cooney, (Family), 157
Cooper, (Family), 157
Cooper, Malcolm E., 301, 302, 303, 311
Cooper, Thomas, 334
Copping, Clifford J., 256
Corbin, (Family), 240
Corey, (Family), 157
Corey, William, 133, 134, 234

Cox, (Family), 157
Cram, Susannah, 117
Crandall, (Family), 51
Crane Hill, 6, 129
Crane's Knoll, 234
Crane, Frederick, 263, 269
Cranton, (Family), 51
Crawford, Warren, 202, 342
Cunningham, (Family), 157
Cunningham, Dick, 219, 220
Cunningham, Florence, 293
Curry, A.W., 231
Curtis, Almond, 125
Curtis, D., 160
Curtis, Daniel, 125, 159, 160
Curtis, John, 160
Curtis, Joseph, 91, 125
Curtis, Zachariah, 22, 49, 100, 159, 348
Cushman, Bob, 314

D.L. Kent & Co., 142, 143
Dalton, (Family), 157
Daly, (Family), 157
Daly, Father John D., 155, 156
Dana, Rev. Robert, 335
Danby, 6, 7, 21, 41, 61, 94, 106, 107, 130, 133, 137, 142, 146, 157, 159, 168, 181, 197, 292
Davis, Ada Lillie, 278
Davis, June, 226
Davis, Wayne B., 10, 11
Deaf Joe Quarry, 132
Dean, William, 281
Deming Pond, 53, 294
Deming, Eliakim, 52, 57, 67, 107
deNottbeck, Miss Cecilia, 202, 214, 217, 218, 223
Depew, Morris, 306, 334
Dern, Claude, 281, 315
deSchweinitz, Mrs. Alan, 283, 240
DeVries, Mrs. Justus (Mary), 202, 327
Dewey, Israel, 40
Dickenson, David B. & Katharine, 239
Dickinson, Harry B., 292
Dillmann, Fritz, 211, 320
Dixon, Francis, 265
Dobson, Percy, 218
Dorset Academy, 105
Dorset Book Club, 171
Dorset Boys Brigade, 210
Dorset Cheese Assoc., 190
Dorset Citizens For Responsible Growth, 362
Dorset Colony House, 202, 263, 265, 286
Dorset Congregational Church, 7, 58, 60, 76, 96, 115, 117, 183, 194, 199, 205, 212, 247,

278, 315, 329, 330, 332, 335, 337, 337, 341
Dorset Conventions, 34, 55, 56, 70, 71, 73, 74, 75, 77, 78, 80, 83, 84, 281, 313
Dorset Corners, 199
Dorset Dairy Assoc., 161, 162
Dorset Docket, 293
Dorset Electric Light Co., 236
Dorset Elementary School, 8, 306
Dorset Field Club, 50, 197, 207, 208, 209, 210, 218, 226, 263, 283
Dorset Fire District #1, 248, 249, 296, 337, 338
Dorset Grange, 189
Dorset Grist Mill, 206
Dorset Hill, 6, 157, 283, 289, 350
Dorset Hill Cemetery, 350
Dorset Historical District, 313
Dorset Historical Society, 222, 312, 347, 362
Dorset History: "1768–1896 Dorset, VT," 165
Dorset Hollow, 4, 6, 12, 18, 49, 50, 52, 67, 101, 109, 111, 116, 149, 156, 157, 161, 162, 183, 202, 204, 205, 226, 236, 266, 268, 275, 296, 306, 321, 324, 326, 327, 335, 347
Dorset Hollow Road, 50, 67, 109, 217, 225, 226, 276, 318, 326, 328, 347
Dorset Home Guard, 211
Dorset Inn, 52, 109, 193, 204, 209, 212, 231, 258, 290, 334, 338
Dorset Iron Co., 158
Dorset Library Association, 173, 218, 226
Dorset Marble Co., 143
Dorset Mountain, 5, 6, 129, 130, 164, 254, 255, 341
Dorset Nursing Association, 211, 308, 332
Dorset Orchard Co., 237, 242, 243
Dorset Peak, 11
Dorset Planning Commision, 362
Dorset Players, 238, 263, 265, 278, 283, 284, 285, 292, 312, 321, 337
Dorset Playhouse, 223, 336
Dorset Pond, 13, 39, 49, 310
Dorset Public Library, 171, 275, 315, 329, 331, 336, 337, 338, 340
Dorset Science Club, 129, 252
Dorset Sportsmen's Club, 298, 339
Dorset Theatre Festival, 263, 265, 286
Dorset Trail, 253
Dorset Turnpike, 133
Dorset Turnpike Company, 107
Dorset Union Store, 109
Dorset Valley, 16
Dorset Village, 7, 8, 47, 50, 61, 67, 157, 219, 303

Dorset Weekly, 334
Draper, Francis, 158
Dreyer, James, 226
Druon, Father, 156
Duane, James, 35, 37, 38, 39, 40, 74
Dunbar, George B., 256
Dunn, (Family), 157
Dunn, Fayette & Mildred, 327
Dunn, Noah, 103
Dunton, (Family), 51, 60, 346
Dunton, Bessie A., 166
Dunton, Elizabeth C., 165, 167
Dunton, Henry L., 96
Dunton, Richard, 96
Dunton, Warren, 180, 203
Dunton, William, 96
Dunton, Major, 67
Durham, (NY Patent), 37, 39, 41

Eagan, Bill, 311
East Dorset, 8, 12, 49, 53, 56, 61, 67, 87, 89, 107, 111, 115, 134, 137, 138, 142, 143, 153, 155, 156, 157, 158, 160, 162, 164, 165, 168, 171, 181, 193, 199, 219, 220, 232, 244, 247, 251, 256, 283, 293, 294, 295, 299, 300
East Dorset Congregational Church, 339
East Dorset Athletic Club, 295
East Dorset Cemetery, 8, 346, 347
East Dorset Creamery, 294, 295
East Dorset Fire District #1, 299
East Dorset Hill, 139
East Dorset Library, 336
East Dorset Union Society, 115
East Road (Route 30), 47, 51, 234, 299
East Rupert, 57, 63, 64, 109, 117, 162, 193, 212, 224, 267
East Society of Dorset, 90
Edgerton, 51, 346
Edgerton Sawmill, 50, 294
Edgerton, Ernest G., 251, 293, 294, 339
Edgerton, Ernest, Sr., 109
Edgerton, Leon, 311, 312
Edmunds, Rev. Ernest F., 330
Edwards, Harriet L., 215, 217, 218
Eggleston, (Family), 295
Eggleston, Ed, 299
Elk Mountain, 41
Emerald Lake, 13, 22, 39, 49, 160, 209, 310, 326
Emerald Lake State Park, 22, 244, 310, 348
Enders, Cleade, 282
Enfield Houses, 221
Engel, Jonathan, 103

Eno, Edward, 311
Equinox School, 299
Erdman, Richard, 283
Ethan Allen Spring, 47, 202, 269
Eugene, (NY Patent), 37, 39
Evans, Mrs. Albert, 215

Fahnestock, Wallace Weir, 219, 253, 264, 276, 277, 278, 283, 284, 306
Farrar, Hannah, 107
Farwell, (Family), 51, 346
Farwell's Tavern, 193, 278
Farwell, Asa, 48, 60, 181
Farwell, Dr. E.J., 161, 164
Farwell, George W., 162
Farwell, Isaac, (Uncle), 48, 60, 181, 182, 183
Farwell, John, 48, 60, 65, 181
Farwell, Thomas, 47
Fassett, Capt. John, 38, 73, 281
Fassett, John, Jr., 55, 74
Faszholz, Jim, 342
Fausett, William Dean, 281, 313, 320, 338
Fay, Jonas, 72, 73, 76, 77, 78, 80, 82
Fay, Michael, 211
Fay, Stephen, 72
Feltus, Olive Hill, 181
Fenton Pottery, 217
Fenton, Christopher Webber, 111, 112, 113
Fenton, Jonathan, 111
Fenton, Richard Lucas, 111
Ferenc, Mrs. Edward, 335
Field, (Family), 345
Field, Alfred, 155
Field, Amos, 53
Field, Charles, 164, 180, 184, 195, 268
Field, Elizabeth, 52
Field, Frederick, 4, 9, 115, 132, 184
Field, Mrs. Charles, 172
Field, Robert, 222
Field, Spafford, 132
Fisher, John, 205
Fisher, Justice, 246
Fisher, Mark, 230
Fisher, Mary A., 166, 173
Fisher, Mrs. John, 203
Fitch, Rev. Hawley, 284, 329, 330
Fitch, William, 74
Fletcher, Col. Samuel, 78
Flynn, (Family), 157
Flynn, John J., 351
Fontaine, Rev. E.C., 212
Foot, Rev. Harry, 330
Foote, Ray, 327

Foote, Roseann, 334
Ford, Sylvester, 133
Fort Ticonderoga, 21, 47, 71, 73, 74, 77, 200, 285
Freedley Quarry, 129, 138, 139, 141, 282, 322, 350
Freedley, George, 244
Freedley, Howard, 219
French, Joseph, 132
Fuller, Noah, Jr., 123
Fuller, Orson, 123, 175
Fuller, William Jackson, 174

Gaffney, Father Thomas J., 157, 350
Gage, George, 54
Gage, Worter, 61
Gager, Oliver, 112
Gallagher, (Family), 157
Galusha, David, 74
Gates, Harold, 202
Gates, Matthew, 202
Gates, Owen, 202
Geer, Abel, 57
Gettysburg Quarry, 141, 181
Gifford, (Family), 348
Gilbert, (Family), 51, 155, 346
Gilbert Brook, 62, 167, 240
Gilbert's Hardware, 307, 331
Gilbert, Alfred Holley, 111, 160, 161, 184, 263, 312, 347
Gilbert, Angie, 172
Gilbert, Anna, 133, 230, 253, 334, 336, 347
Gilbert, Arthur W., 202, 222, 312, 313, 345, 347
Gilbert, Dave, 331
Gilbert, Diana, 155
Gilbert, Dr. George Holley, 141, 248, 252, 253, 254
Gilbert, Elisabeth, 337
Gilbert, Fred, 172, 283, 284
Gilbert, Frederick F., 189
Gilbert, George H., 202
Gilbert, Harriet Holley, 171
Gilbert, Henry M., 255
Gilbert, Huntington, 230, 283
Gilbert, Nora Cunningham, 219, 293, 307, 331, 332
Gilbert, Rufus, 230, 283, 337
Gilbert, Sophronia, 155
Gilbert, William F., 228, 312, 336
Gilbert, William J., 171
Gillette, Dr. Arthur, 315
Glen Farm, 18, 202, 321, 324
Glenn, Carol, 289

Glynn, Father Anthony J., 157
Goes, Matthew, 40
Goodman, Dr. Edwin, 219, 240, 283, 284, 314
Goodman, May, 283, 284, 285
Goose, Larrance, 40
Gormley, (Family), 157
Graham, F.D., 206
Graham, John A., 56, 64, 68
Graham, Mrs. F.D., 204
Grant, Gertrude H., 265
Grant, John, 74
Gray, (Family), 51
Gray's Store, (Clark), 109
Gray's Tavern, 173, 329
Gray, Alvin, 96
Gray, Anson, 96
Gray, Augustus Herman, 180
Gray, Capt. John, 96, 180, 275, 346
Gray, Caroline Rosetta, 180, 181
Gray, Deacon Alonson, 180
Gray, Elijah, 96
Gray, Elizabeth Manley, 183
Gray, Ellen, 180
Gray, Hattie, 173
Gray, Homer, 155
Gray, John, 59
Gray, Marcia K., 172, 180, 204
Gray, Mattie, 172
Gray, Oliver, 96
Gray, Paddock, 96, 97, 183
Gray, Raleigh, 96
Gray, William, 96
Greatbach, Daniel, 112
Green Mountain Boys, 34, 40, 41, 70, 71, 200, 204, 281, 285, 315
Green Peak, 2, 5, 8, 121, 164, 260, 341
Green, Joy, 334
Green, Robert, 320
Greene, Jordan, 248
Griffis, Dudley, 299
Griffith General Store, 251
Griffith, Jack, 244
Griffith, John Kelley "Jack", 251
Griffith, John M. Marley, 155, 251
Griffith, Robert, 180, 181, 315
Griffith, Silas L., 159
Griffith, Bill, 244
Griswold, Rev. John, 105
Grondahl, Mrs. Einar, (Bernadine B.), 218, 286, 312, 315, 331
Grout, Harold, 341
Grover, Joseph, 105
Groves, Arthur, 211

Hagen, (Family), 157
Hamlin, B.P., 242
Hamlin, Henrietta Jackson, 121, 201
Hamlin, Rev. Cyrus, 120, 121, 184
Hanks Hill, 7
Hard, Philo, 74
Harmon, Julian, 64
Harmon, Reuben, Jr., 57, 63
Harrigan, Mrs. Philip B., 336
Harrington House, (Burt), 67
Harrington, Arvin W., 208
Harrington, Connie, 208
Harrington, Joseph, 283, 284
Harrington, Mrs. A.W., 211
Harrington, Peg & Bert, 331
Harrington, Pluma G., 166
Harrington, Roland "Hoke", 208, 255
Harrison, George, 171
Harrison, Gordon, 289
Harrison, Grace, 273
Hart House, 67
Hart, Charles M., 223
Hart, Gilbert, 180
Hartwell, Neil, 297
Harwich, 89, 106
Harwood, (Family), 51, 346
Harwood, Dr. Charles S., 315
Harwood, Dr. Clifford, 315
Harwood, Ed, 315
Harwood, Elmer, 315
Harwood, Fred, 311
Harwood, Horace Greeley, 190
Harwood, P/O Horace Greeley, 297
Harwood, Sam, 297
Hatch, Elizabeth, 274
Hatch, Frances E.S., 271
Hatch, Harrison, 234, 273, 274
Hatch, Lorenzo, 233, 234, 263, 266, 270, 271
Hatch, William C., 271
Hathaway, Jay, 109, 340
Haven, Rev. William L., 212
Hawkes, John L., 337
Hawley, Jabez, 125
Hawley, Jehiel, 38, 50, 72
Haynes, Abigail, 52
Hazelton Cemetery, 348
Hazelton, Hyram H., 348
Hazelton, Leland, 306
Heaton, Jack, 307
Heinz, William C., 289
Henrietta's Elm, 120, 121, 201
Herbert, Mrs. Oliver, 226
Herman, Asahel, 54
Herrick, John, 285

Herrick, Mabel T., 160
Heyde, Charles, 268
Hill, (Family), 157
Hilliard, Ellen, 172
Hilliard, Ira, 172
Hilliard, John H., 217
Hillyard, Isaac, 108
Hislop, Codman, 309, 335, 337
Hitchcock, Edward, 4, 9
Hitchcock, Charles W., 9
Hitchcock, Harold B., 10, 11
Hoctor, (Family), 157
Hodge House, 67
Hodge, Joseph H.C., 161
Hogeboom, (Family), 51
Holberton-Wood, Anthony, 282
Holcumb, Noah, 59
Holley House (Edson and Harvey), 67
Holley, (Family), 51
Holley, Carrie, 263
Holley, E.L., 204
Holley, George B., 164
Holley, Harvey, 109
Holley, J. Frank, 209
Holley, Justus, 52
Holley, Spafford, 136
Holley, Will, 336
Hollister, Heil, 58
Hollister, Laura S., 265
Hollister, Tyrel & Co., 142
Hopkins, Weight (Wait), 74
Houghton, Agnes, 223
Houlahan, (Family), 157
Howe, Carleton, 18, 321, 322
Howe, Dorothy, 289, 321
Hubbard, (Family), 31
Hubbard, Jack, 326
Hudson, Barzilie, 109
Hudson, Cyrus, 186
Humphrey, Zephine, 1, 2, 3, 22, 44, 47, 53, 61, 133, 155, 180, 181, 188, 212, 213, 214, 221
Humphrey, Harriet, 202
Humphrey, Zephaniah Moore, 212, 213
Humphreys, Bea Jackson, 48, 193, 201
Hurd, Phineas, 57

Imperial Quarry, 142, 146
Ingraham, Eunice, 103
Isham, Lincoln, 211

J.K. Freedley Sons, 142
J.K. Adams Co., 300, 301, 302, 334

Jackson Peak, 6
Jackson, Elizabeth, 120
Jackson, Henrietta Anna Lorain, 120, 121, 184
Jackson, Margaret, 120
Jackson, Rev. Samuel C., 120
Jackson, Rev. William, 6, 58, 96, 105, 106, 117, 119, 120, 164, 174, 184, 185, 201, 312
Jackson, Susan, 120
Jarvis, William, 114
Jenks, (Family), 51
Jenner, Edward, 101
John Kent House, 65
John Manley House, 67, 130
Johnson, Austin, 123
Jones, Arthur, 278
Jones, Charles, 297
Jones, John, 310
Jones, Nelson, 161
Jones, Reuben, 82
Jones, Rev. Ezra, 119
Joyce, (Family), 157
Judson, Joshua, 123

Keeler, Robert, 217
Kelleher, (Family), 157
Kelley, Mary A., 155, 181
Kelley, Mrs. William, 205
Kellogg, Don, 312
Kellogg, George F., 201, 203
Kellogg, Titus, 52
Kelly, (Family), 157
Kelly, John, 103
Kelly, Mrs. William, 156, 205
Kelly, Patrick, 350
Kempe, John Taber, 35
Kennedy, Fred, 285
Kenny, (Family), 157
Kent, (Family), 346
Kent & Root Marble Co., 142, 145, 168
Kent & Root Quarry, 150
Kent Hill, 334
Kent House (Martin), 67
Kent Meadows, 71
Kent Neighborhood Historical District, 313
Kent, Abigail, 110
Kent, Alexander, 51, 103
Kent, Cephas H., 185
Kent, Cephas, Jr., 51, 60, 74, 103
Kent, Cephas, Sr., 47, 51, 54, 57, 59, 62, 75, 100, 110, 193, 337, 346
Kent, Charles B., 185
Kent, Clifton, 337
Kent, Dan, 132, 137, 185

Appendix

Kent, Daniel, 51, 52
Kent, Deborah, 51
Kent, E.E., 109
Kent, Hannah, 51, 59
Kent, Henry B., 204, 205
Kent, Jacob, 96
Kent, John, 51, 96, 120
Kent, Juba, 67, 96
Kent, Martin, 51
Kent, Mary, 51
Kent, Mary, 2nd, 51
Kent, Moses, 51, 124
Kent, Rose Lindley, 270, 337
Kent, Samuel, 51
Ketchum, Richard M., 289, 320, 335, 342, 344
King Reid Carnival, 238
King, Larry & Betty, 327, 334
Kinney, Charles, 210
Kirby Hollow, 45, 50, 57, 67, 164, 217, 298, 299, 335, 339, 342
Kissam, Philip, 224
Knowles, Albert E., 255, 298
Koch, Rose Burns, 156
Koch, Walter, 255
Kopituk, Raymond, 67, 202
Koren, H.L.T., 226
Kouwenhoven, John A., 226, 227, 292, 296
Kouwenhoven, John B., 222, 224, 225

Lacey, Isaac, 44, 345
Lackey, Simeon, 103
Ladd, Brazil, 135
Lane Road, 67, 282, 337
Lapham, Amy Ann, 212, 334
Lawrence, W. Hurd, 265
Lay, Charles Downing, 235, 236
Leary, (Family), 157
Leary, Jane, 111, 193
Lebenon, 90
Lee, Charles L., 256
Lee, Elizabeth Sykes, 62
Lee, James W. II, 339
Lee, Mrs. James, W., 201
Lee, Richard, 256
Lefevre, Edwin, Jr., 133, 233, 234, 236, 237, 239, 240, 283, 327, 338
Lefevre, Edwin, Sr., 134, 168, 232, 233, 234, 235, 236, 237, 238, 240
Lefevre, Martha, 234, 236, 238, 285
Lefevre, Reid, 233, 238, 282
Leggett, John, 40
Leigh, W.R., 264
Lepper, Ozzie & Sandy, 220

Liddle, Dr. F.C., 173, 206, 247, 249, 314, 315, 345
Liddle, Gertrude Holley, 315
Liddle, Louise Sykes, 173, 315, 329, 331
Lillie, John, 263, 264, 269, 270, 274, 278, 282
Lillie, Mrs. J.E., 205
List, Eugene, 289
Little Mad Tom, 12
Lockwood, Margaret, 306
Lockwood, Ryland, 210, 283
Long Trail School, 299, 339
Lord, Susan R., 219, 223
Ludlam, George, 115
Lyman, Gideon Esq., 30, 40
Lyman (Proprietors), 31
Lyon, Matthew, 55, 73, 157

Macey, Mary, 226
Mach, Helen, 306
MacIntyre, Rev., 256
Mackey, Dr. John, 315
Mad Tom Brook, 12, 18, 329
Mad Tom Road (Peru Street), 87, 193, 219, 294
Maher, Michael & Diane, 226
Mahlman, Bill, 342
Maillet, Father J.H., 157
Main Street, 204, 206
Mallary, Enoch, Ephrim, 56, 57
Malone, (Family), 157
Maloney, Ellen H., 342
Manchester, 12, 14, 22, 31, 32, 35, 36, 38, 50, 54, 56, 58, 60, 61, 71, 72, 78, 83, 91, 93, 105, 106, 107, 111, 116, 117, 124, 125, 137, 148, 149, 150, 153, 157, 168, 173, 183, 185, 186, 200, 203, 206, 210, 225, 230, 238, 245, 249, 254, 292, 301, 310, 315, 322, 336
Manchester Depot, 146, 149, 150, 168, 203, 206
Manchester, Dorset & Granville RR, 127, 146, 147, 149, 150, 198, 203, 206
Manley, (Family), 51, 234, 346
Manley, George, 96
Manley West Rd. Marble House, 134
Manley's Inn, 193
Manley, Alonzo, 96
Manley, Deacon John, 47, 51, 54, 76
Manley, Edmund, 96, 132
Manley, Fred, 329
Manley, George, 96, 133
Manley, Hiram, 96
Manley, Isaac, 96
Manley, John, 44, 54, 58, 59, 74, 96, 130, 346

Manley, John, Jr., 47, 345
Manley, Judson, 133
Manley, Martin, 96, 133
Manley, Mary, 59
Manley Quarry, 132, 142
Manley, S.D., 132
Manley, Thomas, 58
Manley, William, 61, 96, 183
Manley, William (Curator), 313
Manley-Miller Marble House, 133
Maple Hill, 8, 225, 226
Maple Hill Cemetery, 46, 52, 59, 115, 174, 271, 274, 300, 315, 338, 344, 345, 346, 347
Marble Quarries (list), 137-138
Marion, Cynthia, 306
Marsh, Col. William, 78
Marsh, Felicia, (Meyer), 265, 280
Marsh, Johnson, 96, 125
Marsh, Reginald, 265, 279, 280
Marsh, Sarah, 56
Marsh, William, 53, 56, 57
Martin, Thomas, 325
Martindale, Col. Stephen, 53, 103, 105, 346
Martindale, William S., 123
Martine, Alexander M., 103
Mason, Dr. Sylvester, 164
Matson, Grant, 209, 210
Matteson, Mrs. Charles, 335
McBride, (Family), 157
McBride, George W., 255
McBride, John J., 255
McClaughlin & Tully Grocery, 206
McCooey, Ellen, 332, 334
McCormack, (Family), 157
McCormick, Pat and Tom, 150
McCully, Paul, 334
McDevitt, (Family), 157
McDevitt, Ed, 131, 297
McDonald, (Family), 157, 350
McDonald, Dr. W.D., 297
McFall, Robert, 336
McGuffin, Lloyd & Harry, 330, 331
McGuigan, (Family), 157
McGuigan, Michael, 156
McGuiness, Dr. Gerald, 315
McIntire, Joseph, 57
McIntyre, Robert, 263, 264, 308, 309, 337
McLaughlin, (Family), 157
McNamara, (Family), 157
McNamara Road, 157
McNealus, Carol E., 211
McPhillomy, (Family), 157
McWaync, (Family), 346
McWayne, Bill, 177
McWayne, Nathaniel, 177, 180

McWayne, Paul & Leona, 299
McWayne, Ruth Baldwin, 183, 293
McWayne's West Side Grocery (Don), 334
Meachem, Margaret, 289, 319
Meachem, Sydney J., 332
Meadow Lane, 331
Mettawee Railroad, 245
Mettawee River (Mettowee), 12, 13, 15, 18, 21, 49, 63, 100, 109, 167, 217, 294, 324, 325, 328
Mettawee Valley, 260, 314, 321
Meyer, Anne N., 265, 280
Meyer, Herbert, 264, 265, 277, 280, 309
Miller, Elam, 47, 130
Miller, Jeremiah, 40
Miller, Rev. Hal C., III, and family, 338
Modlish, Edward, 331
Molloy, Ed, 157, 340
Monroe, Francis, 306
Mooney, Mrs. Gordon, 335
Moore Holley & Co., 109
Moore, Buell, 267, 268
Moore, Grove, 60, 105, 267
Moore, Martha, 234
Moore, Philip, 336
Moore, Sir Henry, 40
Moral Society of Dorset, 116
Moresi, Egidio, 263, 283
Morris, Lewis, 67
Morris, Ron, 11, 12
Morse Cemetery, 350
Morse Hill Rd., 8, 18, 46, 127, 157, 239, 240, 258, 303, 329, 347, 350
Morse, Alphons, 124
Morse, Dr. Alpheus, 52, 103, 116
Morse, Ebenezer, ,52, 54
Morse, John, 350
Morse, Noah, 53, 57
Mother Myrick, 2, 5
Mt. Aeolus, 5, 8, 9, 10, 23, 60, 87, 127, 129, 130, 132, 138, 139, 300, 341
Mt. Aeolus Inn, 219, 293, 294, 295
Mt. Equinox, 38, 254, 264, 293, 320
Mt. Tabor, 7, 14, 88, 89, 91, 93, 94, 96, 97, 107, 292
Mt. Tabor Cemetery, 87
Mt. Tabor Turnpike, 14
Murdock, James, 45
Murray, Judith "J.P.", 285
Murray, Warren, 67, 285, 286, 312
Musser, Mrs. John Agnes, 218

Nadeau, Joseph H., 181
Nassivera, John, 286, 287
Netop, 5, 6, 12, 129, 330, 331

New Hampshire Grants, 33, 34, 35, 37, 44, 49, 50, 55, 70, 71, 72, 75, 76, 78, 80, 81, 200
Newel, William, 180
Nichols Hill, 67, 109, 157, 278, 280, 281, 313
Nichols, Sherman, 183
Niles, Elsie & Marjorie, 331
Nobles, John, 74
Nolet, Rene, 18, 294, 295, 339
Norcross, Orlando W., 145, 146, 248
Norcross-West Quarry, 128, 130, 146, 149, 150, 199, 203
Norman, Geoff, 289
Norris, Allen, 223
North Dorset, 17, 22, 100, 110, 133, 138, 141, 153, 157, 159, 160, 161, 199, 219, 310, 332, 348
Norton, Capt. John, 111
Norton, Julius, 112
Norton, Luman, 111, 113
Norton, Mamie E., 166
Not, Theodora, 103

O'Connor, (Family), 157
O'Leary, (Family), 157
O'Neal, (Family), 157
O'Toole, Kevin, 334
Olvard, (Family), 31
Ormsby, Gideon, 60
Orvis, Franklin W., 265
Otter Creek, 12, 13, 18, 21, 39, 159, 160
Overton, Frank, 240
Owl's Head, 5, 8, 129, 164, 274, 306

Pabst, Fred, 14, 322
Paddock, (Family), 346
Paddock, Asa, 49
Paddock, Freeman, 161
Paddock, Harmon N., 161
Paddock, Isaac, 49
Paddock, John, 49
Paddock, Lucy, 49
Paddock, Mary, 49
Paddock, Mercy (Marcy), 49
Paddock, Prince, 48, 49
Paddock, Susannah, 48, 49
Page, George, 44, 345
Palmedo, Roland, 322, 323
Palmer, Peter, 211
Palmer, William A., 119
Parks, Blanche, 223
Parks, John, 223
Parks, Kathe, 301, 330, 332
Parks, Ray, 223, 335

Parks, Russell, 330
Parsons, (Family), 31, 240
Parsons, Brenda, 320
Parsons, Carl, 211, 323, 324
Parsons, Dave, 330
Parsons, Harriet, 324
Patten, Lawton M., 225
Pawlet, 12, 16, 37, 41, 50, 58, 60, 103, 105, 177, 186, 203, 206, 223, 292, 301, 342
Paxon, Evalyn, 283
Payson, Rev. Edward, 121
Peabody, Mary, 296
Peace Street, 217, 218, 281, 335
Peach, Arthur W., 221
Pearce, Agnes, 218
Pearce, (Now Giddings), Moira, 289
Pelsue, Anna W., 336
Peltier's Store, 67, 109, 172, 206, 255, 312, 329, 334
Peltier, Perry, 210, 211, 230, 255, 329, 340, 341
Perkins, Nathan, 58
Perry, Rev. Herbert, 309, 332
Peru, 7, 14, 21, 41, 48, 88, 89, 90, 91, 93, 98, 107, 158, 161, 193, 203, 315, 336
Peters, Edward, 226
Pettengill, Amos, 116
Pfaelzer, Howard R., 219, 283, 297
Phelan, Austin, 249
Phelps, Mrs. Mary, 206
Phelps, Mrs. William W., 204
Phillips, Judson, 289
Phillips, Mrs. Chester, 335
Pinnacle, 8, 166, 208, 215
Pocock, Mrs. James J., 223
Pollard, Martha, 184
Pomroy, (Family), 31
Potter, Oliver, 74
Potts, Rev. J.H., 202
Powell, Felix, 22, 44, 45, 345, 347
Powell, Martin, 75
Powers, Florence C., 265
Powers, Mary S., 265
Pratt, (Family), 51, 346
Pratt, Carrie G., 155, 171, 186
Pratt, Elma, 336
Pratt, John, 130
Pratt, Martha, 186
Pratt, Rev. Parsons S., 58, 119, 121, 155, 171, 172, 175, 176, 177, 181, 182, 183, 184, 186, 188, 189, 194, 197, 199, 201, 215
Prentiss, (Family), 346
Prentiss Brook, 211
Prentiss Pond, 8, 201, 268, 294, 321
Prentiss, Elizabeth P., 121, 194, 195, 196, 197, 361

Prentiss, Rev. George L., 121, 181, 182, 184, 194, 196, 249
Prentiss, Henry, 293
Princetown, (NY Patent), 35, 36, 37, 38, 39, 40, 41
Proft, Matt & Scout, 323
Pruyn, (Pruim-Proprietor), 40
Purday, Charles, 105
Purgatory Pit, 10, 11, 12

Quidor, John, 268

Ramey, Albro, 311
Ramsey, Carl T., 254, 282, 318, 319
Randall, Mrs. S.J., 265
Ransom, Robert, Jr., 337, 338
Rawlins, Harry, 210
Read, Walter B., 111, 299
Reed, Lloyd "Stub", 223
Reed, Orla, 132, 335
Regan, (Family), 157
Reitzenstein, E. Lillian, 265
Reynolds, Ephraim, 54
Reynolds, Louisa, 210
Richardson, Humphrey, 105
Richardson, Susan, 285
Rideout, Samuel, 161
Rideout (Ridout), Timothy, 109, 161
Rinn, J. Philip, 268
Rising, Josiah, 105
Robbins, Rev. Wright, 185
Robert's Store (A.B.), 206
Roberts, A.B., 215
Roberts, Albert, 230
Roberts, Allen C., 106, 107, 108, 135, 136
Roberts, Belle, 166
Roberts, Bruneau, 109
Roberts, Burns H., 180
Roberts, Ern, 266
Roberts, George, 244
Roberts, John Parkinson, 293
Roberts, Lila, 293
Roberts, Lt. Peter, 57
Roberts, Miss, 204
Roberts, Mrs. A.B., 204, 215
Roberts, Olive S., 165, 166
Robinson, John, 103
Robinson, Jonathan, 60
Robinson, Moses, 75
Robinson, Nathan, 175, 176
Robinson, Samuel, 33, 35, 37, 70, 75
Robinson, Samuel, Jr., 75
Rosen, Barney, Flo & Rose, 252

Rowley, John, 45
Rowley, Joseph, 45
Rudolph, R.K., 215, 217
Ruggles, (Family), 31
Rupert, 7, 12, 26, 31, 41, 46, 50, 51, 58, 63, 72, 90, 101, 105, 107, 123, 162, 186, 190, 223, 226, 292, 321
Rutherford, Walter, 35, 37, 38, 39, 40
Rutland Railroad, 14, 146, 149, 193, 206, 219

Sackville, Lionel Cranfield, 26
Safford, Samuel, 74
Salinger, Edgar T., 226
Salmon, Dr. Thomas William, 293
Salmon, Peter, 310
Sanford Quarry, 133, 134, 142
Sanford, Nelson J., 133, 162
Sargent, John, 105
Sawyer, Jesse, 74
Scallop, 7
Schnakenberg, H.E., 265
Schultz, Aunt Margaret, 183
Schwindt, Paul H., 65
Scott, Mrs. Frances, 331, 334
Selden, Alonzo, 96
Sennett, (Family), 157
Severance, Milton, 185
Seymour, Alfred A., 255
Seymour, Fred, 109
Shaw, Aubrey N., 111
Shaw, Robert Alfred, 310, 311
Sheldon, (Family), 51, 158
Sheldon Brook, 167
Sheldon, Allan, 310
Sheldon, Artemus, 114
Sheldon, H.C., 168, 171
Sheldon, Harry & Anne, 219
Sheldon, Helen B., 67
Sheldon, John H., 205, 217, 249, 251
Sheldon, Judge David, 63
Sheldon, Lillian A., 166
Sheldon, Mary, 172
Sheldon, Moses, 162
Sheldon, Mrs. J.H., 204
Sheridan, (Family), 157
Sherlock, (Family), 157
Sherman, Ada Pratt, 215, 257
Sherman, John, 257
Sherman, Stuart P., 256, 257, 258
Shipley, Nathan, 125
Shirlaw, Walter, 263
Shroder, Dr. John, 224
Shroder, Ford, 312
Shroder, Ruth Giffin, 222
Shull, Della, 265

Appendix

Shumway, Anson, 114
Shumway, Capt. John, 53, 67, 105, 109
Sikes, Titus, 105
Sill, Dorcas, 58, 62
Sill, Rev. Elijah, 58, 104
Simmons, C. Herbert, 222
Simmons, Eugene, 231
Simmons, Mrs. E., 202
Sirak, David, 67
Skene, Philip, 83
Skinner, Marchen T., 121, 309, 318, 326
Skinner, Richard, 105
Smith, (Family), 51
Smith, Albert, 265
Smith, Charles, 312
Smith, Daniel, 75
Smith, John, 72
Smith, Nathan, 74
Smith, Phineas F., 124
Smith, Roseanne Foote, 67
Smith, Sandy, 339
Smith, Seth, 59
Snare Associates, 225, 320, 327
Snare, Edith Dulles, 319, 320
Snyder, Helen Smith, 201
Snyder, Mrs. N.E., 185
Snyder, Mrs. H.E., 205
Socialborough, 37, 39, 41, 72
Soper's Tavern, 193
South Dorset, 8, 12, 46, 67, 130, 146, 150, 151, 157, 162, 193, 199, 203, 206, 295, 337, 347
Southern Vermont Artists, 264, 320
Southworth, G.B., 123
Southworth, William S., 123
Spencer, Hannah, 51
Squiers, Vernon, 312
Squires, Isaac, 60
St. Jerome's, 139, 156, 212
St. Jerome's Cemetery, 134, 344, 350, 351
Stannard, Emma, 312, 336, 341
Stannard, Joe, 339
Stannard, John N., 297
Stannard, Mrs. M., 206
Stannard, Ray, 297
Stanton, Joshua, 74
Stemph, Dee, 285
Stephenson, Paul, 285
Stewart, Dr. W.E., 164
Stewart, James, 61
Stewart, Jonas, 131
Stewart, Miss, 258
Stiles, Margaret, 334
Stilwell, Louis, 49
Stone, Guy, 315

Stone, Henry, 295, 311, 315
Stowell, H., 197
Streeter, Frank, 210
Streeter, Fred, 202
Strong, Justice John, 61
Stuart, (Family), 157
Sturges, Elisabeth, 312
Sturges, Peter, 342
Styles Peak, 7
Sullivan, (Family), 157
"Summerville," 226
Sunderland, Peleg, 61, 72
Svetlova Dance Center, 263, 287, 288
Svetlova, Marina, 287
Swezey Sawmill, 295
Swezey, Christopher, 295, 325
Sykes, (Family), 346
Sykes, Anna M., 217, 275
Sykes, Anne, 211
Sykes, Ashbel, 50
Sykes, Aurelius, 172
Sykes, Bernard, 173, 219, 275, 329, 330
Sykes, Carrie, 155
Sykes, Charles, 155
Sykes, Col. Newton, 155
Sykes, Dwight, 51
Sykes, Elijah, 138
Sykes, Gilbert "Gib", 209
Sykes, Gilbert M., 51, 172, 173, 206, 329
Sykes, Harriette "Hattie", 212, 213
Sykes, Hiram, 213
Sykes, Horatio, 96, 115
Sykes, I.N., 162
Sykes, Ira, 50, 109
Sykes, Israel, 50, 96
Sykes, Jacob, 50
Sykes, James, 219
Sykes, Katherine, 276
Sykes, Louise, 171, 173
Sykes, Lyman, 96
Sykes, Oliver, 155
Sykes, Orville, 96
Sykes, Rhoda, 213
Sykes, Rollin, 161, 204, 217
Sykes, Silvanus, 96, 97
Sykes, Simeon, 96
Sykes, Sylvanus, 50, 51
Sykes, Titus, 50, 51, 96
Sykes, Titus, Jr., 50
Sykes, Victory, 50
Sykes, Waldo, 109
Symington Quarry, 142, 146

Taconic Mountains, 2, 14, 87, 200, 314
Taconic Valley RR Co., 245, 246
Taft, Berniss, 297
Taft, Norma S.R., 109, 218
Talbot, Edwin O., 204
Tarbell, Edward, 299
Taylor, Dwight, 162
Taylor, Frederic, 276
Taylor, Ruth, 219
Taylor, Sigrun, 283
Taylor, Stephen, 114
Terry, Emily H., 255
Tetzlaff, Frederick, 325, 326
Theodore, Rev. John, 297
Thompson, Amos, 109
Thompson, Barnum, 132
Tifft, Kimball O., 297, 329
Tifft, Miriam, 296
Titus, Dr. Harry W., 225, 226
Tompkins, Adm. R.B., 334
Towslee, (Family), 51
Towslee, Mrs. C.A., 206
Towsley, Emma J., 166
Towsley, Mrs. E., 206
Tryon, William, 34
Tufts, Rev. Lester, 339
Tully, (Family), 157
Tully, "Yank", 345
Tuohy, (Family), 157
Tyler, Mrs. Walter, 223
Tyler, Terry, 298, 312, 336
Tyler, Walter, Jr., 223

Underhill, (Family), 51
Underhill & Gray, 109
Underhill House (Abraham), 67
Underhill Manley Quarry, 145

Underhill, Abraham, 44, 46, 47, 63, 64, 76, 101, 138, 345
Underhill, Isaac, 47, 127, 130, 208
Underhill, James, 105
Underhill, John, 96, 123
Underhill, Marcy, 47, 101
Underhill, Nathan, 96
Underhill, Return, 109
Underhill, William, 96
Upper Prince Quarry, 181

Vail, John, 105
Vail, Micah, 74
Vail, Robert B., 306
Van Alen, Johannis, 40
van Hoesen, Cornelius, 40
Van Loon, Henry, 238, 242, 337
Vance, Miss, 172
Vanderhoef, F.F., 265
VanOrman, Art, 242
VanVlaanderen, Peter, 226
Vermont Land Trust, 342
Vermont Marble Co., 130, 150
Vermont Republic, 46, 63, 64, 82
Viall, George M., 165
Voorhis, Dinah, 341
Vosburgh, Jacob, 40
Vosburgh, Peter, 40
Vosburgh, Wyndert, 40

Wade, (Family), 350
Wade Inn, 212, 224, 231, 232
Wade, Agnes, 223
Wade, Charles A., 212, 221, 222, 223, 224, 225, 226, 232, 282
Wade, Dan, 306
Wait, Arnold P., 180
Wales, Lucretia, 100
Walker, Rev. Jason F., 188, 189
Walker, Rev. William, 186
Wall, Berry, 211
Wallace, (Family), 157
Wallace, George M., 202, 225, 327, 328
Warner, Robert, 297, 330

Warner, Seth, 34, 52, 53, 72, 73, 74, 75, 83
Warren, Gideon, 74
Warren, Harold, 263
Warren, Miss M.K., 210
Warren, Rev. S.M., 202
Warren, Tom, 65, 249
Webb, Mrs. J. Watson, 110
Weeks, Mrs. George, 204
Weeks, R.W., 203
Weller, Eliakim, 72
Wells, Merwin, 335
Wentworth, Benning, 5, 24, 25, 26, 27, 31, 32, 33, 34, 35, 36, 37, 40, 41, 47, 50, 89, 95, 104
West Cambden, (NY Patent), 37
West Road, 45, 47, 48, 50, 52, 53, 62, 65, 67, 110, 133, 155, 157, 168, 193, 202, 203, 204, 205, 218, 223, 313, 318, 337, 345, 347
West, Augusta, 249
West, Elizabeth, 283
West, Ernest H., 16, 131, 134, 135, 138, 141, 146, 151, 181 203, 209, 210, 211, 336
West, Spafford H., 145, 203
Westminster, 70, 73, 80, 83, 100
Westminster Massacre, 73
Weston, Dorothy, 67
Whalen, Sidney, 111
Whalen, Will, 299
Whalon, (Family), 157
Whalon, Mark, 316
Wheeler, Betsy, 59
Wheeler, Nathan, 59
White, Mary Ann, 268
White, Paul E., 255, 295, 296, 298
Whitehall, 12, 107, 200
Whitney, Ernest, 244
Whitsit, Jesse, 265
Whittemore, Fred, 334
Wickham, Dr. Joseph D., 117, 119, 121, 181, 184
Wideawake, Peter & Merritt, 260
Wieneke, Helen & Kuhrt, 324, 325
Wilbur, James B., 249
Wilkins, Allan, 337
Wilkins, Hal, 294

Wilkins, Seymour, 149
Willard, Jonathan, 75
Williams, (Family), 51, 346
Williams Harness Shop, 180, 206
Williams Store, 180, 206
Williams, C.N., 205
Williams, Frederick Ballard, 263
Williams, George, 180
Williams, Helen E., 166
Williams, Herbert, 180
Williams, Jennie A., 165
Williams, Nelle, 332
Williams, Oliver, 110
Williams, Roy, 52
Williams, William, 110, 180
Wilson House, 219, 220
Wilson, David D., 339, 340, 342
Wilson, Dorothy Brewster, 232
Wilson, Emily Griffith, 232
Wilson, Gilman, 232
Wilson, Robert, 123
Wilson, Widow, 232
Wilson, William G. (Bill W.), 219, 220, 232, 256, 346
Winch, Mary E., 263
Windsor, 54, 70, 82, 83, 158, 159, 281
Wing, Nettie, 172
Woman's Relief Corps, 53, 164, 165, 166, 167, 173, 174
Woodard, Joseph, 76
Woodruff, Henry S., 209
Wormser, Samuel, 226
Wright, Norman B., 282
Wright, Samuel, 48
Wyman, Dave, 255

Young, Dr. Thomas, 82

Dorset

*has been published in a first edition
of twenty-one hundred copies
of which one hundred
have been numbered and signed
by the author.
This is copy number*

and is here signed.